D0520361

Discarded by
Santa Maria Library

781.654
Wood, Ean.
Born to swing : The story o
the big bands
London : Sanctuary
Publishing Ltd., c??

GAYLORD MG

BORN TO SWING

Printed by: Staples of Rochester, Kent.
Copyright: Ean Wood, 1996
Designed by: David Houghton
Published by: Sanctuary Publishing Ltd, The Colonnades, 82 Bishop's Bridge Road, London W2 6BB.

All rights reserved. No part of this book may be reproduced in any form or by electronic or mechanical means, including information storage or retrieval systems, without permission in writing from the publisher, except by a reviewer who may quote brief passages.

While the publishers have made every reasonable effort to trace the copyright owners for any or all photographs in this book, there may be some omissions of credits for which we apologise.

ISBN: 1-86074-154-1

BORN TO SWING

by Ean Wood

intro

"Looking back, what amazes me about those times is that when you think how rough the going got sometimes – the bad hotels, the bad food, the endless nights on the road, the hangovers, the crooked managers, the times when everybody seemed to be broke – somehow out of all that came this music that had so much joy in it, that gave so much joy to so many people. And it still does. It lasts. I get people coming up to me still, remembering when they heard such and such a tune. They were great times, and don't let anybody tell you different. Of course, we were younger then."

trombonist Rufus Gurney

"It don't mean a thing if it ain't got that swing"

Duke Ellington

contents

CHAPTER 1

taking it from the top

The Big Bands of the Swing Era were glorious and exciting to see and to hear: the gleaming brass and saxophones, the coloured spotlights, and the wall of powerful swinging sound these were all an unforgettable delight.

These bands could be sweet and soft, or they could be LOUD!!! It was a matter of pride with brass players – trumpeters and trombonists – to be able to play their notes at top volume without them becoming harsh and unpleasant.

Bands became bigger as the years went by. In the early Twenties the Fletcher Henderson band, with ten pieces, was regarded as fairly big. By the mid-Thirties, bands like Duke Ellington's had about thirteen; by the beginning of the Forties, Benny Goodman had sixteen; and after World War Two some bands, notably Stan Kenton's, grew to have twenty or more.

A typical Big Band at the height of the Swing Era would have something like three trumpets, three trombones, a clarinet, three saxophones (usually alto and tenor, and sometimes a baritone), and a rhythm section of piano, guitar, bass and drums.

The music they played could be slow and sensuous, or fast and exciting. It could be witty or aggressive or tender or brash, but always it swung. And it was because Swing was so popular for so long that bands were able to stay together and work together for long periods. This allowed the musicians in a band to grow together into a team, making the section-work smooth and allowing them to respond instantly to each other's playing, to know each others strengths and weaknesses, and even to anticipate each other, so that, for instance, a drummer would set just the right sort of rhythmic pattern for a particular soloist. With such togetherness, a good band would seem to think and breathe as one.

Such music was too subtle and complex to have grown up overnight. Many influences went into it, and musicians, composers and arrangers worked over several decades to develop it into what it finally became.

From the start, it was dance music.

It always remained that at heart, although by the height of the Swing Era audiences were so attuned to the music that sometimes whole dance-floors of fans would stop dancing and crowd round the bandstand to just listen when something special was being played.

This led some leaders eventually to prefer to play for listeners, who they felt showed more respect and appreciation for their music. Buddy Rich, leading his band at a dance in the late Forties told them, "Let's get the tempo right up and drive these mothers off the floor."

On the other hand there were musicians like Count Basie's great tenor-player, Lester Young, who expressed regret in the Fifties that he no longer got the opportunity to play for dances he felt that his playing drew inspiration from the mood and rhythms of the dancers on the floor.

The great dance explosion that started everything happened during the teens of the Twentieth Century. America went dance-mad, and much of the world followed suit.

The tunes they danced to were the popular songs of the day. During the 1900's there had been a similar explosion of song. Writing song lyrics became an obsession with Americans in all walks of life. Newspapers ran song-writing contests, and the sheet-music industry flourished. Many new popular-music publishers sprang up, most of them in New York and there were so many song-pluggers pounding pianos in the brownstone houses on Twenty-Eighth Street between Broadway and Sixth Avenue that it acquired the nickname "Tin Pan Alley".

Among the songs of the day were 'In the Good Old Summer Time', 'Ida! Sweet As Apple Cider', 'Sweet Adeline', 'Chinatown, My Chinatown', 'Shine On, Harvest Moon', 'I Wonder Who's Kissing Her Now', 'Let Me Call You Sweetheart', 'My Gal Sal', 'In The Shade Of The Old Apple Tree' and 'Take Me Out To The Ball Game'.

Songs like these (and worse) were showcased in music-halls (vaudeville was then at its height), whistled in the streets, and performed in homes and at local dances, mostly by amateur musicians. Many vaudevillians had their own set dance-routines, and used them with whatever song was currently popular.

It was largely because of this that popular song settled into its most usual form of a sixteen-bar verse and an eight-bar chorus.

The songs of that time were rarely topical, and in general they fell into two types, the happy ('Hail! Hail! The Gang's All Here!') and the sentimental ('Will You Love Me In December As You Do In May?'). From the 1890's until after the turn of the century the words tended to be more inventive than the melodies, to the extent that in 1906 the most successful Tin Pan Alley writer said in an interview, "There are no new melodies ever. If they are new they will not be popular. Songs we whistle today are variations of the ones we whistled yesterday."

In the early years of the 1900's, however, the melody got a new lease of life. The young man largely responsible had been a singing waiter called Izzy Baline, but renaming himself Irving Berlin he went on to write hundreds of songs including 'Always', 'A Pretty Girl Is Like A Melody', 'Easter Parade', 'Isn't This A Lovely Day?' and 'God Bless America'.

He also brought into popular song the rhythmic flavour of ragtime, writing such numbers as 'Everybody's Doing It', 'The International Rag' and 'Alexander's Ragtime Band'. (When he was over 100 he was asked by Stephen Spielberg for permission to use the song 'Always' in the film of that title and refused with the words "I got plans for that song.")

Ragtime itself, which was mainly a piano music, had already been responsible for a growing enthusiasm for dancing.

The dance most associated with it was the cakewalk, and around the turn of the century there were often cakewalk competitions. In fact the dance itself had begun years before as a local competition, with a cake for the prize.

The public's enthusiasm for dancing got a further boost in 1907 from the stage musical *The Merry Widow*, by Franz Lehar. This glorified ballroom dancing ('The Merry Widow Waltz') and by 1910 music publishers had started insisting that a song must be danceable for the sheet music to sell. Songs that were without a dance orchestration in strict tempo were given one.

A couple of years later the craze was given great impetus by a stylish and likeable young couple called Vernon and Irene Castle. Vernon, whose real surname was Blythe, was an English eccentric comedian. He had taken his stage surname from Windsor Castle and was working in America in stage musicals, when he met Irene Foote, a would-be dancer, at a swimming party on Long Island Sound. He fell in love with her and got her a job in the musical he was working in. They worked together in a second musical, got engaged, and in 1911 got married.

The following summer they set off for Paris, to try working there as a dance team. For a while they didn't have much luck, but soon went on to become a great success, first in revue and afterwards at the Café de Paris and the Casino de Deauville.

Armed with this success, they returned to New York and opened as a dance team at Louis Martin's Restaurant. There they inaugurated a series of tea-dances that became the rage of high society.

By now there was so much enthusiasm for dancing that in the years from 1912 to 1914 over one hundred new ballroom dances were invented. Most of these had the great advantage over earlier dances of permitting what was denounced as "lingering close contact". They also involved a lot of hip-wriggling and leg-kicking, and so were generally regarded by the upright as sinful.

Many of them were developed in low-life dancehalls in the vice districts of the big cities New York, Chicago, New Orleans and especially San Francisco. They were based on black vernacular dances from the country regions of the southern and western states, considerably simplified, and the names they were given reflected these country origins – the Turkey Trot, the Grizzly Bear, the Bunny Hug, the Possum Trot and the Monkey Glide.

Before then there had been only two types of public dancing – the two-step and the waltz – and even the Bunny Hug and the Turkey Trot bore a strong resemblance to the two-step.

The Castles themselves performed the Turkey Trot in a show called *The Sunshine Girl* on Broadway in 1913, but by 1914 they had discarded it, and similar dances, as jerky and crude. In that year they founded Castle House, a studio for teaching a more refined type of dancing.

A book of instructions they published at that time contained the advice: "Do not wriggle the shoulders. Do not shake the hips. Do not twist the body. Do not flounce the elbows. Do not pump the arms. Do not hop-glide instead." Their style of dancing may have been hectic (it often was), but their aim was elegance.

They went on to invent many dances called, oddly enough, the Castle Walk, the Castle Valse Classique, the Castle Tango, the Castle Last Waltz, the Castle Combination, the Castle Lame Duck, the Castle Maxixe and the Castle Half-and-Half, which proved too difficult to catch on (it was based on alternate bars of 3/4 time and 2/4 time). Most of their dances, however, became fashionable in every American ballroom, and it is fair to say that they changed the whole style of social dancing.

One problem they had when they first founded Castle House was finding bands capable of playing music suitable for the sort of dances they wanted to create. Then, at a private party, they heard the band of James Reese Europe, and were astonished by its rhythms and its instrumental colour.

Jim Europe was a remarkable man. A Negro (like all his band), he had been born in Mobile, Alabama, on February 22, 1881. When he was ten his family moved to Washington D.C., and there he completed his education and musical training.

In 1904 he went to New York, hoping to find a job as musical director and pianist in one of the black touring shows of the day. Ever since the end of the American Civil War, Blacks had provided a large proportion of America's musicians – at first often in minstrel shows, and later in black revues and musicals.

It took Jim Europe till 1906 to get a job in one of these, when he went on the road with a show called *Shoo Fly Regiment*.

Returning to New York in 1909, he scraped a living by accompanying singers, playing in small dance orchestras and giving piano lessons.

Quite a number of excellent black composers and musicians were making their presence felt in New York at that time. Cecil Mack, who wrote 'Runnin' Wild'; Luckey Roberts, who wrote the ragtime piece 'Ripples Of The Nile', later slowed down and converted (with due credit) into Glenn Miller's 'Moonlight Cocktail'; Shelton Brooks, who wrote 'Some Of These Days'; and Chris Smith, whose 'Ballin' the Jack' (a hit in the Ziegfeld Follies of 1913) was one of those dance numbers whose lyric instructed the listener in the steps to do.

Others were Henry Creamer and Turner Layton who together wrote a stream of hits including 'After You've Gone', 'Strut Miss Lizzie', 'Dear Old Southland' and 'Way Down Yonder in New Orleans'. Another partnership, Noble Sissle and Eubie Blake, wrote 'Memories Of You', 'Love Will Find A Way' and 'I'm Just Wild About Harry'. Eubie, like Irving Berlin, lived to be over 100, and was the originator of the line stolen on their hundredth birthdays by both Berlin and Adolph Zukor, the film producer "If I'd known I was going to live this long I'd have taken better care of myself."

Many black musicians of this generation in New York tended to look down on syncopated music, regarding blues (if they ever heard any) as a low down and no-account music, and ragtime as associated with the minstrel shows of an earlier era. Like some jazz musicians of later years, they wanted respectability.

But Jim Europe, who had decided that his future lay in popular music, realised the power of syncopation, even in the primitive form of those days, and made great use of it.

In 1910 he became involved in the foundation of the Clef Club, an organisation formed by black musicians to protect their interests, and to draw attention to the club he formed an orchestra and gave a concert at the Manhattan Casino.

They played light classics, some popular songs of the day, and a few ragtime pieces, and the show was completed by a variety programme and dancing. It was a great success, and was followed by other concerts, each more spectacular than the last. By 1913 one of these concerts attracted an audience of four thousand.

Once the Castles heard Jim Europe, they engaged him as their personal musician, their contracts from then on demanding that only his music be used for their performances.

Although he had good business sense, Europe was a rather quiet and self-effacing man with a likeable personality, and he and his band became society favourites. In March 1914 he even gave a concert at Carnegie Hall, ten years before Paul Whiteman's band played there, let alone Benny Goodman. His extraordinary line-up there included forty-seven mandolins, twenty-seven harp-guitars, eleven banjos, thirteen cellos, eight violins, eight trombones, seven cornets and ten pianos, plus two choirs. (When he played for the Castles at Castle House he normally led a mere sextet.)

TAKING IT FROM THE TOP

The reason for all the mandolins and guitars seems to have been an uncertainty in those early days which were the best instruments to lay down a swinging beat. The flexible and powerful rhythm section of piano, guitar, bass and drums took a while to develop. After all, Louis Armstrong's Hot Five had no drummer, and it took a while for the tuba (taken over from New Orleans marching bands) to be replaced by the string bass, with its lighter and more driving beat.

Another method Europe used to try and generate excitement was to play at enormous speed. Two records he made in 1913, 'Down Home Rag' and 'Too Much Mustard' are played terrifyingly fast, at around 280 beats to the minute, with two notes to each beat.

His programme at Carnegie Hall ranged from religious songs to popular music with a strong ragtime influence. Again it was a great success and it brought his name before an even wider public.

He continued his association with the Castles until in 1916 Vernon returned to England and joined the Royal Flying Corps to fight in The Great War. Having previously taken flying lessons in order to prepare himself, he was made a pilot and sent to Canada as an instructor. When America entered the war in 1917 he was transferred to Texas, and there, on February 15, 1918, while swerving to avoid a mid-air collision, he fell from the plane at fifty feet and was killed.

Jim Europe also joined up when America entered the war. He enlisted in a black New York Regiment, the 369th, known as "The Hell Fighters". He was commissioned a lieutenant and soon was made bandmaster by his C.O. and ordered to organise the finest regimental brass band that he could muster, hiring musicians from around New York.

As he was able to offer far more than army pay, Europe was able to assemble an outstanding group of some fifty musicians, many of whom were also singers, dancers and entertainers.

For drum-major he secured the services of the great tap-dancer, Bill 'Bojangles' Robinson.

From the moment the band arrived in France it was a sensation. General Pershing, commander of the American Expeditionary Force, who had already heard the band at social functions in New York, ordered it to perform at his headquarters, and for the next year it travelled widely, performing for Allied personnel.

In February and March 1918 it made an extensive tour of French cities, performing for civilian audiences, and its exuberant playing created a sensation.

From his civilian popularity and his success as a military band-leader it might be said that Jim Europe was the Glenn Miller of World War One, and he returned to New York to great acclaim. A million people watched his band parade down Fifth Avenue, led by Bill Robinson, to a special Carnegie Hall reception in its honour.

In February 1919, shortly after its return, the band made a dozen or so records, which can claim to be the first syncopated big band recordings ever made. Among them were numbers we still hear today, like 'At The Darktown Strutters' Ball' and 'Ja-da', and while the music is still clearly in the ragtime tradition, with an upright beat and tunes constructed from a succession of different themes, the band has amazing attack, imaginative (if slightly Sousa-ish) arrangements, and makes an enthusiastic attempt to swing. By then mostly brass, it sounds a far cry from the massed banks of mandolins.

It is also playing at slower tempos than his band of 1913. Europe had learned what some of the lesser swing bands never learned right through the Forties, that speed and swinging are not the same thing.

He was also not afraid to use unrespectable idioms in his music. For a start, his recordings include several blues compositions such as 'St Louis Blues', 'Memphis Blues' and 'Hesitating Blues', all by W.C.Handy. Handy had led what was basically a brass dance-band, in a sort of Sousa/ragtime tradition, around the southern states, and in 1917 had come to New York. In the years when jazz was just beginning, he did more than anyone to write down (and copyright) tunes being sung by black blues-singers in the South, and in 1914 his own composition 'St Louis Blues' made him famous.

Also among Jim Europe's 1919 recordings is the number 'Clarinet Marmalade', written and recorded the year before by the Original Dixieland Jass Band (people weren't unanimous about how to spell the word "jazz" in those early days). So Jim Europe was aware of the new sounds of jazz, and enthusiastic about using them. His clarinetists and trombonists in particular have obviously been listening to and learning from the ODJB.

On leaving the Army, Europe kept the band together, and on March 17 they performed at the Manhattan Opera House, beginning what was to have been a tour of the country. But on May 10, during a concert in Boston, Jim admonished one of his his drummers, Herbert Wright, saying, "A little more pep in the sticks"; either that or (accounts vary) he reprimanded Wright for walking across the stage during a number.

Whatever the cause, Wright, who would have won no awards for Most Balanced Personality of 1919, waited for him in the wings as he came off during intermission and knifed him in the neck, killing him. If this had not happened we would certainly have heard a lot more of James Reese Europe.

CHAPTER 2

the roaring twenties

America was less involved in The Great War than the European nations, and for many people there life went on much as usual. By the time it was over, several steps had been taken on the road that would lead to the swing era.

For a start, the dance craze had caused a spectacular boom in the popularity of the phonograph.

Just to get the vocabulary straightened out, in Britain, Edison's original invention, which played cylinders, was called the phonograph; the machine that came along slightly later and played flat discs at 78 r.p.m. was called the gramophone. But in America both were called the phonograph, and it was the disc industry that really took off. Cylinders were tricky to make and cumbersome to store and Edison's cylinder business tailed off, finally ceasing production in 1926.

As some indication of the boom in record-buying, in 1912 there had been three companies making phonographs in America – Victor, Columbia and Edison; by the end of 1914 there were nine, and by the end of 1916 there were forty-six.

The first true jazz band to get itself onto records was the Original Dixieland Jass Band. This group of young white New Orleans musicians had come to New York in 1917 and set the town by its ears. Nothing like them had ever been heard there before. They were young, and this new music they played was brash, lively and enthusiastic. After the initial shock of stunned amazement they caused (was this music at all, or maybe just an elaborate practical joke?), fashionable young people flocked to hear them at Reisenweber's, one of the most famous and expensive restaurants on Broadway.

Two years later they travelled to London, to appear in the revue *Joy Bells* at the Hippodrome. The reception they got was rapturous, partly because the audience included a large number of American servicemen, on their way home from the war. It was Reisenweber's all over again, and they were such a sensation that the star of the show, England's most famous comedian George Robey, demanded that "Either they go or I go."

The producer who had brought them to England, Albert de Courville, hastily took them out of *Joy Bells* and arranged for them to open a week later at the Palladium. Their success grew, and they played at many other places during the following year, including the huge and newly-opened Hammersmith Palais, where they played to audiences of two thousand.

Exactly where the Original Dixieland Jass Band fits into The History Of Jazz is still under discussion. Some critics claim that they simply ripped off what black musicians were doing in New Orleans and, being white, managed to get acceptance for their music first. Others claim that what blacks in New Orleans were playing at that time was much more primitive, and that the idea of a small band with a three-piece front line (trumpet, trombone and clarinet), all playing together in collective improvisation over a flexible rhythmic beat, was the ODJB's and theirs alone.

They were not of course a Big Band (there were originally only five of them, with a drummer added later), but swing developed out of jazz and the ODJB inaugurated the reign of jazz as the popular music of the Twenties.

Jazz, incidentally, simply meant "pep" or vitality. All the various half-informed guesses at its original meaning, many of them hopefully salacious, only arose because the music became so popular. If the band had called themselves The Original Dixieland Pep Band we'd be having the same sort of explanations of "pep".

Many of the numbers they played and recorded (and mostly wrote) have become jazz standards – 'At The Jass Band Ball', 'Livery Stable Blues', 'Fidgety Feet', 'Jazz Me Blues', 'Royal Garden Blues', 'Original Dixieland One-Step', and of course 'Tiger Rag'.

Without records jazz and swing could never have developed as fast and as far as they did. Young musicians learned to play by listening to records of their heroes (the great cornetist Bix Beiderbecke was a big fan of the ODJB). They learned new numbers from new records as they came out, and new ideas in playing and arranging spread through the whole of America (and through every country in the world that had strong ties with America) almost overnight.

Records were also essential in preserving the music. Unlike classical music, jazz and swing cannot be adequately written down in musical notation. There are too many subtleties and shifts in note-length and pitch and rhythmic pattern. A Swing number is a number played by a particular band on a particular occasion. Performance is all, and without records the Swing Era would live on only in the memories of its fans.

Another development during the war was that the dance craze had spread to all sections of society and all areas of the country, creating an enormous demand for live music. Sound systems and amplification had yet to be invented, so the music had to be live. Professional musicians, who until then would have expected to find work mainly in classical orchestras, or in hotels or theatres, suddenly found a new source of employment. Professional dance-bands sprang up all over America. The Twenties were about to start and the "Jazz Age" had begun.

It was the most exciting, irresponsible, despairing, creative, enjoyable decade of the century. In Europe there was a feeling that the nineteenth-century belief in reason and progress and hard work and moral earnestness had led the world into the greatest and most horrible disaster that mankind had ever known, so there must be something wrong with those things. And if there was something wrong with reason, then maybe the healthiest thing to do was follow your instincts. If there was something wrong with moral earnestness, then the sensible thing to be was immoral and flippant, even about death and disaster. This gave people a heady sense of release. The war was over, it had all been about nothing anyway, and all those Victorian rules of behaviour and all that high-mindedness didn't matter a damn.

America shared this feeling of release, but there was also a feeling there of national strength and optimism. As far as the American public were concerned, their Army had gone to Europe and won the victory that the Allies couldn't win for themselves. And once the war was won, the American President, Woodrow Wilson, had been the prime mover in establishing the League of Nations, making America for the first time in history a major industrial world power. The public were feeling devil-may-care and proud, and in a mood to celebrate – and what happened? Prohibition.

On January 16, 1920, the 18th Amendment to the Constitution went into force, proclaiming throughout the United States that no person shall "manufacture, sell, barter, transport, import, export, deliver, furnish or possess any intoxicating liquor except as authorized in this act." The main exceptions were alcohol for medicinal purposes (there were suddenly an awful lot of invalids) and beer containing "half of one percent alcohol" (which was a dismal watery stuff that got the nickname "near beer" and nobody drank without adding something alcoholic to it).

Reisenweber's Restaurant, where the ODJB had played, was so prominent that, when Prohibition came in, it was singled out to be made an example of. The most famous and unlikely of all enforcement agents, Izzy Epstein, with his equally Jewish friend, Moe Smith, turned up there in full-dress tuxedos, each with a gorgeous blonde on his arm. When they ordered drinks, the head-waiter asked for references, and roly-poly Izzy pulled out the first visiting-card he could find in his pocket. It happened to be the card of a rabbi, with which he was hoping to raid a sacramental wine store, but the headwaiter was sufficiently reassured by it to sell them a bottle of whisky. And that was the end of Reisenweber's. As Izzy later said, indignantly, "He deserved to be arrested. Imagine! A rabbi with a blonde and no beard!"

With all places that sold liquor being closed, the stage was set for illicit drinking joints to spring up. Within six months of the start of Prohibition the speakeasy was an established institution. There were far more of them than there had ever

been saloons. By the middle Twenties there were estimated to be 100,000 in New York City alone. Women, to whom the saloon had been socially off-limits, flocked to them as often as men, and they became the fashionable place to go.

Cabarets and restaurants, where much of social dancing had taken place, lost their male clientele when Prohibition prevented them from selling liquor. Almost only other place for a man to dance was the dancehall, where men could take a hip-flask and pay ten cents a time to dance with a hostess of their choice. During the Twenties, dancehalls sprang up in their thousands.

Dancehalls had developed out of brothels, and especially the brothels of the red-light district of San Francisco, the so-called "Barbary Coast". This district had originally sprung up to take advantage of the huge number of surplus males among the miners of the 1849 Gold Rush (men such as the father of Clementine).

Starting out as simple shacks with a bar which was often just a plank of wood across two barrels, they soon developed a standard pattern – a saloon with dancing downstairs and rooms for the whores upstairs. In the saloon, hostesses would dance with the customers in order to get them into the mood to visit the other girls upstairs.

Many that were not quite brothels used the gimmick that an "instructress" would charge ten cents a "lesson" to make everything legal. They were known as "creep joints", and a creep joint might have as many as fifty hostesses, nicknamed "taxi dancers", each dancing something like sixty times a night. The dances were kept short, usually lasting little over a minute, and the girls got to keep four cents out of every ten for themselves.

Considering how much has been written about the way jazz was born in the brothels of New Orleans, it's alarming to think *Come Dancing* has an even more direct pedigree from such places.

Even before Prohibition, slightly more respectable dancehalls had been springing up all round the country. In 1919 a New York dancehall on Seventh Avenue admitted averaging $1,500 a week. In San Francisco there was one six stories high, with dancing on every floor. By 1921 there were 1,000 in the East, and New York alone had applications for licenses for 1,800 more.

The development from "creep joint" into respectability took place very quickly. By 1922, for instance, the famous Trianon Ballroom was opened in Chicago. It cost a million dollars to build and paid a band $5,000 for a six-day engagement, enormous sums for those days. By 1923 some dancehalls were featuring two bands, and thus offering continuous music. As the dance boom continued, theatres and picture houses found themselves losing business.

By 1925, dancehalls began to give way to "modern ballrooms". These were designed to attract an even more respectable clientele. They had ringside seats and balconies where family groups could sit to watch exhibition dancing, novelty bands, and other entertainments.

And by 1925 big band music was well under way. Even before the ODJB had their New York success, black jazz bands from New Orleans had made their way to the dancehalls of San Francisco. As early as 1912, white musicians there were struggling to learn this exciting new music, and a hotel bandleader, Art Hickman, started trying to use a few of its rhythms and voicings in his band.

He was aided by a young musician called Ferde Grofé, who wrote his arrangements. Although Hickman's dance-band never even began to swing, Grofé has a strong claim to have been the first big-band arranger.

His family were originally French Huguenots, and they had a strong musical tradition. His maternal grandfather, Bernhardt Bierlich, had

been solo cellist for the Metropolitan Opera in New York; an uncle, Julius Bierlich, was for a while concertmaster of the Los Angeles Symphony; and his mother played violin, viola and cello, sometimes professionally. His father was a comedian and baritone.

Grofé told one interviewer that he started learning to play the piano when he was five, and studied composing at nine. When he was young, his father died, and he and his mother moved from New York to San Francisco, where her brother Julius was with the Symphony.

In his late teens Ferde was also briefly in the Symphony, playing viola, but to make a living in music he also had to work in popular music, and so became familiar with the new sounds. Although he never became a great jazz player, he was one of the very few musicians at that time thoroughly at home in both jazz and classical music. He joined Art Hickman in 1915 as pianist and arranger, and using some of the simpler devices of symphonic music, created the first modern dance-band arrangements.

Hickman's own great contribution, in the light of what came later, was introducing the saxophone into the dance band. This happened in 1918, when Hickman heard a two-man saxophone team playing in vaudeville.

The saxophone until then was regarded rather as a novelty instrument. The whole family of saxes – soprano, alto, C-melody, tenor, baritone and bass – had been invented by the Belgian instrument-maker Adolfe Sax in the 1840's. Sax was described by his biographers as "a handsome, charming, arrogant perfectionist, skillful at everything except business." Among other things, he was trying to develop an instrument that would combine the speed of playing of a woodwind with the carrying power of brass.

He succeeded, but the sound it produced was

not good (nobody had worked out how to play it properly). As late as 1927 the *London Daily News* wrote "The saxophone is a long metal instrument bent at both ends. It is alleged to be musical. As regards markings, the creature has a series of tiny taps stuck on it, apparently at random. These taps are very sensitive; when touched they cause the instrument to utter miserable sounds suggesting untold agony. At either end there is a hole. People, sometimes for no reason at all, blow down the small end of the saxophone which then shrieks and moans as if attacked by a million imps of torture. The shrieks issue from the large end. So do the moans."

As a result of attitudes (and playing) like this, its use was restricted for years to the larger military bands and vaudeville. It should also be noted that saxophones of those early days were not quite the same as now. Once jazz and swing players learned what a splendid instrument the sax could be, the instrument-makers helped by widening the bore, giving modern saxes a fuller, richer sound. This happened to other wind-instruments as well, notably the trombone. The narrow-bored "pea-shooter" trombones in the Jim Europe band could produce a shrill whinnying sound almost impossible to reproduce on a modern instrument.

The most successful saxophone-players in vaudeville were The Six Brown Brothers, who played the whole family of instruments; but another troupe, even more famous, who used a saxophone were The Three Keatons. Buster's mother, Myra, had found an alto in a pawnshop and was billed as "America's first lady saxophonist".

The two performers Hickman heard were Clyde Doerr and Bert Ralton, and they were using the saxophone not as a novelty instrument, but integrated into the orchestra, sometimes with a hard staccato attack, and sometimes more legato, producing almost the effect of strings.

Hickman realised that in the posh hotels his band worked in, this legato playing would be more acceptable than the brashness of brass, so he hired Doerr and Ralton. In 1919 his band was brought to New York by Columbia records (who wanted to record them), to play at the Biltmore Hotel. They were such a hit that Florenz Ziegfeld hired them for the roof-restaurant of his New Amsterdam Theatre, where patrons could dine and see a second show after the main show.

All the musicians and arrangers in New York were talking about the playing of Doerr and Ralton, and from then on the saxophone was an essential in the dance-orchestra. As well as having an interesting new sound, it looked exciting and exotic. Between 1919 and 1925, around a hundred thousand saxophones were sold in America, and sheet-music for saxophones began to far outsell sheet-music for pianos.

Art Hickman looked as if he was on the road to stardom. But he became homesick for San Francisco and took the band back there, in spite of being offered $2,500 a week by Ziegfeld to stay. Once back in California, his band dropped out of the running, and by the time Hickman died, still fairly young, in the Thirties, he was almost forgotten.

As for Doerr and Ralton, they both left Hickman in 1921. Doerr, after leading his own band for a while, became a session-man for radio. Bert Ralton, who was additionally famous for being able to smoke a cigarette and play a saxophone solo at the same time, came to London to run the famous Savoy Havana Band at the Savoy Hotel. In 1927 he was accidentally shot dead while big-game-hunting in South Africa. Even for a band-leader this is a strange and exotic way to go.

Ferde Grofé had left Hickman before the Hickman band left for New York. He continued to work in San Francisco, and there, in about 1920, he met the man who was to become by far the most famous big-band leader of the Twenties, Paul Whiteman.

Paul Whiteman was a large portly man, weighing around 300 pounds and somewhat resembling a taller Oliver Hardy, with one of those pencil-thin moustaches that were unaccountably fashionable in the Twenties and Thirties. Like Grofé, he had a classical music background, his father, Wilberforce Whiteman, being conductor of the Denver Symphony and head of music education for the Denver schools. And like Grofé, he had some appreciation of jazz.

Born in Denver in 1890, he was trained to professional standard on both the violin and the viola. But he rebelled against the sort of musical career his fond parents had in mind for him, and by 1915 had made his way to San Francisco, where the Panama-Pacific Exposition was providing work for musicians.

Being an affable man who liked drinking and associating with women, he spent a good deal of time in the dance-halls of the Barbary Coast. There he encountered jazz and Ferde Grofé. Aware of the success that Art Hickman was having, he decided to form a band himself, and asked Grofé to join him, again as pianist and arranger.

Grofé did. Whiteman formed his band, talked the Alexandria Hotel in Los Angeles into hiring it, and was on his way. The Victor Phonograph Company hired the band to compete with Columbia, who were recording Art Hickman, and almost his first records were an enormous success. His coupling of 'Japanese Sandman' and 'Whispering', recorded in 1920, sold two-and-a-half million copies, and his record of 'Three O'Clock In The Morning' sold three-and-a-half

million. One for every second phonograph in the country.

By 1924 the Whiteman band was getting $7,500 a week to appear in vaudeville; by the end of 1925 it was getting $9,000 a week to perform in picture-houses; and by the end of 1927 it was getting $12,000 a week, with transportation thrown in for Whiteman and (as *Variety* put it) "his thirty-three melodians".

Most of the thirty-three were performing members of the band, because by any standards the Whiteman band was huge. It had grown from the septet that recorded 'Whispering' to a ponderous aggregation of about twenty-five, which not only could play the popular tunes of the day for dancing, but could provide a whole evening's entertainment, including singers and a solo rendition of 'Stars And Stripes Forever' on a bicycle pump by one of his trombonists, Willy Hall.

It was far and away the most successful band that America has ever had, and it would probably qualify as the biggest-ever swing band, if only it had swung. Only it didn't. Or at least, not often and not much.

Both Whiteman and Grofé liked the new rough music they were hearing. As well as being aware of its commercial popularity, they realised it was capable of being both exciting and emotionally expressive, and they thought that the best way to bring out these virtues would be by using the techniques of nineteenth-century classical music.

This is only true up to a point. What was needed for successful big-band arranging, it turned out, was to use techniques similar to those of classical music, but not exactly the same.

Neither Whiteman nor Grofé ever really got away from their classical backgrounds. Whiteman genuinely thought he was doing jazz a favour when he hired the young composer, George Gershwin, to write a piece of "symphonic jazz". This, when Grofé had arranged it (Gershwin was still learning), turned out to be 'Rhapsody In Blue', and it was premiered at a concert to celebrate Lincoln's birthday at New York's Aeolian Hall in February 1924.

Whiteman later reported that "men and women were fighting to get into the door, pulling and mauling at each other as they sometimes do at a baseball game, or a prize fight, or in the subway".

The concert opened with a dixieland-style rendition of the ODJB number 'Livery Stable Blues', intended as an example of the raucous sort of music that "symphonic jazz" was going to improve on. Unfortunately, many people afterwards agreed that this was the most exciting number of the evening. But it is undeniable that it was 'Rhapsody In Blue' that got all the media attention.

Considering that jazz had hardly got going (Louis Armstrong and his Hot Five were still a year away), 'Rhapsody In Blue' is a creditable work, although there is some truth in the English composer Constant Lambert's later remark, that all such "symphonic syncopations ... remain the hybrid child of a hybrid. A rather knowing and unpleasant child, too, ashamed of its parents and boasting of its French lessons."

The great thing that Whiteman did achieve by commissioning such works, and by publicising himself as "The King Of Jazz", was to give jazz a veneer of social acceptability. In his own words, to "make a lady out of jazz". This allowed the more daring among the respectable to listen to anything called "jazz" without feeling they had to apologise more than a bit, and it did much to allow a hearing for the real thing.

After the Aeolian Hall concert it was obvious to everyone that the dance-band of the future would be playing some sort of arranged jazz.

Grofé continued to import the techniques of classical music into his arrangements, as he had done with Hickman. Swinging or not, he was one of the first to lay down many of the basic techniques of the Swing Band. Whiteman's orchestra was divided into sections brass, reeds and rhythm, with the brass sometimes further divided into trumpets and trombones.

These sections could be used to play phrases in turn, in a call-and-response pattern, or they could play different themes at the same time, one section in counterpoint to another. Where Grofé rather fell down was in having too many sections playing different things at the same time. His arrangements tend to have too many layers of sound. They lack the clean simplicity of a good swing band – those simple call-and-response figures that are deceptively hard to do well.

In among Whiteman's section-work were instrumental solos, players with a rhythm-section backing – sometimes they were improvised, sometimes a written-out variation on the melody, and sometimes simply the melody itself. All in all, exactly the sort of musical patterns that became the patterns of swing.

Whiteman flourished throughout the Twenties, and his style was much imitated by bands both in the U.S. and abroad. During the Thirties his band played more and more for radio shows and Broadway shows, and less for dancing, and when swing became the thing it was no longer a contender.

Probably this is due to the fact that Whiteman never really understood what jazz is about. In 1930 a fine reed-player and arranger called Fud Livingstone (he went on to do arrangements for both Tommy Dorsey and Benny Goodman) joined Whiteman as a clarinetist. When the date came for him to join the band he had just recovered from a severe illness, and he was not sure he could stand up, let alone play.

To his dismay, on his first night in the band, Whiteman called on him to play a hot clarinet solo. He stood up and tried, but all he could produce were a succession of squeaks and squawks. As he struggled to play, he could see the horror on Whiteman's face, and was sure he was going to be fired that night. But when he sat down the entire band rose and applauded him. Whiteman looked as if he was in some sort of unbelievable nightmare.

More or less the same thing happened throughout the following week, his playing getting only a little stronger. And he wasn't fired. Instead, Whiteman gave a press interview in which he urged people to come and hear the amazing new playing of his new clarinetist.

Although Whiteman carried on leading bands and making records into the Fifties, today his band is mostly remembered for two of its members during the Twenties. One, a member of his trio of vocalists, The Rhythm Boys, was Harry Lillis Crosby, nicknamed by the band "der Bingle", after a comic-strip character. The other was the great cornetist, Bix Beiderbecke, who joined the band in 1927.

Self-taught on both piano and cornet, Bix had patterned his cornet-playing on the records of Nick LaRocca, the leader of the Original Dixieland Jass Band, but Bix was in another league as a musician. His tone was clear and bell-like, with plenty of rhythmic punch, and his ability to improvise coherent solos with form and structure (as well as beautiful phrases), was the wonder and delight of his contemporaries. So much so that his style of playing seemed, in those early days of jazz, to offer the only possible alternative to trying to play like Louis Armstrong.

Born in 1903, in Davenport, Iowa, Bix was slightly above medium height, boyish-looking, and stronger than his lanky frame suggested. He was well-mannered and polite, and usually had a slightly abstracted air, as if he was mentally somewhere else. The only thing that mattered to him in life was his music. The clothes he wore, his studies at school and college, even the girls he knew, all faded away into a misty background behind the vibrant and exciting music he loved.

Unfortunately, his middle-class family, in spite of their reverence for classical music as a spiritual experience, regarded being a musician (of any sort) as not quite a respectable way to make a living, and regarded what he was doing as of no value. Late in his short life he made a trip home to Iowa and found copies of his records, proudly mailed home, in a cupboard, their packages never opened.

Being naturally modest, he was always a little surprised that people valued his playing so highly, and having the background he had gave him a touch of the Paul Whitemans. Looking uncertainly for a way to develop his music further, he eventually took to working out rather drifting and vaporous sub-classical improvisations at the piano, using harmonies that were modestly adventurous for jazz at the time, but would have been nothing unusual in the classical concert-hall.

His other problem was alcohol. From what had no doubt started as a joyful and sociable pastime, his drinking became a crutch, and an escape from his shyness and frustration. He swallowed quart after quart of dubious Prohibition rotgut until, when he was still in his twenties, his body began to weaken, and his control over his instrument, including the beautiful golden tone, began to desert him.

Whiteman valued him so highly that when, in 1930, Bix got too sick to tour with the band,

Whiteman kept his chair in the band open for him. He kept it open until, his system weakened by the drinking, Bix died of pneumonia in 1931.

As jazz (or at least a watered-down form of it) spread throughout the Twenties, new dances continued to be invented – the Shimmy, the Charleston, the Black Bottom.

The Shimmy was really an exhibition dance. Ordinary folk in the early Twenties mostly danced the fox trot. Then in 1925, a dance from a show caught on with the dancing public and largely wiped out the distinction between dances to watch and dances to dance. The show was a black musical called *Runnin' Wild*, and the dance, to a number composed by the great stride pianist, James P. Johnson, was the Charleston.

In the show it was danced by the chorus boys, billed as "The Dancing Redcaps" and they danced very much what had been danced in the southern states for years, done in the show to a simple accompaniment of hand-claps and foot-stamping. Poet James Weldon Johnson, who saw it, wrote "The effect was electrical. Such a demonstration of beating out complex rhythms had never before been seen on a stage in New York."

It took the country by storm. Children danced it on the streets for theatre queues for pennies. The Pickwick Club in Boston, a rather low-down joint, collapsed under the hammering of Charleston dancers, and fifty people died.

A year later, in 1926, the Charleston itself was supplanted by the Black Bottom. This dance had been featured in a black Harlem show called *Dinah* a couple of years before, but had made little impression. George White, Ziegfeld's rival, saw it, bought it for his show *Scandals Of 1926*, had the famous song written for it by DeSylva, Brown and Henderson, and had it danced by the small and lively white dancer, Ann Pennington.

The rhythm of the Black Bottom is based solidly on the Charleston, and like the Charleston, its original steps and movements had to be refined quite a bit until it was considered suitable for the ballroom. The chief gestures that survived were a few hops forward and back, and a genteel slapping of the backside.

Interestingly, the earlier show version, in *Dinah*, also had a song, 'The Original Black Bottom Dance', written by Perry Bradford in 1919. Its tune was a fast twelve-bar blues, and its lyrics gave elaborate instructions on how to dance it.

Such instructional songs were common in the Teens and Twenties. Perry Bradford had published 'Stewin' The Rice' in 1915, 'The Possum Trot' in 1915, and 'Scratchin' The Gravel' in 1917. In the same year Shelton Brooks published 'Walkin' The Dog' and Spencer Williams published 'Shim-Me-Sha-Wabble'. Others still remembered are 'Ballin' The Jack', written in 1913 by Chris Smith and Jim Burris, and 'Pinetop's Boogie Woogie', recorded by pianist Pinetop Smith in 1928.

Among songs written for specific dances, but without instructions in the lyrics, are 'The Varsity Drag', again by DeSylva, Brown and Henderson, and Duke Ellington's 'The Mooche', as well as his original theme 'East St Louis Toodle-oo' (pronounced "toed-low").

The Twenties was a prolific time for songs, many became standards, both in the Swing Era and since, and a great many more mercifully sank without trace. The crop for 1919 included 'Take Me To The Land Of Jazz!', 'How Ya Gonna Keep 'Em Down On The Farm', 'I'm Forever Blowing Bubbles', 'April Showers', 'Ma! (He's Making Eyes At Me)', 'Chicago', 'Way Down Yonder In New Orleans', 'Dardanella' (which had proved unsaleable under its original title 'Turkish Tom Toms'), 'Daddy, You've Been A Mother To Me' and 'Goodbye Teddy Roosevelt, You Were A Real American'.

In the early Twenties came 'Margie', 'Rose Of Washington Square', 'If You Knew Susie', 'Yes, We Have No Bananas', 'You Gotta See Mama Every Night', 'China Boy', 'Wabash Blues', 'Wang Wang Blues', 'My Man', 'Ain't We Got Fun?', 'Dear Old Southland' and 'Oogie-Oogie Wa Wa', which claimed to be an Eskimo love song.

Later came 'Limehouse Blues', 'Who's Sorry Now?', 'California, Here I Come', 'Dinah', 'Charmaine', 'Diane', 'Ramona', 'Jeannine (I Dream Of Lilac Time)', 'I'll See You In My Dreams', 'If You Knew Susie', 'Always', 'What'll I Do?', 'In A Little Spanish Town', 'Pretty Baby', 'Old Man River', 'Hallelujah' and 'My Blue Heaven', which sold so many copies that it made singer Gene Austin the most famous crooner before Crosby, 'Pagan Love Song', 'Sonny Boy' and (from the title of a film) 'Woman Disputed, I Love You'.

With jazz beginning to find itself, with bands and ballrooms in every corner of the land, with a flourishing record industry, the abundance of new songs and dances, and the eagerness on the part of almost everybody to have a good time, the stage was set for the birth of swing.

CHAPTER 3

fletcher henderson

Fletcher Hamilton Henderson, Jr was a tall, handsome, courteous, light-skinned Negro. An educated man, he was so unassertive he might almost be called supine, and yet he managed to lead the first important swing band, filled over the years with great names like Joe Smith, Tommy Ladnier, Rex Stewart, Henry "Red" Allen, Buster Bailey, Charlie Green, Benny Carter, John Kirby, Dicky Wells, Ben Webster and Coleman Hawkins.

Not that it started out swinging. On the earliest records by a Henderson band of any size, made in 1923, there is probably less drive and lift than the Jim Europe band had four years earlier. But Henderson, like Jim Europe, had been born and raised in the southern states, and possibly this helped him to appreciate and use the more propulsive sounds arriving in New York from the south sooner than most.

He had been born in 1897 in the town of Cuthbert, Georgia, where his father, beginning a distinguished career in education, was then teaching at Douglas Academy, and his mother was a pianist and music-teacher. Even by the white standards of those days, Fletcher was well-educated, and by black standards he was exceptionally so, majoring in mathematics and chemistry at Atlanta University.

Obtaining a degree in chemistry, however, was one thing. Pursuing a career as a chemist was, for a black man before 1920, quite another. Having come to New York with that idea in mind, he soon decided it was hopeless.

Luckily, his mother and father had taught him to play light classics on the piano, and to read music, and he began to support himself by using those talents to demonstrate sheet music for the black music publishers, Pace and Handy. "Handy" was the already-famous W.C.Handy – Harry Pace was an executive with a black insurance company who occasionally composed songs.

Henderson was only one among a number of well-educated blacks of his generation who found popular music to be their best way of making a living. Jimmie Lunceford had studied classical music at Fisk University, although without taking a degree; Don Redman, who was to become Henderson's arranger before going on to lead bands of his own, had studied music at conservatories in Boston and Detroit; bandleader Claude Hopkins had a degree from Harvard and had gone on to study music at a conservatory; all at a time when few Americans, even whites, went on to college.

To their families who had worked hard to attain this considerable degree of respectability, the music of "lower class" blacks would have been anathema. They would have had almost no contact with the gospel singing of the Sanctified Church, let alone the blues and field hollers of the rural South. In 1920, about all that musicians in the north of America would have known of jazz were the blues compositions of W.C.Handy and the recordings of the Original Dixieland Jass Band. Furthermore, New York musicians saw themselves as sophisticated members of the capital city, with little to learn from the backwoods, and were already by the early Twenties developing a bright, brittle, rather unswinging beat that was intended as an improvement on the hectic and now old-fashioned rhythm of the ODJB

In New York at that time it was mainly the pianists who were heading in the right direction. Men like William Henry Joseph Bonaparte Bertheloff (Willie the Lion) Smith, Luckey Roberts and James P. Johnson were beginning to import a new rhythmic freedom and a certain amount of improvisation into their playing, developing it from ragtime into what was to become known as "stride". In fact in 1922, when Fletcher Henderson was about to work for a while as accompanist to Ethel Waters, she made him listen to James P. Johnson piano rolls so that he could learn how to play in the latest style.

By 1922 the fad for the sort of hoked-up jazz performed by the ODJB's imitators was passing. The new craze was for blues, although nobody then had much idea what a blues was, beyond the fact that it was jazzy and popular. This craze explains why so many songs published in the Twenties had "blues" in the title without being any such thing 'Jazz Me Blues', 'Limehouse Blues', 'Wang Wang Blues', etc., etc.

This had all started in 1920 when Mamie Smith, a black vaudeville entertainer, made the first solo blues recording with her band, which constantly changed its personnel, but was always called her "Jazz Hounds". The number was called 'Crazy Blues', and within six months it had become a surprise million-seller. In fact it sold so fast in

Harlem as soon as it was released that the record company (Okeh) sent people up there to check that somebody wasn't giving copies away for nothing. By 1921 at least half-a-dozen other black singers had been recorded, and by 1923 there were hundreds of blues and near-blues singers being recorded.

In 1921, Harry Pace had split off from W.C.Handy to form the first black record company, Black Swan, and took Fletcher Henderson with him as a sort of musical handyman who could accompany singers, hire bands, and write simple arrangements.

While Fletcher Henderson probably started out almost as ignorant as most New Yorkers then of what blues was about, the considerable amount of work he did accompanying blues singers, including Alberta Hunter, Bessie Smith and Clara Smith (no relation), helped him to get a feel for it. In 1922, working as accompanist to Ethel Waters, he recorded with her and went on a promotional tour round the country, leading a small group called The Black Swan Troubadours. (His parents were not at all happy about him accompanying a "low-down" blues singer, and came all the way from Georgia to New York to investigate the whole affair before giving him their approval to go.)

The tour included a visit to New Orleans and there, in a little dance hall, he heard a short, shy, tubby, determined young cornetist called Louis Armstrong (Louis didn't start his switch to the more brilliant-sounding trumpet until 1925).

Louis was already an accomplished player, and Fletcher was impressed. He asked Louis to join the tour with the Troubadours, but Louis wouldn't leave without his friend and drummer, Zutty Singleton, and either Zutty wouldn't leave New Orleans, or Fletcher wouldn't fire his own drummer, so that was that.

Nonetheless, the exodus of musicians north

from New Orleans was by then well under way. The move had started in 1917, after the closing down of Storyville, the official red-light district of the city and named after Alderman Joseph Story, who had sponsored the legislation to set it up in the 1890's.

It was America's only official red-light district, and it seems that while prostitution was not exactly legal there, it was somehow less illegal than anywhere else. It was in Storyville that all the famous sporting-houses were situated immortal names like "Gypsy Schaeffer's", Josie Arlington's "The Arlington" and Lulu White's "Mahogany Hall".

These houses were not for blacks. Not in the southern states in those days. They catered to a white clientele, employing white or mostly-white girls and, contrary to legend, it is now believed that few early jazz musicians played in them.

Where they did play, and where jazz was born, was about three blocks away, in an area that was informally recognised as the "black Storyville". To say it was a rough area would be an understatement. It was an area of dives and creep joints, where drunken fights were frequent, where knives and guns were in common use, and murder was not unusual.

In 1917, the U.S. Navy objected to young sailors training for the war getting into fights in the official Storyville, and the U.S. War Department had it closed down.

Probably at that time there was pressure put on all the low-down joints in New Orleans, and work for musicians began to become scarce. The main thoroughfare out of the city was the Mississippi, and musicians, some of them finding work on the riverboats, some not, began to migrate up-river to the cities further north dash Memphis, St Louis, Kansas City and, most of all, Chicago.

It was to Chicago that Louis Armstrong went when he himself left New Orleans, in 1923. He went there to join his mentor, cornetist Joe "King" Oliver, who had been working around Chicago off and on for two or three years past and had returned there in April 1922 to play at a black dance-hall called the Lincoln Gardens (previously the Royal Gardens) with his newly-formed Creole Jazz Band.

While the Creole Jazz Band was a great band, and the men in it became models for young musicians to imitate, it did not have much influence, as a band, on the development of arranged swing. Its arrangements, instead of being based on section-work (the band was only eight strong), were a worked-out counterpoint (interspersed with improvised solos) that imitated the interplay of cornet, trombone and clarinet in the bands of New Orleans. Nor were they written down. They were what swing musicians called "head arrangements", worked out in rehearsal (and often developed further in performance) and memorised.

Meanwhile, his tour with Ethel Waters over, Fletcher Henderson was back in New York and had started to put together small bands to play at dances or cabarets. In 1923, he heard that the Club Alabam, a well-known cellar club on West 44th Street near Times Square, was auditioning for a dance-band. This was part of the increasing vogue among white folks in the Twenties for black entertainment (the Club Alabam had a whites-only policy) and, true to his character, Fletcher Henderson at first did nothing about it. But fortunately the musicians in his band talked him into taking the audition, and they got the job.

The most important member of his band at that time was Don Redman, who played clarinet and alto saxophone, and became the band's arranger. This was very much with Fletcher's approval, but there was a certain amount of muttering at first from some of the musicians, who were proud of their ability to extemporise, and felt that written arrangements would hamper their creative freedom.

Redman was a little, warm-hearted man, liked and admired by his fellow-musicians. Born in 1900, he had been a child prodigy, able to play almost all the conventional instruments, and had already done some arranging before he joined Henderson. He is the other contender (along with Ferde Grofé) for the title of first effective big-band arranger.

Grofé was earlier, and he was certainly heading in the right direction. In fact, some of Redman's earliest arrangements for the Fletcher Henderson band sound as if he had been listening to Grofé, but Redman quickly took things further.

He had a good grounding in musical theory, and a rare ability for creating interesting melodic phrases. He developed the interplay between sections essential to good swing, and he kept things simple. If he had a fault it was that the phrases he gave each section in turn tended to be a little too short, giving some of his work an over-busy, fussy texture.

Two important techniques for a swing band were beginning to become clear. First, the longer a band played together, the better they got to know each other (and the better they got at reading music). Second, the way to organise a section was to have one member of it lead – that is, play the melody and set the phrasing with the other members following his phrasing as closely as possible. As the swing era developed, good section-leaders, who could give a band life, became highly-prized and well-paid.

The band had only been at the Club Alabam a few months when Roseland, the most prestigious ballroom in New York, suddenly also needed a resident band. This had come about because

Roseland had been featuring two bands, a white group led by Sam Lanin and a creole band from New Orleans (not really a jazz band) led by Armand Piron. Suddenly Piron and his boys had decided they didn't like New York – it was too cold and they were homesick and they were going home.

Roseland offered Henderson and his band the job, and like a flash he did nothing. And probably would have continued to do nothing, if his saxophonist, the newly-joined 19-year-old Coleman Hawkins, had not got into a dispute with the management of the Club Alabam. He was refused extra pay for accompanying a singer, the band either quit in protest or was fired for protesting, and they took the job at Roseland.

Roseland, at 51st Street and Broadway, had a big dance floor, with a large refreshment area off to the side where you could buy soft drinks or near beer. The admission charge was around a dollar. The policy at Roseland too was "whites only", but apart from that, anyone was welcome – single men, single women, or couples. Hostesses were available for single men who wanted to pay a dime a dance, but Roseland made sure to keep its reputation spotlessly clean. It was no house of assignation.

The year was now 1924, and blues was the thing, and Henderson decided that what his band needed was a hot soloist. His favourite hot cornetist was the beautifully-toned Joe Smith (who was also Bessie Smith's favourite cornetist), but Joe, who played (and recorded) with the band off and on, refused to join permanently.

Fletcher remembered Louis Armstrong. He knew that Louis had moved to Chicago to play at with King Oliver, and knew that his reputation was rising fast, so he sent a telegram inviting him to join the band.

He didn't really expect Louis to accept, but as

luck would have it, Louis' new wife Lil (King Oliver's pianist), anxious to build up her husband's confidence and get him embarked on a career where he was not simply a second cornet, was talking him into quitting the Oliver band. She wanted him to realise that with his talent he could be a leader and a star, and joining an up-and-coming New York band seemed to her like a good move. So in around September 1924 Louis set off for New York (with Lil) to become Fletcher Henderson's third trumpet.

And what sort of band did the nervous provincial young Louis find when he arrived in the big city? Well, they were young (their average age was about twenty-two), they rather fancied themselves as Broadway swells, and they were fairly wild and undisciplined (Fletcher was no disciplinarian). Referring to the band of a few years later, Duke Ellington said, "That was probably one of the partyingest bands there ever was."

Conscious as they were of being sharp big-city boys, Louis, in his old-fashioned suit, long underwear down to his socks, and clumping great shoes, looked to them like a hayseed. (It wasn't long before younger players, like cornetist Rex Stewart, wanting to emulate their hero in every way, would be buying clumping great shoes so as to look like Louis).

Louis first met the band while they were rehearsing at a club in Harlem. Feeling very conscious of being the new boy, he took his seat on the stand and stared down at his music, conscious of every eye being on him and thinking, "This bunch of old ... stuck up ...".

Just then, Ralph Escudero's bass fell against Big Charlie Green's trombone, and Charlie Green yelled, "Why, you hit my horn, you son-of-a-bitch!". In a moment they had their coats off and were really going for each other. Fletcher managed to get them calmed down and Louis thought to himself, "Oh, I'm gonna like this band."

Reading the band's written arrangements was at first a little difficult for him after playing head arrangements with the Creole Jazz Band. At an early rehearsal they were rehearsing what Fletcher Henderson later described as "a medley of beautiful Irish waltzes" (which says something about how uncertain the band was of their direction in 1924). The dynamics were all marked on the music, and at one point there was a fortissimo (ff) followed by a diminuendo down to pianissimo (pp). Everybody followed these instructions except Louis, who continued blasting away at full volume. Fletcher stopped the band and asked him if he didn't see the "pp". "Oh," said Louis innocently, "I thought that meant 'pound plenty'." Everybody fell about laughing, and that was the moment when the band decided they liked Louis.

That was before they really heard him play. Whether because he was concentrating hard on reading the parts, or whether he was still a little unsure of himself in this fast company, it wasn't until he had been in the band for a few weeks that he really let go.

By then a fellow New Orleanian, clarinetist Buster Bailey, had joined the band (bringing their number up to eleven), and his presence helped Louis feel more at home. On a version of 'Tiger Rag' he was allotted four solo choruses immediately after a chorus by Bailey, and really let rip. Then they knew what they had.

Rhythmically and musically Louis was by then streets ahead of everyone. One of the earliest his solos with the Henderson band is on 'Shanghai Shuffle', recorded in November 1924, and his ability to swing is obviously something that the rest of the band have yet to learn.

During the rest of his time with the band he

was their featured soloist, soloing on almost half their records. He also begged Fletcher to let him sing, but Fletcher never did, apart from allowing him a few shouted remarks at the end of a version of 'Everybody Loves My Baby', which are the earliest example of his voice on record. Fletcher's explanation was that he couldn't see what Louis could possibly do with "that big fish-horn voice of his".

Nor did all this exposure make Louis a star. His way of playing was too emotionally raw and too different from anything that had been heard before to be accepted immediately by the general public. With musicians it was another matter. They were awed by his talent, and flocked to hear him, and tried to learn to play like him. Not just the trumpeters, but musicians on every instrument. Black musicians of course could not enter the whites-only Roseland, but there was a tiny window backstage through which you could hear the band from the outside, and they used to scramble to get near it and listen.

It was while Louis was still with the band, in May 1925, that the Sam Lanin group suddenly quit Roseland. James Lincoln Collier, in his book "Louis Armstrong", says that he feels they may have resented working opposite blacks, but he admits there is no concrete evidence of this. Maybe they were alarmed by Louis. Whatever the reason, they were not replaced, and Henderson had somehow drifted into leading the number one house band at one of the most important locations in New York.

Nonetheless, Louis himself was not entirely happy with the band. Many of the musicians were sports and high spenders. Making the considerable sum for those days of seventy-five dollars a week, they spent their money as fast as it came in on fine clothes and fast cars. Many were unpunctual, often turning up for performances late or drunk or both. Louis had grown up in bars,

and he saw nothing glamorous in speakeasies. More to the point, he was deadly serious about his music, and hated all the "goofing and boozing".

His wife had gone back to Chicago to form a band, and she wanted him in it (and with her), so at around the end of October 1925 he left Fletcher Henderson, after being in the band for a little over a year.

His legacy to it was immense, in showing just what this new music was capable of. But he was not the only influence in bringing the sound of New Orleans to New York. By now there were others, like soprano saxophonist Sidney Bechet, who in 1925 was playing with the embryonic Duke Ellington band, and Ellington's first great trumpeter, Bubber Miley who, although he was not from New Orleans, but from Carolina, had been much influenced by King Oliver, especially in the use of the mute, which was almost an Oliver invention.

Another Oliver contribution to the scene was his famous tune 'Dippermouth Blues', which Louis had brought with him to Henderson and which became Henderson's first great record hit, and his own favourite record by his band. This great number, also known as 'Sugar Foot Stomp', was to be recorded by almost every major band of the swing era – Bob Crosby, the Dorsey Brothers, Benny Goodman, Glenn Miller, Artie Shaw, Chick Webb, and Louis himself. Fletcher Henderson recorded it three times once featuring Louis in 1925, and twice with his replacement, Rex Stewart, in 1931 (for two different record companies, one under the name of "The Connie's Inn Orchestra").

Rex, being a fervent disciple of Louis', was delighted when Louis phoned him at the Nest Club in Harlem and asked him if he wanted a good job. Rex had heard a rumour that Louis was starting a band of his own, and said, "Sure."

"Fine," said Louis, "you take my place with

Fletcher in two weeks."

At that Rex made a rapid switch from delighted to terrified. He was working at the Nest Club with a group led by banjoist Elmer Snowden and Rex stayed in the group for another six months, until Snowden, in desperation, fired him to get him to take the job.

Even then, after sitting in what he thought of as Louis' chair in the Henderson band for nine months, he couldn't stand the pressure, and one day sneaked off on a train to Washington and disappeared for two months, part of which he spent playing in a band that Fletcher's younger brother, Horace, had formed in 1924. Horace was seven years younger than Fletcher. He had majored in music and, following in his brother's footsteps, had also become a pianist, arranger and bandleader. At his time he was leading a touring band, based at his old university, Wilberforce College.

After his two months away, Rex came sneaking apologetically back to Fletcher. He stayed with the band on and off until 1933, playing his own particular and very individual brand of vocally-inflected cornet, before joining Duke Ellington in 1934.

The other major musician in the Fletcher Henderson band was Coleman Hawkins, who in his way was almost as influential as Louis. He had joined in 1923 (after being a member of Mamie Smith's Jazz Hounds) and stayed for ten years. During that time he effectively invented the tenor saxophone. Which is to say that he worked out how to get a good rich tone out of it, and established it as a powerful, expressive voice.

This took him a little while. When he joined the band he was only nineteen and still, according to himself, not taking music seriously. He had been born in St Joseph, Missouri, although his family moved to Kansas City while he was still in junior school. He started learning to play the piano at the age of six, played cello for a while, and took up the tenor when he was nine.

After leaving school he studied music at Washburn College, Topeka, Kansas, and in Chicago, going to as many classical concerts as he could, and learning about jazz from records. In Chicago he heard Louis Armstrong and the great pianist and future bandleader, Earl Hines. By sixteen he was playing professionally around Kansas City.

His own explanation of the full tone he developed was that he always used a stiff reed anyway, and had to learn to play loud to make his solos heard over seven or eight other horns. This developed the fullness of his sound, so that eventually he found it was still full when he played softly.

In addition to his rich tone he had a formidable knowledge of harmonic theory, of resolutions and inversions and chord sequences, and developed his own method of improvisation, running up and down the notes in each chord as it came along. Maybe it was from listening to Louis, or maybe it would have happened anyway, but serious about his music he now was. Certainly it was from Louis that he learnt to swing as hard as he soon did.

All in all, he became for years to come the man to beat. Years later, in the Fifties, after all the changes and subtleties of swing and bop, of Lester Young and Charlie Parker, a young fast tenor-player newly arrived in New York ran head-on into Hawkins at an informal session and later complained to Cannonball Adderley that Hawkins had scared him. "Man," said Cannonball, "Hawk is supposed to scare you."

Up-and-coming tenor-players had been laying for Hawk for years. About the only time he seems to have come off worst was in around 1934, when he was on tour with the Henderson band in

Kansas City and went off for an after-hours blow at a club called the Cherry Blossom. Possibly not even Hawkins had realised what a strong scene was then growing up in Kansas City. Word went round that he was at the Cherry Blossom, and within a short time he was faced by Lester Young, Ben Webster, Herschel Evans, Herman Walder and one or two other tenor-players, all after his blood.

Even Hawk was overwhelmed by this aggregation of talent, although he kept blowing all night and into the next morning to try and assert his supremacy. The Henderson band was due to play in St Louis that night, and he so far overshot his leaving time that he had to drive like fury to get there, burning out the engine of his brand new Cadillac in the effort to make it.

Which brings in another aspect of life in the swing era – the road. Fletcher Henderson was the first bandleader to take seriously to touring. Because he was so early on the scene, there were at first no booking agents, and he and his wife Leora did all the organisation themselves, writing letters and telegrams, and phoning all over the north-east of America.

Later bands used buses, and sometimes trains, but the Henderson band were proud owners of big cars, and toured in those. Fortunately the Twenties was also the decade of the automobile, and during the decade there was a gradual upgrading of America's road system from what in 1920 had been three million miles of mostly cart-tracks, to a surfaced network from coast to coast, complete with gas-stations, roadside diners, motels and Burma-shave ads.

When the band was in New York, Roseland was the place to be. Among the famous names who often dropped by to hear the band were Cole Porter, columnist Walter Winchell, gangster Legs Diamond, boxer Benny Leonard, and New York's mayor, Jimmy Walker.

Another regular listener from the early days was a young Harlem pianist, a disciple of James P. Johnson's, Fats Waller. Fats, among all his other musical talents, had a gift for arranging, and used to have long discussions with Don Redman. One day Redman went into "The Hamburg King", next door to the Rhythm Club on 132nd Street, and there was Fats, broke and hungry. He brightened up on seeing Don, and said, "Have a seat and buy me a hamburger." Don bought him two, and as a favour in return Fats tried to sell him eight numbers he'd just written for ten dollars each.

They were great numbers, and Don talked Fats into taking them to Fletcher and getting a fair price for them. Fats did, and Fletcher bought most of them, and several of them got recorded by the band.

One of those tunes, with Fats himself on piano, is 'Henderson Stomp' (admittedly credited to Fletcher as composer, but he and Fats were friends and that sort of thing never seemed to affect their friendship). In those days (the mid-Twenties) Fats often sat in with the band, on recordings and at live performances. Fletcher was well aware that Fats was ten times the pianist he could ever hope to be, and while he (Fletcher) was a useful accompanist, he would never have the attack to properly control a big band from the keyboard.

The band continued from strength to strength, and by 1927 had reached its peak. Coleman Hawkins was its star, his only rival for the crowd's favour being Big Charlie Green (the trombonist of Bessie Smith's song 'Trombone Cholly'), an ex-carnival musician with perfect command of his horn and a tone that ranged from sweet to strident.

Hawkins had a trick for cooling off Charlie's playing when he felt like it. Charlie was a jealous husband, and Hawk would mutter to other musicians on the bandstand, in Charlie's hearing, "I guess I'd better call my old lady. It's not that I don't trust her, but I want her to know I'm thinking about her." This never failed to upset Charlie, who would hit the gin bottle, and during the evening his playing would get sadder and sadder.

The band continued to play at Roseland, and at other dance-halls round New York, and they toured and made records. A sad fact is that, from the accounts of those who heard it, it never managed to capture its full excitement on record. A possible explanation of this is that in live performance its numbers tended to last for about ten minutes, building the tension higher and higher, and this was difficult to reproduce in the three minutes of a 78.

Coleman Hawkins once said that the only recording that came close to the excitement of the live band was its 1934 version of 'Limehouse Blues'. It's certainly an amazing performance, taken at a blistering tempo, and Hawk's remark is a considerably charitable when you realise that the long tenor solo is not his, but is by his disciple, Ben Webster, sounding in those days as like Hawk as he could possibly get.

By 1934, however, the great days were over. The decline started in 1927, when Don Redman, who had effectively run the band since he joined it, left to go to Detroit and be musical director of the band called "McKinney's Cotton Pickers". He had done all the Henderson's arrangements since 1923, except for a few contributed by Coleman Hawkins, and Henderson had to scrabble round hurriedly for a new arranger, with no real success.

Then, in 1928, Fletcher was in a car-crash. He was down in Kentucky, on the way to visit his wife's mother in Louisville, driving his big black open Packard roadster and having as passengers Coleman Hawkins, Big Charlie Green, and trumpeters Bobby Stark and Joe Smith. Avoiding a woman driver who wouldn't pull over, he went off the road and the car fell fourteen feet into a ditch and turned over. By a miracle, none of the passengers was hurt, but Fletcher got a bad knock on the head and a damaged shoulder.

As his wife, Leora, said, after that he seemed changed. Everything seemed comical to him, and he lost what little ambition he had ever had. He didn't even seem to care if the band sounded in tune.

Fortunately, the band had great morale, and great affection for Fletcher, and did a lot to hold things together themselves. Then, in 1929, came the real disaster. The band was hired to go to Philadelphia and play for a revue whose musical director was Vincent Youmans, composer of 'Tea For Two', 'I Want To Be Happy', 'Sometimes I'm Happy', 'I Know That You Know', 'Time On My Hands' and many more.

The band was to be augmented for the occasion by about twenty white musicians, mostly string players, and Youmans suggested that, as Fletcher had no revue experience, an experienced conductor should be brought in. Possibly the reason for this request was that the white musicians would resent having a black conductor, but whatever the reason, Fletcher (as usual) made no objection. He continued not to object when the white conductor began firing the members of his band, or giving their parts to the white musicians, and didn't even object when his closest friend in the band, drummer Kaiser Marshall, was fired. The band broke up in some bitterness, and most of them never worked for Fletcher again.

To give Fletcher credit, he worked hard over the next few years to rebuild the band and its reputation, and by 1931 again had a fine collection of musicians, still including Coleman Hawkins, Rex Stewart and trombonist Jimmy Harrison, who either was a great influence on Jack Teagarden, or else was greatly influenced by Jack Teagarden, but either way, between them (and they became close friends), they led the way for the trombone from being an accompanying instrument, mostly playing great smears, to being a viable solo instrument, phrasing more like a trumpet.

By now Fletcher was able to get occasional arrangements written by Benny Carter and others, but more and more he was forced into becoming his own arranger, and he turned out to be the best his band ever had. His style was sparer and simpler than Don Redman's (possibly from laziness), and made the music seem effortless.

His brother Horace also joined the band in 1933. He played piano on some of the band's recordings, and did quite a bit of arranging, but it is hard to be sure exactly what his role was. He left, and came back, and left again more firmly in 1937 to form a big band of his own. It is said that he felt somewhat bitter because his arrangements were always assumed to be by Fletcher.

In 1934, Coleman Hawkins abruptly decided to leave the band and go to England. Quite why his decision was so abrupt is hard to say. Maybe he was aware of the reception that both Louis Armstrong (in 1932) and Duke Ellington (in 1933) had received there, and wanted some of the applause for himself. Or possible he was getting a bit tired of being the fastest draw in town and wanted to be somewhere where he would be applauded without being challenged for a while.

Whatever the reason, he sent a telegram to British bandleader Jack Hylton that simply said, "I am interested in coming to London." His reputation was such that Hylton wired him back a good offer next day, and he left a week later.

Then followed one of the ironic moments in jazz history. Searching for a replacement, Fletcher, who had a fine talent for recognising talent, sent for one of the Kansas City tenor-players who had given Hawkins such a hard time earlier in the year. It was the next great giant of the tenor saxophone, Lester Young, and the appointment turned out a disaster.

At this time, Hawkins had been the dominant voice in tenor-playing for nearly ten years. He had worked out how the instrument should be played, and almost every up-and-coming tenor-player strove to sound like him. Among the dozens of Hawkins clones were several exceptional players Ben Webster, Chu Berry and Herschel Evans among them. But Lester was something else.

He had found his own way to play, lighter and with less vibrato than Hawkins, and with a spare, wry method of improvising that owed nothing to anyone. As far as the Henderson band were concerned, he played wrong.

Leora Henderson, Fletcher's rather domineering wife, and a trumpeter herself ("circus trumpet", according to Lester), even took it upon herself to sit Lester down at nine every morning and play him Coleman Hawkins records, in an attempt to set him straight.

The rather shy and diffident Lester stayed with the band for only a few miserable months and then was off back to Kansas City. The band, with a sigh of relief, hired Ben Webster.

Nonetheless, things were moving on. New bands were coming up all over the place, the music was changing, Fletcher no longer had the pick of the best musicians, or the drive to move on. The musicians he had no longer felt committed to the band the way the earlier men had, and one by one they drifted off. Eventually, in 1935, broke, he sold a batch of his best arrangements to a young white bandleader called Benny Goodman. But that's another story.

CHAPTER 4

white bands of the twenties

Throughout the Twenties the place that had the hottest bands, both jazz and dance, was Chicago. Prohibition had made possible the lucrative business of bootlegging. When it was first enforced, Big Jim Colosimo, owner of a chain of brothels and a fashionable restaurant, had had the town in his pocket for a decade. He was the first to see the commercial possibilities of supplying illegal liquor to a thirsty population, and set about doing so.

Unfortunately he did not live to reap the rewards of his imagination and resource. He made the mistake of hiring as his bodyguard a dapper New York gunman named Johnny Torrio. Torrio decided to take over Colosimo's empire, and in May 1920, when Colosimo went to a cafe to take delivery of one of his first consignments of illegal whisky, he was gunned down.

His extravagant funeral attracted five thousand mourners, and the procession was led by three judges, two Congressmen, one Assistant State's Attorney, and eight Chicago aldermen, illustrating the link between politics and commercial enterprise. (There were also a number of opera singers. Colosimo had a passion for opera.)

Chicago during the rest of the Twenties was like a feudal society where robber barons fought and killed each other for supremacy. Gangs led by such as Dion O'Banion, Al Capone, Hymie Weiss

and the Genna brothers carved up the town between them. The revenue from the liquor industry gave them enormous wealth and power, enabling them to buy off police and politicians to an even greater extent than before.

If you are in the liquor business, it helps to own places where it can be sold, and the gangs opened and owned clubs and speakeasies and restaurants and dance-halls, none of which paid very much attention to licensing laws or hours of opening. And the bands flourished.

In big dance halls like Dreamland and the Trianon and the Merry Garden they played almost non-stop. There were dance contests and exhibition dances, and where new steps were introduced. Skirts were getting shorter, dancing was close, and life was exciting.

By 1920, in the wake of the Original Dixieland Jass Band, an army of young white musicians who wanted to play jazz had appeared all over America, and Chicago in the early Twenties had the band that was regarded as the ODJB's natural successor – the New Orleans Rhythm Kings. Their front line of Paul Mares (trumpet), George Brunies (trombone) and Leon Roppolo (clarinet) were all from New Orleans. They had left there separately, but came together in Chicago, found a rhythm section of young men from other places, and formed the band.

Basically they played the same sort of music as

the ODJB, but they were also greatly influenced by the King Oliver's Creole Jazz Band. As a result they played with a less jerky rhythm and a considerable feeling of relaxation. Two members of the band's rhythm section would go on to have a great influence on the development of swing – the bassist, Steve Brown and the drummer, Ben Pollack.

Mares was a good driving trumpeter; Brunies (who later shortened his name to George Brunis on the advice of a numerologist) was a useful trombonist who became very active in the jazz revival of the Forties; but Roppolo was by far the best player in the band. An inventive player, he used subtle variations in tone and, by contrasting the clarinet's plaintive upper register with its rich lower one, he played with an emotional quality rare among his contemporaries.

Although his career was short (he had a nervous breakdown in 1925 and retired to a sanatorium), he influenced many clarinetists, notably one kid who was occasionally allowed to sit in with the band, even though he was only fourteen. His name was Benny Goodman.

Near-contemporaries of Goodman's, all three or four years older than he was, were the amazing collection of young enthusiasts known to jazz history as the Austin High School Gang.

Only a few of them had actually attended Chicago's Austin High School – trumpeter Jimmy MacPartland, his brother Dick (a guitarist), bassist Jim Lanigan, and tenor-player Bud Freeman – but around them had gathered a number of other future stars, among them clarinetist Frank Teschemacher, guitarist Eddie Condon, and Dave Tough, who in the Thirties and Forties would become one of the greatest drummers of the Swing Era, playing with Tommy Dorsey, Benny Goodman and Woody Herman. There was also a slightly younger drummer hanging around, the

same age as Goodman. His name was Gene Krupa.

They spent all the time they could hanging around the clubs where jazz was being played, especially the clubs in Chicago's black quarter, the South Side. There was King Oliver's Creole Jazz Band, with Louis Armstrong, trombonist Kid Ory, clarinetist Johnny Dodds, and Johnny's younger brother Baby Dodds, on drums (In the Sixties, when Gene Krupa was being interviewed by Rudi Blesh, he went out of his way to say, "When you write this up, remember Baby Dodds, will you?")

Among the dozens of small bands there was one led by another New Orleans clarinetist, Jimmy Noone. There was local pianist Jimmy Blythe, with his State Street Ramblers, and there were two other pianists who at that time were leading the way in the whole of jazz – there was Earl Hines, playing in the black dance-bands of Sammy Stewart, Erskine Tate and Carroll Dickerson, and there was Hines's chief rival, Teddy Weatherford, who would be better-remembered today if he hadn't emigrated to the Far East in 1926.

And at a battered, rat-infested joint called the Paradise Club there was Bessie Smith. This was the real thing, a world away from what the dancing public thought of as blues. Bix and Eddie Condon went to hear her night after night, and one night Bix pulled out every penny he had in his pockets and gave it to her to keep her singing.

Although Chicago was the great swinging town, New York was still the Big City, and had its own scene going, and many hopeful young bands that had sprung up naturally headed there. One such was made up of young musicians from Ohio and Pennsylvania, although it had named themselves the California Ramblers because "it sounded good".

They had been brought together by a banjoist called Ray Kitchingman and, scuffling for work in New York, he brought the band in 1921 to audition for an independent record producer and talent booker called Ed Kirkeby, now probably best remembered as Fats Waller's manager and biographer.

Kirkeby was in his early twenties. and had started his career in 1916 as an assistant recording manager for Columbia Records where his job had been to organise bands for recording sessions. It was for such a session that he was auditioning in 1921 on his own account. He was looking for a young peppy band to accompany a straight singer called Eva Shirley.

When he heard the California Ramblers, he liked them. He not only used them with Eva Shirley, he also fixed them an audition with the B.F.Keith vaudeville circuit.

Benjamin Franklin Keith and his partner, Edward Albee, had been for years (for decades) the most powerful management team in vaudeville, and almost before they knew it the Ramblers found themselves booked into the most prestigious vaudeville house in America – the Palace Theatre, New York – the place that acts spent their careers trying to get booked into. Not only that, they were on the same bill as Singer's Midgets.

Kirkeby then got them a season at the Post Lodge in Larchmont, New York. Their reputation continued to grow, and things began to go wrong. On-stage, the band was fronted by their violinist, Oscar Adler, who was a good showman. He was also very ambitious, and began complaining to Kirkeby that he wasn't giving the band enough of a build-up. He complained so much that Kirkeby stopped representing the Ramblers. Kirkeby also went to his friends at the B.F.Keith office and got the band blacked from appearing in any Keith-Albee house.

This was no joke. Keith-Albee owned so many of the best places of entertainment, and had so much influence everywhere, that work virtually dried up for the Ramblers, and within a few months they were forced to disband.

Fortunately, however, Ray Kitchingman refused to give up. He came back to Kirkeby and asked him to help in re-forming the band (without Oscar Adler). Kirkeby agreed, and using a nucleus of the original members, plus a number of other talented young musicians, the California Ramblers were back in business.

Kirkeby eventually hunted out so many good young musicians that he built up a considerable pool of talent for making records. Using anywhere from nine to fourteen musicians, with constantly shifting personnels, the band recorded prolifically, usually as the California Ramblers, but sometimes under such names as the Golden Gate Orchestra, and, in smaller groups, as the Goofus Five, the Five Birmingham Babies, the Vagabonds, the Varsity Eight, and Ted Wallace's Orchestra.

Over they years they not only recorded for major companies like Columbia, Edison, Pathé, Victor, Vocalion and Paramount, but also for lesser-known labels with names like Banner, Bluebird, Emerson, Arto, Bell, Cameo, Harmony, Apex, Regal, Clarion, and finally, in 1937, Variety. In sixteen years they waxed over six hundred sides.

Once the band had got re-launched, Kirkeby started looking round for a venue they could call their own. In Pelham Bay, a well-to-do district at the north end of the Bronx, he found a restaurant with a dance-floor called the Pelham Inn. He had it renamed the California Ramblers Inn, one of the versions of the band moved in, and the place became a great success. As Kirkeby himself said fifty years later, "the society crowd used to dance their heels off". And not only was the music new and good, the Inn also served a fine seafood dinner of steamed clams, lobster, broiled chicken, salad and dessert, all for one dollar fifty.

The main audience for the California Ramblers was the white college crowd. It was among these young people at the Ramblers Inn that a characteristic phenomenon of the swing era first began to appear – fans who came to listen avidly to the music rather than to dance.

Although they were among the pioneers of big band jazz, the Ramblers had no arranger of their own. By the early Twenties there were so many bands in existence, both professional and semi-professional, that music publishing houses had started issuing band parts for their songs. The Ramblers used these stock arrangements as a basis, adding touches of their own and superimposing solos.

These solos were often of high quality, which is hardly surprising when you consider some of the names among the regular players. There was clarinetist Fud Livingstone (who later joined Whiteman, and went on to arrange for Tommy Dorsey and Benny Goodman). There was cornetist Red Nichols, whose 1927 recording of 'Ida, Sweet As Apple Cider', by his famous Five Pennies, was to become the first million-selling jazz record.

There was trombonist Miff Mole, who joined Nichols in the Five Pennies. Mole in the early Twenties created the first distinctive solo trombone style, expanding the use of the trombone from its previous role as an accompanying instrument. He played with a pure-toned, precise style, using short notes and leaps in pitch rather than using great hoarse glissandos, as the New Orleans trombonists tended to do.

Also in the Ramblers was saxophonist Jimmy

Dorsey, who would later be joined by his younger brother, Tommy. It was using their reputation with the dancing public, first built up in their days with bands like the Ramblers, that eventually allowed them to set up their own band, using another ex-Rambler, Stan King, as their drummer.

In the mid-Twenties Jimmy was a more finished player than Tommy, who had not yet perfected the smooth trombone tone and perfect breath-control of his later years. Jimmy had much more technical control of his instrument than most other saxophonists of the time, whose intonation tended to be insecure, and he became a considerable influence on others, in spite of the fact that he was somewhat lacking in invention. Musicians are able to recognise technique when they hear it, and tend to admire it for itself alone. Among those in later years who expressed admiration for his playing were three giants – Johnny Hodges, Charlie Parker and Ornette Coleman.

Another influential musician that Kirkeby discovered, and certainly the most unusual, was a young pianist and xylophonist called Adrian Rollini. Rollini was born in 1904 and had been leading his own band in New York at the age of fourteen. He was one of those musicians who can play anything, and Kirkeby, who had decided the band needed a bass saxophone, got him to learn to play one.

Rollini succeeded triumphantly on that ungainly and unforgiving instrument (for a start it has an appreciable time-lag between the time you blow into it and the time the note comes out). He learnt to play it with surprising ease and lightness, and although his improvised lines were not usually all that interesting, he had a real feeling for how to swing.

Not content with mastering the deepest of the reeds, he also took up the shrillest, a miniature clarinet about a foot long, with no keys (only holes, like a recorder). This he called his "hot fountain pen".

He also played what appeared to be a saxophone with piano keys on it, but in fact was a sort of harmonica. This was properly called a couesnophone (it was made by a French firm called Couesnon & Cie.) but people found this name too difficult so Rollini started referring to it as a goofus. Hence the Goofus Five.

In their early days the California Ramblers mostly recorded for Columbia. On the rival Victor label at that time one of the most popular bands was the Benson Orchestra of Chicago, which was then among the crème de la crème of society bands. It was only one of a number of dance-bands being run by an entrepreneur called Edgar Benson, and one his regular musicians was a charming and sophisticated young pianist called Jean Goldkette.

Goldkette had been born in France in 1899. Something of an infant prodigy, he had already been trained in Greece and Russia as a classical pianist before he was twelve, when some relatives in Chicago suggested he might do well in the U.S., and he moved to live with them.

Benson noticed Goldkette's charming manner, which was by no means hindered by his soft-spoken French accent, and he began using him to front some of his bands.

Goldkette quickly became popular. Capitalising on this, he left Benson, moved to Detroit, and set up his own organisation, modelled on Benson's, with a stable of bands, a booking agency, and with its own ballroom, the Graystone.

How he came by this was that a group of Chinese businessmen had started building a huge restaurant, found themselves unable to complete it, and put the building on the market. Goldkette learnt about the property from banker friends, managed to drum up enough finance to take over the lease, and the Graystone Ballroom was born.

It was described (in its own house newsletter) as "the most beautiful ballroom in the middle west, if not the land". It had a Spanish-style entrance lobby, and the ballroom itself had a canopied mezzanine around it, with "inviting chairs and divans where guests may rest and lounge while enjoying the music and a full view of the dancers below".

Like other band-leaders, Goldkette realised the pulling-power of hot musicians, so he scoured the surrounding middle-west to find them. One he heard of in 1924 was an amazing young cornetist from Iowa called Beiderbecke.

Bix was then twenty-one, playing with a group of young Chicago musicians called the Wolverines, and Goldkette listened to some recordings they had made for the Gennett label.

Gennett was owned by the Starr Piano Company of Richmond, Indiana, who had decided in 1915 to start up an independent recording company and get in on this new-fangled phonograph business. Their recording quality was pretty terrible, but they left their musicians alone to play what they wanted (Jelly Roll Morton and King Oliver among them). Goldkette liked what he could hear of Bix, so he made an unannounced trip to New York to hear him live.

Bix was playing at the Cinderella Ballroom, on 48th Street and Broadway. It had only been recently opened and had hired the Wolverines on a three-month contract in an effort to lure customers away from the Roseland, three streets away, where Fletcher Henderson (with Louis Armstrong in his band) was such a big attraction. For the run of their engagement the management renamed the band "The Personality Kids".

It was the height of the Charleston craze, and while the Personality Kids were there, the Cinderella was the place to go to dance it.

At this stage in the development of dance music, jazz was still regarded as "novelty music". In the words of a local journalist as late as 1929 – "Plinky-planky-plinky moans! Crooning tones! Ear- tickling, piercing, soul-wrenching melodies – that's jazz!" A dance-band arrangement might allot a half-chorus, or even a chorus, to a hot soloist, and there were a few syncopated semi-ragtime bands around playing "peppy" music, but a group like the Wolverines, playing straight-ahead jazz, was still something unusual.

Goldkette heard Bix and liked his playing. He went round backstage, introduced himself, and offered Bix a job in his band in Detroit.

For a few days Bix agonised over the decision. New York was the place to be, and he was being feted there. Young white musicians were coming to hear him in the same way that young black musicians were going to the Roseland to hear Louis Armstrong. Even musicians who had already made something of a name for themselves, like fellow-cornetist Red Nichols, of the California Ramblers, were coming by to hear and admire him.

Also there was so much exciting new music for him to hear. In Harlem there were lavish jazz-flavoured revues. Louis Armstrong was at the Roseland with Fletcher Henderson. Even nearer, a block away, on 49th Street, there was the Kentucky Club, where a pianist from Washington called Duke Ellington had a good little band.

Also he didn't want to abandon the Wolverines, seeing as he was their star player. But he discussed the matter with them, and they, realising that he was too good to stay with them for ever, gave him their blessing to go. In October 1924, he went.

Unfortunately, their magnanimity brought the Wolverines little luck. At around the time that Bix left, the manager of the Cinderella Ballroom decided that there were more people in New York dancing the more sedate older dances than there were dancing the Charleston, and that the energetic Charleston dancers, with their sideways kicks that could catch you on the shins, were keeping the others away. His solution was to change the ballroom's musical policy, and the Wolverines were told that their three-month contract would not be renewed.

The band Bix found in Detroit was a dance-band with a few hot players in it. Among them were clarinetist Don Murray, violinist Joe Venuti, and trombonists Bill Rank and Tommy Dorsey (who had not yet moved to New York to join the California Ramblers). They loved Bix's playing, as did Jean Goldkette, but nonetheless he didn't last long with the band. Two months, in fact.

The main reason was that, having played only in jazz bands, he was not good at reading music (he never became really proficient). The band had a regular broadcasting date on a local radio station, so they constantly had to rehearse new numbers, and it soon became clear that Bix was unable to cope. Instead of carrying two trumpets, Goldkette found the band had to carry three – two to play the scores and Bix to play his hot solos. So Bix's salary was on top of the band's usual payroll.

In December 1924, Goldkette and his partner, Charlie Horvath, were planning to rearrange the band (they were temporarily splitting it in two to provide an extra band to play at a newly-opened hotel), and this seemed a good time for them to let Bix go. Goldkette gave him the news, but advised him to brush up on his reading and become more of an all-round musician, and there was every chance he would be back.

For over a year, Bix played in other bands – with Charlie Straight, with Nat Natoli, with the California Ramblers, with Merton "Bromo" Sulser and his Iowa Collegians.

In April 1925, when he was playing with Charlie Straight's band at the Rendezvous Cafe in Chicago, he ran into some of the Goldkette boys, and as a result was hired for the night of May 1 to play with them at the annual Indiana University prom. Bix had a strong following among the students there, led by a piano-playing student named Hoagy Carmichael.

His problem was, he had no tuxedo. Guitarist Eddie Condon and his brother Jim helped fit him out with (in Condon's words), "Jim's jacket and trousers and shirt, my studs and tie. For good measure and the cool spring nights we gave him a topcoat and a hat. A few days later he returned and brought us the borrowed articles. There was a tuxedo, complete with studs, tie and shirt. But the tuxedo was not Jim's, the shirt was not his, and the studs and tie were not mine. The topcoat and hat also differed from those we had given him. 'Did you have a good time,' we asked politely. 'I don't know,' Bix said."

Eventually, in September 1925, Bix joined an eleven-piece band led by his friend Frankie Trumbauer, known to everyone as Tram, at the Arcadia Ballroom, St Louis.

He had first heard Trumbauer's playing in 1922, when Tram was in the Benson Orchestra of Chicago, and they had met in New York when the Wolverines were playing the Cinderella Ballroom.

Trumbauer mostly played C-melody saxophone. In pitch the C-melody comes between the alto and the tenor. Originally a military-band instrument, it dropped out of jazz early (its function being adequately covered by the other two), and almost nobody except Trumbauer continued to play it. He developed a light singing tone, and a poised and delicate style, with unusual turns of phrase (although he was never a great improviser, preferring to work out his solo variations carefully in advance and criticising Bix for playing spontaneously, on the grounds that it made him (Bix) nervous on the bandstand).

Like Jimmy Dorsey and Adrian Rollini, Trumbauer was a considerable influence on other saxophonists, in particular on Basie's great soloist, Lester Young, who claimed Trumbauer as almost his only influence.

The Arcadia Ballroom, where the Trumbauer band was playing, was due to close down for the summer at the beginning of May 1926, so at the end of March Bix went to Detroit to talk to Jean Goldkette and see whether Goldkette would hire him and Tram and some of the other musicians in their band during the lay-off.

Goldkette said he would certainly think about it, and in April his partner, Charlie Horvath, came to the Arcadia with a proposition. Goldkette wanted to take a break from leading the band to concentrate on other aspects of his business (the Graystone Ballroom, his booking agency, and a music school he had started). Would Trumbauer take over leading the band and act as its musical director? And would Bix come back permanently as featured cornet soloist?

They would, and did. Goldkette's plan was for his full band to play a string of prom dates, then to be split in two, with a few added players, to play at two summer resorts. The smaller band with Bix and Tram in was to play at an inn on Hudson Lake, Indiana. As well as them it had a number of other young hot musicians in it, the most famous in future years being the quirky clarinetist, Pee Wee Russell.

They had a wonderful summer, lazy and relaxing, living in rented bungalows along the lakeside and drinking awful corn mash brewed by two elderly spinsters on a nearby farm. The band got better and better, as did Bix's playing, and he and Trumbauer learned to take choruses together as improvised duets.

After their lazy summer, things suddenly hotted up. At the end of August the men added for the summer, including Pee Wee Russell, left, and the rest were called back to Detroit where the full Goldkette band was to be reassembled. Goldkette had managed to arrange a three week tour of New England, followed by a ten-day booking at the Roseland Ballroom in New York, temporarily replacing Fletcher Henderson, who he had booked into the Graystone Ballroom in Detroit.

There was a lot of work to be done, and they had only two weeks to do it in. The two halves of the band had been playing apart all summer, and each half had developed a slightly different style. Furthermore they were very short of arrangements featuring the new hot players.

Fortunately, a young saxophonist called Bill Challis had sent the band a sample of his arranging work (the tune was 'Baby Face'), and Eddie Horvath sent for him to come and join the band. They were already a week into their tour when he arrived, and one by one his new arrangements started to appear.

They were intelligent and harmonically inventive, and left plenty of space for the soloists, and the band got even better.

When they set off on their New England tour the wife of their second trombonist, Spiegle Willcox, was expecting a baby, so he stayed behind and back into the band came Tommy Dorsey.

They opened at the Roseland on Saturday, October 6, but the big event of their stay was to be a week later, when the Henderson band, back from Detroit, was to engage with them in a "battle of the bands".

That next Saturday, the two bands were seated on bandstands flanking a central stage, Goldkette's on the left, Henderson's on the right. The dance-floor was packed, with lines of listeners in tuxedos, mostly musicians, crammed twenty-deep round the stage.

Some of the men in the Henderson band were a little anxious because, during their stay at the Graystone, Charlie Horvath had gone out of his way to tell them they were going to get "one helluva shock" when they heard the Goldkette Victor Recording Orchestra.

One who was especially anxious was the nineteen-year-old Rex Stewart, still nervously occupying what he thought of as Louis Armstrong's trumpet chair. But Coleman Hawkins reassured him. "Bunch o' li'l ol' white boys from out there where all that corn grows. Nope. Ain't got nothin' to say to me."

The Goldkette band was to play first. Trumbauer, realising that the Henderson men would expect them to begin with an up-tempo flag-waver, had come up with a plan. He raised his hand for silence, trumpeter Ray Lodwig stamped off the beat, and they went into a 6/8 arrangement of the Spanish march, 'Valencia'.

There was a moment of stunned silence, then the audience began to laugh and clap and cheer in a crescendo of applause. From that moment the Goldkette band had the audience on their side. They followed 'Valencia' with 'Tiger Rag', 'My Pretty Girl', 'Blue Room', 'Baby Face', working their way down the new Bill Challis scores, and even slipping in the occasional waltz or tango.

The Henderson band did some muttering among themselves about how this wouldn't have happened if Don Redman had been here on alto (he was off visiting his parents in West Virginia), but they were licked, at least for that night, and they knew it.

An important reason why the Goldkette band had became so good was their bass-player, Steve Brown – he who had been a member of the New Orleans Rhythm Kings. He had been in the other half of the band from Bix during the summer, and it was his way of laying down the beat that really gave the band something new.

Up till then most bands (including Fletcher Henderson's) had used the tuba to lay down the bass rhythm. With Steve Brown's plucked bass the beat was more driving and flexible. Also he was something of a showman, who was quite happy to come out front and play a solo, and dance a Charleston at the same time.

Not only that, his rhythmic instincts led him to play on all four beats of the bar, not just two. He had started doing this in the New Orleans Rhythm Kings as early as 1923, and by now was doing it often. This was the start of the switch from playing 2/4, like most Twenties bands, to playing the smoother 4/4 beat that was essential to the great swing of the Thirties and Forties.

From then on, the bass quickly replaced the tuba in all dance-bands. Other bands also noticed that the Goldkette band had three trumpets (Bix still wasn't all that hot at reading music) and, not knowing the reason, quickly began to employ three trumpets as well.

The Roseland engagement was really the Goldkette band's finest hour. Within slightly under a year it had effectively ceased to exist.

There were several reasons. In 1927 they were engaged on an ambitious nationwide tour, which included theatre shows. At one of these, at the end of May, a French variety act complained that the music was wrong for them. One of the band's lesser arrangers, a volatile drinker called Eddie Sheasby, took offence and failed to show up at the band's next engagement. Not only that, he had taken with him all the band's arrangements, and they were never seen again. With no written music, the band busked along as best it could, but it was soon obvious that most of the rest of the tour would have to be cancelled.

Also, some of the theatre managers had begun to complain that the band might be all right for dancers or other musicians, but that nowadays thee-ay-ter audiences wanted entertainment as well, perhaps a few comedy skits. As Irving Riskin, the pianist, said, "Who does he think we are – the Keystone Cops?"

Towards the end of July the band returned to the Graystone, where it was clear that not all was as it had been. By now Goldkette was running a number of other bands, and had built an empire of ballrooms on such a scale that he had become the most important impresario in the huge area bounded by Buffalo, Chicago, Toronto, and New Orleans. But he had over-reached himself, and there were rumours of breakup and financial disaster.

One thing that might stave it off was a booking that Goldkette was after, at a new club due to open in New York, to be called the New Yorker (the magazine of that name was then two years old and becoming fashionable). In fact it was the old Cinderella Ballroom remodelled.

Unfortunately for Goldkette, Adrian Rollini was also after the booking for a ten-piece band he was forming himself. Bix and Tram had from time to time been making the magnificent small-group recordings for which they are best known, and Rollini had been on some of them. And to make things worse for Goldkette he wanted them in his new band as well. And so did Paul Whiteman, who had heard rumours that the Goldkette band might be breaking up and had made them both an offer.

As things turned out, Rollini got the New Yorker job. Bix and Tram, leaving the struggling Goldkette band, joined him. They (and the club) opened on September 22. The attendance was poor, and mostly composed of fellow-musicians, and on October 15 the club closed.

This was a shame, because on the evidence of the records that Bix, Tram and Rollini were making at that time, it must have been an outstanding band. (Incidentally, one of the records that Bix and Tram made while they were still with Goldkette was the classic 'Singin' The Blues'. It's easy now to appreciate Bix's stunning 32-bar solo, with its perfect structure and unusual harmonies, but what is less obvious today is that this is one of the first great slow numbers in jazz. The group, and Bix in particular, showed other musicians that it was possible to play hot without using an up-tempo rhythm.)

Rollini's band hung together for a week or so while he tried to find other work for them, then Bix and Tram joined Paul Whiteman.

Goldkette's fortunes continued to decline.

Receipts at the Graystone, usually around $12,000 a week, by September 1929 had dropped to half that. Eventually he was left with thousands of dollars of debt and the band, deprived of its financial support, eventually folded completely.

Too proud to become bankrupt, he struggled for years to repay his debts, but never did. He ended up working as a booking agent, occasionally assembling bands for recording purposes. Musically, in spite of his appreciation of jazz, he was never able to play it well, although he remained a fine pianist and continued to make occasional appearances on the concert platform.

Most white big bands of the Twenties, like Whiteman and Goldkette, used hot musicians as part of an overall policy aimed at pleasing as wide a public as possible. The first leader to give real prominence to jazz-musicians and jazz-flavoured scores was Ben Pollack. He led the first "hot dance band", the immediate ancestor of the swing band.

Pollack himself was a drummer. Born in Chicago in 1903, he played in his school band, then in various obscure groups around Chicago. From time to time he began to sit in with the New Orleans Rhythm Kings. They liked the way he played and asked him to substitute on a record date for their regular drummer, Frank Snyder. This went so well that they fired Snyder and took Pollack aboard permanently. This was in 1923.

Now that he was playing regularly with a good band, his drumming got even better. One night, when they were playing for a show, the M.C. asked him to leave out all the press-rolls and fancy accents he had carefully worked up, as it was confusing the act on-stage. So he just played rhythm, and the band found to their surprise that they could swing more easily. In his own words, he learned that the secret of swinging for a drummer is to feed the band rather than compete with it.

His family (his father was a respectable furrier) were extremely unhappy about his musical interests. In 1924, in an attempt to lure him away from the music business they offered him a three-month vacation on the far side of America. He took them up on it and went to California, but while there he got a job in a dance-band led by one Harry Bastin.

After he had been away for eleven months, his family threatened to disown him, so he left the band and came reluctantly home to join the fur business. He stuck it for exactly one day and then fled to the music scene in New York. There a telegram somehow reached him saying that Harry Bastin was ill, and would he come back to

California and take over the band?

He would, and did, in 1925. Leading a band of his own was just what he wanted, and he knew exactly what sort of band it should be (a hot dance band). He also knew that he didn't have the necessary musical training to build one. Fortunately for him there had been another young Chicagoan in the Bastin band in 1924, an alto-player named Gil Rodin. Rodin was only an average alto-player, but he had ambitions to be an arranger, so Pollack hired him as musical director. A little later he hired two other budding arrangers, clarinetist Fud Livingtone and trombonist Glenn Miller. The band was coming together nicely.

Discussing other likely players, Pollack told Gil Rodin about the young clarinetist who used to sit in with the New Orleans Rhythm Kings, Benny Goodman. The kid was probably still only about sixteen, but he could read music fluently was was a talented hot improviser. With his background playing New Orleans jazz, Rodin wanted his band's solos to be improvised.

Rodin hadn't heard Goodman, but he was about to make a trip east, and promised he would check the kid out.

Reaching Chicago, he tracked him down playing in a dance-band at the Midway Gardens, in a white section of the South Side. This venue, as well as having an indoor dance-hall, had an outdoor "garden", which was used for dancing in the summer and was a place where respectable girls could go unaccompanied to hear the music and meet their friends.

It was playing in the garden that Rodin found Benny Goodman. He liked what he heard, and told Goodman that there would be a job for him in the Pollack band if opportunity presented itself.

Fortunately for Goodman, it was only a few months before Fud Livingstone wanted time off. In August 1925 Pollack sent for him, and he took the train to California, joining the band at the Venice Ballroom in Los Angeles. He was excited about going to California, where all those movie stars lived, and he was excited about joining the Pollack band. Even though the band hadn't yet built a public reputation, musicians knew about it, and those in the band felt they were in on the start of something special.

The band soon began to to build up a reputation, at least in California, but then it emerged they had a problem. The easterners in the band were getting homesick. As comedian Fred Allen said, "California is a great place if you're an orange." So in January 1926 Ben Pollack took his band back to Chicago.

Naturally, some of the men from the west preferred to stay there. One was the bass player, and Benny Goodman grabbed the opportunity of levering his brother Harry, who was a tuba player, into the band. He suggested this to Pollack, but Pollack was aware of what Steve Brown was doing with the Goldkette band, and said he would hire Harry only if he switched to string bass. Harry agreed to make the switch and was hired, gradually phasing out his tuba.

In Chicago, where it was almost unknown, the band had a hard time at first getting established. Some of the musicians, Goodman among them, took work from time to time with other bands, but they stayed loyal to the band they thought of as their own. At last Pollack landed the job that would make them, as resident band at the prestigious Southmoor Hotel. They all reassembled, and they were on their way.

As word of its new hot playing got around, Jean Goldkette arranged for them to get a recording contract with Victor. From the Southmoor they moved to the Rendezvous, and then to the Blackhawk, two of Chicago's most famous clubs. And new hot musicians continued to join. In 1927 in came trumpeter Jimmy MacPartland, of the Austin High School Gang, who by 1925 had become good enough to be some sort of replacement for Bix in the Wolverines.

In Goodman and MacPartland, Pollack now had two top-rank soloists, at least, for a while, because he and Goodman, both prickly personalities, had slight disagreements, and Goodman left the band in early 1928 to go with the dance-band led by Isham Jones. At the time he said it was because the money was better.

The Isham Jones band was popular, especially in the Midwest, and could play fairly hot when necessary (when Jones finally left the band business in 1936, some of its members formed the core of the first Woody Herman band), but nonetheless it was not as exciting a band as Pollack had, and Benny Goodman was persuaded by Gil Rodin to return after only a couple of months.

The particular reason why Pollack wanted him back was that the band had been offered a chance to play at a well-known club in New York, the Little Club. This was a chance not to be passed up, especially as things were changing in Chicago.

Big Bill Thompson, who had been mayor of Chicago since the Great War, had got himself elected on a platform of an open city, regardless of what the federal government said about the sale of alcohol, and had virtually turned Chicago over to the mobs to run. Serious crime was run like a business, albeit a business where opposition could be discouraged with a tommy-gun.

But by 1928 the people of Chicago were beginning to get tired of gangsters gunning each other down all over the place. It had been exciting for a while, but now there was growing agitation for reform. Bill Thompson might have held on, but just before the 1928 mayoral election, somebody bombed the homes of two prominent reformers. This swelled the tide of opinion against him. At the end of the year he was voted out and "Moral Chicago" was born.

Prohibition was firmly enforced. Clubs, cabarets, dance-halls, gambling joints and brothels were closed by the police hand over fist, and the party was over. Work for musicians dried up, and over the next two years almost all of them left for New York, which by 1930 had taken over as the place where it was all happening.

As well as Goodman, for his move to New York Pollack hired tenor-player Bud Freeman. About five years before, when Freeman had joined the Austin High School Gang, he had been the only one with no musical training. As a result, he was slow picking up the music. He began by just playing rhythm, getting one note and playing it over and over until the others would yell at him, "Change the note."

Frank Teschemacher, the clarinetist and the best-trained musician, wanted to throw him out of the group, but MacPartland and the others refused. They recognised that Bud had one thing, a terrific beat. As the years passed he learned more and more what to do, and eventually became almost the only tenor-player of the Twenties to develop a style independent of Coleman Hawkins, playing smooth supple lines with very little vibrato (and still a terrific beat).

The job at the Little Club lasted three months, then there was a period of scuffling for work until Pollack landed a booking at the famous Million Dollar Pier in Atlantic City. Glenn Miller had found another job and wasn't available, so Pollack needed a trombonist, and he was lucky enough to find the best possible replacement.

Weldon Leo Teagarden, tall and slow-spoken and known to the world as "Jack", was born in Texas in 1905. His mother was a classically-trained pianist who liked to play ragtime, and his father was a fairly good amateur cornet and baritone horn player. Jack showed an early interest in music – when he was five or six he was much taken by the black revivalist congregation that used to sing spirituals in a tent on a vacant lot alongside the Teagarden house – and when he was seven his father bought him a trombone for Christmas.

His idea was simply that his young son would play duets with him, but it soon became obvious that what he had on his hands was a real musician. After Jack had had his trombone only two months, they were playing along together when his father blew a bum note. Jack covered his ears with his hands and ran into the next room shouting, "First valve, first valve!"

Naturally Jack got into the school band, and at this point his mother got a teacher for him. But the teacher gave up after three months, saying, "I can't teach that lad anything." Instead, Jack taught himself, mainly by listening to the blues singers and guitar-players that seemed to be everywhere in Texas at that time.

When he was thirteen the family moved to Nebraska, then to Oklahoma, where he listened to Indian war-dances. And when he was fifteen an uncle back in Texas sent for him to come and help run the theatre he had in San Angelo.

He began to play in local dance-bands, then in small groups, most notably in a band called "Peck's Bad Boys", led by a legendary Texas pianist called Peck Kelley. He was a swinging, imaginative player with formidable technique, and the only reason he never became widely famous was because he preferred not to leave home and never made a record.

In the late Thirties the Will Bradley band, a white band that made a habit of playing swing numbers based on the rhythms of boogie-woogie piano, had a bit hit with a number called 'Beat Me Daddy, Eight To The Bar!' Its lyric contains the words, "In a little honky-tonky village in Texas, there's a guy who plays the best piano by far", and for many years this was believed to be a veiled reference to Peck Kelley. In fact, Kelley himself once thanked the band's drummer, Ray McKinley, for such a welcome piece of publicity. But McKinley, who was part-author of the song, admitted that the whole thing was just a coincidence – they didn't have any particular piano-player in mind.

When, in about 1922, the clarinetist left his band, Kelley sent Jack Teagarden to New Orleans to find a replacement. He didn't find one who was willing to go to Texas, but he did hear the young Louis Armstrong, and was knocked out. He introduced himself to Louis, and promised himself that some day they would play together.

By the time Peck's Bad Boys broke up, in 1923, Teagarden's very personal style (both on trombone and singing) was basically formed. His acquaintance with blues, work songs and spirituals showed itself in his sense of pitch – he was one of the first white players to use "blue notes", those slightly flattened notes that are the essence of jazz – and in his sense of rhythm, weaving lazy arabesques of melody all round the beat.

After playing with various bands all over middle America – Oklahoma City, Kansas City, Memphis, California – he eventually made the big move to New York City in 1928, when he was in his early twenties.

Pee Wee Russell, the clarinetist, had toured in Texas and heard Jack there. When Jack arrived in New York, Pee Wee went round telling everyone he knew that a great musician had arrived. Either Bud Freeman or Gil Rodin told Ben Pollack, and Ben Pollack went looking for him.

He tracked him down to a dingy lodging-room where a New Orleans trumpeter called Johnny Bayersdorffer was reading a newspaper by the light of a gas-jet. He enquired after this guy Teagarden, and Bayersdorffer indicated a figure asleep on a small cot against the wall. "Can he read?" asked Pollack.

"He's the best," said Bayersdorffer. He shook the sleeping figure but the only response he got was grumbling. He said, "Jack, you got a job in Atlantic City tonight. Wake up." "Man, I just got here," said Teagarden, "I don't wanna go nowhere."

After that, no amount of shaking could rouse him, and Pollack, getting mad, turned to leave. "There goes your job with Benny Pollack," said Bayersdorffer. Teagarden was awake like a shot. "Man, are you Benny Pollack? When do I leave."

The Atlantic City job was a success. Then there was another lean period for the Pollack band before they landed a job in the ballroom of the prestigious Park Central Hotel. They had to add some strings to the band, and play a lot of toned-down dinner and dance music, but the exposure they got made it bearable. At last they had made it in New York.

At the end of 1928 they were hired as pit band for a new musical called *Hello, Daddy*, written by the famous team of Dorothy Fields and Jimmy McHugh, and Ben Pollack decided at this point to turn over the drumming to somebody else and conduct the band from the front. The drummer he hired was a nineteen-year-old called Ray Bauduc, whose father, a cornetist, led a band in New Orleans.

Now the band was rolling. As well as the hotel job and the show, they were making records and appearing on the radio. The stars of the band were making about $650 a week, the lesser lights about $300, at a time when good dance-band musicians around New York were making anywhere from $125 to $150.

And then the problems started. Or at least, the problem, which was that Ben Pollack was beginning to act like a bandleader. In those days, and right through the Swing Era, bandleaders assumed a certain right to be autocratic. They could give their musicians uniforms to wear, tell them to get their hair cut, prohibit them from smoking or chewing gum on the bandstand, and fire them for lateness or poor attitude or anything else that seemed to call for it.

Most band musicians accepted this as part of the natural order of things. After all, a certain degree of polish and presentation was needed to survive in a competitive business and, after all, that was the way things were.

The trouble with the Pollack band was that, without thinking, he had filled it with jazz musicians. These are a notoriously difficult group to dictate to. They tend to care about nothing but their music, and as long as they play well, nothing else is anybody's business. Furthermore, they regarded the Pollack band as a co-operative venture, which they had stuck with through the lean times because they were proud of the noise it made, and whereas they were happy to have Pollack as a front-man, they didn't want a boss.

Pollack told Teagarden off for showing up drunk at rehearsals and unable to play properly, which was probably true, but if he wasn't that sort of guy he probably wouldn't play the beautiful way he did. He told Jimmy MacPartland off, either for not wearing sock-suspenders on stage, or for having scuffed shoes, and after an exchange of views Pollack threatened to fire him. Benny Goodman, always inclined to be cranky, said that if Jimmy went, he went.

Things went on in this vein until Pollack heard that Goodman and guitarist Dick Morgan had gone to the Park Central Hotel management and offered them the services of the Ben Pollack Band without Ben Pollack. Pollack managed to block this deal and he set about finding excuses to fire those he saw as mutineers, one by one. Among the first to go was Harry Goodman.

Then the band acquired a singer, Doris Robbins. She and Pollack began an affair, with the result that he started featuring her singing more and more, at the expense of the jazz numbers. There were more defections from the band, and more firings. Fortunately for him, Pollack retained his instinct for finding talent, and among the replacements he found were clarinetist Matty Matlock, trumpeter Yank Lawson and tenor saxophonist Eddie Miller.

This went on until one day in 1934, when the band was in California, the musicians in it decided to quit and form a band of their own. One by one that night they called by Ben Pollack's place and dropped off their band-books. Going back to New York, they set about building a new band and repertoire. At first it was something of a struggle, until agent Cork O'Keefe had the bright idea of hiring the brother of the biggest name in popular music at that time as their (nominal) leader. This they did, and as the Bob Crosby Band they went on to great success.

Ben Pollack rebuilt his band and soldiered on. His ear for good players did not desert him and in later years he hired, among others, trumpeter Harry James, clarinetist Irving Fazola and saxophonist Dave Matthews. But all these had their greatest successes under other leaders – Harry James with Goodman, Irving Fazola with Bob Crosby, and Dave Matthews with Harry James.

Gradually Pollack slipped out of sight. When the Swing Era got under way he was not part of it. By 1942 he was directing a touring band for Chico Marx. He later ran a booking agency for a time, and a short-lived record label. He led various small dixieland bands, opened a club in Los Angeles, and occasionally instituted lawsuits for breach of copyright against various big bands. For a time he ran a restaurant in Palm Springs, and in 1971, aged sixty-eight, he hanged himself.

For its brief moment, his band had been the best there was. Not because of its arrangers – Fud Livingstone and Glenn Miller were not nearly as adventurous as Bill Challis had been with Goldkette, or Don Redman with Henderson, or even Ferde Grofé with Whiteman – but because it had such outstanding young musicians. Goodman, Teagarden, Freeman, MacPartland – these were who the fans came to hear, and they were ably supported by the rhythm section – Pollack himself on drums, Dick Morgan on guitar (to which he had switched when other bands, including Henderson, were still using the less subtle banjo), and Harry Goodman, playing the smooth four-beats-in-a-bar he had learned from Steve Brown.

The band's recorded output tends to fall into two halves. Recording for Victor, under its own name, it made rather toned-down, respectable versions of numbers, played as it would for the Park Central Hotel. For smaller labels like Banner, recording under such pseudonyms as "The Kentucky Grasshoppers", "Jimmy Bracken's Toe Ticklers", "Lou Connor's Collegians", "Ted White's Collegians", "The Southern Night Hawks", "The Ten Black Berries", "The Lumberjacks", "The Dixie Daisies", "The Whoopee Makers", or "The Hotsy Totsy Gang", they re-recorded the same numbers with all the jazz feeling they were capable of, which was plenty.

In spite of his early rebellion against his family, Ben Pollack's band in some ways turned out to be less adventurous than it might have been, but he did come up with one major contribution to the years ahead.

From time to time during his band's performances he would summon out to the front Benny Goodman, Jack Teagarden and Jimmy MacPartland to play a number accompanied by the rhythm section alone. So he was truly the originator of the band-within-a-band that became so much a feature of the Swing Era.

CHAPTER 5

black bands of the twenties

All over America, wherever there was a group of young black musicians, bands were springing up. Often these groups came about because of an outstanding music-teacher, or a successful local bandleader, or a school or orphanage that had a policy of training musicians. There was a general feeling among educationists at the time that music was a civilising influence, and that putting musical instruments into the hands of young potential tearaways would make the world a safer place.

Birmingham, Alabama, had a great teacher called Fess Whatley ("Fess" being short for "Professor"). From a poor background, in 1917 he became an instructor at the Industrial High School and formed a school band which became so highly regarded that it performed before President Harding.

In the early Twenties he formed the first "society" dance-band to play in Birmingham, and he went on to form a succession of bands throughout his life, the finest being his curiously-named Vibra-Cathedral Band, which existed from 1937 to 1943, and was from all accounts the finest big band in the Southern States. Whatley's repuation as a teacher was such that during World War Two the service bands would accept his pupils without testing them.

Although he was still leading a big band when he retired from music in 1962, neither the Vibra-Cathedral band nor any of his others ever recorded. From them, however, came a procession of musicians who went on to make their names in the famous black bands.

In Charleston, South Carolina, there was the famous Jenkins Orphan Home School, where there was an actual policy of producing school bands. The music teaching was not as good as it might have been (the school was run on charity, so the teachers' pay was small, and they had no Fess Whatley), but it was strict and thorough, and produced good enough musicians for some of the members of School Band Number Five to form themselves into a professional dance-band, calling themselves the Carolina Cotton Pickers (unlike the famous McKinney's Cotton Pickers, they were perfectly justified – the orphans really did have to pick cotton from time to time).

They had a hard time making ends meet at first, but gradually things got better and the band stayed in existence from 1929 into the mid- Forties. Its most distinguished alumnus was William Alonzo "Cat" Anderson, trumpeter in the big bands of Claude Hopkins, Lionel Hampton and (above all) Duke Ellington.

There were dance-bands in Alabama, in Tennessee, in Florida (Miami was the home

51

town of the Ross De Luxe Syncopators, and it was as members of that band that clarinetist Edmond Hall and trumpeter Cootie Williams first came to New York).

Among the New Orleans dance-bands (quite apart from the hundreds of jazz-bands) was the one led from 1927 by trumpeter Sam Morgan. This was unusual in that instead of the more usual arrangements it tended to play New Orleans-style counterpoint, only with rather more instruments than usual (it had a six-piece front line – two trumpets, two trombones and two saxes).

In Missouri from 1927 there was Walter Page's Blue Devils, which had a trumpeter called Oran "Hot Lips" Page (no relation), and in 1928 acquired a singer called Jimmy Rushing and a pianist called Bill Basie. Rushing would become Basie's vocalist, Hot Lips one of his trumpeters, and Walter Page his great bass-player. And two of his tenor-players, Herschel Evans and Buddy Tate, would come out of a Texas band called Troy Floyd and his 10,000 Dollars Orchestra.

There were bands in California, in Nebraska, in Kansas, in Oklahoma – in every state of the Union. In the south-west, one of the best was the Alphonso Trent band. Trent was born in Arkansas in 1905 (strange to think that that was only four years after Butch Cassidy and the Sundance Kid fled the south-west, and that they still had six years to live as outlaws in South America).

After having piano lessons as a child, and playing in local bands, Alphonso Trent got together a band of his own in 1925, to perform at the Adolphus Hotel in Dallas. It was an octet that soon became a ten-tet, and eventually grew to fourteen or fifteen pieces and played all over the America – in Memphis, in

Cincinnati, in St Louis, in Pittsburgh, in Buffalo, in Oklahoma City – before it folded in 1934. Unfortunately, it only ever recorded nine titles (one of which was never issued), but it was from all accounts an outstanding band that could play anything from jazz to ballads to 'symphonic' numbers.

Fletcher Henderson was so impressed by the band that he encouraged Trent to bring it to New York, and it played such a successful week at the Savoy Ballroom in Harlem that a prominent booker offered Trent a New York residency. Trent turned it down, afraid that if his band was permanently in New York, other bands would poach his men. Hardly an unjustified fear when you consider that in his band he had such musicians as trumpeter Harry Edison, although from the way his band's personnel changed so little over the years, it seems he inspired a great deal of loyalty.

Part of the reason may have been the fact that he paid them well. Trent came from a reasonably well-to-do family, and his band had an impressive array of touring cars, a variety of band uniforms, and gleaming golden instruments that were the envy of other bands. Unfortunately it seems that his wealth was also the reason why the band never became nationally famous – he simply didn't need the money.

Having broken up the band in 1934, he came back into music in 1938 leading an octet which again travelled widely, and which should be remembered in swing history for first bringing to public attention its young guitarist, Charlie Christian.

A trumpeter who had worked with Trent in other people's bands in the early Twenties, but went on to form a band of his own, was called

Terrence Holder. His "Dark Clouds Of Joy", formed in 1927 and lasting till 1933, had through it an amazing succession of names that would become famous – at one time or another he had trumpeter Bill Dillard, trombonist Keg Johnson, altoist Earl Bostic, tenorists Budd Johnson, Herschel Evans and Buddy Tate and pianist Mary Lou Williams, tuba- player and future bandleader Andy Kirk.

One bandleader who became famous in the late Twenties was not born in America at all. His name was Luis Russell and he was born in Panama in 1902. He studied violin, guitar, piano and organ with his father, who was a music teacher, played piano in a silent movie theatre and in clubs and, when he was seventeen, won $3,000 in a lottery.

In 1919, using this windfall, he moved with his mother and sister to New Orleans (what happened to his father is not recorded). He found jobs playing where he could, took over the leadership of a small band from clarinetist Albert Nicholas in 1924, and later the same year took a job he had been offered with a sixteen-piece band led by pianist/arranger Doc Cooke at the Dreamland Ballroom in Chicago.

After only a few months, however, he left to join King Oliver's Creole Jazz Band, as the replacement for pianist Lil Hardin, off to New York with her new husband (and Fletcher Henderson's new cornetist) Louis Armstrong.

Luis stayed with King Oliver until the summer of 1927, when he left to go to New York himself, to work at the Nest Club in an octet led by a drummer called George Howe. In October of that same year he took over the leadership of the band, and during the next year replaced Howe and a couple of the others, bringing in trumpeter Louis Metcalf, trombonist J.C.Higginbotham and New

Orleans drummer Paul Barbarin. He also brought in another old New Orleans friend, Albert Nicholas.

With this band he did two recording sessions (the second under the title of The Jungle Town Stompers), which reveal it as a pleasant useful band whose main interest is its soloists.

Shortly after the second session, however, he made two important changes.

Firstly, he replaced his bass-player with another New Orleans player, Pops Foster. There has probably never been a more driving bass-player than Pops Foster. By the standards of what came later, technically and musically, his playing is extremely simple and straightforward, but no other bassist ever had such a driving beat.

Secondly, Russell replaced Metcalf with the great New Orleans trumpeter (and son of a New Orleans trumpeter) Henry "Red" Allen. Born in 1908, and thus several years younger than Louis Armstrong, he had at first been influenced by Louis, whom he had heard playing in his father's band, but by the time he joined the Luis Russell band he was already developing his own highly individual style, playing in short, almost disconnected phrases that wander all around the beat but have a fierce drive of their own, using a whole arsenal of tonal effects, of trills and smears and rips and growls.

It was joining the Russell band that first made Red Allen famous. To musicians he was a sensation, and he did as much as Louis to set the standard for big-band trumpeting in the early Thirties.

A large, amiable man, he differed from Louis in liking to drop in at clubs for a bit of competitive blowing. Clarinetist Kenny Davern tells a story of seeing him drop in unannounced at Minton's Playhouse in Harlem in the Fifties. The place was packed, listening intently to an introspective bebop band, which had been playing the same cool number with great involvement for about half an hour. Red walked in, "all spiffed up with his shirt, tie and jacket.

"'Hey, Red! Hey, my man!'

"And he's putting his hand out, like he's mayor of Harlem. He walked right up to the bandstand ... thumped his case onto the stand ... took out his horn and, while these guys are still playing he's warming up: paa paa paapaa paapaa. And then he stopped them in the middle of the tune and said, 'Rosetta. Womp, womp.' And he started playing 'Rosetta', walking through the crowd playing to all the people. These cats were in a tempo half of 'Rosetta' and all of a sudden they're in 'Rosetta'. Whether they knew it or not didn't matter.

"When he got finished playing he just took his mouthpiece off, put the horn in the case, slammed the case shut, and says, 'Goodnight, y'all. What a ball, what a ball.' He was shaking hands and went out the door. These cats were back on and one of them says, 'What are we doing? Who was that?'"

On records made with his new band, Russell's arrangements are simple and unambitious, but they provide just the support needed for his great soloists – Allen, Nicholas and Higginbotham.

The band worked around New York, at the Nest Club, at the Saratoga Club, at the Savoy Ballroom, and at Connie's Inn. In 1929 it acted for a while as accompanying group for Louis Armstrong. It toured a lot during the early Thirties, and in 1935 it became Louis' regular band. In fact it became the Armstrong band to such an extent that in 1943 Luis Russell left it to form another big band, which alternated touring with New York residencies in much the same way as his earlier band until he retired from music in 1948.

The Armstrong band during the Swing Era was mainly there as a backing for Louis. The other members of the band got little solo space, and the arrangements were perfunctory. Louis himself was magnificent, both singing and playing, but the band remained outside the mainstream. In fact, because it had already been playing much the same way for several years before the swing era got going, and because Louis made little attempt to adapt to the new style, the young swing fans were inclined to regard it as yesterday's news, and it always came well down the polls.

A band that was well on the way to becoming a swing band came out of Paducah, Kentucky in the late Twenties. Formed by a black circus-drummer called William McKinney, it started as a quartet, and at first it was a kind of novelty band – the musicians wore paper hats and made joky noises with rattles and whistles. But as its reputation spread it turned more and more to playing straight dance music. It grew into the "Synco Septet", then into the ten-piece "Synco Jazz Band", and worked all over Michigan and Ohio.

In 1926, at White Sulphur Springs, West Virginia, it played a special date for the Prince of Wales, later Edward VIII, who sat in on drums for a set. In that same year (and probably nothing to do with the Prince of Wales) McKinney replaced himself with a fine drummer called Cuba Austin and gave up playing to devote himself to the business side.

By now the band was becoming experienced and efficient. An engagement at the Green Mill in Toledo brought them a wider public. They played short residencies in Michigan, Baltimore and Detroit, where they appeared at the Arcadia Ballroom, situated not far from Jean Goldkette's Graystone.

A little later that year, following Fletcher Henderson's success at the Graystone, Goldkette began looking for a black band that could play in the Henderson style. He hoped that such a band might help bail the Graystone out of its looming financial difficulties by appearing there when his own band was working elsewhere.

He had heard the Synco Jazz Band at the Arcadia, and sent a telegram to McKinney in Dayton, Ohio, where the band then was. Goldkette's proposition was that if McKinney upgraded his band with more and better musicians, he could have the job. McKinney too had heard the Henderson band and been impressed, and he agreed.

It took him a few months, but in that time he assembled a core of good musicians (mostly from Virginia and West Virginia) and the upgraded band opened for a trial run at the Graystone. They were a great success, and Goldkette took control of the band, renaming them McKinney's Cotton Pickers and relegating McKinney to a managerial role.

Manager or not, it was McKinney who had the idea of luring Don Redman away from Fletcher Henderson to be the band's musical director (and alto-player). It took him a whole year to manage it, but eventually Redman arrived, in July 1927. From the few sides the Cotton Pickers recorded before he joined them, it is obvious that they were already a fine swinging band, but once Redman took charge they became outstanding. Using the Graystone Ballroom as their base, they were soon embarking successfully on tours to major centres like New York, Philadelphia, Atlantic City and Chicago.

A probable reason why Redman and McKinney's Cotton Pickers worked so well together was that he found them a better vehicle for his arrangements than the Henderson band had been. It was by now filled with skilled musicians, but not with temperamental stars, so he was able to impress his ideas firmly on the band and set its style. More than most, it was an arranger's band.

Redman was by this time probably the most outstanding arranger in America. His intricate scores, as well as exchanging phrases between sections, had begun to contain passages blending reeds and brass in unusual ways. He tended to write strongly for the brass and sweetly for the reeds, contrasting the one against the other, and overall he aimed a light texture and a lively swinging rhythm. This the band was well able to provide, in spite of still having a tuba and a banjo in the rhythm section, rather than a bass and guitar. Fortunately, Ralph Escudero on tuba was an exceptional player, able to get a light bouncy rhythm out of his grunting instrument.

If the band had a weakness, it was a lack of really strong soloists, although it was strengthened in this respect in the summer of 1929 when trumpeter Joe Smith joined the band.

Joe Smith had been in Mamie Smith's Jazz Hounds in 1922, and had been on recording sessions with Fletcher Henderson as early as 1923. Something of a wanderer, he had been in and out of the Henderson band since 1925, and also appeared on many of Bessie Smith's recordings. He was by far her favourite trumpeter. She even preferred him to Louis Armstrong, possibly because his playing was less assertive than Louis'. Joe had a firm but gentle way of playing, with a beautiful tone using a great deal of blues inflection.

He stayed with the Cotton Pickers until November 1930, when he was in a car crash in which the band's saxophonist and vocalist, George "Fathead" Thomas was killed. Joe was so disturbed by this that he left the band and went back to Fletcher Henderson. Then, when Henderson's drummer, Kaiser Marshall, left to form a small band of his own, Joe went with him, and stayed with him for a spell before rejoining the Cotton Pickers late in 1931.

In 1928 and 1929 the band had acquired a few better soloists. One was trombonist Claude Jones, who went on to work with Fletcher Henderson, Chick Webb, Cab Calloway, Benny Carter and Duke Ellington. Jones also taught his brother-in-law to play the trombone, and he too joined the band. This was Quentin Jackson, who went on to join Cab Calloway, Lucky Millinder, Duke Ellington, Quincy Jones, Count Basie, Charlie Mingus, Louie Bellson and, in 1971, the Thad Jones-Mel Lewis Orchestra.

In 1930 it acquired Edward Inge, who played a driving imaginative clarinet and went on to become an arranger, playing in bands led by Andy Kirk, Jimmie Lunceford, Fats Waller and Louis Armstrong.

When the band made some records in New York, Redman shrewdly beefed it up by co-opting a number of strong soloists – Coleman Hawkins and Rex Stewart from the Henderson band (on one occasion in 1929 he co-opted almost the whole Henderson band), pianists Fats Waller and James P. Johnson, and altoist, clarinetist, trumpeter, arranger and future bandleader Benny Carter.

In 1931 Don Redman got the opportunity of leading his own band at the famous New York club, Connie's Inn, and left the Cotton Pickers. His place as musical director was briefly taken by Benny Carter, but somehow the band was never ever quite as good again, and it folded in 1934, at which time it included the man who would become the greatest trumpeter of the Thirties, Roy Eldridge. (McKinney himself formed another "Cotton Pickers" the following year, and it staggered on until 1940, but it never amounted to anything much and McKinney then left the business).

Redman went on to lead his own excellent band throughout the Thirties, and after that, in a long and successful career, to arrange for many big bands, including Count Basie, Cootie Williams, Jimmy Dorsey and Harry James. In 1951 he became musical director for Pearl Bailey and her husband, Louie Bellson, and remained so for the rest of his life, from time to time assembling groups under his own name to make records. He died in 1964.

Another black band came from St Louis, Missouri. Eventually they were to call themselves "The Missourians", but in about 1923, when they arrived in Chicago after some years touring the midwest, they were known as Wilson Robinson's Syncopators.

Compared to New York bands like Fletcher Henderson's, and compared to white bands like Jean Goldkette's, they had a looser and harder-swinging beat. Their arrangements were based on simple repeated riffs, in the style that would later be refined by bands around Kansas City, such as Count Basie.

In 1924, under the leadership of a violinist-singer-entertainer called Andy Preer, they were brought to New York to be the resident band at a new Harlem club, to be called The Cotton Club (nobody seems quite sure why – possibly partly as a reflection of its whites-only policy, and partly from some dimly-perceived notion of the romantic deep south, where all that hot music came from). Preer was a charismatic leader, and he had been appointed by the management of the Cotton Club to take over the running of the band. And when the management of the Cotton Club made an appointment, it was as well to go along with it, because the club was owned by a gangster called Owney Madden.

It stood on the north-east corner of 142nd Street and Lenox Avenue. Originally built in 1918 as the Douglas Casino, it was on two floors – on the ground floor there was a theatre, showing silent films and occasional vaudeville acts, and upstairs there was a vast room originally intended as a dance-hall.

It was not very successful as a dance-hall, and in 1920 it was rented by the famous Jack Johnson, amateur cellist and bassist, sometime vaudevillian, and former world heavyweight champion. He turned it into a supper club, calling it "The Club Deluxe", but even with Johnson's name it failed to prosper, part of the reason being that black Harlem resented him for openly parading his white wife. So Johnson was relieved when Owney Madden's gang came around looking for a suitable spot to entertain white night-clubbers, and to serve them "Madden's Number One" beer. They offered Johnson a deal – they would take over the lease and operate the place, and he could stay on as a "manager". He eagerly accepted.

Owney Madden was not actually present at these negotiations. He was at the time serving ten to twenty years in Sing Sing for the manslaughter of Patsy Doyle.

Born in England in 1890, his family had emigrated to New York when he was eleven, and by the time he was seventeen he had acquired the nickname "Owney the Killer". By the time he was eighteen he had taken command of one of the factions of the Gopher Gang, the largest gang in Hell's Kitchen, a Manhattan ghetto in the Forties on Sixth Avenue with a large black population. His specialties were protection rackets and various forms of theft.

A small, slim, dapper, soft-spoken young man, he was known for having the gentlest smile in New York's underworld. Also for being prepared to kill anyone who seemed to be thwarting his often-expressed desire to be king of all the gangs.

This naturally brought him enemies. There were several attempts on his life, but none came near to succeeding until he visited the Arbor Dance Hall on the night of November 6, 1912. There his attention was so taken by an attractive young woman that he failed to notice eleven men closing in to surround him. By the time they finished firing he had six bullets in his body.

He had to spend months in hospital recuperating, and while he was in there other ambitious gangsters started making moves to take over his territory. One was Patsy Doyle, who started spreading rumours that Madden was permanently crippled. This seemed to annoy Madden. As soon as he was released he set out after Doyle and killed him. This was in 1914.

For some reason he was arrested, convicted, and sent to Sing Sing. His imprisonment modified his attitude somewhat

– from then on, while exercising considerable power in the underworld, he kept a much lower profile, avoiding as much as possible confrontations with those on either side of the law.

From Sing Sing he continued to run his syndicate. When Prohibition came in he entered the liquor business, and having done so, realised that running a Harlem cabaret could only be a good thing.

More tables were crammed into the Club Deluxe, raising the number of seats from under 500 to around 700. The tables were arranged in a horseshoe shape around the tiny stage, on two levels, and the side walls were lined with booths. A "jungle décor" was applied, complete with artificial palm-trees – this was to conform with the white audience's notion of primitive abandon – and all the fixtures and fittings were sufficiently luxurious to permit charging hefty prices.

When the club first opened, in 1923, they used a succession of local bands, including the New Orleans creole band of Armand J. Piron, which later that year preceded Fletcher Henderson into the Roseland. But in 1924 they they started looking for a regular house band that could play good lively music for shows.

It was Owney Madden's policy in the early years of the club to hire all his staff from Chicago – cooks, waiters, busboys – on the grounds that staff from Chicago were unlikely to hold any allegiances to gangs in New York who might prove unfriendly. So what with this policy, and the fact that in 1924 Chicago was the place to look for good swinging bands, it was to Chicago that the management looked.

They decided to hire Wilson Robinson's Syncopators, who were at that moment playing an engagement in Buffalo. They got in touch with them there, hired them, renamed them Andy Preer's Cotton Club Orchestra after their leader, and brought them to New York.

They also hired Boston songwriter Jimmy McHugh to write songs for the shows (he had been one of the twenty-two song-pluggers in the Boston office of Irving Berlin Music before coming to New York, where he had already had a hit with 'When My Sugar Walks Down The Street').

The Cotton Club shows were lavish fast-paced revues, with a new one every six months. The chorus-line were beautiful high-yaller girls who had to be at least five feet six inches tall, not over twenty-one, and able to carry a tune.

The shows always had plenty of hoofing, and were designed to be a Harlem version of the Negro stage revues that for several years past had been packing them in on Broadway. Broadway socialites who had seen these revues came uptown en masse to get a closer look, and as soon as it opened the club was a roaring success.

It was such a success in fact that in June 1925 it was busted for violating Prohibition. Not by the local police, who usually had some sort of working agreement with the club owners, but by the Feds. The club was padlocked and Owney Madden, who by now was out of Sing Sing, and a little-known pickpocket called Sam Sellis, who was nominally president of the owning corporation, were charged with forty-four violations of the Volstead Act.

They assured the judge that they had both tried hard to make good since their last sentence, and were let off fairly lightly. They were not sent back to prison, but the club was heavily fined, and lost a lot of revenue during the three months it was out of business.

When it reopened, a new young producer called Dan Healy was hired, and the shows got even better. Healy's shows would last between an hour-and-a-half and two hours. In a typical show there would be band numbers, with and without the chorus-line, and acts including a comedian or eccentric dancer, a star singer, such as Ethel Waters, and a specialty singer, whose songs would include some of the sexual innuendo the audience expected.

Healy also increased the lavishness of the productions, he was possibly the first to introduce actual miniature sets, with elaborate lighting, onto a night-club stage. And above all, as he later said, "The chief ingredient was pace, pace, pace!"

The club continued to prosper, and all was going well when, in 1927, the bandleader, Andy Preer, died. The management considered that without him the band would not have enough pulling power, and they decided that the only thing to do was to find a replacement.

Once more looking to Chicago, they offered the job to King Oliver, whose Dixie Syncopators were just coming to the end of their engagement at the Lincoln Gardens, but Oliver turned the offer down. Not enough money for a ten-piece orchestra, he said.

As the Cotton Club performers were the highest-paid in Harlem, this can't have been the true reason. Possibly he was worried about his band's ability to play for a sophisticated New York show, or possibly he was worried about his worsening embouchure (his teeth were giving him trouble, partly because he was suffering from pyorrhea and partly because he was such a glutton for sugar that cafés where he ate regularly would hide the sugar-bowl). Whatever his reason, it was undoubtedly the

worst decision he ever made.

From then on his bookings became fewer, and he had difficulty holding his bands together. In the early Thirties he toured with obscure dance bands around small towns in Tennessee and Kentucky, then wound up in Savannah, Georgia, at first running a fruit stall, then working as a janitor in a pool hall. He always hoped to make a come-back, but died of a cerebral haemorrhage, with his hopes unrealised, in 1938.

The only good thing about his unfortunate turning-down of the Cotton Club job was that it opened the way for another band. The opening night of the new show had already been postponed to December 4, and Harry Block, the club's manager, was getting desperate. Then Jimmy McHugh said he knew of a band that could play the kind of music he wanted for the show. They weren't from Chicago, but they'd been at the Kentucky Club for a year and were now at a vaudeville theatre in Philadelphia. They were called Duke Ellington and his Washingtonians.

The management weren't keen. Who knew what sort of music came out of Washington? But McHugh persisted, and Jack Johnson backed him up, and eventually Harry Block said all right, he would give them an audition. But he was going to audition a couple of other bands as well, just to be on the safe side.

Ellington's problem, when he was called to audition, was that the only six of the Washingtonians were playing in Philadelphia, and the club engagement needed ten or eleven. The audition was called for noon, and by the time he had got to New York and scraped together the rest of the band it was after two in the afternoon.

They went to the Cotton Club and played,

and were hired, the reason being that Harry Block had got there late as well, and hadn't heard the other bands. As Ellington said, it was a classic example of being at the right place at the right time with the right thing before the right people.

CHAPTER 6

duke ellington - part one

The urbane Duke Ellington, who developed more poise and graciousness than any member of the natural-born aristocracy ever possessed, ran the most inventive and enjoyable band in the world for almost fifty years.

Through it passed a procession of outstanding soloists, most of them with strongly individual sounds, and many of them staying with him for years on end. Cootie Williams, a total of 22 years; Paul Gonsalves 24 years; Lawrence Brown 29 years; Sonny Greer 31 years; Johnny Hodges 41 years; Harry Carney 47 years.

Duke was born in Washington in 1899 and christened Edward Kennedy Ellington, Kennedy being his mother's maiden name. His father, James Edward, known as "J.E.", worked first as coachman, then as butler, to Dr M.F.Cuthburt, a society doctor whose patients included high-class families like the Morgenthaus and the Du Ponts.

Young Edward's mother, Daisy, was light-skinned, pretty and refined. The daughter of a captain of police, socially she stood only a little below the daughters of the college professors, doctors and lawyers at the top of black Washington society. Their whole life was a world apart from the squalid black ghettoes that also existed in Washington. (Many Blacks had moved to Washington in the years after the abolition of slavery, feeling that as it was the government that gave them freedom, they were more likely to be treated as equals in the government's own city.)

J.E., like any good Edwardian butler, had an aristocratic air. He liked to dress elegantly, to give his wife and family the life-style he felt they deserved, and generally to live the good life, both at home and out on the town. As a result he was often rather hard-up. Nonetheless, he managed to afford his own home, and in his capacity as butler learned about wines and food and about famous makers of chinaware and cutlery. Many pieces of fine tableware, cast off by Dr Cuthburt, made their way into the Ellington home.

As his competence grew, J.E. (and various other brothers and cousins of the extended Ellington family) began catering for some of the great houses around Washington. Once at least he served at the White House.

Young Edward Kennedy Ellington, raised in this civilised environment, was an only child until he was almost adult, and his mother Daisy doted on him. As he once said, "My feet were not allowed to touch the ground until I was eleven years old."

From his early days he felt (and was encouraged by his mother to feel) that he was extremely special. He inherited his father's elegant taste in clothing, and his lordly but gracious manner, and while still at school was nicknamed "Duke".

His musical background as a child was much closer to that of a white child than a black. His mother, who played the piano a little, played sentimental Victorian parlour pieces, and both his parents, striving after gentility, loathed the vulgar low-down music of the black working-class.

When he was about eight, Duke was given the piano lessons that were obligatory to any boy or girl brought up in a genteel and respectable household, black or white, but at that age he had no interest in music. He skived out of the lessons whenever he could, and they were abandoned after only a few months. All the same, it is possible that they were the reason why, when he did become interested in music, it was the piano he opted for. And it is pleasant to remember that his teacher's name was undeniably Mrs Marietta Clinkscales.

His real interest in music was first awakened when he was fourteen. Like almost all respectable families in those days, it was the Ellington family's practice to spend the hot summer months away from the unhealthy miasma of the city, preferably at some coastal resort. They would stay with relatives at Asbury Park, Atlantic City, or Philadelphia, and it was in Philadelphia in 1913 that he heard a ragtime pianist called Harvey Brooks.

Born in Philadelphia, Brooks was only about ten weeks older than Ellington himself. He went on to have a solid but unspectacular professional career, playing for instance in Mamie Smith's Jazz Hounds.

Whatever Brooks was playing in 1913, Duke was impressed. He went home and started practising again, helped shortly afterwards by a cold which confined him to the house for a week or two. He also composed a piece called 'Soda Fountain Rag' (he had been working as a soda jerk at the Poodle Dog Cafe, on Georgia Avenue).

Armed with this piece, and another he wrote a little later called 'What You Gonna Do When The Bed Breaks Down?', he started playing at parties and social gatherings for his high school friends, and quickly learned that "when you were playing the piano there was always a pretty girl standing down at the bass clef end." A remark which probably gives an accurate explanation of why he became a piano-player in the first place – not so much for the music as for the life it offered – fun and girls and a bit of spending money.

Over the next two or three years he continued to play and practise, picking up a smattering of musical knowledge in a rather haphazard manner (all his life he remained deeply suspicious of formal training). He played well enough to occasionally be asked by older pianists to substitute for them at parties, but admitted himself that he really wasn't up to it "I knew three or four numbers. I played them fast, slow and medium."

Being suspicious of formal education, he hadn't done especially well at school, and at sixteen he entered Armstrong Technical High School to study commercial art.

Among the students at Armstrong Tech were other musicians, and he and a few of them got together and formed a small band to play at dances. What sort of music they played we can't be sure, but it would not have been jazz at that early time and in that place – presumably it was a sort of syncopated raggy playing of popular tunes of the day, with little improvisation.

Duke was still no great shakes as a pianist at this time in fact he was certainly better as an artist. He lettered signs and painted backdrops for the Howard Theatre, and in 1917 he won a poster contest sponsored by the N.A.A.C.P. the National Association for the Advancement of Colored People.

The prize was an art scholarship to the prestigious Pratt Institute in New York, but he never took it up. Firstly because he never succeeded in graduating from high school, secondly because in the summer of 1917 he got his neighbour and schoolmate Edna Thompson pregnant. He married her in the July, and their son Mercer was born in March 1918.

Now that he had a family to support, Duke took on a partner and opened a small sign-painting business. But he continued to work as a musician whenever possible.

One day a local professional, Louis Thomas, sent Duke out as his dep to play at a reception. He told Duke to keep ten dollars of the fee and bring him the rest. When Duke learned that the total fee was to be a hundred dollars, he was astounded. Next day he booked large adverts in the yellow pages of the phone book for "The Duke Ellington Orchestra", and shortly afterwards found he was able to work continuously – in fact, more than continuously – such was the demand that soon he was sending out several bands under the same name on a single night. After all, nobody knew what Duke Ellington looked like.

By 1919 he was doing well. He bought a house for his family, and a car. The dance-music business was looking more and more to him like a good idea, especially because it was then one of the few ways into fame and money open to Blacks. (It was still fashionable in society in those days to have black servants, dance-band musicians were regarded as servants, and therefore black musicians, such as James Reese Europe, had almost a monopoly at fashionable functions.)

Among the young musicians around him by now were several whose names would remain associated with him. One was Otto Hardwick, whose first name was pronounced "Oh-toe" which his many friends somehow modified into "Toby".

Some five years younger than Duke, he lived in the same neighbourhood and went to the same school and their fathers were friends.

When he was about fourteen he took up the string bass, but found it heavy to lug around and switched to the C-melody sax, then to the alto, possibly at Duke's suggestion, and soon he was a member of Duke's pool of musicians. His playing tended to be pure and smooth-toned, and he was at his best on the sort of slow wistful numbers that Duke always liked. In person he was gentle and engaging and unreliable, always liable to disappear drinking and socialising for a few days at a time. Ellington all his life was inclined to have band-members a bit like that, whom he not only put up with but positively seemed to encourage, feeling that they played the way he liked because of the way they were.

Another musician, of about the same age as Otto Hardwick but of extreme reliability, was Arthur Whetsol, whose family had come to Washington from Florida, where he was born. His part-Mexican father was a Seventh Day Adventist and, possibly because of this, he grew into a dignified and serious young man. His ambition was to become a doctor, and he began attending Howard University as a premedical student. Music to him was not a career, but a way of helping pay his tuition fees.

He set about learning to play the trumpet in his usual correct and serious way, and became one of the few of Ellington's early musicians who could read music fluently, developing a pure, gentle, precise tone that was almost the equivalent of Hardwick's on the alto.

A third arrival was drummer Sonny Greer, born in 1902. Greer was not from Washington but from Long Branch, New Jersey. His father was a master electrician on the Pennsylvania Railroad and his mother was a modiste. Nobody in his family was musical ("including me", he said, and he became a drummer almost by accident.

In his early teens he was a fairly conventional school boy who had a paper round and delivered groceries, but at the same time he had something in him of the hustler. He had a charming, out-going manner, and liked the idea of becoming a fast-talking cat in a sharp suit. In his spare time practised playing pool at the local pool-hall, and became pretty good at the game.

Then a drummer from a show that was passing through town dropped into the pool room looking for a game. He played a few games with Sonny, saw how good he was, and offered to teach him the drums in exchange for a few tips. Sonny took him up on it, learnt enough about drumming to join the school band, and when he left school decided to make music his career.

By his late teens he was gigging around Asbury Park, New Jersey with a band in which he was the only Black, and rehearsing in New York with the famous Clef Club orchestra. In Asbury Park he met a couple of Ellington's young fellow-musicians, who suggested he visit Washington.

This he did. He found Frank Holliday's poolroom, next door to the Howard Theatre, and started to hang around there. It wasn't long before somebody dashed in from the theatre shouting, "Is there a drummer in the house?" The drummer with the theatre band, evading an alimony subpoena, had fled. Sonny took the job, and became the regular drummer at the theatre, doubling at the Dreamland Café with a small band that included pianist and future bandleader Claude Hopkins.

The Dreamland Café was a hot spot, frequented by bootleggers and gamblers, and with ten waitresses who all sang the blues. So now Sonny was a prominent part of the Washington music scene. He had intended to stay for only a few days, but found work so plentiful that he stayed three years.

Quite early on in those years he met Duke Ellington, and they hit it off instantly, to the extent that Sonny once said that they were like brothers. Duke felt the same. He was always attracted by showmen and hustlers, and Sonny was certainly in that mould. He also had the attraction of being, to the Washington boys, a sharp character from New York.

More and more Duke was finding himself being drawn to New York. It was, after all, the entertainment capital of the world. Even movie companies were mostly based there in 1919.

It mattered little to these young Washington musicians that the northern city for hot music was Chicago. They weren't really aware of hot music. What Duke and his colleagues were basically playing was a form of polite ragtime, and his friend Sonny had been trained by a show drummer. In fact he always remained more of a show drummer than a jazz drummer. He had a flashy stage personality, sang quite a bit in a light voice with traces of Al Jolson, and liked to play rolls and rimshots and cymbal crashes to highlight performers and soloists. A few years later, when the Leedy Drum Company gave him a complete set of all their kit, complete with chimes and vibes and Chinese blocks and cowbells and tympani and two huge cymbals, he was in his element "I didn't have to play them. All I had to do was look pretty."

Ellington's first move to New York was triggered by the appearance at the Howard Theatre, towards the end of 1922, of the black clarinetist Wilbur Sweatman. Sweatman, born in 1882, was of an earlier generation than Ellington and his colleagues. His background was circus and vaudeville (he was best known for his ability to play three clarinets at once) and ragtime (he was the composer of 'Down Home Rag'), and at the time he came to Washington he was trying hard to pick up the new popular rhythms.

The band accompanying Sweatman at the Howard Theatre (Flo Dade's Acme Syncopators) was without a drummer, and Sonny, as house drummer, filled in. Sweatman liked his playing enough to ask him to come to New York, where he was about to begin an engagement at the most prestigious black theatre in America, the Lafayette Theatre in Harlem. Sonny, being Sonny, said he would only go if Sweatman would hire his friends Duke and Toby as well.

Sweatman agreed, but Ellington hesitated. After all, he was making good money with his little bands in Washington, and he had a family to support. He let the others leave without him, but after a few months the lure of New York proved too strong, and he followed them in time to play in Sweatman's band for his last week at the Lafayette.

Ellington was bowled over by Harlem. As he said at the time, "The world's most glamorous atmosphere. Why, it's just like the Arabian Nights." Among his hundreds of compositions he was to write dozens of songs with titles referring to it 'Drop Me Off In Harlem', 'Jungle Nights In Harlem', 'Harlem Air Shaft', 'Harlem Twist', 'Harlem River Quiver', 'Echoes Of Harlem', 'Harlem Flat Blues', 'Harlem Speaks', 'Uptown Downbeat', 'Harmony In Harlem', 'Boys From Harlem', 'Blue Bells Of Harlem', 'Heart Of Harlem', 'Shades Of Harlem', 'A Night In Harlem', 'A Tone Parallel To Harlem' and 'Harlem'.

In its earliest days, from about 1658, Harlem had been a farming village carved out of the wilderness by Dutch settlers. It changed only slowly, being some way north of the growing centre of New York, but by the 1870's it had become a middle-class suburb of mostly Germans. Then, between 1878 and 1881, Manhattan's three

elevated railroads pushed north, almost reaching it, and further extensions were being planned.

Speculators moved in, buying land as fast as they could and erecting hundreds of expensive town houses and high-rent apartment houses. So strong was the feeling that this would become a moneyed neighbourhood that in 1889 Oscar Hammerstein I built the Harlem Opera House, the first New York theatre north of Central Park. The famed and fashionable architect Stanford White was commissioned to design a row of elegant apartment-houses on 139th Street between Seventh and Eighth Avenues. These apartments were so desirable in the Twenties that they became known as "Strivers' Row".

Stanford White, incidentally, never lived to see the Twenties. In June 1906 he became the victim of one of the most notorious crimes of the era when he was shot dead by young, rich and mentally unbalanced Harry Thaw, then newly wed to Stanford White's young ex-mistress, Evelyn Nesbit, "The Girl On The Red Velvet Swing".

At the time White was seated at a table in roof garden of the original Madison Square Garden (which he had promoted and designed). He was attending the first night of a rather tedious musical (which he had backed), called *Mamzelle Champagne*. As Thaw's three shots rang out, the composer's mother, who was in the audience, screamed out, "My God – they've shot my son!"

Unfortunately for the speculators, the rich and respectable turned out to be in no hurry to move into expensive property in Harlem. In the early 1900's, in an attempt to recoup their losses, and to the horror of the white residents, they started renting and selling to Blacks.

Up to the start of the Great War, most of the black inhabitants who moved in were well-to-do professional people, including many entertainers, or else quiet middle-class families delighted to find a quiet neighbourhood with wide well-lit streets, such as they could not hope to find anywhere else in New York.

From that time, the name "Harlem" began to acquire an almost magical aura among black Americans. Advertised as "The Land Of Refuge", not only was it seen as a place where Blacks could live in dignity and equality, but as the source and centre of a new black consciousness.

The real flood of immigration there came with the war. Many recent immigrants from Europe went back to fight for their native countries, leaving the American war-effort severely short of labour. This shortage was met by a mass migration north by Blacks only too happy to escape from the racist South.

Harlem changed from a quiet middle-class community to a seething lively cauldron of all the black classes. By 1930 there were half a million living inside its six square miles, in housing designed for 75,000.

Because of the strong component of creative people, right from the first wave of black residents, a strong artistic movement sprang up. This was in a day when cultured black Americans looked to white Europe as their model, rather than to black Africa, and there were painters and singers and actors and musicians and poets and novelists, all full of pride and excitement in what they saw as a new dawn for their race.

Also caught up in this feeling were an increasing number of whites. Black entertainers had been highly regarded in the States for years, but in the early Twentieth Century a change of attitude occurred. Blacks changed from being seen as carefree and childlike (when they weren't being armed and dangerous) to being seen as noble savages, in tune with the dark mysteries of the soul and the unconscious. And still entertaining as well.

At first a few white bohemians, then an increasing number of the brave but fashionable, made their way to Harlem nightspots. The proprietors of these nightspots were of course glad of the business, but there was some edginess on the part of the black clientele, who began to get the feeling that they were in some kind of zoo. This led eventually to whites-only nightspots like the Cotton Club being opened, allowing the black entertainment to be safely segregated on the stage.

Among the highest-regarded black entertainers in 1923 were the Harlem stride pianists, who were at that time playing better and more original jazz than anyone else in New York. Sonny Greer being quite fearless about cheerfully introducing himself to anyone he wanted to meet, the three Washingtonians soon found themselves hob-nobbing in clubs and cabarets with such piano giants as James P. Johnson and Willie "The Lion" Smith, and their young protégé, Fats Waller.

Ellington, as a pianist, was bowled over by what he heard, and the rather aggressive Willie the Lion seems to have been kindly disposed to the three newcomers, possibly because as a proud Negro he approved of their middle-class good manners.

Ellington took the Lion, more than any other piano-player, as his model (it gives one a fair idea of what a late starter Ellington was to realise that the well-established Lion was less than two years his senior).

In spite of his aggressive manner, the Lion was more inclined to patches of prettiness in his playing than the other stride pianists, and this vein of prettiness continued to outcrop in Ellington's playing for the rest of his life.

When Wilbur Sweatman finished his engagement at the Lafayette Theatre, he asked the three Washingtonians to go with him on tour, but they elected to stay behind in the heady Harlem atmosphere and try to find work. It is a further indication of their lack of prowess at that time that they failed, in spite of the enormous demand in 1923 for musicians of any aptitude at all.

Becoming seriously hard up, they were relieved when Ellington found fifteen dollars lying in the street. They used the money for train-fare back home, but remained determined to find their way back to Harlem. To keep in practice they took a job at a place called the Music Box in Atlantic City. This job was organised by another of their Washington colleagues, Elmer Snowden.

Snowden had been born in Baltimore in 1900, had taken up the guitar and the banjo as a boy, and by the time he was a teenager had been playing there professionally.

Coming the short distance to Washington, he soon established himself there as one of the best rhythm banjoists around. Having a couple of years more working experience than most of Ellington's other colleagues, he also saw himself as something of a leader.

The Atlantic City band he organised was a quintet – Snowden, Hardwick, Greer, Ellington, and trumpeter Art Whetsol. They called themselves the Washington Black Sox, as a topical allusion to the recent baseball scandal, when members of the Chicago White Sox team were convicted of taking bribes to throw the World Series and nicknamed in the press "the Black Sox".

Although this little band simply played its Atlantic City gig and returned to Washington, its importance is that it turned out to be the nucleus of the first Duke Ellington band.

Back in Washington, they ran into Fats Waller. He was touring there in a band backing a vaudeville comedian, Clarence Robinson, and he was bored. He said that the rest of the band were bored too, and that when they got back to New York they were going to quit, and that perhaps the Washingtonians, as they were now calling themselves formally, could get the job.

This was just what they were looking for, but after Fats got back to New York he sent them a wire saying that he'd decided not to quit himself, so there was no job for a pianist, but that some of the band had, so there were jobs for Greer and Hardwick. Sonny and Toby went.

Then Fats sent a second wire saying that he was quitting as well, so Duke went. His father, J.E., had lent him some money to start him off, so he took a train, spent all the money in grand style on a parlor car and a big dinner in the diner, and arrived in New York to find that the whole job had evaporated and the three of them were exactly back where they'd been last time.

Fortunately another job soon materialised, at an important black cabaret in Harlem called Barron's Exclusive Club.

This famous club was owned and operated by Barron Wilkins, who was practically the only club-owner in Harlem who was not a gangster. He had opened his club in around 1915, before Prohibition came in. When it did come in, and gangsters started opening clubs, he naturally had to buy his liquor from bootleggers.

This worked fairly satisfactorily until around the end of 1925, when he objected to the quality of a consignment (given the nature of most bootleg liquor, it must have been a horrendous fluid) and refused to pay for it. The bootleggers arranged for a well-known local junkie called Yellow Charleston to knife him to death outside the club early one morning in 1926.

The club closed shortly after, but it had been so well-regarded and successful that soon afterwards it was reopened by a consortium of prominent Harlem show folk, including the great ragtime pianist and composer Eubie Blake, and renamed the Theatrical Grill.

As the Theatrical Grill it was never as successful, but in 1923 it was still Barron's Exclusive Club and still at the top of the tree.

Appearing there, just when Duke and his friends needed work, was a handsome woman singer called Ada Smith, who would in a few years emigrate to Paris and become internationally famous as "Bricktop". She had met Duke and the others in Washington when she was touring there, and liked them as well-mannered respectable young men. So she persuaded Barron Wilkins to let his current band go and hire the Washingtonians instead.

What the Exclusive Club aimed for was a genteel atmosphere, and what the Washingtonians provided there was what Ellington later described as "under-conversation music", which was basically the sort of music the band would continue to play for the next few years.

Ellington now decided that from now on New York was his home (a decision he never went back on). He brought his wife Edna from Washington (leaving the infant Mercer to he looked after by his grandparents) and they started living in a series of rented rooms. Because Harlem rents were so high, most of these were the spare bedrooms of large apartments, and one of them they rented from a white producer of black shows called Leonard Harper.

Harper was asked to put together a show, to be called *Harper's Dixie Inn*, at a Times Square cabaret-club called the Hollywood Inn, located at Forty-ninth Street and Broadway. He needed a band, hired the Washingtonians away from Barron's, and in September 1923 they moved downtown from Harlem and opened at the Hollywood Inn. They would be based there for four years, during which time the club would change its name to the Kentucky Club.

It was situated in a basement room with a ceiling so low that the bandstand was only five feet six inches (1.66 metres) from the ceiling, so it was not possible to play a string bass up there, and Ellington had to play his piano and conduct from the dance floor. The dance floor was also tiny, but somehow they managed to run a modest floor-show, with even a small chorus-line.

The club was open from about eleven at night to seven in the morning, and because of these late hours it attracted a lot of musicians from the Broadway shows. Bix Beiderbecke used to come in when he was working at the Cinderella Club with the Wolverines (re-named the Personality Kids). Tommy Dorsey and other member of the California Ramblers came in. Members of the Paul Whiteman band, working almost next door at an elegant club called the Palais Royale, would drop in, Whiteman himself among them, affably buying drinks all round.

During their four years at the club, various important changes took place in the band.

The first was that Art Whetsol decided to go back home and resume his medical studies at Howard University. (He never completed them, possibly through ill-health, and he rejoined Ellington in 1928, staying with the band until 1936.)

Whetsol was replaced by an outstanding trumpeter, Bubber Miley. A cheerful round-faced young man with gold fillings in his teeth, and another member of the band with a fondness for drinking and partying and having a good time, he was one of the first of the young New York players to properly assimilate the sounds and rhythms of jazz.

He had actually been born in South Carolina (in 1903), but his family moved to New York when he was six. His father played the guitar a little, so he was aware of music early and took up the trombone and then the trumpet. By 1920 he was playing professionally, and by 1921 he was a member of Mamie Smith's Jazz Hounds.

In 1922 the Jazz Hounds were touring in Chicago and he went, with clarinetist Garvin Bushell, to hear King Oliver's Creole Jazz Band at the Lincoln Gardens. They were stunned by what they heard, and went back every night for the week they were there. As Bushell said, "The trumpets and clarinets in the East had a better 'legitimate' quality, but their sound touched you more ... Bubber and I sat there with our mouths open."

Miley quickly absorbed what he had heard. Adopting the use of mutes, like Oliver, he began to play "growl" trumpet. Even more than Oliver, in a way, because he either invented or learned from somewhere else the technique of actually growling in his throat as he played, giving his sound even greater fire and attack.

Considering that the Washingtonians were essentially still playing "under-conversation music", it is a bit of a mystery why they hired such a dramatic player as Bubber. Possibly it was an awareness on their part that hot music was the coming thing the same awareness that would cause Fletcher Henderson to send for Louis Armstrong the following year.

Whatever the reason, Miley was almost single-handedly responsible for the success of the Washingtonians. His playing was a sensation, and Ellington said later, "Our band changed its character when Bubber came in. He used to growl all night, playing gutbucket on his horn. That was when we decided to forget all about the sweet music."

Shortly after Miley, the band acquired another growl specialist, trombonist Charlie Irvis, a boyhood friend of Bubber's (and an adult drinking-partner), who had played with Willie "the Lion" and who, according to Ellington, had learned to growl independently.

The band also lost a member – its nominal leader, Elmer Snowden. The most likely story of how it happened seems to be that, as leader of what was supposed to be a co-operative band, he was walking off with more than his share of the wages. This came to light when Sonny Greer asked the manager, Leo Bernstein, when he was going to give the band a raise. Bernstein said, "I just raised." Snowden hadn't seen fit to pass on this information, and the others voted him out.

Bernstein suggested that Sonny become the new leader, but Sonny said, "No, I don't want the job. Give it to Duke." Which is how Duke Ellington became a bandleader (he was bound to sometime).

Snowden's career after that was all downhill. He formed another band immediately, to play at the Nest Club. That was the band that the young Rex Stewart was in before Snowden had to fire him to force him to go with Fletcher Henderson.

He went on to lead a succession of small bands with many fine jazz musicians in them, but in the early Thirties he got into a dispute with the New York branch of the musicians' union, and was barred from the area. After that he worked around Philadelphia and gradually dropped from sight, somwhat embittered at the success of the band he felt he had originally put together.

New York clubs like the Hollywood Inn did poorly in the hot summer weather, so it was the habit of the management to arrange to have a serious fire around the beginning of May, often considerably warning their musicians to take their instruments home tonight. Then they would collect the insurance, close for redecoration, and reopen in the autumn.

Fortunately for the Washingtonians, at around

the time of the first of these fires they obtained a regular summer booking at a ballroom called the Charleshurst, recently opened by two young brothers called Charlie and Cy Shribman in Salem Park, near Boston. So that was all very convenient all round.

It was after that first summer fire, in 1924, that the Hollywood Inn was renamed the Kentucky Club. And it was during 1924 that they acquired two more key men. The first was guitarist Fred Guy, who was to remain a mainstay of the Ellington rhythm section for twenty-five years. The second stayed for only a couple of months, but he remained to Ellington for the rest of his life the greatest and most extraordinary musician in jazz – Sidney Bechet (pronounced "Bash-ay", except in France where, because he was American, they decided it must be "Betch-ett").

Bechet, clarinetist and soprano saxophonist supreme, was New Orleans born and bred. A powerful and passionate improviser with a ravishing tone and driving rhythm, he was three years older than Louis Armstrong and comparable only to Louis as a jazz originator.

He was also touchy and hot-tempered, a musician who would not compromise about the music he wanted to play, and a wanderer who spent most of his life travelling from town to town and from America to Europe, spending little time in one place until in 1951 he settled in Paris, where he lived until his death in 1959.

Ellington had heard him first in Washington, possibly in a black vaudeville show at the Howard Theatre, and been "knocked out". As he would have been the first outstanding jazz musician Duke could have heard, and as he was so considerably outstanding, this is hardly surprising.

With the Washingtonians, Bechet and Bubber Miley would engage in cutting contests, playing to try and outdo each other over five or six choruses each at a time. Bechet did more than anyone to show the band how jazz should be played, and he gave Ellington a lifelong taste for musicians from New Orleans. He quit after so short a time because (he said) of feuds with Bubber and Charlie Irvis, but as everyone else in the world got on with those two amiable drinking-buddies, it seems most likely that Bechet's own prickliness was the true problem.

By 1927 the band was becoming fairly well-known. One factor in this was the new medium of radio. Quite early on in the days of broadcasting it was realised by the station heads that live music offered plentiful cheap programming. Many clubs were connected to the studios by land-line, and the Kentucky Club was one of these from around 1925. The Washingtonians made regular broadcasts and acquired a considerable audience.

Also by 1927 the band had subtly changed from being a co-operative to being Ellington's band. Partly this was because he was ambitious, and a natural-born leader, partly it was because, as pianist, he was the most natural one to work out arrangements on new numbers, but mostly it seems that some time during 1926 he simply decided that what he was from now on going to lead the band. With Ellington's characteristic impatience, to think was to act and, quite suddenly it seems, he surprised the band by starting to produce arrangements. And the band started to acquire its own personal sound.

Not that he was yet any great shakes as an arranger – that came gradually, and even when it did, the band would always remain to a surprisingly large extent a soloists' band. In fact, a great part of Ellington's genius was in hiring soloists with strongly individual and contrasting voices.

Among the musicians he hired towards the end of his time at the Kentucky Club were New

Orleans bassist Wellman Braud (a Creole name, pronounced "Bro"), who at first played tuba, and New Yorker Joe "Tricky Sam" Nanton, who replaced his friend Charlie Irvis both on trombone and as Bubber Miley's drinking buddy.

Tricky Sam became the greatest and most expressive growl player the band had in those early days, to the extent that his voice in the band became almost its trademark and he rarely played on the open horn.

Trumpeter Louis Metcalf, a well-schooled player from St Louis, with some experience of the New Orleans style, joined, as did Chicagoan clarinetist and saxophonist Rudy Jackson, who had worked with King Oliver.

With Toby Hardwick and Rudy Jackson, the band now had two saxes, but in the summer of 1927 Ellington decided to acquire a third – a three-man sax section was not only becoming fashionable, it was also better musically, as even a simple full chord requires three notes.

The third saxophonist he hired was the seventeen-year-old Harry Carney, who would stay with the band for the rest of his life. Originally from Boston, he had studied piano for a while as a boy, then clarinet, to which he had later added the alto.

Unfortunately, Rudy Jackson was the band's hot clarinetist, and Toby Hardwick played alto, so the young Carney was persuaded to take up the baritone. He learnt by listening to Coleman Hawkins on tenor and to Adrian Rollini on bass sax, and eventually became the best baritone-player in jazz (although he always continued occasionally to play both clarinet and bass clarinet).

Never a great improviser, he nonetheless had a formidable sense of harmony and a strong beat, and his tone became so rich and sonorous that in later years it was remarked that "Ellington has two sax sections – the sax section and Harry Carney."

By the end of its stay at the Kentucky Club the band had developed a long way musically, but from a practical business point-of-view the most important development was Ellington's association with music publisher Irving Mills, who became the band's manager in 1926.

Irving Mills was small and neat and energetic and Jewish. In the Twenties it was hard for Jews to get to the very top of the show business world, but they could get higher than Blacks, and thus could act for black performers as agents and intermediaries.

Having started in the business as a song-plugger (he was not too bad a singer in the style of the day), Mills had risen in the wake of the success of Mamie Smith's "Crazy Blues" by buying and publishing any blues any black musician cared to bring him. He became the Washingtonians' manager basically because he wanted a black band to play the songs he was publishing, and because he realised that Ellington could also write publishable songs (or at least, the music, to which Irving Mills, as an ex-song-plugger, would be quite happy to add words).

Mills's association with Duke lasted until the end of the Thirties. Many people later criticised him for having his name on the copyright of Ellington's compositions, and thus claiming royalties on them, and generally for sponging off the success of the band. But there is a lot to be said on his behalf. For a start, he did make some contribution to the compositions – adding lyrics in some cases, or tidying up Duke's arrangements when they got too dense, as they sometimes did and he was already a successful music publisher when their association started, while Duke was still very much a beginner.

One thing is sure, Duke's great success was to a large extent due to Irving Mills's management, and Duke always acknowledged this. (Furthermore, Mills was a hustler, and Duke always enjoyed being around hustlers).

Certainly one of Mills's earliest influences was in the frequency of the band's recordings. In 1925 the band had visited the recording studios three times; in 1926 it was six times; in 1927, the year after Mills became manager, thirteen times.

In the autumn of 1927 the band was away from the Kentucky Club, playing an engagement at Gibson's Standard Theatre, on South Street in Philadelphia. Or at least, six of them were, when the call came to audition for the Cotton Club.

After they got the job, and the contract was agreed with Irving Mills, there still remained the problem that their engagement at the Standard Theatre still had a week to run after the already-delayed Cotton Club show was scheduled to open.

The Owney Madden gang, owners of the Cotton Club, solved this by contacting a Philadelphia gangster named Boo Boo Hoff. At their request he sent round to the theatre an emissary named Yankee Schwartz, who said to the manager, "Be big, or you'll be dead." The manager found it in his heart to be big.

At the Cotton Club, with its policy of giving its white patrons the illusion that they were seeing raw savage jungle emotions straight out of the heart of Africa, the band was renamed "Duke Ellington's Jungle Band". As far as most of the patrons were concerned, the jungle was what the growling of Bubber Miley and Tricky Sam Nanton was all about.

Playing for shows, as they now were, much more than for dancing, Sonny Greer was in his element. Using every piece of percussion in his kit – cymbals and kettle-drums and tom-toms and all the rest of it – he could conjure up images of tribal warriors and sabre-toothed tigers and Ubangi fertility-dancers wearing coconut-leaves and feathers and not much of those.

During their long residence, the band (and Ellington himself) grew in excellence, and the famous names continued to arrive.

First of all, however, clarinetist Rudy Jackson went, after falling out with Duke over a tune. In the autumn of 1927 Jackson had brought him a tune that he had based on Jimmy Noone's clarinet solo on a King Oliver recording called 'Camp Meeting Blues'. Ellington modified the tune further, arranged it, copyrighted it in his own name, and called it 'Creole Love Call'.

Recorded in October 1927, with a wordless vocal by Adelaide Hall, it became one of Ellington's best and most famous early records, and is another example of his quickness to make use of unusual tone colours the band had been playing the number on-stage and he had heard Adelaide singing wordlessly along with it in the wings. Liking the sound, he immediately arranged for her to do the same thing on record.

When the record came out, King Oliver sued Duke for infringement of copyright. His suit failed, because his own claim on the copyright was not clear, but the whole business left Duke with the feeling that somehow Rudy Jackson had double-crossed him. So Rudy had to go, and in January 1928 was replaced by Barney Bigard.

Bigard was a New Orleans clarinetist who had played with King Oliver (and with Luis Russell) and who, like most New Orleans clarinetists of his day, played the Albert-system clarinet. Most clarinetists of later years use the Boehm-system clarinet which, by redesigning the pattern of the keys, allows faster playing. It also, however, has a narrower bore, and the wider bore of the Albert clarinet gives it a rich woody tone, especially in the lower register. Bigard's use of this tone became a valuable colour in the band.

The next new arrival, in May 1928, less than six

months after the move to the Cotton Club, was altoist John Cornelius Hodges, known sometimes in the band as "Jeep" (after a small magical animal in the *Popeye* strip), but mostly as "Rabbit" (he himself said he got the name from being fast on his feet, but others said he got it either from being fond of lettuce-and-tomato sandwiches or from looking like a rabbit).

Born in Cambridge, Massachusetts, in 1907, he spent his boyhood in Boston. All of his family played a bit of piano, himself included, but he decided he preferred the drums, and "beat up all the pots and pans in the kitchen." Then he decided he liked the look of the saxophone, and got hold of an old curved soprano (unlike Bechet's, which was straight, although musically the same). A friend taught him to play scales, and from then on he taught himself.

He had heard a lot about Sidney Bechet, who was then playing in Boston at a burlesque house called "Jimmy Cooper's Black and White Show". When he had had his soprano only two days he went to see the show, carrying it with him wrapped up in a sleeve cut off an old coat. Summoning up all his nerve, he went backstage after the show and not only got to meet Bechet, but played a tune for him, 'My Honey's Lovin' Arms'. Bechet was sufficiently impressed to give him a few tips.

As it happened, he lived only a couple of blocks away from Harry Carney, who was three years younger, and the two of them (plus a third friend, Charlie Holmes, who would go on to play alto sax in the big bands of Luis Russell, Chick Webb, Louis Armstrong and Cootie Williams) used to listen to records and practise together, Hodges very much under the influence of Sidney Bechet and Louis Armstrong, and thus passing the New Orleans influence on to Carney.

A couple of years later, when the Washingtonians started playing their summer dance engagements at Salem Park, he used to go and hear them, and sometime around the same year (1924), Duke Ellington dropped in at a small club where Hodges was playing for two-and-a-half dollars a night. By this stage he had also taken up what was to be his main instrument, the alto.

Duke offered Hodges a job in the Washingtonians, but Hodges refused, being shy of going to New York. The shyness disappeared a few months later when he was asked by Bechet himself to come and work in a club he had just opened in Harlem, calling it the Club Basha.

He stayed at the club for several weeks, duetting with his hero, then for two or three years divided his time between Boston and New York, playing with a number of well-known black bands, including the one led by a cousin of his, Chick Webb.

In May 1928 Toby Hardwick was in a taxi-cab accident and went through the windshield. His face was badly cut, and Duke urgently needed a replacement. This time Hodges went. He stayed with the band for a total of forty-one years, never really learned to read music well and, as well as playing the most ravishing alto in jazz (at any tempo), contributed many tunes to the band's book, both by formally composing them, and by improvising phrases in his solos that Duke would frequently develop into whole new numbers.

Although shy and generous, he was also a somewhat prickly character. He insisted on being paid at the end of every day for the whole of his forty-one years, and on-stage appeared completely bored and impassive. When his turn came to solo, he would sit expressionlessly in his chair until it seemed nerve-wrackingly impossible he would ever make it forward to the mike in time. But four or five efficient steps later, there he was, reaching the mike on the exact beat to begin pouring out an effortless and passionate flow of music.

Having now got an excellent sax section, Duke turned his attention to the trumpets, and again decided there should now be three. In late 1928 Art Whetsol, having abandoned his medical studies, came back to replace Louis Metcalf, and the third man arrived in the shape of Freddy Jenkins.

Jenkins, who came from New York, was a short, feisty man – a flashy dresser – who played his trumpet left-handed, having lost the tips of two fingers of his right hand in an accident. When he stood to play solos, he struck an attitude, with one foot forward, his elbows raised and his head thrown back. He claimed that this was correct trumpet technique, but the band nicknamed him "Posey". Posey was a good section man rather than a soloist – he could read well and had a strong upper register that Duke used often.

And that would have been that, except that Bubber Miley was becoming increasingly unreliable. A happy-go-lucky character, it was nothing for him to break down in the middle of a solo in a fit of giggles at something that had just occurred to him, and often he would appear drunk and dishevelled on the stand after a night and day on the town. Or even sometimes to not appear at all – in November 1927 he failed to show up for an important recording-session, and Jabbo Smith (a flashy pyrotechnic trumpeter who was briefly hailed as a possible rival to Louis Armstrong) had to be hastily summoned to fill his place.

Reluctantly, as he had been so great a part of establishing the band's success, Duke decided he would have to be replaced. But by who? Hodges suggested that there had been a trumpeter with him in Chick Webb's band that would do. "Why don't you get Cootie Williams?" he said.

By then, Cootie had joined the Fletcher Henderson band, at that time still the top black band in the country, but when Cootie was approached he readily made the move to "Duke Ellington's Jungle Band". Duke, he felt, was coming up.

Charles Melvin "Cootie" Williams had been born in either 1910 or 1911 in Mobile, Alabama. Mobile is only 150 miles from New Orleans, and musicians often travelled between the two, so he played New Orleans style jazz like a native.

His mother died when he was seven or eight, and he and his brothers (he was the third of four sons) were raised by their father, a man who was so big and strong that someone offered to train him up to fight Jack Johnson. He turned down the offer and instead opened a gambling saloon. Unfortunately he was a gambler himself, lost all his money at the races, and had for a while to find work in Texas as a strikebreaker. Eventually he settled down and became a minister.

Fortunately, he respected music and insisted all his sons study it. At school Cootie tried various instruments, but by the time he was nine had settled on the trumpet. (He had got the nickname Cootie when he was about five. Somebody asked him what the music he had heard at a concert had been like. "Cootie, cootie, cootie," he said.)

Beside his school trumpet lessons, he also took lessons from a man named Charlie Lipscomb, who ran a local cleaning-and-pressing shop and played in the local concert band. Charlie detested jazz, and would give young Cootie a smack round the head if he caught him trying to play it, but it was worth it because he also gave him a firm grounding in correct trumpet technique, a foundation that few early jazz players were lucky enough to afford, or get.

As regards jazz, Charlie didn't have a chance, because Cootie was soon listening to the records of King Oliver and, even more important, of Louis

Armstrong's Hot Five. These records, which burst onto an astonished jazz scene in 1925, moved the emphasis of jazz from ensemble playing onto the soloist, and furthermore showed what a rich range of expression it was capable of. Cootie learned many of Louis' solos off by heart, and could still be heard quoting them from time to time for the rest of his career. Following Louis' example, Cootie when he joined Ellington played mostly open horn, while Whetsol or Jenkins played the growl solos. Diplomatically, Ellington said nothing, and neither did anybody else, but one day it dawned on Cootie that if he had been hired to replace Bubber, he had been hired to growl.

He had never heard Bubber, but he listened to Tricky Sam Nanton's trombone, and he practised at home with the plunger mute, and within a few months he was using it in the band. Eventually he developed a subtlety and power beyond even Bubber Miley, and became the best trumpeter Ellington ever had. Benny Goodman, whose band he joined for a while in the Forties, said that Cootie was by far the most versatile player he ever had in his trumpet section, a fast reader with the biggest tone and unlimited power.

In spite of his raw and emotional playing, Cootie was as reliable and dependable as Bubber was not. He did not drink, was always there on time, and cared passionately about the music. As a result, he soon became a sort of foreman in the band, glaring at those he felt were not giving their full attention to the performance. Finally, in building up the band that he was inventing for himself, Ellington added a second trombone, choosing a Puerto Rican named Juan Tizol.

Tizol had been born in 1900, and his family had in it a number of professional musicians, as well as lawyers and respectable businessmen. His uncle, Manuel Tizol, who was the director of the San Juan Symphony Orchestra, played the cello, trombone

and bassoon, and of these young Juan elected to take up the trombone. Not the slide trombone, which is usual in jazz and swing, but the valve trombone, which has the same pitch but is keyed like a trumpet. It is harder to play in tune than a slide trombone, but having keys makes playing faster passages easier.

Tizol had a full musical education, played as a teenager in the municipal orchestra of San Juan, and in 1920 came to America with a group of other young Puerto Rican musicians to play a long engagement at the Howard Theatre in Washington. It is said that while they were there he heard a small Ellington group play an intermission set, and that he and Duke briefly met. What is certain is that he liked America, and its new music, and decided to settle there. He opened a small delicatessen in Washington with his wife-to-be, Rose, and began playing when he could in bands both there and in New York.

In September 1929, the Ellington band was hired to play for a stage show called *Show Girl*, written by George Gershwin. This would mean reading professionally written-out scores, rather than the scrappy notes and memorised parts that they were used to (and would continue to use throughout Ellington's career).

Ellington decided he needed to find another good reader. Whetsol reminded him of Tizol, and when Ellington sent for him, Tizol came, leaving Rose to run the delicatessen. With his classical background, Juan Tizol was never an improviser: his solos tended to be straight renditions of the written melody, played flawlessly and with a pure tone. The contrast with Tricky Sam was enormous, and Duke had another tone-colour in his musical palette. He also had a skilled copyist, who both wrote out band-parts, and transposed them from one key into another. Duke had him copying parts from the day he joined the band.

The band as it was after Tizol joined remained almost unchanged right through the Thirties. The first of Ellington's great musical talents to show itself was his ability to assemble a band of musicians with unusual and contrasting sounds. The next was his extraordinary skill at arranging, which he was able to develop during the three years' stable employment of his first spell at the Cotton Club.

Having avoided formal training, he had picked up hints about arranging and the theory of music here and there as opportunity presented itself. In about 1926, at the time when he swiftly and definitely took control of the band, he began deliberately to pick the brains of more schooled musicians. Two were established black leaders of an earlier generation Will Vodery, who for decades was musical director for the great showman, Florenz Ziegfeld, and Will Marion Cook, a graduate of Oberlin Conservatory, who around 1900 had written the first important black musical, *Clorindy, or the Origin of the Cakewalk*.

Ellington and Cook used to hire a taxi and be driven round Central Park while Cook gave him elementary lectures in arranging, teaching him such basic tricks as reversing the melody, or turning it upside down. "First," he said to Duke, "find the logical way, and when you do find it, avoid it and let your inner self guide you. Don't try to be anybody else but yourself."

Duke didn't need any telling to break rules, and many of his most inspired effects come from doing so. As John Lincoln Collier points out in his excellent book on Ellington, if he was told you were not supposed to use parallel fifths, he would find a way to use them. If he was told that major sevenths must always rise, he would write a piece where they fell. And so on.

He tended to arrange piecemeal, starting with a basic tune and adding a phrase here and a phrase there, putting the slightly dissonant notes that he liked into a chord here and a chord there. Some of the little theory he knew he had picked up from the concert pianist, occasional movie actor, and acerbic wit, Oscar Levant.

Around 1926, when both Ellington and Levant were peddling songs they had written, they would run into each other in music-publishers' offices. While they were waiting, Ellington would engage Levant in long technical discussions. Some years later, after years of success, Ellington met Levant and said, "You know, Oscar, you gave me certain chords that I've been able to use again and again in my work." Levant, who had achieved considerable failure as a songwriter, said, "Duke, I'd appreciate it if you'd return those chords to me. I certainly could use them."

There were two very individual traits in Duke's composing and arranging. First, he tended to write not for a particular instrument, but for a particular musician in his band – he didn't write for a trombone, he wrote for the individual voice of Tricky Sam Nanton, or for Juan Tizol; he didn't write for an alto sax, he wrote for Toby Hardwick or for Johnny Hodges. This approach brought out strongly the personal sounds he had so carefully brought together. Second, which grew out of the first, was that in writing a chord to be played by three instruments, he didn't do the obvious thing and give the highest note to the highest instrument you might find that the lowest note was coming from Barney Bigard's clarinet and the highest from Harry Carney's baritone. In the immortal words of André Previn, "Stan Kenton can stand in front of a thousand fiddles and a thousand brass and make a dramatic gesture, and every studio arranger can nod his head and say, 'Oh, yes, that's done like this.' But Duke merely lifts his finger, three horns make a sound, and I don't know what it is!"

into the thirties

As the Twenties modulated into the Thirties, the world of popular music in America began to change. By 1927 the idea of the "name" band had come into being. Previously, hit songs had dominated the popular music industry – now the fans were beginning to realise that a good band would have a style of its own, and they would flock to hear a band and buy its records quite independently of the tunes it played.

This attitude on the part of the fans would become a fundamental part of the Swing Era, when they would follow the broadcasts and recordings and appearances not only of favourite bands, but also of favourite soloists, noting when they moved from one band to another, or formed bands of their own.

Another feature of the late Twenties was that jazz became unfashionable and "sweet" bands, playing more romantic music, came to the fore.

Partly this was simply a matter of fashion. Jazz was no longer a novelty. The Jazz Age with its "shebas" and "sheiks", "the bee's knees" and "the cat's pyjamas", was a stale playback. A new generation of young people wanted to find a new music of their own.

For a long time it was thought that the shift to sweet music was caused by the Depression – that after the Wall Street Crash of October 1929 people's lives became so much poorer and harsher that in a world of unemployment, of breadlines and soup-kitchens, people wanted a gentler and more reassuring music, not the confident cheerfulness of popular jazz. But in fact the shift had started as early as 1927, and to a large extent it was caused by the new and powerful medium of radio.

Radio sets had begun to appear in people's homes in the early Twenties, and by the end of the decade, although radio was still something of a novelty, it was well-established right across America. Sales had risen from less than two million dollars in 1920 to six hundred million in 1930, by which year there were 618 radio stations in business and the four big networks (NBC Red, NBC Blue, CBS and Mutual) were broadcasting coast to coast.

This meant that the average audience for radio was much more rural and provincial than the audience for the big dance-bands had been. Sweet bands and crooners were more to its taste, and as the power of radio grew, the sales of records and sheet music reflected that taste. Music-publishers and record-companies, following the trend, shifted their publicity away from the hot bands, which entered something of a lean period.

When the Depression that followed the Crash began to bite, record companies entered an even leaner period. With a radio you could hear the hits of the day played by top musicians for almost nothing, and record sales dropped so far that people began to believe that records were a thing of the past, a mere fad of the Twenties. The whole business of winding up the phonograph every three minutes and replacing worn-out needles was considered hopelessly clumsy and old-fashioned. American record sales fell from a-hundred-and-four million in 1927 to six million in 1932, and companies like Victor switched their production almost completely from making phonographs to making radios.

Among the vast number who had become professional musicians in the boom days of the Twenties, many started having a hard time. Hot musicians disliked having to play in big sentimental bands, and the out-and-out jazz musicians, who saw their music as a cause, suffered even worse. The great Sidney Bechet in 1933 even left music altogether for a while, opening "The Southern Tailor Shop" in New York with his friend, New Orleans trumpeter Tommy Ladnier. (It wasn't much of a tailor shop – they mostly did cleaning and pressing – and it didn't last more than a few months.)

Nonetheless, hot bands did keep swimming against the tide, and some even had some success. One was a white band from Detroit, called the Casa Loma Orchestra. It had grown out of one of Jean Goldkette's stable of bands, and when it was first formed in 1927, under a leader called Henry Biagini, it called itself the Orange Blossoms.

In 1929 a new nightclub, specially erected for a visit by the Prince of Wales, was to be opened in Canada. It was to be called the Casa Loma, and the band was booked for the opening. Unfortunately, the opening never happened, but the band (not surprisingly) liked the name Casa Loma better than the one they had, so they adopted it.

Finding work hard to come by, the band-members left Biagini and formed themselves into a co-operative, with saxophonist Glen Gray as their president and with Cork O'Keefe, who had been a band-manager for the Jean Goldkette organisation, as their manager. They were the first, but not the last, struggling big band to set themselves up in this way.

In the autumn of 1929 O'Keefe, who had moved to New York to set up as a booking-agent, succeeded in getting them a booking at the famous Roseland Ballroom, while the Fletcher Henderson band was playing elsewhere. There they were heard by a talent-spotter from Okeh Records, and their recording career was launched.

The Wall Street Crash came on Black Tuesday, October 28, 1929. The next day the Casa Loma Orchestra went into the studios to make their first three recordings, one of which was the new song 'Happy Days Are Here Again'. (Some of the cheerfulness of the Twenties lingered on for quite a while after the Crash. It took a couple of years for the real depth of the Depression to strike home.) The song became a great hit, and for a few years the band was regarded as among the best, especially by college students.

Although none of the band was an outstanding musician, and their rhythm section was rather plodding and uninspired, they played a mixture of up-tempo numbers and extremely slow sentimental ballads that appealed to young dancers. This, much enhanced by their stylish presentation, did a lot to pave the way for the Swing Era to come. When the Dorsey Brothers formed their first big band in 1934, it was the Casa Loma Orchestra (with a bit more swing) that they were hoping to sound like.

One of its alto-players in the early days, and an occasional singer, was Ray Eberle, who became one of Glenn Miller's most famous vocalists. Over its long recording career the band did well for singers – they recorded with Connee Boswell (the arranger and lead singer of the Boswell Sisters), Mildred Bailey (the best white singer of the Thirties, with a pure powerful voice and a rocking beat), Lee Wiley (the only girl singer that Chicago jazzmen like Eddie Condon found bearable), with Hoagy Carmichael and with Louis Armstrong.

Unfortunately for the Casa Loma, by the time the Swing Era got under way they had been around for five or six years, and in their turn were regarded as last year's news. By that time they were working under Glen Gray's name, and although they survived until 1945 and made a comfortable living, from about 1934 on they always remained well down the polls.

Even in the early Thirties, there were some places in America where hot music continued to thrive. One was Kansas City, Missouri. The other half of the city – Kansas City, Kansas – was too respectable, so musicians from there used to have to travel the five or six miles across the state border if they wanted to be where it was all happening. And by around 1930 it was happening more in Kansas City than any other place, any time.

The city had become a focus, attracting black musicians from all over the South and South-West of America. Partly this was because they found little racial prejudice there, but mostly it was because in those days Kansas City was what was known as a "wide-open" town. Its affairs were firmly in the hands of the crooked politician, "Boss" Tom Prendergast.

Boss Prendergast and his gangster cronies had Kansas City sewn up. They were hauling in cash hand over fist from the sale of liquor (even during Prohibition) and drugs. (He was also an early patron of Harry Truman, and gave Harry a judgeship). As part of their operation they encouraged the opening of clubs, large and small. All the clubs had live music, even if it was simply a

pianist, and most of them never seemed to close, day or night. As Basie's drummer, Jo Jones, once said, "You could be sleeping one morning at 6 a.m., and a travelling band would come into town for a few hours, and they would wake you up to make a couple of hours' session with them until eight in the morning."

With musicians dropping in at each other's clubs to blow informal jam sessions, the ability to phrase and swing and invent interesting new ideas developed rapidly. That was why Coleman Hawkins ran into so much trouble there in 1933.

One of the best bands in Kansas City in the early Thirties was led by a competent but not outstanding musician called Andy Kirk, who had been born in 1898 in Newport, Kentucky. During his boyhood his family had moved to Denver, Colorado, and in his late teens he studied piano and alto sax. He did not begin to work as a musician until the early Twenties, when he joined a polite Denver dance-band led by one George Morrison. By this time he was playing the tuba and the bass saxophone.

He first came to appreciate hot music in about 1924 when he heard a seven or eight piece band out of Amarillo, Texas, that came to Denver on tour. They were called Gene Coy and his Happy Black Aces, and from all accounts they were a hard-driving band. Gene Coy himself was the drummer, and his wife, Ann, played powerful piano (John Lewis, pianist and leader of the Modern Jazz Quartet, heard her in 1927 and was much impressed).

At around the same time that he heard the Happy Black Aces, and still in Denver, Andy Kirk heard Jelly Roll Morton playing solo piano. Jelly's approach to rhythm, he later told an interviewer, influenced him greatly.

Possibly he felt he needed time to get used to playing hot music, or possibly he wasn't a good enough musician to get work, but for whatever reason Kirk worked for a while as a postman before (in 1925) accepting an offer to go to Dallas, Texas and join trumpeter Terrence Holder, who had just given up being a featured soloist in the Alphonso Trent band to form a band of his own, calling it the Dark Clouds of Joy.

The band toured all over the Middle West, and Andy Kirk stayed with it, still playing tuba and bass saxophone. Then, one day in January 1929, when they were in Oklahoma City, Terrence Holder had some sort of sudden domestic problem and had to leave. Kirk offered to take over the leadership of the band, and all but three of the band-members agreed to stay if he did.

Somehow the band managed to survive, and that summer they were playing at the Crystal Park in Tulsa when they were heard by singer and bandleader George E. Lee (brother of singer and pianist Julia Lee), who helped Kirk to get them a booking at one of the leading ballrooms in the country, the Pla-Mor Restaurant in Kansas City.

There they were approached by Jack Kapp and Dick Voynow of Brunswick Records, who asked them to hold a rehearsal so that they could be auditioned for recording. At the rehearsal the band's pianist, Marion Jackson, failed to appear. Kapp began to get impatient and Andy Kirk, in desperation, asked one of his alto-players if he could get his wife to come and sit in on piano. He could, and she did. The alto-player was John Williams, and his wife was Mary Lou Williams.

Kapp liked the band, especially Mary Lou's playing, and arranged a record date for them at a local radio station. Andy Kirk felt that as Mary Lou had saved the day, it was only fair that she should be on the date. She said that would be fine, and by the way she had written a number of pieces that she would like him to hear. Of the six numbers they recorded over three days at the radio station, four were wholly or partly written and arranged by Mary Lou Williams.

Kapp was pleased with the results, and set up other recording dates, the first to be in Chicago whenever Kirk thought he had sufficent new material ready. When the record date came round, Kapp observed that the band was using its own pianist, Marion Jackson, and not Mary Lou. He insisted that Kirk send for her. This sort of occurrence led to Mary Lou for a while sharing the band's piano work with Jackson, but this was never really satisfactory, and in 1931 Marion Jackson quit and Mary Lou Williams became the band's pianist and arranger.

In spite of the success of the band's 1930 recordings, they were not asked to make any more until 1936. During those years they continued touring, even appearing at Harlem's Savoy Ballroom twice during a tour of the eastern states that lasted almost two years. In 1934, however, they settled back in Kansas City. Two famous tenor saxophonists, Ben Webster and Buddy Tate, did spells in the band, and it settled into a routine of constant touring, interspersed with occasional residencies of a few weeks at a time at the city's leading clubs and ballrooms.

Black bands scored for fewer of the best residencies than white bands did, and consequently had to spend more of their time touring, but nonetheless Kirk kept his cheerful band together right through the Swing Era, finally having to disband only as late as 1948, after a severely unsuccessful post-war tour. They remained a fine band, their rather simple riff-based playing given variety and interest by the arrangements of Mary Lou Williams, who went on to arrange for Earl Hines, Benny Goodman, Tommy Dorsey and Duke Ellington.

In later years (she left Kirk in 1942), she mainly led small groups, featuring her own piano playing, and continued doing so right through the Seventies, apart from a brief period in the late Fifties when she contracted religion.

The other great centre for hot music was of course Harlem, but even Harlem was changing by the end of the Twenties. For a start, high society was beginning to stay away. Hot music fans would continue to go there, but Blacks were no longer seen as chic and fashionable.

At the same time, black shows on Broadway, which had encouraged people to go to black clubs in Harlem, underwent a rapid decline in popularity. Partly this was the effect of a fad running out of steam, but partly it was the fault of the shows themselves. By 1930 they had run out of new ideas and were beginning to repeat themselves. Worse, they were starting to borrow ideas from white shows which had borrowed ideas from them in the first place, and so were beginning to look like poor imitations of imitations.

In addition, as the Depression took hold and money began to dry up, the supply of white visitors to the Harlem clubs began to dry up even further. And with the general rise in unemployment, Blacks were hardest hit. By 1934, eighty percent of the residents of Harlem were unemployed and on relief. They could not afford to shop in the white-owned stores, or even get jobs in them, and they began to feel trapped and resentful. The streets of Harlem became filled with the unemployed and disenchanted, and such white club-goers as did appear were increasingly liable to be mugged.

Then, in 1933, Prohibition was repealed, slightly to the regret of the young night-clubbing set, who felt that being able to buy drinks legally was taking a lot of the excitement out of life. The effect of this in Harlem was that the gangs, already suffering from the economic squeeze of the Depression, lost their major source of income and, finding the going tough, they began increasingly to fight among themselves. Although it was only among themselves, there was always the chance that a sightseer might get in the way of a stray bullet, and the streets of Harlem became ever more dangerous.

Then, in 1935, a sixteen-year-old black Puerto Rican called Lino Rivera pocketed a ten-cent knife in the Kress department store on 125th Street.

He was seen, and grabbed, by a white employee of the store. There was a scuffle, and another employee came up and helped hold him. A crowd of shoppers, mostly black, gathered round the disturbance, at which point Rivera bit one of his captors severely on the thumb. The man, losing his cool, shouted, "I'm gonna take you down to the basement and beat hell out of you!"

It isn't clear whether he ever attempted to carry out this threat, but within minutes the rumour spread through the streets of Harlem that a white man was beating a black boy to death. Then an ambulance was heard and seen heading for the store. It had actually been called to attend to the man with the bitten thumb, but that was all the confirmation of the rumour the crowd needed. Harlem exploded in a night of burning and looting such as had never been seen. The heady "Arabian Nights" days of the Twenties were over, and things were never to be as free-spirited and optimistic again. High society and celebrities stopped going there, and in February 1936, bowing to the inevitable, the Cotton Club moved downtown to Broadway.

In the great days of the Twenties there had been three big clubs in Harlem – the Cotton Club, Connie's Inn, and Smalls' Paradise.

Connie's Inn was a large basement cabaret on the corner of 131st Street and Seventh Avenue.

Originally opened in November 1921 by an entrepreneur called Jack Goldberg, it was then called the Shuffle Inn (a name based on a highly successful black musical, written by Eubie Blake and Noble Sissle, and called *Shuffle Along*). One of the celebrities who went there regularly was Al Jolson.

In 1923 Jack Goldberg sold the club to two brothers, George and Connie Immerman, who renamed it "Connie's Inn". Over the next ten years it would feature many of the greatest bands, including those led by Fletcher Henderson, Horace Henderson, Luis Russell and Don Redman, but its high point was its 1929 revue, *Hot Chocolates*, with all its numbers written by Fats Waller and Andy Razaf, and featuring (among others) Louis Armstrong. This was the show that introduced to the world the songs 'Black And Blue' and 'Ain't Misbehavin''.

Connie's Inn moved to Broadway in 1933. Smalls' Paradise, however, never moved. A basement club offering music and dancing, it was opened in 1925 by Edwin A. Smalls, a former elevator operator from South Carolina. Advertised as "The Hottest Spot In Harlem", one of its claims to fame was its singing and dancing waiters.

The house band for almost all of its first ten years was Charlie Johnson's Paradise Orchestra, a band said at the time to be comparable to Fletcher Henderson and Duke Ellington. Unfortunately it suffered from under-promotion and from the ill-health of its leader, Charlie Johnson, who had to give up full-time band-leading in 1938, aged only 47, but through its ranks passed a procession of first-rate players, including Benny Carter, Jimmy Harrison, Charlie Irvis, Jabbo Smith, Hot Lips Page, and Edgar Sampson.

Charlie Johnson's band left in 1935, but Smalls' Paradise carried on and on for year after year. During the Forties small jump bands played there; during the Fifties rock 'n' roll groups joined them. Smalls himself retired in the late Fifties, and the club was owned for a while by the famous basketball-player, Wilt "the Stilt" Chamberlain. It kept going right into the Eighties, and closed only in 1986. By the end of the Twenties, the big three clubs had been joined by another venue, which in the Thirties would prove to be the most influential of all – the famous Savoy Ballroom.

CHAPTER 8

stompin' at the savoy

The vast Savoy Ballroom was built on Lenox Avenue, on a site previously occupied by streetcar barns. Billed as "The World's Most Beautiful Ballroom", the dance-hall itself occupied the first floor of the building and ran the whole length of the block between 140th Street and 141st Street.

Passing the muscular bouncer and in under the lighted marquee, you descended into the basement to check your hat and coat at one of the ornate check-in counters, then climbed two flights of marble stairs, between mirrored walls, to emerge into the dance-hall. On the wall facing you as you entered was a double bandstand, and before you was the gleaming expanse of polished floor, teeming with dancers. The floor, which was specially sprung to be resilient under the dancers' feet, was completely relaid every three years.

Opposite the left-hand band-stand was a ticket-booth, and lurking alongside it were a dozen or so attractive young ladies in evening gowns, who would dance with you for ten cents a dance. Most of them in fact were the wives or girl-friends of members of the bands, but they tended to keep that a secret.

The grand opening took place on March 12, 1926, and the first band to play there was Fess Williams and his Royal Flush Orchestra, with the Fletcher Henderson band as guests on the other bandstand. One of the big features at the Savoy, was battles of the bands – one band on each bandstand, vying with each other for audience approval.

Over the thirty years that the Savoy existed, almost every important band of the Swing Era played there, some for a night, some for long engagements – Goodman, Ellington, Henderson, Whiteman, Lucky Millinder, Erskine Hawkins, King Oliver, Jay McShann, Cab Calloway, Jimmie Lunceford, Benny Moten, Andy Kirk – even the sweet band of Guy Lombardo played a night there, and unexpectedly made the all-time attendance record.

A band that had several engagements there in 1927 was the Missourians. After being replaced by Duke Ellington at the Cotton Club in 1928, they went on to became the Savoy's house band. Their punchy middle-western style of playing went down well for a year or so, but by the beginning of 1930 the ballroom's manager, Charles Buchanan, decided their appeal was fading, and that something was needed to pep them up.

From the late Twenties on, several big bands adopted the practice of having a sort of front man, who was not necessarily the leader, and who did not play an instrument, but who announced the numbers, introduced the soloists, and built up the excitement by reacting enthusiastically to the music, urging on the band, often dancing a few steps, and sometimes singing.

In the early Thirties Chick Webb had a front-man called Bardu Ali. In the mid-Thirties singer and dancer Willie Bryant put together a band made up to a large extent of the recently-disbanded McKinney's Cotton Pickers. He called it the Willie Bryant band and did his own fronting. But earlier than these had been a band called the Alabamians, who in 1928 had played a short engagement at the Savoy, using as front man a young singer and dancer called Cab Calloway.

Cabell Calloway, Jr had been born in 1907 in Rochester, New York, where his father, Cabell Sr, was a prosperous lawyer and real-estate broker. The family soon moved to Baltimore, where young Cabell sang in the choir of the Bethlehem Methodist Church and became such a successful baseball and basketball player that for a while he considered turning professional.

He was also stage-struck. When he was sixteen he got a part-time job as a steward at the Century Theatre roof-restaurant. He also developed into a useful dancer, and occasionally sang in a group calling themselves the Baltimore Melody Boys. But his family had plans for him to become a lawyer like his father, and when they moved to Chicago in the mid-Twenties they sent him to study law there at Crane College. While studying law, he also began learning to play the drums.

Unfortunately for the legal profession, he had an elder sister, Blanche, three years older than himself, who was well enough established as a singer by November 1925 to have recorded a couple of sides in Chicago with Louis Armstrong, just after he returned from his year in New York with Fletcher Henderson. At around that time she was appearing at the Loop Theatre in a show called *Plantation Days*. She got her young brother a singing spot in the same show, and that was the end of the studying.

He went on to appear with Blanche at the Dreamland Ballroom, then in a show at the Sunset Café, where he got his first big break. Adelaide Hall, who was also in the show, felt too ill to appear one night. Cab volunteered to substitute for her in a big production number, singing and dancing, and was such a success that from then on he was official understudy to the entire cast, and began substituting for somebody almost every night.

One evening the M.C. didn't show up, and Cab took over for him as well, so effectively that he later became permanent Master of Ceremonies. There he was spotted by Marion Hardy, the boss of the Alabamians, and was hired to front them for their booking at the Savoy.

The Alabamians were rather a flop there, but Cab was a success and went on to do a further short stint at the Savoy fronting the house band, the Missourians. Their first sight of Cab in action stunned the Missourians. From the first note of a number to the last he was a whirlwind of movement. With hair and coat-tails flying, he dashed from orchestra to microphone, from one side of the stage to the other, spinning and grinning and dancing and scat-singing.

He went back to Chicago to front the Alabamians again at the Sunset Café. He did that for about a year, then left them and came back to New York to appear in the Broadway show *Blackbirds Of 1928*, singing 'I Can't Give You Anything But Love, Baby' as his big number.

He went on to appear at the famous Connie's Inn, playing the juvenile lead in *Hot Chocolates*, and stopped the show every night with his rendition of 'Ain't Misbehavin''.

It was while he was there that he was spotted by Irving Mills, who became his manager and did a deal with Charles Buchanan for Cab to become the permanent front man for the Missourians at the Savoy.

Unfortunately for Buchanan, this soon backfired. While Cab and the band were playing a temporary gig at a Broadway club called the Crazy Cat, four men in broad-brimmed hats and overcoats walked in and told him that he and the Missourians were going to take over from Ellington for a while as the house band at the Cotton Club, and that rehearsals started tomorrow afternoon, and be there.

What had happened was that the Ellington band had been offered the chance of going to Hollywood to make a movie. It was to be called *Check And Double Check*, and was to star the popular radio comedians, Amos 'n' Andy.

To call Amos 'n' Andy "popular" is rather an understatement. They were so popular during the Thirties that every week-day evening, during the quarter-hour they were on, phone usage dropped by fifty per cent and many movie theatres actually stopped showing films to pipe in the show. (The black characters Amos 'n' Andy had actually been created by two white comedians, Freeman Gosden and Charles Correll, and to make the film they had to black up. So did the light-skinned Barney Bigard and Juan Tizol.)

Quite why Owney Madden decided to let the Ellington band take time off is not clear. Certainly Ellington, after two-and-a-half years at the Cotton Club, was now nationally famous. The almost daily CBS broadcasts from the club, coast-to-coast, had seen to that. But even with such a high profile, if Owney had insisted the band stay, it would have stayed.

We can only assume that either he reasoned that the band's appearance in a film would be a great piece of publicity for the club, or that the band and Owney's gang were on amiable terms. After all, as Sonny Greer said years later, "I keep hearing how bad the gangsters were. All I can say is that I wish I were still working for them. Their word was all you needed. They had been brought up with the code that you either kept your word or you were dead."

Whatever the reasons, in the summer of 1930 the Ellington band went off to Hollywood, and the Missourians came back to the Cotton Club, now fronted by Cab and renamed "Cab Calloway and his Orchestra". It was clear that what the club really wanted was not its old band back, but Cab himself, with a band to back him.

The club don't seem to have seen him as a permanent replacement for Duke, only as a temporary substitute, but he turned out to be such a smashing success that from then on, throughout the Thirties, the Calloway and Ellington bands alternated as the Cotton Club house band. Which suited everybody, including Ellington, who had begun to feel the urge to write more complex music than was suitable for a Cotton Club show, and was glad of the opportunity to perform in other places.

It also suited Irving Mills, because he was managing both bands, and on the few occasions when neither Duke nor Cab was available to appear the the club, he booked in a third of his bands. Not the Hotsy-Totsy Gang, which was a name he stopped using in 1930, but a black band that had been formed in that year by a New York drummer called Willie Lynch. Originally called the Blue Rhythm Band, it became for a while the Cocoanut Grove Orchestra, from the New York club where it was appearing. Several times it accompanied Louis Armstrong under that name, but when Mills took it over as manager in 1931 he reverted to the original name, but with a subtle addition. It became The Mills Blue Rhythm Band.

It was a fine and spirited band, and a number of great musicians spent some time in it, notably in the trumpet section, which at one time or another contained Henry "Red" Allen, Charlie

Shavers, and Basie's future trumpeter, Harry Edison. It existed until 1934 when, like the Missourians, it took on a front-man, and took his name. From all accounts he was so hyper-active on-stage that he made Cab Calloway look as if he was standing still, and his name was Lucky Millinder. The Millinder band went on to become one of the greatest swing bands of the Thirties, Forties and Fifties.

Cab Calloway's success at the Cotton Club was helped along enormously by Irving Mills, who decided that what Cab needed was a special song to showcase his scat-singing. Together they wrote 'Minnie The Moocher'. The song became so famous that Minnie (and her man, Cokey Joe) almost became figures in folklore.

Among those who flocked to see Cab was George Gershwin, who so admired his colourful vocabulary and flashy dress that he used him as the basis for the character "Sportin' Life" in his operetta *Porgy And Bess*. He always hoped that Cab would play the part when it opened in 1935, but Cab was too fully booked to be able to make the time. He did eventually play it in 1952, in a revival.

Cab's attitude to what had now thoroughly become "his" band was very much his own. Although he was neither a composer nor a musician, he could tell a good musician when he heard one, and as a result the band gradually acquired a number of fine players. Once he had hired them, Cab had the sense to leave them alone to develop their music themselves. As a result, his became one of the best swing bands of the late Thirties.

Among the great musicians who passed through it were bassist Milt Hinton; drummer Cozy Cole; trumpeters Doc Cheatham, Shad Collins, Jonah Jones and Dizzy Gillespie; trombonists Claude Jones, Quentin Jackson and Tyree Glenn; tenor saxophonists Ben Webster, Walter "Foots" Thomas and, above all, Leon "Chu" Berry (in his early twenties he grew a goatee beard and moustache that an altoist called Billy Stewart decided made him look like Chu Chin Chow).

"Chu" Berry, born into a musical family in Wheeling, West Virginia, in 1908, was inspired to take up the tenor by hearing Coleman Hawkins. He became so good that by 1935 he was himself in the Fletcher Henderson band, leaving it in 1937 to join Cab. Starting out (like almost every other tenor-player) as a Hawkins imitator, he developed a style of his own. He was not as fluent an improviser as Hawkins, but he had almost as rich a tone, quite as much knowledge of musical theory, and he swung even harder.

He became quite an influence in his own right in the later Thirties, while Hawk was away in Europe, and was still improving when, in 1939, he was killed in a car crash. The Calloway band had played a one- nighter in Brookfield, Ohio, and were driving to their next night's date in Toronto, Canada. Chu was in a car with trumpeter Lammar Wright and saxophonist Andy Brown when they skidded and hit a concrete bridge. The other two were more or less unhurt, but Chu sustained severe head injuries and died four days later without regaining consciousness. The whole band flew to Wheeling to attend his funeral.

Soon after the Missourians left the Savoy, the house band there became the band that remained most closely associated with it during almost the whole of the Thirties – the band led by drummer Chick Webb.

William Henry "Chick" Webb was born in Baltimore, Maryland, in 1909. A dwarfish hunchback, with a deformed spine, he was amiable, proud and determined. His family were poor, and by the time he was nine he had left school and was earning a living selling newspapers. Every Sunday on his way to church he saw a parade band, and he became entranced by the drums. By the age of ten he had his own drum-kit, and soon he was playing alongside established semi-professional musicians.

With no training in music, he learned by listening. He progressed to playing with a group calling itself the Jazzola Band, on excursion boats making trips across Sheepshead Bay, and in 1925, when he was sixteen, he set off to join the music scene in New York.

Freelancing around, he impressed several of the big city musicians, among them Benny Carter, Coleman Hawkins and Duke Ellington. It was Ellington who got him his first job as a leader. How it happened was that the Ellington band had been offered a five-month residency at a club called the Black Bottom, but Duke preferred to stay where he was, at the Kentucky Club, so he reverted the the practices of his Washington days. He got together a quintet, appointed Chick as leader, and got them the job. They got $200 a week, of which Duke took $30 commission.

Chick was then seventeen, and became a leader only with great reluctance, never having had the urge to be any such thing.

After their five-month stint was up, Duke got him a similar deal at the Paddock Club (below Earl Carroll's Theatre on Seventh Avenue at 50th Street). Here the band's reputation began to grow, and it expanded to an octet, but the job was cut short at the end of 1926 when the club accidentally caught fire.

Offered a twelve-month residency for the band at the Savoy Ballroom, he was still young and uncertain enough to hesitate, but fortunately was talked into taking the job by the alto-player then in his band, his two-years-older cousin, Johnny Hodges.

While his band was there, on May 15, 1927, it was pitted in a four-way battle against the bands of Fess Williams, King Oliver and Fletcher Henderson, and it says a lot for the Harlem Stompers, as they were now named, that their little eight-piece band was by no means outclassed.

When the Savoy contract expired, the band went touring for a while. They had been asked to return to the Savoy for a further engagement, but Chick asked the management if they would pay for him to add two extra musicians to the band. They refused, so instead he took a residency at the rival Rose Danceland, employing the two extra musicians he wanted (and replacing a band there that was billing itself as The Original Dixieland Jazz Band, solely on the strength of the fact that their drummer was Tony Sbarbaro of the original ODJB).

While he was at the Rose Danceland, Webb's inexperience (he was still only eighteen) once more let him down. Somebody came and offered him a booking to tour for several months in vaudeville. This was purely a put-up job to get him away from the Danceland. The Danceland offered him more money to stay, but no, he decided to take the tour. Not only did the tour soon fold, leaving the Harlem Stompers unemployed, Chick also found that the Rose Danceland had lost so much money because his band had left that they refused ever to employ him again (a decision based more on pique than on sound business sense).

With no work available, things got rough for the band. Fletcher Henderson borrowed Chick's lead trumpeter, Bobby Stark, then refused to return him when the band had an audition for another ballroom, the Arcadia, so they lost that job too.

As a replacement for Stark, Chick found the young Cootie Williams (like Cab Calloway, he had a genius for picking good musicians). But in an attempt to get work for the band at another ballroom, the Alhambra, Cootie criticised the band then playing there, led by one George DeLeon, to the management (he said it was wrong that a good orchestra was in the street and a ham-fat bunch was working). DeLeon had Webb and Williams hauled up before the union, and they were prohibited from ever working together again.

Chick, who by now had become proud of leading a fine band, turned down offers of work for himself with both Ellington and Fletcher Henderson, and hung on with a nucleus of his musicians, starving and rehearsing and hoping for a break, and meanwhile all sharing one room, living on whatever money any among them could bring in from casual gigs.

At last the break came when Chick was signed on as a client by entrepreneur Moe Gale (Moses Galewski), who also happened to be a major stockholder in the Savoy. Under Gale's management the band was booked into the famous Roseland Ballroom at $1,500 a week, a huge sum for 1929, and appeared for the all-white clientele there regularly over the next two years, from time to time also returning to the Savoy for a "battle of the bands".

Chick, with his amiable willingness to think the best of anyone's motives, continued from time to time to stumble. At the end of March 1931, during one of his stints at the Roseland, he did an unusual exchange of personnel with Fletcher Henderson, in which they each gave up and gained an alto-player and a trombonist, apparently to their mutual satisfaction. The alto-player that Chick got was regarded by many people as the best around at that time – Benny Carter, who also played the trumpet and the clarinet, and was an accomplished arranger.

Moe Gale was suspicious of Carter's intentions in joining the band, and advised Chick to get rid of him, but Chick loyally refused. The band left the Roseland and did a brief tour, then were faced with a two-week lay-off. As soon as it started, Benny Carter left, taking half of the band with him to start a band of his own. It took Chick several months to find good replacements and rehearse them into shape.

By now his band had twelve members. Moe Gale booked them back into the Savoy, renamed them Chick Webb's Savoy Orchestra, and in October 1932 they set a new attendance record for a breakfast dance when 4,600 showed up. All through 1933 and 1934 they continued to improve, delighting the dancers and beating all comers in band battles. Well, almost all comers.

As the band's long-serving trombonist, Sandy Williams, recalled in a *Down Beat* interview, "We used to go into training like a prizefighter. We'd have special rehearsals. The brass used to be downstairs, the saxes upstairs, and the rhythm somewhere else. We had the reputation of running out any band which came into the Savoy. But not Duke's. The place was packed and jammed the night he came, and when we opened we broke up the house. Then he started, and he'd go from one tune right into another. The whole room was swinging right along with him. I looked and saw Chick sneaking into the office. 'I can't take it,' he said. 'This is the first time we've ever really been washed out.'"

This was a feat that neither Count Basie nor Jimmie Lunceford ever managed. Partly this might have been due to the home crowd at the Savoy always being on Chick's side, but mostly it was the effect of Chick's drumming. He was believed by many, including Gene Krupa and Buddy Rich, to be the best of all the big-band drummers of the Thirties.

What impressed drummers were the crispness of his playing, and his ability to shade and colour his sound. Regardless of which item of kit he was striking – cymbal, cowbell, wood block, snare drum rim, snare drumhead, small tom-tom, low tom-tom or bass drum – each stroke had exactly the right weight and placing (on his recording of 'Squeeze Me' he plays all those instruments perfectly in one fast four-bar break). What makes this technically remarkable is that each instrument is made of a different material, so the stick will rebound from each at a different speed, which needs taking into account, and each needs hitting with a slightly different strength to get a proper balance of sound.

What impressed the general public was his flow of ideas, and his immense drive and swing. His crisp attack enabled him to drive a big band without playing loudly, a trick that even some excellent swing drummers never mastered.

As well as his drumming, Chick had also developed into a good leader. With his strong sense of rhythm and structure, he was able to guide the musicians he had hired into a tight and coherent unit. He was one of the first to give his band as a whole a dynamic shape, shifting easily between loudness and softness, a technique later taken to extremes by Glenn Miller.

Among the musicians in the Chick Webb band in 1934 (the year it began recording for the newly-formed Decca Record Company) were trumpeters Taft Jordan and Mario Bauza (who came from the Havana Symphony Orchestra and needed special coaching from Chick before he could learn to swing), trombonist Sandy Williams, and altoist Edgar Sampson, forever associated with the Savoy for writing its theme-song, 'Stompin' At The Savoy'. He also wrote for the Webb band the number that Benny Goodman later made famous, 'Don't Be That Way'.

Sampson provided many of the band's arrangements, and Chick bought others from top arrangers like Benny Carter and Don Redman. But still the band seemed unable to develop an individual sound, one that the public could instantly recognise and that would take it into the big time. It was a star band at the Savoy, and appreciated by other musicians, but as far as becoming widely popular, like Ellington and Henderson, it seemed to have levelled off and be getting no further.

Once the band was firmly established at the Savoy, in an attempt to build up its popularity, Chick acquired his front man, Bardu Ali, who tumbled and conducted and made the band's announcements. At around the same time, now that the band was making money, he was able to afford a baritone crooner, Chuck Richards, replacing him in 1934 by Charles Linton, a handsome "Indian-looking" singer, who sang slow ballads in the then-fashionable falsetto style. His good looks went down well with the dancers, and he was also capable of standing in for Bardu Ali as M.C..

But still the band seemed to be standing still, and Charles Buchanan (in his capacity as a director of the Moe Gale Agency) began urging Chick to employ a girl singer as well. She could do the up-tempo numbers that Charles Linton wasn't so happy with, while he handled the ballads.

Chick was willing to try anything (by now he had become determined that his band should be a big success), and got Charles Linton to start putting the word around that he was after an attractive girl singer. What he got was Ella Fitzgerald.

Ella was seventeen. Shy and self-effacing, she was nevertheless fiercely determined to make her way as a dancer or singer.

She had been born in Virginia in 1917. Her

mother, Temperance (known as "Tempie"), was not married at the time, and her father, William, soon disappeared from the scene. While Ella was still an infant, Tempie met and married a Portuguese immigrant called Joe DaSilva, and soon afterwards the family of three moved to New York.

While still at school, Ella acquired her passion for dancing and singing. She listened to records, and the radio, patterning her singing very much on the hard-swinging white Boswell Sisters from New Orleans. As she got older she would also sneak off to the Savoy whenever possible to learn the latest dance steps. Her usual partner was a boy from the same apartment block called Charles Gulliver, and together they would earn a few dollars dancing as a couple to provide entertainment in small clubs.

Then, in April 1932, her mother Tempie died of a heart attack, aged only 38. Relations became strained between Ella and her stepfather, Joe, and she moved uptown to Harlem to live with her mother's married sister, Virginia. Then, in the same year, Joe too died of a heart attack.

Competing for attention with her Aunt Virginia's children, Ella became fractious and difficult. She dropped out of school and started hanging round in the seedier areas of Harlem, acting at various times as a look-out for a sporting-house and as a runner for the numbers racket. (This was an illegal lottery based on placing small bets on what the last three digits of one of the day's stock exchange closing prices will be, and it had a surge in popularity during the Depression.)

After a serious row with Aunt Virginia, she moved out, hoping to be able to move in with another aunt. But the other aunt turned her away and for a while she lived rough, making a few pennies by singing and dancing in the street. She also began to enter amateur talent contests, of

which there were so many at that time at Harlem's bigger clubs and theatres that you could enter one every night of the week.

Ella's first-ever stage appearance was at the Apollo Theatre's Amateur Night on Wednesday, November 21, 1934. She had intended to enter as a dancer, but finding at the Monday audition that she would be in competition with one of Harlem's top dance duos of the day, the Edwards Sisters, and contrasting their sequinned dresses and dance-shoes with her street-rough cast-off clothing (including men's boots), she suddenly elected to sing instead. At the show, accompanied by Benny Carter's band, she sang two numbers, 'The Object Of My Affection' and 'Judy', and won.

The Apollo Amateur Contest had the unusual feature that the prize for the winner was a week's booking on the next week's bill, but because of her shabby appearance Ella never got her booking.

A few weeks later she entered the contest at the Lafayette Theatre, which had originated such contests. Unfortunately she got lost in her song and was booed off. At the end of January 1935 she entered the "Amateur Hour" at the Harlem Opera House, which had then just changed over to being a vaudeville house and was intending to compete with the famous Apollo. Again she won, to rapturous applause, and this time the management (copying the Apollo) gave her a week's booking.

The audiences were wildly enthusiastic about her singing, but for some reason she never got paid for the week, possibly because the house had to costume her and deducted the cost from her fee. But it wasn't long before news of her two successes crept along the grapevine to Charles Linton.

He put out word that she was to come and see him at the M & S Theatre, where the band was then playing, and a couple of nights later, after the performance, she appeared. He asked her to sing. She sang 'Judy', and he took her upstairs to introduce her to Chick.

Chick was horrified at her gauche and dishevelled appearance, and hissed in Linton's ear, "You're not puttin' that on my bandstand, no, no, no, out." Then Charles Buchanan came in and Chick explained the situation to him, and Buchanan said much the same thing. Charles Linton then threatened to quit if she wasn't given a chance, and Buchanan caved in to the extent of offering her a two-week trial when they went back to the Savoy. If the audience liked her, O.K. If they didn't, out and no pay.

With a little coaching from Linton about the routine of singing with a band, she went on at the Savoy early in 1935, and did well. It took Chick a few weeks to make up his mind to put "that old ugly thing" permanently on his payroll, but with a bit of prodding from Fletcher Henderson's drummer, Kaiser Marshall, he finally did.

The Moe Gale Agency agreed to pay for her to live in a Harlem hotel, and gradually she learnt how to dress and move on-stage. She made her first recordings with the band in June 1935, and it was soon obvious that Chick Webb knew that in Ella he had the public image he was looking for. After she joined the band, it recorded only fourteen instrumental numbers, as opposed to eighty-one with Ella, many of them issued under her name.

Musically, the band became blander and less interesting. Ella had an enormous hit with her own song. 'A-Tisket, A-Tasket' and, in an attempt to catch the great white audience, Chick began to commission arrangements from successful white arrangers of the day, ironically at a time when white bandleaders like Artie Shaw were headhunting successful black arrangers to give their bands extra life and lift.

All this put Ella in a unique position as a singer. Other band singers were regarded as subservient to the band. In a day when fans listened to music rather than words, singers, male and female, were there to add a little variety to an evening's programme, to add a bit of glamour, and to give the hard-blowing musicians a chance to have a bit of a rest. They had to cope with whatever key the band wanted to play in, and were very much an afterthought. The standard phrase on record-labels, "with vocal refrain", summed up the situation pretty accurately.

Ella, on the other hand, virtually had her own band, playing arrangements tailored to her requirements. Which became even more so in 1939 when Chick Webb, after some years of considerable pain, died of tuberculosis of the spine.

Now the band became Ella Fitzgerald and her Orchestra, with Bill Beason replacing Chick Webb on drums. It carried on much as before, except that gradually it began to dawn on the band-members that things had changed. From a being a co-operative attempt to create something they could all be proud of, and starve if necessary to do it, the band had become a large and increasingly unadventurous backing-group. They drifted away in ones and twos, and in 1942 it disbanded. "The best thing that ever happened to it," said bassist Beverley Peer, but of course he wasn't right. The best thing that happened to it was its years as the house band at the Savoy Ballroom.

When the Savoy had opened in 1926, its policy at first was that energetic dancing was verboten, with two burly bouncers to enforce the rule. Perhaps Charles Buchanan was remembering the state of affairs at the Cinderella Ballroom a couple of years before, when Bix and the Wolverines played there and the management felt that

Charleston dancers were keeping the more staid majority of dancers away.

Because the Charleston was still popular in 1926, and early dancers at the Savoy wanted to dance it, in spite of the ban, they invented a fast-travelling step called "the run", which enabled them to escape the bouncers without stopping dancing.

To many of the young people who went there, dancing was a whole way of life. They lived and breathed dancing, and the Savoy became the centre of their lives. To the regulars it was known as "The Track", allegedly because in its early days, before the management realised what a treasure they had on their hands, they occasionally used to run dog-races there.

The atmosphere at the Savoy was different on different nights of the week. Naturally the busiest night was Saturday, when the place was packed and there was no room to dance properly. That became known as "square's night" (squares could easily be identified because they emphasised the first syllable of "Savoy").

On Wednesday and Friday nights the place was usually booked privately by social clubs or fraternal organisations, so you couldn't go. Thursday tended to be the night when people in domestic service got their evening off and went, so it was known as "kitchen mechanics' night". To a good dancer wanting to practise, this was not a bad night as the floor was usually not too crowded.

Tuesday was the night for dedicated dancers, and it was a fine night to be there – with plenty of floor space and plenty of other dancers to watch, to enjoy their steps and to pick up hints.

But the best night of all for a good young dancer was Sunday, when it wasn't as crowded as Saturday, and when the Savoy's publicity agent used to round up and bring in celebrities and movie-stars from downtown. They were always good for a tip if you danced with them, and furthermore, Sunday was the night of the "Opportunity Contest", first prize, ten dollars; second prize, five dollars.

A stocky young dancer called Shorty Snowden (he was five feet two), won the Opportunity Contest so often that eventually the management asked him to kindly stay out of it.

Shorty used to dance at the Savoy at least five nights a week, and by any standards became a remarkable dancer. In 1928 he entered one of the biggest dance-marathons ever held, at an enormous New York ballroom called the Manhattan Casino. The music was provided by a phonograph by day and by a band at night, and the contestants would dance for an hour, then rest for fifteen minutes, for as long as they could keep it up.

After eighteen days, when the contest was stopped by the Board of Health, only four couples were still on their feet to share the $5,000 prize money. Shorty and his partner were among them, and unlike the other competitors, he had begun to gain weight.

During the contest, spectators were allowed to liven things up by offering a five or ten dollar prize for a short contest between the remaining couples. During one of these contests, Shorty decided to do a flashy breakaway, separating from his partner to improvise a few fast steps of his own. (At the Savoy, he was known as a fast dancer, able to cope with a number like 'Tiger Rag' when it was played at four choruses a minute).

Shorty's breakaway electrified everyone – the audience, the other dancers, and even the orchestra. He continued to dance breakaways from time to time, winning all the short contests, and journalists like Walter Winchell and Ed Sullivan started to mention him in their columns.

Fox Movietone News arrived to film the event, and shot close-ups of his flying feet. Their interviewer, who seemed to have gained the impression that Shorty was somehow out of his mind and dancing in some sort of inspired confusion, asked, "What are you doing with your feet?" "The Lindy," Shorty told him, not missing a step.

This dance, the Lindy Hop, had been known around Harlem as the Hop for some time before Lindbergh made his famous 1927 flight across the Atlantic. It has a short basic pattern – a sort of syncopated two-step accenting the off-beat – which a pair of dancers do together before separating into a breakaway in which any steps the dancers feel like creating can be done before they come together again. Unlike earlier jazz dances, which tended to bounce up and down, the Lindy flowed more horizontally and smoothly.

Before setting off to enter the dance-marathon, Shorty Snowden had asked Charles Buchanan if he could enter it as an official representative of the Savoy, and was firmly told "No". But when he came back a star, Buchanan presented him with a gold lifetime pass.

That was also when he decided to change the Savoy's policy, allowing everyone to dance the Lindy. Its slogan changed from "The World's Most Beautiful Ballroom" to "The Home Of Happy Feet", and from that moment the Savoy went on to become the main birthplace of Swing Era dancing.

The truly creative part of the Lindy was the breakaway. Steps could be, and were, borrowed from everywhere.

At first dancers used a lot of elements of the Charleston, but as time went on they would get ideas from vaudeville, from ballet, from Russian dancing, from accidentally slipping and almost falling, from watching the way people walked in the street, from anywhere.

The dancers were creating a new dance style to suit the rapidly developing music of swing, and the bands that played at the Savoy were creating new rhythms and phrasings to reflect the dancers on the floor. This led to the music becoming more flowing and propulsive.

Leon James, a dancer who was one of the Savoy elite in the Thirties, tells of the young Dizzy Gillespie playing there in the Teddy Hill band in 1937 – "A lot of people had him pegged as a clown, but we loved him. Every time he played a crazy lick, we cut a crazy step to go with it. And he dug us and blew even crazier stuff to see if we could dance to it, a kind of game, with the musicians and dancers challenging each other."

It was around 1937 that a big development took place in the Lindy. Dancers started using air steps, where the girl partner's feet left the ground in increasingly acrobatic moves that owed something to the science of ju-jitsu. These moves, like most of the steps developed in the Lindy, acquired names – the Hip to Hip, the Side Flip, the Back Flip, Over the Back, Over the Head, the Snatch – and quite suddenly the Lindy was airborne.

The strange thing is that the Lindy, or as it later became known, the Jitterbug, remained for quite a long time the possession of a small clique, almost a secret society, of amateur dancers in a few of the big cities of America. The Lindy itself, named in 1926 and danced in Harlem even earlier, didn't become popular among the great majority of swing fans for about ten years.

Part of the reason for its slowness in spreading was of course that in the days before video it was much harder to pass on a new dance-step than a new musical idea. Music could spread via records, but dancing had to be passed from person to person. In that way the steps slowly spread through the black dance-halls. Later, adventurous young white dancers would go to those dance-halls, pick up a few steps and take them back to teach to their friends.

It was only after the Swing Era had got well under way that some of the dancers from the Savoy were shown to the world on film. (One group is in the 1937 Marx Brothers film *A Day At The Races*. Leon James is the young man who gets given a big grinning close-up.)

With the steps there to be danced, and the bands there to be heard, the stage was set for the Swing Era to burst into full flower.

CHAPTER 9

benny goodman

It was Benny Goodman's band that led the way into the full flowering of the Swing Era. During the late Thirties his was the most popular band in the world, and right to the end of his life (he died in 1986) he was able to fill concert halls all over the world with the bands, big and small, that he would from time to time assemble.

Benjamin David Goodman was born in Chicago in 1909. His father and mother were both Jewish, and both came from big-city ghettoes in Eastern Europe his father, David, from Warsaw; his mother, Dora, from Lithuania.

Both emigrated to America, where they met and married in Baltimore in the early 1890's. There they produced a daughter and two sons, before moving in around 1903 to the immigrant slums of Chicago, where they produced two more daughters, two more sons, another daughter, and four more sons twelve in all. Benny was number nine.

The family was not only large, it was also extremely poor. Clothes were second or third or fourth-hand, worn-out and repaired repeatedly until they fell to pieces. Food was scarce breakfast for the family was usually coffee and rolls (milk for so many was out of the question), and at times there was no food in the house at all.

David Goodman got work where he could, slaving twelve to fourteen hours a day at whatever poorly-paid job he could get. He had some skill at tailoring, and got work sometimes operating a sewing-machine in a sweatshop or doing piecework at home, but not even that was steady employment, and at one time he had to find work in the Chicago stockyards, shovelling around unrefined lard from the carcases.

In spite of his hard life he was a kindly, caring father, determined that his children should have a better education and a better life than he was having. Benny's sisters, for instance, studied to become book-keepers and stenographers, and, as each child left school and began work, they tended to stay within the family unit, contributing to its income, a common practice in such families at that time.

The family moved frequently, from one dark cramped apartment to another, sometimes even living in cellars. Not all had indoor toilets, and some were without running water. The effect of this poverty on young Benny was that he grew up determined to earn his way to a better life, and to provide a better life too for the father he admired.

When he was ten years old, his father became friendly with a neighbour who also worked in the garment business, and discovered that this man's sons were earning the odd dollar by playing musical instruments. Even if his own sons never became great musicians, David Goodman felt that playing music was a step up from working in a sweatshop or shovelling lard.

He learned that a nearby synagogue had a boys' band, renting out instruments for a modest fee and providing some instruction. He at once took Benny and his two next-oldest brothers, Harry and Freddy, there, and they were allotted instruments in order of age and size. Harry, being the oldest, was given a tuba, Freddy a trumpet, and ten-year-old Benny an Albert-system clarinet.

All three received some instruction from the bandmaster at the synagogue. Harry and Freddy turned out to be not much more than all right on their instruments, but Benny turned out to be a natural-born clarinetist. Unfortunately, after less than a year the band was discontinued for lack of funds.

David Goodman at once set about finding a replacement, and learned that by good fortune a Chicago settlement house called Hull House was about to form a band.

Settlement houses were philanthropic enterprises that arose at around the turn of the century to help immigrants assimilate into American society. Their basic programme was to teach such things as cooking and domestic science, but often they were much more than that and Hull House had an active programme promoting appreciation of the arts, offering classes in dance, sketching and music.

Here too Benny was loaned an Albert-system clarinet (and a smart new band-uniform, which he admitted was part of the attraction), and in the band played marches, simple overtures and some of the popular songs of the day.

At Hull House he received some tuition, although probably only as part of a group of clarinetists. But at around this time he also began two years of private lessons with an outstanding

teacher called Franz Schoepp, who was so well-regarded that he used to coach members of the Chicago Symphony. With such a solid formal grounding, far beyond what most jazz musicians of that day would have had, young Benny acquired a formidable command of his instrument.

Schoepp also had a social conscience. This led him to accept both black and white pupils, which was almost unheard-of in those days. A fellow-pupil of Benny's was clarinetist Buster Bailey, eighteen years old to Benny's eleven. Schoepp occasionally used to have them practise duets together, and Buster Bailey would go on to play with King Oliver, Fletcher Henderson, the Mills Blue Rhythm Band, and many others, spending the last two years of his life (he died in 1967) as a member of Louis Armstrong's All-Stars.

In 1921, when he was twelve, Benny first became aware of jazz. The family had somehow got hold of a second-hand phonograph, and the band that attracted his attention was the small group led by clarinetist Ted Lewis.

Ted Lewis himself was only nineteen at the time, but had already arrived at the corny semi-vaudeville style of playing that he was to preserve unaltered over a long and commercially successful career. A career during which he did at least provide long term employment for a few outstanding white jazz musicians, notably cornetist Muggsy Spanier, and trombonist George Brunies of the New Orleans Rhythm Kings.

Benny soon learned to play a very fair imitation of Lewis's whinnying vibrato, and in the same year, when there was an amateur "jazz" night at the Central Park Theatre, his eldest brother, Charlie, got him onto the bill. He played his Ted Lewis imitation to great applause, and a few weeks later, when the theatre manager was short an act, he sent for Benny to fill in. Benny, who never seems to have suffered from stage-fright in his life, was pleased to be asked but matter-of-fact about the whole thing. He played the job and was paid five dollars – about a working man's daily wage in 1921.

Fortunately for his growing interest in jazz, he was also beginning to hear better clarinetists. At eleven or twelve he would have been too young to go to the sort of dives where bands like the New Orleans Rhythm Kings were playing, but they made their first records in the summer of 1922, and he was able to hear their fine clarinetist, Leon Roppolo.

It is said that in those early days he was also influenced by a white New Orleans clarinetist called Doc Berendsohn, who recorded in the early Twenties with a New York band called (for the purposes of the record) Bailey's Lucky Seven. Their real name was the Original Memphis Five, but they were nothing to do with Memphis either.

In 1922, when he was thirteen, Benny started going to Harrison High School where he fell in with two fellow-pupils who were a pianist and drummer, and the trio started playing for the school's dances. Somehow, through other young fellow-musicians, he met the members of the Austin High School gang – Bud Freeman, Jimmy McPartland, Jim Lanigan and the others, all three or four years older than he was and amazed at his youth and musical fluency. The strange thing was that, according to Bud Freeman, Benny at that age had no real idea of the extraordinary talent he possessed.

Another member of the group was Dave Tough, who would become Benny's drummer after Gene Krupa left his band in the late Thirties. Tough was an unusual and thoughtful character, steeped in literature and the arts, and

it seems likely that he did more than anyone to encourage the attitude among the Austin High School gang of the jazz musician as an outcast artist, keeper of the mystic flame and perpetually in quest of the musical Holy Grail.

Benny never subscribed to this attitude. Coming from the poverty-stricken background he did, music was and always remained first and foremost a business, no matter how much enjoyment he got from it.

By 1923 he was playing at small local functions, and his reputation among young white musicians was growing. Early in the year he was heard at a dance by a young would-be promoter called Murph Podolksy (his real first name was Charles, but for some reason at that time Jews were frequently nicknamed "Murph"). Murph was booking small bands for gigs around Chicago, mainly at schools and colleges, and he offered Benny some bookings.

As these bookings were on a professional basis, this meant that Benny would have to join the union. This involved a playing test and a reading test, and the union officials must have been a bit startled to be faced with a thirteen-year-old applicant, but Benny was plainly well-qualified, and he got his ticket.

Armed with his union membership and a tuxedo organised for him by his sister Ethel, who had become a book-keeper for a clothing firm, he began working several nights a week, and was soon earning around eighty to a hundred dollars a week, a goodly sum for those days. He bought himself a saxophone, and his sister Ethel again helped him out by helping him to buy a new clarinet (still an Albert).

Working meant staying up until one or two in the morning, which made getting up for school difficult. For a couple of months he transferred to a school set up to cater to young professionals, which didn't start in the mornings till eleven-thirty, but even that was hard going, and when he turned fourteen in May and could legally leave school altogether, he did.

Now that he didn't have to get up in the morning, he was able to explore the booming jazz night-life of Chicago. He heard Leon Roppolo with the New Orleans Rhythm Kings, Johnny Dodds with King Oliver, and the other great New Orleans clarinetist in Chicago at the time, Jimmie Noone, then playing in Doc Cooke's Dreamland Orchestra. But he went out and about less often than the other young white beginners. Benny was something of a loner all his life, and night-clubbing was not really for him. Most of his listening he still did off records. Nonetheless, influences of Roppolo and Dodds and Noone did feed into his growing style.

Between 1923 and 1925 he worked fairly steadily in various groups at various cabarets and dancehalls. In 1925, when he was sixteen, he bought another new clarinet, switching this time to the more modern Boehm system. This he probably did because microphones were coming increasingly into use, both for recordings and for radio, and the more brilliant-sounding Boehm was more effective with a microphone. But in his later years he did admit that he felt that rich lower tones of the Albert were a loss.

By this time (1925) he had already developed his own distinctive tone and phrasing, his playing instantly recognisable as the fiery, fluent and swinging Goodman style of later years. His reputation continued to grow, and in that same year he was playing in the Midway Gardens Restaurant when the call came for him to go to California and join Ben Pollack.

At around this time, Benny made a trip home to Chicago and told his father that, now there was plenty of money coming in, there was no need for him to keep working. David Goodman looked him in the eye and said, "Benny, you take care of yourself, I'll take care of myself."

However, Benny was not the only one of the family making a good living at this time. His brother Harry was also in the Pollack band, and several of his other brothers and sisters were in secure jobs. So they all got together and, out of gratitude for all that their father had done for them, at least arranged for him the easier job of running a newsstand at the corner of California and Madison streets.

The plan backfired. One day in 1927, not long after he took over the newsstand, David Goodman, either going to or coming from his work there, was knocked down by a car and killed. Benny was deeply shocked. His father had only been in his early fifties, and it was Benny's regret to the end of his days that his father never lived to see and enjoy his son's great success.

The time Benny spent with the Pollack band was important in his career. As well appearing with it in hotels and dance-halls, he was heard on its records, and by 1929, when he finally fell out with Pollack and left the band for good, he was well established as one of the best young reed players of the day, with a small but growing reputation among hot dance fans.

Furthermore, being in the Pollack band gave him some idea of what the day-to-day business of running a band involved, and having been in it during the brief time when it was leading the field in hot dance music, Benny would also use its sound as a model for what he wanted from a band of his own.

After leaving Pollack he worked for several years as a freelance musician, working in clubs and at dances and at recording sessions. Even though the record industry was dwindling, between 1929 and 1934 he appeared on almost five hundred sides.

About fifty of these were with the cornetist Red Nichols (another disciple of the ODJB) and basically they were jazz-flavoured dance numbers. The bands would have eight to ten members, playing written arrangements with spaces in them for improvised solos, much as Pollack's band band had done. But Nichols was a stricter leader than Pollack.

His father, who had taught him to play the cornet, was a firm believer in musical discipline, and he had taught Red that as well. As his manager, George Tasker, said, "(He was) considered by many as one of the roughest taskmasters in the business. It wasn't unusual for him to call section rehearsals as well as band rehearsals time after time to improve intonation, phrasing and technique on material that the band had been playing for months."

This was exactly the sort of approach that Benny Goodman would adopt as a bandleader. Very likely he would have adopted it anyway, for these were very much his attitudes, but having Nichols as an example could only have reinforced them.

He first worked in a band led my Nichols in January 1930, when Nichols had organised the pit band for a Gershwin show called *Strike Up The Band*. In the band were also Gene Krupa and Glenn Miller, as well as a fine tenor-player two years younger than Benny, Irving "Babe" Russin, who would go on to play not only in the Goodman band, but also with Tommy Dorsey, Jimmy Dorsey and Bunny Berigan.

Being in a pit band led by Red Nichols was a good situation for Benny. Nichols was popular with the young white dance crowd, so it would get him further exposure. And a pit band's hours would leave him plenty of time during the day to keep up his freelance work in radio and record

studios. But in spite of this he didn't stay long because this was the time when the Pollack band were trying to get themselves booked into the Park Central Hotel without Pollack, and Benny left to join in the plot. He gave Nichols two weeks' notice and was replaced by Jimmy Dorsey.

The Pollack plot failed, and Goodman found himself out of work. He picked up jobs where he could a bit of studio work, and a stint in a pit band under radio bandleader Don Voorhees for a show called *The Nine-Fifteen Revue*, which opened on February 11 and closed on the 17. Fortunately Voorhees was using the same band for his radio work, so that kept some money coming in.

In the autumn of that same year Nichols was asked to form a pit band for another Gershwin show, *Girl Crazy*, and he again he hired Benny, along with quite a few familiar faces. Jack Teagarden was there, along with his brother Charlie on trumpet. So were Glenn Miller and Gene Krupa. Again it was a good job for Benny to have, and it also paid well. He was making somewhere between $350 and $400 a week. But here once again he fell out with his bandleader.

The incident happened at around the end of April 1931. Benny himself later said it was during intermission, but most likely it was during the performance, and what he did was to start having a bit of fun by deliberately playing in the old Ted Lewis style. Nichols told him off and Benny, attempting to smooth things over, said, "You know I was just kidding." Which would have been fine except that he added, "You know how I sound when I'm kidding? Well that's how you sound all the time."

Further words were immediately spoken. Benny either quit or was fired, and at the end of his two weeks' notice was again replaced by Jimmy Dorsey. His main work now was in radio bands, and within a few months had had similar altercations with two influential radio band-leaders, one of them being Don Voorhees.

Something was obviously eating him. All his life he had a tendency to be moody and irascible, but at this period he seemed worse than usual. Possibly he was feeling that his career was going nowhere. No longer was he the amazing boy prodigy, earning a man's wage at the age of fourteen. No longer was he the star clarinetist with the hottest white band in the country. He was merely one of a large number of highly competent session musicians, albeit one of the best, freelancing around the radio and record studios, or in pick-up bands for short engagements.

He seems to have had no ambition at this time to lead a band of his own, although he may have toyed with the idea, but in the spring of 1932 he was asked to form a band to back the crooner Russ Colombo, at that time being promoted as "NCB's Romeo Of Song" in the hope that he would become a rival to Bing Crosby, who by now (thanks to radio) was well on his way to the dominant position in popular song he would hold throughout the Thirties.

Among the men that Benny hired for the band, as well as his brother Harry on bass, were trumpeter Jimmy McPartland, tenorist Babe Russin, drummer Gene Krupa, and a Chicago pianist of around his own age called Joe Sullivan, who was conservatory-trained and had also played in vaudeville before getting involved with the Austin High School gang.

This was Benny Goodman's first real experience of being a band-leader, although this was a very conventional band. He had been responsible for hiring the men, and on-stage had to set the tempos, appoint the soloists, and control the overall sound of the band, its light and shade and voicing.

How well he managed on this maiden outing is not recorded. He obviously managed to do the job well enough, because the band continued to back Russ Colombo through all that summer, but he made at least one odd decision. He restricted Gene Krupa to drumming with brushes only. Krupa was so indignant that he swore he would never work for Benny Goodman again in his life, ever.

After this engagement, work for Goodman started to dry up. As by now he was the sole support of his mother and his two youngest brothers, whom he had installed in a house in the pleasant neighbourhood of Jackson Heights, in Queens, the situation must have caused him some worry. But things were shortly to change, and the man responsible was John Henry Hammond, Jr.

There was no-one in the history of jazz quite like John Hammond. Over a long and successful career he arranged Bessie Smith's last recording session, discovered Billie Holiday, Charlie Christian and Count Basie, and as an executive of Columbia Records went on in the Sixties to advance the careers of Aretha Franklin, Bob Dylan and Bruce Springsteen. He was a tireless propagandist for good jazz. The only trouble was, he had a god-given belief that he was the only one who truly knew what good jazz was. Fortunately, he was often right.

He also believed that if a musician was any good he would take John Hammond's advice about what to play and who to play with, and if he wouldn't take it, then he couldn't be any good. Hence he wasn't too keen on the work of Duke Ellington, who in 1939 moved from Columbia Records to Victor to get away from Hammond's well-meant interference.

This irritating but on the whole admirable

man had been born in 1910 into the best of American society. His paternal grandfather had been a Union general during the Civil War, and his mother was the great- granddaughter of Cornelius Vanderbilt. She was deeply religious, with a mission in life to put the world to rights, and her son either inherited this trait or acquired it by example in his formative years.

He was a tall, sparely-built man with an aristocratic sense of his own rightness and a crew-cut. He first became interested in jazz while on a visit to London at the age of twelve, when he heard a San Franciscan pianist called Arthur Schutt. Schutt went on to record with Bix in a band called the Chicago Loopers, and to work with Red Nichols and the Dorsey Brothers.

By seventeen, Hammond was visiting Harlem clubs to hear black jazz and blues. He never seemed to feel that black jazz was better than white (or vice versa), but he did begin to feel that black musicians were getting a raw deal in the music business. For the rest of his life he would devote much of his crusading energy to the cause of black equality.

He entered Yale in 1930, but soon dropped out to pursue his obsession with jazz. He began to write enthusiastic and not entirely reliable articles for two British periodicals, *Gramophone* and *Melody Maker*. (It was Hammond who was responsible for the inaccurate account of the death of Bessie Smith, saying that she had been refused admission to a white hospital after a road accident, and had bled to death as a result).

In 1931, when he turned twenty-one and came into a fairly solid inheritance, he moved into an apartment in Greenwich Village, and began standing his favourite musicians drinks (he himself was a lifelong teetotaler) and subsidising small recording sessions. His ambition was to break into the American record industry as a record producer, but he was having no success, so in 1933 he made an extended trip to England. There he got himself introduced to Sir Louis Sterling, the president of the English Columbia Record Company.

He convinced Sir Louis that it would be a good idea to have someone (John Hammond) in America producing jazz records for the British market, and returned to the States with a contract to record eight sides by Fletcher Henderson, eight by Benny Carter's big band, four by a sextet led by violinist Joe Venuti (formerly with Paul Whiteman), and four for a group led by Benny Goodman.

Why he decided on the relatively little-known Goodman is not clear. Certainly he admired Benny's playing. The jazz writer James Lincoln Collier suggests that Hammond chose Benny so as to use him to front a racially-mixed group of his (Hammond's) own choosing, and thus to start breaking down the racial barrier that then existed in the music business.

Whatever the reason, on returning to New York Hammond wasted little time in hunting down Benny. He found him in a famous 52nd Street jazz joint called the Onyx Club, introduced himself and said that he had a contract with Columbia to produce four Goodman sides. "You're a goddamn liar," said Benny, with that new-world charm for which he was famous, "I've just been up to see Ben Selvin at Columbia and they're nearly bankrupt and can't afford to use me."

Hammond explained that he meant English Columbia, not American Columbia (although the records would have a good chance of also being released in the States), and once Goodman understood, he agreed to the deal.

Almost immediately, he wished he hadn't. Hammond, using his authority as producer, explained that this was to be a racially-mixed group, using Coleman Hawkins and Benny Carter, with a rhythm section of pianist Joe Sullivan, guitarist Dick McDonough, and Gene Krupa on drums. Benny was appalled. You could offend the whole record industry by doing a thing like that, and in any case, they probably wouldn't let you. He suggested that Hammond come and hear a small group of radio musicians he'd been rehearsing with (as ambitious musicians with not much work tended to do).

Hammond agreed, but with not much optimism, and his lack of optimism was justified. The group was bland and "commercial" not what he was contracted to provide and not what he wanted to provide. Benny explained that hot improvised jazz was no longer what the public wanted and you had to compromise.

Eventually they did compromise and agreed on a band that had Hammond's excellent white rhythm section, but no Blacks. Instead they happily agreed to use Jack Teagarden on trombone, which meant using his brother Charlie on trumpet, because Jack would insist. As a second trumpet Benny chose Manny Klein, a New York trumpeter of about Benny's age who was not only a useful player but also was (and remained all his life) a reliable studio musician who controlled a lot of work. They also enlisted a saxophone-player called Art Karle.

The next thing was for Hammond to phone Boston, where Krupa and Jack Teagarden were both playing in the Mal Hallett dance-band, to arrange a day for them to come to New York to record. Krupa repeated his emphatic decision never to work for Benny Goodman again, so there was nothing for it but for John Hammond to take a train to Boston, meet Krupa face-to-face, and change his mind.

This, being John Hammond, he did. The band recorded four cheerful and musicianly sides, which Ben Selvin of Columbia indeed thought highly enough of to release them in the States. One coupling, 'Ain't Cha Glad' and 'I Gotta Right To Sing The Blues' (with a typically disarming vocal by Jack Teagarden), was even a minor hit, selling five thousand copies. Most of these were probably bought by college students, the very group which would later form the core of Goodman's fans.

The success of this record was a great help to Hammond in his determined attempt to shoehorn himself into the record industry, and over the next couple of months he produced fourteen record sessions, including the first appearance on record of his new discovery, Billie Holiday, backed by a group that included both Teagarden and Goodman.

Neither John Hammond nor Benny Goodman were men who made friends easily Hammond was socially rather shy, and Benny had a strangely detached personality that indicated he was barely aware of the existence of other people at all. A story often told is of him having assembled a few musicians for a rehearsal at his house, which had a private recording studio adjoining it. The day was cold, and the studio heating was turned down, and eventually one of the shivering musicians pointed out to Benny that the room was freezing. Benny looked a little surprised, then agreed and set off into the house. A few minutes later he returned, wearing a sweater.

But in spite of Hammond's shyness and high-handedness, and Benny's self-centredness, by the end of 1933 they had become friends. Possibly Hammond was to some unconscious extent congratulating himself on his broad-mindedness in making friends with a Jew (the caste he came from regarded Jews as only marginally better than Blacks). Nonetheless, the friendship was genuine.

Benny, for his part, had an aspiration to climb as far as possible from the ghetto, and John Hammond's friendship not only provided him with an entrée into the best society, but also with a role model. Increasingly he would dress and speak in a style based on Hammond's.

By the beginning of 1934, the amount of work Benny was getting was falling off. Fewer and fewer records were being made, and he had offended so many radio leaders that by the autumn of that year he was down to one forty-dollar job, as fourth saxophone in the band on a single radio show. That, and maybe one record session a month.

He had a standing offer from Paul Whiteman to join his orchestra, but that would be a last desperate measure, what with all the travelling to one-nighters and getting to play only the odd solo.

Perhaps the answer was to form a band of his own. Despite the continuing Depression, there was now a new man in the White House, Franklin Delano Roosevelt, and his firm and buoyant confidence was beginning to spread through the country. Perhaps it was still possible for a good dance-band to make money. After all, the Casa Loma band was doing so.

At this point, early in 1934, the Ben Pollack band, with his brother Harry still on bass, returned to New York to take up a residency at a mob-owned club called the Casino de Paree, on 54th Street. The club manager was Billy Rose, then just beginning his long career as a showman, and Harry Goodman heard that Rose was about to open a similar club in the empty Manhattan Theatre nearby, calling it Billy Rose's Music Hall.

As Billy Rose himself later wrote, in an article deriding his own reputation for spotting talent:

"A succession of press agents have claimed I gave Benny Goodman his start. Don't believe it. It's true I gave his band its first job at the Billy Rose Music Hall, but it only filled in while the other band was catching a smoke in the alley. When the whole country went crazy about B.G. and his Cats, I took a few bows here and there, but I never knew what all the hollering was about."

When Benny decided to get a band together to audition for Billy Rose, he was sufficiently well-known and respected in the music business for word soon to get about. He started rehearsing. A steady stream of musicians showed up to audition, and gradually he assembled a band. Mainly he chose men from the radio studios, rather than hot players, and his choice was considerably curtailed by the fact that he had little money to offer (around fifty dollars a week), and only a half a chance of an engagement.

Among the better players he gathered in were Hymie Shertzer, who would go on to become one of the top alto-players of the Swing Era, playing on and off with Goodman until 1945; Adrian Rollini's brother Art, who would be Benny's tenor-player for five years; guitarist George Van Eps, whose famous father Fred had been recording ragtime banjo solos as far back as 1897; and pianist Claude Thornhill, who from 1940 would lead a fine big band of his own. And then, at his last audition, appeared the performer who would make a huge contribution to the band's eventual success singer Helen Ward.

Helen Ward, although she was only eighteen, had been singing professionally for two years and already had a small reputation. She auditioned for Benny as a favour to him, and not initially to be a full-time member of the band.

Having got his band together, Benny got Oscar Levant, whom he knew from his studio work, to arrange an introduction to Billy Rose.

The band auditioned for Rose twice, the second time with Helen Ward, and after the second audition he hired them.

By now Benny seems to have become excited about being a band-leader. It felt right to him, it felt like a fresh start, and he was anxious for this first engagement to be a success.

The club was to have dining and dancing and a floor-show, admission two dollars fifty, and, according to Benny, the show included a lot of out-of-work vaudeville acts that Rose could get cheaply tumblers, fire-eaters, trained dogs and the like.

Of the two bands he hired, Billy Rose certainly seems to have preferred the other one, which was led by songwriter Harold Arlen's brother Jerry. It was decided at the first rehearsal that the Arlen band would play the scores for the floor-show, while the Goodman band would play for dancing.

The band did reasonably well, although nobody connected with it had much good to say about it in later years. A lot of the reason was that Benny hadn't been able to afford much in the way of arrangements, so they had to manage as best they could with what they'd been able to work out in rehearsals, plus a lot of solos with rhythm section accompaniment.

Nonetheless, the job went smoothly enough. The band even recorded several sessions for Columbia, one of its best numbers being 'Music Hall Rag', a thinly-disguised version of the old Twenties war-horse 'The World Is Waiting For The Sunrise'. Then, in the autumn, after it had lasted six months, the job abruptly folded. Billy Rose vanished to Europe, possibly after a difference of opinion with the mobsters backing him, and the new management fired the band.

Fortunately, just before this happened, the seeds had been sown for the big break-through Benny was looking for.

NBC Radio had been having difficulty selling advertising for Saturday nights, because advertisers believed that nobody stayed in on a Saturday night to listen to the radio. So they got together with the McCann-Erickson advertising agency, who handled the account of the gigantic National Biscuit Company, and developed the idea of a special Saturday night "dance party" programme, the idea being that people would gather in somebody's house for the evening, dance to the radio, and hear lots of lovely advertising for the new "party cracker", the Ritz biscuit.

The show, which was to be called *Let's Dance*, would last three hours, in half-hour segments, and there would be three bands one sweet, one Latin, and one hot each having a spot in each segment. On the very last night that the Goodman band was at Billy Rose's Music Hall, executives from McCann-Erickson came to see if it was good enough to be considered as their hot band. They liked what they heard and invited Benny to bring the band to a competitive audition with several other bands.

At the audition, which was held at NBC, the bands played in one room and their music was fed out through a loudspeaker in another, where an audience of young staff members of NBC and the agency listened and danced to the music, then voted. The Goodman band won the hot band spot by just one vote.

The Latin spot was won in a similar way by Xavier Cugat, and the sweet band was put together by the agency itself, under the leadership of a young studio violinist called Murray Kellner, who for the purposes of the programme would be known as Kel Murray. This was partly in the hope that audiences would confuse him with a popular entertainer called

Ken Murray, and partly because the agency thought that "Murray Kellner" sounded too Jewish. Oddly enough, nobody seems to have thought this about "Benny Goodman".

This was the biggest break that Goodman and his band could have hoped for. Radio then was at the height of its power, and to be on a three-hour show every week, transmitted from coast to coast, could make them into a household name almost overnight (which happened with Xavier Cugat, but not with "Kel Murray").

Also they were on a good salary. Goodman was on $250 for each show, and the members of the band each got $125 for rehearsing and playing the show. In addition, Goodman was allowed a weekly budget of $250 to buy arrangements. This was essential, because each week the band would have to play about a dozen numbers, most of them new, and Benny didn't have enough grounding in musical theory to do much arranging himself.

The first show was to be aired in December 1934, which gave Goodman about a month to get the band ready. As was his habit all his life, he embarked on a routine of hiring and firing. The Ben Pollack band had just broken up, and from it came arranger/altoist Gil Rodin, trumpeter Charlie Spivak, who would later lead a successful swing band of his own, and brother Harry.

Benny and Spivak soon had words, and Spivak quit, taking with him Gil Rodin to go back into the Ben Pollack band, which had decided to re-form. Brother Harry stayed, and was joined in the rhythm section by drummer Stan King.

Stan King, born in Hartford, Connecticut in 1900, had played gigs with local bands and worked in an insurance office before coming to New York in 1920 to become a full-time professional. A steady and reliable musician, he worked constantly. Among the bands he played with were the California Ramblers, Jean Goldkette and Paul Whiteman. Later on with he would play with the Dorsey Brothers, and in hundreds of pick-up bands that wanted a steady reliable drummer.

Unfortunately, while his beat too was steady and reliable, it was not very exciting, and a repeated pattern in his life was to be employed in a band when it was starting off, only to be replaced by a more driving drummer as soon as success raised its head. Eventually he became somewhat embittered by this.

Fortunately for Goodman, before the first broadcast of *Let's Dance* Helen Ward also joined the band permanently. Goodman was not the first band-leader to employ a girl singer (Mildred Bailey for instance had spent some time with Paul Whiteman, and the recently-formed Dorsey Brothers band already had Kay Weber), but in 1934 band singers were usually male. Helen was a pleasant singer, pretty without being stunning, and with a girl-next-door quality (visually and vocally) that appealed greatly to the band's core audience of male students.

Let's Dance was designed to have the feel of a real ballroom. It was broadcast from the largest studio NBC had, before a live audience. The studio could seat about 1,500, but people came and went during the evening, so that each week maybe 3,000 people passed through. The show also attracted a sizeable audience, certainly enough to satisfy the sponsors. People from the music business began dropping in to the studio to hear the Goodman band, and a feeling began to grow that something important might be beginning here.

Naturally at this time Benny was anxious to develop a distinctive sound for his band. With his $250 a week allowance he bought arrangements from a whole slew of arrangers Fud Livingstone,

Deane Kincaide, Jimmy Mundy, Edgar Sampson, Benny Carter, Gordon Jenkins and George Bassman, who arranged his opening theme 'Let's Dance', among them. But two in particular did a lot to form the band's style.

The most famous was Fletcher Henderson, whose own band was falling on hard times, and who was urged by John Hammond to make a bit of money by selling some of his arrangements to Benny. This he did, including among them 'Down South Camp Meeting' and 'Wrappin' It Up'. He also wrote some new scores for the band, as did his brother Horace. Among Horace's early arrangements were 'Always' and 'Dear Old Southland'.

Because Fletcher was so famous, and because John Hammond went around loudly saying so, it became accepted that he almost single-handedly gave the Goodman band its sound. But at least as influential was Benny's staff arranger, Lyle "Spud" Murphy, who wrote around a third of the band's arrangements during its formative years, including at least fifty for *Let's Dance*. Among his best were 'Get Happy', 'Restless', 'Limehouse Blues', 'Darktown Strutters' Ball' and 'Anything Goes'.

During the run of *Let's Dance*, the Goodman band did a couple of recording sessions for Columbia Records. At the second of these, in April 1935, they recorded 'The Dixieland Band', with a vocal by Helen Ward. This sold fairly well, and got a considerable amount of air-time on the radio, helping to build the band's reputation.

It was now becoming apparent to Goodman that the band was on its way, and what he needed was a good agent to handle contracts, publicity and bookings. He approached the gigantic and powerful Music Corporation of America to see if they would represent him, but MCA refused on the grounds that they were only interested in commercial music.

Fortunately for MCA, a little while later, in about February or March of 1935, they took on a young musician from Philadelphia, Willard Alexander, to help them book bands. Willard was aware of the current success of the Casa Loma band, and of an interesting band recently formed by the Dorsey Brothers, and felt that MCA ought to have an equivalent hot band. He had heard and liked the Goodman band's records, so he stuck his neck out and signed them, aware that his superiors weren't really keen.

The Casa Loma and the Dorsey Brothers had recently joined the new record company, Decca, which was making big inroads into the somewhat depleted record industry by pricing its discs at thirty-five cents instead of the more usual seventy-five. Their main market was a new generation of young people, and Willard was aware that Victor was eyeing this market as a way of rebuilding its record division. So he got them to sign the Goodman band.

Victor immediately got them to re-record their biggest hit, 'The Dixieland Band', and in a series of further sessions produced several numbers that would become Goodman standards, including Fletcher Henderson's arrangement of 'Blue Skies'.

Willard Alexander also arranged for the band to take part in several "battles of the bands" against Chick Webb at the Savoy, although there was no way that the Goodman band at that time could defeat Chick Webb, whose band was then at its best. As Cab Calloway's pianist, Bennie Payne, said: "It was reputed that the Chicklet had three different books, or types of musical program. The third was mild stuff, number two was hot stuff, and number one would blow you away. Chick used his number three book on Benny Goodman; he and his band didn't even work up a sweat."

Sometime around May 1935 a party was held by singer Mildred Bailey and her then husband, xylophonist Red Norvo. Among the guests were Benny, John Hammond, Mildred's cousin Carl Bellinger, who was an amateur drummer, and pianist Teddy Wilson, a young Texan who had worked in Chicago with Jimmie Noone and Louis Armstrong, and come to New York in 1933 to join the Benny Carter band.

Benny and Teddy Wilson started jamming. Carl Bellinger joined them, playing with his brushes on a suitcase, and the party came alive. It was obvious that such a group ought to be recorded, and in July the first of the Goodman small groups went into the studio – the great trio of Benny Goodman, Teddy Wilson and Gene Krupa, recording 'After You've Gone', 'Body And Soul', 'Who?' and 'Someday, Sweetheart'.

Over the next few years Goodman's small group records would provide a substantial part of his success, eventually selling around 50,000 copies each. This not only helped his career, and the band's, but proved to record companies that there was an audience out there for a new style of improvised hot jazz.

While this was happening, disaster had struck *Let's Dance*. In May 1935, the employees of the National Biscuit Company came out on strike. The company saw no point in advertising biscuits it could not provide and the programme lost its sponsorship and folded. Goodman was immediately faced with the problem of keeping what was now a well-drilled band with a considerable repertoire together. Willard Alexander, in desperation, had them booked into the Hotel Roosevelt, which previously had been home to the soothing music of Guy Lombardo. The Goodman band were not trained to play that kind of music, and Benny himself admitted that

out of sheer bloody-mindedness he didn't do much to soften down his music. The waiters went around holding their ears and the band was given two weeks' notice the first night.

Despite these setbacks, the band was determined to soldier on. They were all still in their twenties, and their youthful optimism kept their morale high. On July 1 they went into the recording studios again, laying down four Fletcher Henderson arrangements, 'Sometimes I'm Happy', 'Between The Devil And The Deep Blue Sea', 'Jingle Bells' and Jelly Roll Morton's 'King Porter Stomp'.

Willard Alexander was aware that their record sales were good and growing, and he felt it was only a matter of hanging on for the success he believed was sure to come. He worked hard to set up a tour that would take the band from place to place right across America, ending with a month's engagement at the Palomar Ballroom in Los Angeles.

Meanwhile, Benny continued hiring and firing his personnel, and the first great Goodman band began to take shape. He got rid of Stan King and brought in Gene Krupa. Krupa was of course an immensely exciting drummer, but his time-keeping was never rock solid, and Harry Goodman was never a great bassist, so Benny was lucky at the same time to acquire one of the best guitarists of the whole Swing Era for his rhythm section.

His previous guitarist, George Van Eps, realising that the band would soon be thinking of going on the road, and not wanting to travel, brought along as replacement his twenty-year-old pupil Allan Reuss, who up till then had been driving a laundry truck.

Reuss did more then anyone to give the band its lift and swing. James T. Maher, a writer who got to know Goodman well in the latter years of his life, once said to him that he'd never realised how important Reuss was to the band until he was gone. "Neither did we," said Benny.

He also brought Bunny Berigan into the trumpet section. Berigan, born in Wisconsin in 1908, had played in an orchestra there led by his grandfather, then in several college bands, before coming to New York in the early Thirties, just in time to be in at the birth of swing.

By then he had become the hottest white trumpeter in jazz, much influenced by Louis Armstrong, and hailed by many as the new Bix Beiderbecke. Unfortunately he was as heavy a drinker as Bix, and after a meteoric career in which he added greatly to the bands of Paul Whiteman, the Dorsey Brothers, and Tommy Dorsey, as well as leading bands of his own, he died of drink-related illnesses in 1942. Louis Armstrong, always disapproving of unprofessional conduct, said, "Bunny had no business dying so young."

There was one other crucial replacement. John Hammond had been dissatisfied for a long time with the band's pianist, Frankie Froeba, whom he felt tended to rush the beat. He had heard of a pianist working in Chicago, a white disciple of Earl Hines called Jess Stacy.

Stacy was just a little older than the rest of the band. Born in Bird's Point, Missouri in 1904, he had got interested in music when he was about ten and heard a woman neighbour playing such numbers as 'St Louis Blues' on the piano.

By a stroke of good fortune, his mother took in an orphaned girl who had inherited a piano. She was taking lessons, and after she would do her exercises, young Jess would run to the piano and copy them. His mother offered him lessons too, but he was happier teaching himself.

When he was about fourteen his family moved to another Missouri town, Cape Giradou,

on the Mississippi. He began to hear the bands that played on the riverboats – he heard Louis Armstrong, Johnny Dodds, Baby Dodds and Henry "Red" Allen, although he didn't then know their names.

Going to work in a music store, he heard the records of the ODJB, and became a member of a quartet (saxophone, violin, piano and drums) playing local dances. They called themselves the Agony Four.

He became good enough to play piano in dance-bands on the riverboats himself, and even played the calliope, the great brass-keyed organ of steam-whistles that could be heard for miles and warned towns ahead of the boat's arrival. (You had to play a calliope with thick gloves on, because the brass keys got too hot to touch).

In 1921 he joined a touring dance-band and wound up with it in Chicago, where so much was going on that he stayed, playing piano in little clubs and speakeasies. He was strongly influenced by Bix's piano-playing, and by Earl Hines, and became a powerfully swinging player. He was playing for twenty-one dollars a week at a large but seedy club called the Subway when Benny Goodman phoned him there and invited him to join the band. He didn't need much persuading.

So the band that set off on its cross-country tour was made up of Nate Kazebier, Bunny Berigan and Ralph Muzillo (trumpets); Red Ballard and Jack Lacey (trombones); Benny Goodman (clarinet); Hymie Shertzer and Bill De Pew (alto saxes); Dick Clark and Art Rollini (tenor saxes); Jess Stacy (piano); Allan Reuss (guitar); Harry Goodman (bass); Gene Krupa (drums); Helen Ward (vocalist). The pay on the tour would not be good, but was an incentive to keep on trying, and it would end in California, where all those suntanned Hollywood movie-starlets lived.

It was as well they were all young and resilient, because the tour was far from a triumph. At the Stanley Theatre In Pittsburgh the band was well-received – a few young couples even danced in the aisles. In Milwaukee there was a good attendance, many of the audience being enthusiastic musicians from the Chicago area. Salt Lake City wasn't too bad, but Denver was a disaster.

At Denver, Willard Alexander, for want of anywhere better, had got them booked into a taxi dance hall called Elitch's Gardens. By 1935 taxi dance halls were well on the way out, but somehow Elitch's had survived. As patrons were charged ten cents per dance, the management expected each number to last no more than a minute, which was a problem for the band as all their arrangements ran for around three minutes.

Furthermore, bands in such halls were expected to play a variety of dance-rhythms, including waltzes and rhumbas, and the Goodman band simply did not have such numbers in its book. They were given notice the first evening.

Benny was ready to give up. The tour hadn't been at all the triumphal progress he had hoped for, and now again the band had been fired on its first night. He phoned Willard Alexander in New York and told him he was ready to break up the band.

Willard encouraged him to do no such thing, and then several of the band said the same, with the result that he went and had a talk with the management of Elitch's, and it was agreed that if they cut their numbers down in length and played a lot of waltzes they could see out their two weeks. They managed the waltzes by having them played by a small group including Bunny Berigan and with Helen Ward playing the piano.

From Denver they went to California. They drew a good crowd at McFadden's Ballroom in San Francisco, a poor one at Pismo Beach, and an enthusiastic full house at Sweet's, in Oakland. So when they finally arrived at the Palomar they had no confidence in what they might expect.

Accounts vary about some of the details of what happened there on the famous first night, August 21, 1935, but it does seem that the band started out rather hesitantly, playing the mild arrangements of current pop songs that Benny had come to believe was what the public wanted.

The place was filling up slowly and steadily, and whether the band became aware that they had a responsive audience, or whether they simply got fed up and decided to go out with all guns blazing (one quite believable account has Bunny Berigan yelling, "Let's cut out this shit! Let's get out 'Bugle Call Rag'"), the fact remains that the band did cut loose on something like 'King Porter Stomp'.

The audience greeted it with a roar of approval, and the evening, part of which was broadcast, became a major triumph. Their one-month engagement at the Palomar was extended to two, and the publicity generated by their success sent the Goodman band, and the Swing Era, firmly on their way.

Why such a success there and then? James T. Maher, the writer who knew Goodman in his later years, and who researched his life in detail, came to the conclusion that it was largely due to a new breed of radio presenter, the disc-jockey.

The term "disc-jockey" didn't come into existence until after World War Two, but such presenters of records on radio were well established by 1935. They were becoming increasingly influential, and several of the Goodman band's records, especially his early ones for Columbia, had received a lot of playing on the West Coast, creating for the band a ready-made and expectant audience.

While the band was at the Palomar, word got to Goodman about a fine new musician playing at a rough sailors' joint called the Paradise Club, on Sixth and Main. He was playing an unusual instrument, the vibraphone, and his name was Lionel Hampton.

As Hamp later recalled, "One night I heard all this clarinet playing, looked around, and there was Benny Goodman." They played together that night into the small hours, and shortly afterwards Benny brought along Teddy Wilson and Gene Krupa to see how the four of them would sound together. They sounded good, and soon Lionel Hampton joined the others in a recording studio, and the trio became a quartet.

After the band finished its two months at the Palomar, Bunny Berigan left it. Whether it was because he was tired of travelling, or whether Benny finally had to fire him for persistent drunkenness (and he was one of the few musicians whose playing Benny admired unreservedly), is not clear. But Bunny sent his horn back to New York ahead of him, went home to Fox Lake, Wisconsin, for a week's rest, then followed it. His place in the band was taken by Pee Wee Irwin. The band too headed back east. En route they played a few club dates, then a short residency in the Urban Room of the Congress Hotel in Chicago. This important venue was usually home to more sedate bands, but the previous year there had been an outbreak of amoebic dysentery in several Chicago hotels. Business had fallen off, the the Congress Hotel was looking for a hot attraction to bring it back.

An attraction the band now was. While it was at the hotel a group of influential fans called the Chicago Rhythm Club hired them (and the Urban Room) for a Sunday afternoon dance. At least, it was advertised as a dance, but so many people came that extra tables almost covered the dance-floor. Furthermore, these were serious listeners, and those few who had attempted to dance were booed off the floor. The knowledgeable hepcat had arrived on the scene.

It was at this Sunday dance that the trio played in public for the first time – an event often spoken of as the first racially-mixed public performance ever given in America. It wasn't, but it was the first in a major big-city venue. Benny had to be urged into presenting a mixed group, but to do him credit he put his new-found success on the line by going along with the idea. And nobody really noticed. The half-feared fuss never materialised, and the event paved the way for other bands to do the same.

Teddy Wilson's appearances in the Goodman trio and quartet led to his becoming the most important model for young pianists of the Swing Era. His style was less powerful than other models like Earl Hines and Fats Waller, and nobody in their right senses was going to try and imitate Art Tatum. Wilson's light and sparkling style seemed easier, and hundreds of young pianists tried to play like him, among them the one who was to be the major pianist in be-bop, Bud Powell.

The Congress Hotel booking, originally scheduled for one month, extended to six, and during that time the band won the *Down Beat* magazine's poll as best "All-time Swing Band" (the term "swing" had come into existence somewhere in 1935). They began getting radio spots, and in March 1936 replaced the Casa Loma band on the popular and prestigious programme, *Camel Caravan*. And Willard Alexander got them signed to make a movie appearance in *The Big Broadcast Of 1937*.

Meanwhile, Benny as usual kept tinkering

with his personnel. Chris Griffin joined the trumpet section, and the great arranger Jimmy Mundy, who had been with the Earl Hines band, became a full-time staff arranger.

When the band got to Hollywood, Benny fired the fine trumpeter Dick Clark because he was losing his hair, and Benny wanted his band to look young. As he said to Art Rollini, "When we get to California I'm going to get rid of the bald-headed son of a bitch."

He also had words with another of his trumpeters, Nate Kazebier, during the shooting of the movie. Kazebier quit and had to be temporarily replaced by the businesslike Manny Klein, who had moved to Hollywood to work in the film studios.

While the band was in California it was booked back into the Palomar (at three times the fee they had got the year before), and while they were there Art Rollini came to Benny with news of a fine tenor-player he had just heard. He was playing at a club in Balboa Beach in a little band led by Gil Evans (later a celebrated jazz composer), with Stan Kenton on piano, and his name was Vido Musso.

Musso had been born in Sicily in 1913, and his family emigrated to Detroit in 1920. In the late Twenties he began playing clarinet, later switching to tenor. Before joining Gil Evans he had had spells with various leaders, and a spell fronting his own band, and his tenor-playing had developed a rich tone and a fiery attack. As well as his exciting playing he became famous in the big band world for his shaky grasp of the English language. Watching an undersea movie one time, he remarked, "Gosh, those octopuses put their technicals around you just like a boa constructor."

When Art Rollini told Benny about him, Benny said, bring him in. So one night Musso turned up for the last set at the Palomar. Benny asked him to sit in with the band and called for 'Honeysuckle Rose'. He gave him a long solo and Musso tore it apart. Benny was impressed. Riding home after the performance a few nights later with his brother Eugene he said, "What do you think of Vido Musso? I'm thinking of adding him to the band." Eugene, who wasn't a musician, did his best to answer. "Well, Benny," he said. "He can't read music. And if he can't read, what good will he be to the band?" This wasn't the answer Benny wanted. He put Eugene out of the car and made him walk the rest of the way home.

He hired Musso, and Musso struggled with the written parts. As he once explained, "It's not the notes I can't read. It's the rest-es." Rest-es or not, he was a fine addition to the band, and went on later to work for Bunny Berigan, Tommy Dorsey, Gene Krupa, Harry James, Woody Herman and Stan Kenton. In the Forties he three times won the *Down Beat* poll as best tenor sideman.

Meanwhile, Goodman still had two trumpeters to replace. Half a dozen came and went before, in September 1936, when the band was back east playing a short tour that included the Steel Pier in Atalantic City, Goodman's attention was drawn to a powerful trumpeter in the Steel Pier's resident band, Ziggy Elman.

Ziggy, whose real name was Harry Finkelman, had been born in Philadelphia in 1914 and raised in New Jersey. Self-taught, he was a versatile player who could not only lead a section but also play a hard-driving solo. Four months later, Benny found his second replacement, the most famous sideman he would ever have, next to Gene Krupa – Harry Haag James.

Harry's family were travelling circus folk. His father, Everett, was director and trumpet soloist of the band of the Mighty Haag Circus, and his mother was a trapeze artist. He was born in 1916 while the circus was on tour in Albany, Georgia, and by the age of eight was playing trumpet. By nine he was in the circus band, and by twelve was leading a small circus band of his own.

His family gave up travelling in 1931 and settled in Beaumont, Texas. While gigging around there he was heard by Ben Pollack, and by 1935 was in the Pollack band. There he was heard by Benny's brother Irving, who told Benny he ought to hire him, and in January 1937 Benny did. The great Goodman trumpet section was now in place – Harry James, Ziggy Elman and Chris Griffin.

There were a few other changes. In September 1936, Lionel Hampton had become a full-time member of the quartet, and in December 1936 Helen Ward left to get married. After a succession of other singers, Benny finally found one he was happy with – Martha Tilton, and the band he always would consider his best was ready for his next (and slightly unexpected) big moment – the opening at the Paramount Theatre in Times Square, New York, on March 3, 1937.

The Paramount was pioneering a new idea, to present big swing bands on-stage, not for dancing or as part of a show, but simply as themselves, often as part of a double-bill with a feature film. At this booking, made by Willard Alexander, the band was to share the bill with an otherwise unfamous movie, *Maid Of Salem*, starring Claudette Colbert.

Nobody was expecting anything special from the occasion. It was just another gig. But when the band turned up at 7 a.m. to rehearse they were amazed to find hundreds of customers, mostly students, lined up at that early hour waiting for the box office to open. Before dawn there had been six or seven hundred, dancing

and shouting and lighting fires, and by seven-thirty mounted police had to be called to keep control.

The band rehearsed and took a break, and as the first showing of the movie reached its end, they took their places on the Paramount's famous rising bandstand. At ten-thirty a.m. they went into the band's theme, 'Let's Dance', and as the bandstand rose slowly into sight, with Benny's liquid clarinet spiralling up out of the powerful wall of sound, the three thousand fans packing the auditorium went wild. Many began dancing in the aisles and crowding round the bandstand demanding autographs.

The manager and the ushers panicked, trying vainly to restore calm. It was useless. Each of the five shows that day was the same, and the same scenes were repeated for the whole engagement. By the end of the first day, twenty-one thousand fans had been admitted. Originally booked for two weeks, the band was held over for three. At later shows, fans wanting to jitterbug even clambered up onto the stage, where there was more room.

Not only was Goodman a star, the Swing Era had begun. For the first time since the jazz age, hot music was the most popular music in the world, and it was popular among a much wider audience than jazz had ever been. It dawned on musicians that now you could play good music and get paid for playing it.

According to John Hammond, at this point Benny was wandering around in a daze. Three years before he had been struggling to make three hundred dollars a week. Now he was pulling in a hundred thousand dollars a year. From sharing a small apartment with fellow-musicians he was now living in a three-room suite in the luxurious Hotel Pennsylvania.

Towards the end of 1937, with Goodman now

firmly enthroned as the King of Swing, the advertising agency that was promoting the *Camel Caravan* dreamed up a publicity stunt. The Goodman band would give a concert at Carnegie Hall, the highly respectable home of "serious" music. "Are you out of your mind?" said Benny. "What the hell would we do there?"

Somehow they talked him into co-operating, but he remained nervous, even suggesting at one point that the famous comedienne, Beatrice Lillie, be hired as M.C. He even approached the lady herself with the suggestion, but mercifully she had the good sense to turn it down. Even Miss Lillie would have had a hard time not being upstaged by the 1938 Goodman band in full cry.

It was decided that the concert would mostly consist of the band's regular repertory, the numbers on which its success was based, but the music critic Irving Kolodin, who would later collaborate with Benny on his early autobiography, "The Kingdom Of Swing", suggested that the programme also include a sort of capsule history of jazz till then. It would include numbers associated with, and played as far as possible in the style of, the Original Dixieland Jass Band, Bix Beiderbecke, Ted Lewis, Louis Armstrong, Duke Ellington and Benny Goodman.

The main problem with this was soon realised. Nobody could play Ellington numbers like the Ellington band could. So for the evening they hired Johnny Hodges, Harry Carney and Cootie Williams (Ellington himself was invited, but declined, not wishing to appear as a guest on somebody else's bandstand).

As nobody in the Goodman trumpet section could play anything like Bix, they also hired in cornettist Bobby Hackett (later famous for his solo on Glenn Miller's 'String of Pearls'.)

In addition, John Hammond, who was not otherwise involved, managed somehow to wangle a spot on the programme for some members of a band he had just discovered and was promoting – Count Basie. To accomodate these an ad lib jam session was added to the programme, adding to the others present Buck Clayton (trumpet), Lester Young (tenor), Freddie Green (guitar), Walter Page (bass), and Basie himself on piano.

When the big evening arrived (Sunday, January 16, 1938), the musicians were extremely nervous. As Harry James whispered just before the curtain went up, "I feel like a whore in church." He needn't have worried. The house was packed with enthusiastic fans, and when the curtain did go up and the band roared into Edgar Sampson's arrangement of a number he had written for Chick Webb, 'Don't Be That Way', it was immediately obvious that this was going to be a historic and enjoyable evening. Jazz was finally confirmed as an art, and as *Time* wrote in its review, "(Mr Goodman is) a far more serious artist than Mr Whiteman."

Inevitably, some of the spots in the two-hour concert were less good than others. The 'History of Jazz' fell a bit flat (although the quiet and romatic Ellington piece, 'Blue Reverie', was outstanding), and the jam session (using 'Honeysuckle Rose') had so many musicians in it that the ensembles were muddy and the string of solos seemed endless. Nonetheless, Lester Young's tenor solo was by some way the best performance of the evening.

The pieces that did work best were not the ones involving additional performers, but the numbers played by the band itself, interspersed with those by the Goodman trio and quartet. And the undoubted climax to the evening was the band's extended workout on the Louis Prima number 'Sing, Sing, Sing'.

This extended number, which had been recorded by the band six months earlier on two sides of a 78, had no real arrangement. The band had first played it on its second visit to the Palomar, in 1936, and since then it had gradually grown up in performance. It basically consisted of roaring choruses by the full band interspersed with solos backed by the rhythm section and with Gene Krupa pounding away on his tom-toms. The climactic solo was usually given to Harry James's trumpet, but on this evening, after James had finished, Goodman called unexpectedly on Jess Stacy to take a piano solo.

Quite why he did this has never been clear. Maybe he felt that the enormous excitement that had been generated needed cooling down, or maybe be was annoyed at Jess Stacy (he often was) and wanted to put him on the spot. Whatever the reason, it turned into an electrifying moment as Stacy embarked on a thoughtful, intricate and understated solo. The whole place erupted into applause, and when the band finally came roaring back in, it was clear that there was nothing left to say.

The publicity generated by the Carnegie Hall concert was enormous. Goodman's name was everywhere. Swing was the thing, and Goodman was on top of the heap, and well on the way to making his first million.

The curious thing is, he didn't entirely seem to enjoy it. He enjoyed the music all right, but the screaming mobs of fans, unlike anything ever seen before, he neither had expected nor welcomed. At a second concert a few months later, at Symphony Hall in Boston, he was so exasperated by all the screaming that he shouted at the audience, "For heaven's sake, shut up!" (or words to that effect).

This seems to be the reason for his otherwise inexplicable break with Gene Krupa. It seems that he was inclined to feel that Krupa's drumming was too exciting, and that Krupa was to blame for rousing the rabble. Words were spoken between them, even occasionally on-stage, and in March 1938, after a blow-up at the Earle Theatre in Philadelphia, Krupa quit. Lionel Hampton filled in on drums for three weeks (and nobody seemed to notice that for the first time there was a black musician playing in a white band) and then Benny succeeded in luring Dave Tough away from the band that Bunny Berigan had formed.

Tough was not as exciting a drummer as Krupa, but he was still a better drummer, and made the band itself sound looser and more exciting. His timekeeping was impeccable, he could play unbelievably fast, and his bass drum did not cover up the notes of the bass-player, as Krupa's often did (fortunately Harry Goodman's bass notes were no great loss).

Krupa's was the first defection from the great Carnegie Hall band, but there would be many others. Third trumpeter Chris Griffin, a good hot soloist, got tired of never getting a solo (they all went to Elman and James), and in 1939 he too left, to go and work as a studio musician for CBS radio.

The story of his leaving is one of the classic illustrations of Benny Goodman's strange remoteness. Chris, who Benny liked, had told the band's road manager, Leonard Vannerson, that he was quitting. Driving Benny home from a gig in Benny's car, Leonard finally plucked up courage to tell him this news while they were pulling up for a meal in a diner.

Benny didn't say anything, just walked to the diner, went in, and ordered scrambled eggs. When they arrived, he tipped up the ketchup bottle over them and the top fell off. Instead of lifting it off the eggs, he carefully ate all round it, leaving only the portion underneath. Their meal finished, still without a word from Benny, they got back into the car and drove on.

Some time later, at about five in the morning, a farmer's horse-drawn milk-wagon unexpectedly pulled out of a side road in front of them. Leonard jammed on the brakes, but the car hit the wagon with a tremendous crash. There were broken milk-bottles all over the place. Both the horse and the farmer were screaming. At which point Benny said, "Now what would Chris want to do a thing like that for?"

The defections continued. Harry James left to form a band of his own. Babe Russin, who had replaced Vido Musso on tenor, was in his turn replaced by Bud Freeman. Allan Reuss was doubly upset at being replaced as guitarist for a Goodman sextet session by Basie's Freddie Green and by not being told that he had been, and he too quit.

Unlike, say, Ellington or Fletcher Henderson, who hired musicians who were promising and brought out their full abilities, it was always Benny's habit to try and hire replacements who were already completely formed. And if he didn't like the way they played at once, to replace them and try someone else. This meant that his personnel was continually shifting, and the band after 1938 never properly settled into a unit.

More and more his best work was done with his small groups, and especially, from 1939, with his sextet. The growth of the quartet into a sextet was again due to the inspired interference of John Hammond.

Hammond, in his tireless search for talent, had heard from Mary Lou Williams of an amazing young guitarist playing in Oklahoma City. His name was Charlie Christian and an unusual thing about him was that he played electric guitar, a

rare instrument in 1939.

Charlie had been born in 1916 in Texas, and all his family were musical. His mother and father provided the music for the silent movies at the local cinema, she on piano, he on trumpet.

When Charlie was about two, they moved to Oklahoma City, to live in a wooden tenement. Although they were poor, his family was always "respectable", and although his father went blind soon after the move, he still continued to earn a meagre living by playing the guitar or mandolin, and singing.

Charlie's elder brothers, Edward and Clarence, were also musicians, and while he was still at elementary school Charlie was building cigar-box "guitars" for himself and playing them.

At his senior school, music was a major part of the curriculum, even including a four-year course in harmony, and by his early teens Charlie (who now had a real guitar) and his father and brothers would make up a strolling quartet to entertain in the better-off streets of the city. The music they played was of all sorts, even including light classics.

Sometime in the early Thirties Lester Young came touring through the city. Charlie was much influenced by his playing, and taught himself to play Lester's recorded solos on his guitar.

In the mid-thirties he became a profesional musician, and was already good enough to be invited by Alphonso Trent to join his prestigious band as a bass-player. He did spells in other bands, then returned to Trent as a guitarist.

In 1937 the Count Basie band visited Oklahoma City, and Basie's great arranger and trombonist, Eddie Durham, who was also a guitarist, introduced Charlie to the instrument he would make famous, the electric guitar. Not the solid-bodied instrument that is now common, but a conventional acoustic guitar with electrical amplification. For the first time the guitar had enough volume to function in a big band as a solo voice.

Soon Charlie had developed his own unique style of playing – long flowing single-string lines ending in unexpected places, a crisp bell-like tone, light rhythm, and endless invention.

By 1939 he had left Trent and was playing in the Ritz Cafe in Oklahoma City in a small band led by one of his brothers. When John Hammond got there and heard him, he was captivated. He immediately arranged to fly Charlie to Los Angeles, where the Goodman band was about to open at a restaurant called Victor Hugo's. Charlie wasn't that keen either to join Benny Goodman or to leave Kansas City, and neither were his family, knowing that he was already suffering from TB, but Hammond was as usual unstoppable.

However, when he descended on Benny Goodman with his new discovery, Goodman was not impressed. For a start, Charlie Christian was dressed like an Okie, with a big broad-brimmed hat, pointed yellow shoes, a green suit and a purple shirt with a garish tie.

Hammond had just succeeded in luring Goodman away from recording for Victor to recording for Columbia, and they met at the Columbia recording studios, where Goodman was about to record his first session for them. He looked at the apparition before him, and reluctantly agreed to a short audition, refusing, however, to let Charlie use his amplifier.

After about two minutes of playing 'Tea For Two' on his clarinet with Charlie's acoustic accompaniment, he curtly stopped the audition and walked out of the studio, saying this was another of John Hammond's "pointless enthusiasms". But Hammond was not giving up. That evening at the Victor Hugo there was to be

an hour's performance by the Goodman quartet between two performances by the band. After the band finished their first set, Benny went table-hopping for a few minutes and Hammond, with the help of Benny's then bassist, Artie Bernstein, sneaked Charlie in through the kitchen with his amplifier and got him and it rigged up on the stand.

When Benny came back and saw Charlie sitting there he was livid. He had no option but to include him in the performance, and out of vindictiveness chose the rather complicated number, 'Rose Room', expecting that Charlie would be unfamiliar with it. He wasn't. After three choruses by the others he called on Charlie to take a chorus, and it was Benny's turn to be electrified. Charlie went on to take twenty choruses, to rapturous applause, and the number went on for forty-three minutes.

Benny invited Charlie to play with the band when it came back for its second set, and soon the sextet was formed, with Charlie as composer in residence, writing such numbers as 'Seven Come Eleven', 'AC-DC Current', 'Air Mail Special' and 'Flying Home'.

The personnel of the sextet changed from time to time, but its other major acquisition came in 1940 when Benny decided that what his sextet needed was Cootie Williams. To even think it possible that he could entice Cootie away from the Ellington band was chutzpah of a high order, but as it turned out Benny was right to try.

He got his brother Irving to sound Cootie out, and although it took Cootie some soul-searching, he eventually agreed. There were two reasons – one was that the money Goodman could offer, being the most popular white bandleader of the day, was far beyond anything Duke could come up with; the other was that he was getting rather fed up with Sonny Greer, both with his indiscipline (he was so senior in the band that even an on-stage glare from Cootie had no effect) and with the looseness of his beat. Cootie felt it would be nice for a while to play in a driving band like Goodman's.

What Ellington felt is not recorded. It was beneath his dignity to beg favours from his employees, even to ask Cootie Williams to stay in his band, and with ducal panache he even conducted the negotiations for Cootie's Goodman contract himself.

From Goodman's point of view it was worth it. The sextet recordings with Cootie (and Charlie Christian) are among the best recordings he ever made.

The Goodman band continued into the war years, increasingly in competition with the hundreds of other bands that had sprung up in the wake of its success, several of them led by its own ex-members, but very much holding its own.

By the late Thirties a whole youth-culture had sprung up around the music, with a uniform of its own — almost all the girls wore saddle shoes, short white "bobby sox", a blouse or sweater, and a fairly short pleated skirt that swirled out on the dance-floor; the boys tended to be more conventional – only the heppest wore the zoot suit, with its pegged trousers (wide-kneed and narrow-cuffed) and its long single-breasted jacket with narrow waist and wide shoulders.

Fans followed the fortunes of bands and of the star musicians in them with knowledgeable keenness. They grew to recognise the sounds of individual soloists on records (in a day when a player of any worth not only prided himself on developing his own individual sound, but would have been looked down on by other musicians if he sounded like anyone else), and followed their progress from band to band. If, say, Bunny

Berigan moved from Goodman to Tommy Dorsey, or Vido Musso from Harry James to Herman, the news would pass along the grapevine and be eagerly discussed.

All over America, fans gathered round their radios to hear the weekly broadcasts of their favourite bands, and on Saturdays to listen to *Your Hit Parade* to learn what were the top ten hit tunes of the week (in those days the top ten was still based on sales of sheet music for tunes, not on record sales).

And the record industry took on a new lease of life, mainly due to the invention of the juke box. In every town, large and small, young fans would gather in ice cream parlours and soda fountains, feed nickels into the juke box and hear the latest releases. Sales of records to juke-boxes became enormous, and were increased further by fans buying records they heard on them for themselves.

From around 1934, when record sales had started showing signs of recovery, phonograph companies like Victor and Columbia built on the technology of radio to market record-players that were electrically driven and amplified. Some were designed to plug into radios, the more sophisticated were part of integral units called radiograms.

Eventually there were auto-change players, that would play through a stack of eight or ten 78's (playing the top side of each), and even some very elaborate models, based on the technology of the juke-box, that would turn each disc over. These, however, were very expensive and slightly unreliable, and aquired the unkind nickname "platter-busters".

The Swing Era probably generated more slang than any other musical era before or since. A musician who played for business, not enjoyment, was a clock puncher. Hot musicians were clambakers, killer-dillers or solid senders. A fluent improviser was a ride man, famous for kicking out. Square musicians were longhairs, mouldy figs or wheat benders, and a square band would be a long underwear gang. A female band-singer was usually a canary, and one with a pronounced tremolo was nervous.

As for the fans themselves, they were jitterbugs, alligators, hepcats, rug-cutters, scobo queens and zeal girls.

A square, of course, was a stale adventurer, a gesture taker, a discharge. In fact an undecided bringdown. But if you were on the beam and in the groove, and could shag and truck and suzy-Q to the noodling of the agony-pipes, it was a golden time to be alive.

CHAPTER 10

the dorsey brothers

James and Thomas Dorsey (Tommy) were born in 1904 and 1905 respectively in the heart of the coal-mining district of Pennsylvania. The town they were born in was Shenandoah, forty-five miles south of Scranton, but soon after Tommy was born the family moved twelve miles east to Lansford. There their younger sister, Mary, was born and there they grew up.

Their family was close-knit and Irish, and their father, Thomas F. Dorsey, who worked for the mines, also became the bandmaster of the town band, which was recalled by a local journalist as "a damn good marching and concert outfit".

He was also an enthusiastic music teacher, and insisted that all his three children learn to play instruments. There was a family story that their mother used to hide the boys' shoes so that they would stay in the house and practice, but they needed little encouragement, both being enthusiastic musicians from their earliest years.

Eventually both boys would learn to play almost every instrument in the band, Jimmy started on slide-trumpet and cornet at the age of seven, and Tommy started on trumpet shortly afterwards. Although Jimmy became famous as a clarinetist and alto-saxophonist, and Tommy as a trombonist, both continued to play cornet or trumpet all their lives, usually for relaxation.

A feature of their childhood practice sessions was the family quartet, with father on baritone sax and cornet, Jimmy on cornet and alto, Tommy on tenor sax and euphonium, and Mary on the tenor horn (a brass band instrument whose bell points upwards). A curious sidelight on Jimmy's playing, once he had taken up alto at the age of eleven, was that he played sax on one side of his mouth and cornet on the other, so as to develop two separate embouchures.

By 1919 in the era of the dance craze, small dance-pavilions were cropping up all over America, and anybody who could play an instrument ended up playing in a string of small combos. Jimmy, aged fifteen, and Tommy, aged fourteen, could be found at that time playing in a local six-piece group called the Syncopators. Jimmy at that time already had considerable facility on both cornet and alto. At the age of twelve he had confidently performed the famous cornet piece 'Carnival In Venice' in front of a large crowd in the town pavilion. Tommy, on trombone, took a little longer to develop, but only a little.

Whether they had already formed the idea of becoming professional musicians is not clear. Certainly Jimmy had left school at fourteen and did a spell down the mines. This we know because in 1937, when his band had become famous and was playing at a dance in Pottstown,

Pennsylvania, a huge burly customer came determinedly off the dance floor during an intermission and headed towards the bandstand.

Jimmy, seeing him approach, fled backstage. The man demanded to see Jimmy, and singer Bob Eberly, going backstage to fetch him, found out the situation. In 1919 Jimmy had accidentally hit the man over the head with a sledgehammer while working underground. It eventually turned out the man wanted to thank him. "Back home," he said, "I've been famous for years as the guy who was hit on the head with a sledgehammer by Jimmy Dorsey."

However long Jimmy (or both brothers) worked in the mines, it couldn't have been long, because in 1921, after playing in a number of regional outfits with names like the Scranton Serenaders and occasionally leading their own small bands like Dorsey's Novelty Six and Dorsey's Wild Canaries, they joined a professional band called the Scranton Sirens, which had been organised two years before by violinist/leader Billy Lustig.

It was a good band, several of whose members would go on to join Jean Goldkette. An early admirer of it was a young Scranton trumpet-player called Bob Stephens, who would later become the first A & R man (responsible for artistes and repertoire at recording sessions) of American Decca when that company was formed in 1934. For Decca he would record the Dorsey Brothers band and, later, the Jimmy Dorsey band. One thing that he remembered about the Scranton Sirens was that, even as early as 1921, their drummer, Joe Settler, was moving towards the swing era feeling of playing four beats in a bar instead of the jazz-age two.

The big dance-hall in Scranton was called the Armory. Scranton was a prosperous town and could support a dance there every night of the week. Among the famous bands that visited it were the Original Dixieland Jass Band and Paul Whiteman. When the Sirens played there they acquired another young fan, still at school in Wilkes-Barre but already a saxophonist and would-be arranger – Bill Challis.

Bill, while still at school, was playing in a little band led by a local pianist called Freddy Smalls. Smalls arranged for him to sit in with the Sirens, and they were sufficiently impressed to invite the schoolboy to play with them at weekends.

Then the Sirens got more ambitious and began to venture out of their home neighbourhood. Reaching New York, they played for a dance at the St Nicholas Rink. This was across from what is now the Lincoln Center, and was one of those venues that mounted all kinds of events, such as boxing-matches, roller-skating derbies, and jazz.

At the St Nicholas Rink the band was heard by Ed Kirkeby, who was then hunting for good new musicians for the California Ramblers. In the summer of 1924 Jimmy moved to New York and joined the Ramblers, followed shortly afterwards by younger brother Tommy.

This would be a pattern that they would frequently repeat during the next ten years, as they freelanced around from band to band – Jimmy joining a band, and Tommy following later – it would happen with the Ramblers, with Goldkette, and with Whiteman.

Being raised together in a closely-knit family, and growing up together as fellow-musicians, Jimmy and Tommy developed strong emotional ties to each other. Jimmy always called Tommy "Mac", Tommy always called Jimmy "Lad", but to others they always referred to each other as "the brother".

They had temperaments that were very similar, and very different. Both were emotional, but Jimmy was more level-headed, Tommy more impulsive and aggressive. Both were quick tempered, in spite of each having a strong sense of humour, but while Jimmy would become cold and insinuating, Tommy would rage and storm. Both were generous and warm-hearted, but where Tommy was outgoing, Jimmy was reticent. Their tastes in music were almost identical, but whereas Tommy took naturally to leading a band and became an astute businessman, Jimmy, much as he loved his band, became a leader with reluctance.

In spite of their closeness they fought continually. In 1925, when they were both in the Jean Goldkette band, one of manager Charlie Horvath's unofficial chores was to try and keep the peace between them – a difficult task, because both would turn and rend an outsider that interfered between them. Jimmy McPartland once tried and was set on by both of them.

On one occasion when the Goldkette band were on tour in Hazelton, Pennsylvania, Jimmy and Tommy got into a ferocious argument in their room at the Hazel Hotel. Jimmy had a new gold-plated saxophone there and Tommy threw it on the floor and jumped on it. After that the fight really started.

It wasn't only with Jimmy that Tommy fought. When Charlie Horvath left the Goldkette organisation he was replaced as manager by Cork O'Keefe (who would later manage the Casa Loma band through his New York agency Rockwell-O'Keefe). One day O'Keefe got an angry phone-call from the manager of the Book-Cadillac Hotel in Detroit, where one of the Goldkette bands was playing, demanding that Tommy Dorsey be fired immediately.

Apparently the band had been being pestered all evening to play requests, especially by one gentleman who asked repeatedly for the 'Missouri Waltz'. Eventually Tommy had spoken up from the body of the band telling the gentleman "No" and enlarging on what he could do with his request. Unfortunately the gentleman belonged to the rich and powerful Fisher family, a power in the world of General Motors, and thus not a person to be offended in Detroit. Tommy was moved to another Goldkette assignment.

The emotional tie between the brothers, even expressed as aggressively as it was, was so close that in 1926, when Tommy married his wife Mildred, Jimmy broke down and cried, lamenting the loss of his roommate.

But the closeness remained. In 1927, after the Goldkette band had broken up and the brothers were both with Paul Whiteman, Bill Challis, who was rooming with Jimmy, forgot to wake him before leaving for a theatre performance. Jimmy didn't arrive until after the first show was over, and was promptly fined fifty dollars by Whiteman. Tommy, without pausing to speak to Jimmy, marched angrily up to Challis and demanded, "How come you didn't wake up the brother?"

Jimmy was equally protective of Tommy. Both tended to be heavy drinkers (at least in their early years), although they seemed to take it in turns to go on a bender. On one occasion Tommy was brought back drunk to an apartment they were sharing in New York. Jimmy, opening the door, rounded on the two musician friends who had brought him home, blaming them for having been so inconsiderate as to have got "the brother" drunk.

In 1928, Jimmy also got married, to Jane Porter, who had been Miss Detroit of 1927. Neither of the brothers' marriages lasted, partly no doubt due to the pressures of big-band life, but also partly because their greatest emotional commitment was always to each other.

When Jimmy married, Tommy had already left the Whiteman band and headed for New York. Jimmy followed him. Both had decided that they weren't getting enough exposure with Whiteman, and they wanted more of all that recording work that was going on in the big city.

In 1928, the informal headquarters for freelance jazz musicians was a speakeasy on West 53rd Street, under the elevated railroad. Originally known as Plunkett's, it eventually got listed in the phone book as the Trombone Club. Eddie Condon claimed it was renamed in honour of Tommy, and certainly it was apt – one day somebody happened to glance along the bar and every customer seated there was holding a trombone case.

If anyone assembling a band wanted a particular musician, the place to phone was Plunkett's. If he wasn't there, somebody would know where he was. This was becoming increasingly important with the growth of radio, which meant that capable musicians were in increasing demand. The phone at Plunkett's never stopped ringing, and the call board next to the phone was always plastered with messages.

As well as radio, there were pit bands needed for shows (a show Jimmy particularly enjoyed working for was the 1930 production *Rain Or Shine*, starring comedy headliner Joe Cook – juggler, acrobat, sharpshooter, wire-walker, multi-instrumentalist, dancer and deadpan monologuist). And the college circuit offered a continual flow of work for small jazz groups.

Both brothers enjoyed playing jazz, even though they were not so steeped in it as the New York or Chicago-based musicians among their contemporaries. Possibly this was what prevented either of them from ever becoming first-rate jazz soloists.

When he was first working in New York with the California Ramblers Tommy had been impressed and influenced by the trombone-playing of Miff Mole. Mole, born in New York State in 1898, was arguably the first trombonist to develop the trombone as a solo voice in jazz, playing short precise notes and using considerable leaps in pitch. He had a pure tone, and good ideas, but was a little short on dramatic interest.

Shortly after joining Jean Goldkette in 1925, Tommy had gone to the Gennett Studios in Richmond, Indiana, and recorded in a sextet assembled by his fellow band-member Bix Beiderbecke (the band got so drunk that of the four numbers they tried to record, only two were ever released). He learnt from listening to Bix, and he also began listening to as much Louis Armstrong as he could lay his hands on. When he was with the Whiteman band in 1927, he would entertain the band between shows by playing Louis' choruses on a little C cornet he carried round with him. Bill Challis said years later, "He seemed to know everything Louis ever did, as well as – on trombone – everything Miff ever did."

Unfortunately for any ambitions Tommy may have begun to entertain of becoming a great jazz trombonist, in 1928 Jack Teagarden arrived in New York. Tommy heard him, and had the good sense to realise that Jack was in another league. From then on he concentrated on developing his pure and beautiful tone and immaculate phrasing, leaving inventive improvisation to others.

His respect for Teagarden, whom he nicknamed "the master", lasted for the rest of his life. In January 1939 *Metronome* magazine arranged a recording session for the winners of the first of its annual polls (the Swing Era was great on magazine polls for the best musicians, bands and recordings of the year – *Esquire* ran a poll each year that led to concerts and poll-winner's recordings; *Down Beat* ran two polls, one among its readers, one among the critics).

In this first *Metronome* poll, Jack and Tommy were the two trombone winners. They duly turned up to record the two sides planned. The first was Edgar Sampson's tune 'Blue Lou', and when it came to the second, a straightforward blues, it was suggested that Tommy take a solo. For one of the few times in his life he became uncertain and flustered. "Nothing doing," he muttered. "Not when Jack's in the same room."

It was pointed out to him that it would look silly if he was the only poll-winner not to take a solo, and eventually he was talked into playing one chorus.

He played it straight, and absolutely beautifully, while Jack improvised arabesques around him.

Jimmy's main influence in his formative years had been a popular virtuoso alto-saxophonist called Rudy Wiedoeft, who produced a torrent of records in the period just after the Great War, all played with enormous facility and a complete absence of swing. Echoes of this style would crop up in Jimmy's playing all his life, especially on flashy numbers like 'Oodles Of Noodles' or 'Dusk In Upper Sandusky'.

Fortunately he later also came under the influence of Johnny Hodges (who, oddly enough, in turn expressed an admiration for Jimmy's undoubted technique), and learned to play what was at least recognisable as a pale imitation of the Hodges sound.

In fact, imitation was in a way Jimmy's strongest point. In his clarinet-playing can be heard echoes of (among others) Benny Goodman and Artie Shaw, Johnny Dodds and Barney Bigard. This enabled him to play convincingly in a wide variety of styles.

Between 1928 and 1933 the brothers, being among the most technically proficient players around, had spent a lot of time working as radio studio musicians. But during the same period they had frequently got bands together themselves and made recordings under the title of "The Dorsey Brothers Orchestra".

By the beginning of 1934 they had issued over sixty sides, which had sold increasingly well, and they decided it was time to trade on their growing reputation and form a full-time band. Cork O'Keefe's agency, Rockwell-O'Keefe, agreed to represent them.

Both brothers were musical perfectionists, and long hours of rehearsal were put in at the Rockwell-O'Keefe offices. Tommy in particular was very demanding and, like Benny Goodman, a considerable martinet. Only, where Goodman would show his displeasure with a baleful unnerving glare (known to both musicians and fans as the Goodman ray), Tommy would fly off the handle.

After a couple of weeks of rehearsal, when the band was in reasonable shape, it began touring outside New York while it continued to settle in.

News of its formation had reached the ears of Glenn Miller, who was at that time touring the west in a band led by Texan singer Smith Ballew. Ballew had suffered a succession of cancelled dates, and was thinking of giving up his band, and Miller called Tommy and said that not only would he soon be available, he could also recommend several other members of the Ballew band.

The result of this call was that in April Miller joined the Dorsey Brothers' band as trombonist and arranger, and it would be Miller who did most to set the band's style. Ballew's female vocalist, a fine ballad-singer called Kay Weber, joined at around the same time he did. Drummer Ray McKinley came in to replace Stan King (as usual) in July, and in August was followed by tenor saxophonist Skeets Herfurt, trombonist Don Mattison and guitarist Roc Hillman.

With so many ex-members of the Ballew band now with the Dorsey Brothers, it is hardly surprising (though a bit puzzling) that a side they had recorded back in May ('On Accounta I Love You') was released as by "Smith Ballew & his Orchestra" (Ballew was not present).

In July the band, still in the process of coming together, had begun a summer residency at the Sands Point Bath Club on Long Island, and in August it began recording for the newly-formed Decca Record Company, where they were pleasantly surprised to find that their recording director would be their old fan Bob Stephens from the Scranton Sirens days.

With Miller, Mattison and Tommy, the band had three trombones, but oddly enough, only one trumpet, George Thow. The rest of the line-up was orthodox – three reeds, piano, guitar, bass and drums. Glenn Miller became its main arranger, and as both he and Tommy were trombonists, they may simply have enjoyed voicing with trombones.

The band was designed purely as a hot dance band, and its aim, according to Tommy, was to develop a style somewhere between the sweet band of Hal Kemp and the more swinging sound of the Casa Loma.

As well as Kay Weber it had a male singer in the person of Bing Crosby's younger brother, Bob, and these two handled the vocal work on straightforward dance-band versions of the popular songs of the day.

Bob had been allotted to the band by the Rockell-O'Keefe office, who were also handling him and Bing. He was sent to replace a tenor that had briefly sung with them. Everybody agreed that the tenor wasn't very good with the band, but Tommy resented being told by the office who the band's male singer was going to be, and tended to take out his resentment on the rather nervous twenty-one-year-old Bob.

As well as popular songs, the band played dixieland-style versions of jazz standards like 'St Louis Blues', 'Milneburg Joys', 'Dippermouth Blues' and 'Basin Street Blues' (Glenn Miller and Jack Teagarden had written the words for that back in 1931, for a band assembled by Benny Goodman to record under the name of "The Charleston Chasers").

There were also in the band's repertoire a few original compositions that, although still slightly dixielandish, were beginning to sound a bit smoother, like portents of the Swing Era to come. Among these were such numbers as 'Stop, Look and Listen' and 'By Heck'.

When they formed the band, the problem naturally arose as to which brother should act as leader. Should they perhaps take turns? It was quickly obvious that the natural choice was Tommy. He was outgoing where Jimmy was rather retiring, and he was more diplomatic with the customers. Jimmy was inclined to be curt and dismissive with people who wanted the band to play 'Happy Birthday', but on the other hand he was the better musician. So it was arranged that Tommy should stand out in front, acting as leader, and that Jimmy should be the star soloist.

This would have worked except that Jimmy soon began to resent Tommy standing out front and getting all the glory. Tommy, who was immensely capable and energetic, was not only fronting the band but also compiling the radio programmes and doing all the other things a leader does. Jimmy began drinking heavily, and this made Tommy mad because he was carrying too much responsibility to do the same.

Jimmy began to needle Tommy by sitting in the sax section saying things like, "Smile, Mac. You're the big star," and Tommy, the determined and demanding band-leader, began to feel like an outsider.

Once, a few months after the Sands Point booking finished, he was driving to a gig in his car. Passing the band bus, he signalled it to stop, then climbed on board, obviously very upset, and blurted out, "Why don't you guys like me?"

After an embarrassed silence, drummer Ray McKinley spoke up. He said, "Tommy, you always say this is a band of hand-picked musicians. Then why don't you treat us with respect? That's all we want."

Sands Point had been a good venue for the band's first residency. One reason was that it had a radio link, and by 1934 air-time was essential to any real success for a band. Unfortunately, on the night they were to have their very first network broadcast, there was a fierce thunderstorm and all the lights went out.

Before the broadcast part of the evening, the band tried playing the arrangements from memory, then switched to jamming on old favourites. Tommy decided that the only solution was candles, and set all hands to grabbing them from waiters who were trying to distribute them among the customers. Using the candles, the broadcast began and, possibly because all the excitement had released a lot of adrenalin, the band played exceptionally well.

The brothers seemed to be on their way, and that summer Tommy and his wife Mildred bought a large house on a 22-acre estate at Bernardsville, New Jersey, which he would live in and develop for the rest of his life, even installing a huge model-railway layout for himself on the top floor, fifty feet of track representing the route from New York to Los Angeles, complete with working signals and switching, and accurate topography. In that house they would raise their two children, daughter Patsy and son, Tommy Jr., and hold open house for friends and band-members.

After the summer job at Sands Point finished, Glenn Miller left to assist British bandleader Ray Noble, who had recently moved to the States to work. He was replaced as trombonist by Joe Yukl, and the band embarked on a string of one-nighters that would carry them through until they took up the summer job they had landed for the next year, at the famous Glen Island Casino in New Rochelle on Long Island Sound.

At one of these one-nighters, in the spring of 1935, the band was playing for a police ball in the Armory in Troy, New York. There they were introduced to a local boy, from nearby Hoosick Falls, who was a singer and had recently won comedian Fred Allen's Amateur Contest on the radio. His name was Bob Eberle, and it was his good fortune that Bob Crosby had just decided he would take up an offer to leave the Dorseys and front a band made up of the remnants of the Ben Pollack band. Tommy asked Bob Eberle to join the band as their male singer, and he did, changing the spelling of his surname to "Eberly".

Bob Eberly was good-looking, with a fine rich voice, and is regarded by many as the best of all the band singers of the Swing Era, who could have gone much further if he'd wanted to. But he was loyal to Jimmy (who became his close friend) and not especially ambitious.

The Glen Island booking was a coup, because for the previous two summers the Casino had featured the Casa Loma band, and thus had built up an enthusiastic clientele. The band's opening night there was a grand affair, with fans and friends swarming in from all directions. Jack Teagarden was there, and actor John Barrymore. Lena Horne and Connee Boswell were there, and most of the New York Yankees, including baseball's all-time star, Lou Gehrig.

The band looked set for a fine summer, but the resentments between Jimmy and Tommy kept building up. They had only been at the Casino for two weeks when Tommy, on the night of May 30, called for the band to play 'I'll Never Say "Never Again" Again', and counted off the tempo. "Mac, that's a little fast, isn't it?" said Jimmy. Instantly, without a word, Tommy turned and walked off into the night. And that was it. The Dorsey brothers had split.

Jimmy later explained that in that number he and fellow-saxophonist Jack Stacey had to switch to cornets to join trumpeter George Thow in a three-cornet chorus, and he felt the tempo was too fast for them to handle comfortably. Tommy said that nobody had any idea what it was like trying to lead a band with that fellow sitting there all the time criticising you with his eyes.

As soon as Tommy left, the Casino's manager, Ed Dorn, phoned the band's agent, Cork O'Keefe, who was having dinner at the nearby Wykagyl Country Club. Cork hurried to the Casino and sought out Jimmy, who was calmly smoking a cigarette and staring off into the distance as if nothing had happened. "Where's Tommy?" demanded Cork. "He's gone," said Jimmy.

After Cork had heard what happened, it was agreed that Jimmy would take over leading the band while Cork hunted down Tommy. He was especially anxious to find him as he was trying to pull together an important deal for the band.

Radio schedules were being fixed for the year ahead, and the Kraft company wanted to sponsor Bing Crosby for a series to be called *Kraft Music Hall*, to begin the following January. Bing's affairs were also handled by Rockwell-O'Keefe, and along with Bing they wanted to sell Kraft the Dorsey Brothers band. But before they could sell it to Kraft, they had to sell it to Bing, and he hadn't heard it yet. Nor would he come to the Glen Island Casino to hear it, because he didn't like crowds in the first place, and in the second place crowds would mean he would have to wear his despised toupee.

Unable to find Tommy, Cork suggested to Bing that the band, under Jimmy, do a recording session, which Bing could attend and hear the band. Bing agreed, but said he'd prefer to hear it with both brothers.

Fortunately Cork managed to track down Tommy, who told him he had no intention of coming back to the band, and was planning to form a band of his own. Cork asked him if he'd at least show up for the recording. "I'll do it for you," said Tommy, "but not for that shithead."

Bing came to the recording, which turned out to be pretty much of a shambles, with nobody really sure what tunes they were proposing to play. So nothing got recorded, but Bing heard enough of the band to decide he liked it, and would accept a band led by either brother, or both.

Cork made a last-ditch attempt to bring the brothers back together, and they agreed to meet at his office, Tommy making it quite clear that as far as he was concerned the whole meeting was pointless. At the meeting, Cork asked him point blank if he wouldn't reconsider. Tommy rose from his chair, walked slowly to the door, turned and said, "I wouldn't go back with that asshole if I had to drop dead." Then to Cork he added, "And you – what I won't do to you!" Then he left.

Jimmy turned to Cork with tears in his eyes. "What'll I do?" he said. "From now on," said Cork, "you're the boss." So Jimmy reluctantly became a solo leader.

His most pressing problem, while they played out the summer at Glen Island Casino, was to find a trombonist to replace Tommy. Finding one who could play his book wasn't easy. For a while there was a parade of trombonists through the band, mostly old friends from the radio studios helping out, among them two future bandleaders, Jack Jenney and Will Bradley, and a future comedian, Jerry Colonna.

Then Jimmy remembered an occasion the previous winter when the band was playing an engagement at the Fox Theatre in Detroit. They had been invited to visit the Cass Technical High School, and Tommy had sat in with the school band, led by a sixteen-year-old trombonist called Bobby Byrne.

In return, Bobby had been invited to the theatre to see the show (arriving to find Tommy and Jimmy having a furious row backstage), and had later sat in with the band for a dance at a nearby Air Corps base. He had been good, and Jimmy now sent him a wire inviting him to try out with the band.

He arrived, still aged only sixteen, bringing his instruments – three trombones, a flute and a concert harp. He had no problem reading Tommy's parts, his tone was beautiful, and he was the answer to the problem. He seemed to be able to play in any style, sweet or hot, and with Bobby Byrne's firm lead, Jimmy's became the best trombone section in the business.

Jimmy won the contract to provide a band for the Kraft radio programme. This would mean moving to Hollywood, where Bing was, and in theory he could have taken a few hand-picked musicians there and made up a band with local musicians. But, being Jimmy, he decided to take everybody, even singers Kay Weber and Bob Eberly, neither of whom would be needed for the radio show. This sort of loyalty on Jimmy's part gave the band an immense esprit de corps, and many of its members remained with it for years.

They all made the cross-country pilgrimage in a collection of cars, stopping en route to play a few weeks in Houston (young Bobby Byrne had spent all his money on a new car and arrived in Houston flat broke and a day and a half ahead of everybody else – it was a very hungry day and a half).

In December, Bing and the band broadcast a few trailer spots for the Kraft Music hall, and in January 1936 the series started. In the same month the band played an engagement at the Palomar ballroom in Los Angeles, where Benny Goodman had had his first big success the year before.

The Jimmy Dorsey band would remain in Hollywood working with Bing on the radio for the next eighteen months, and being on the air every Thursday night, the nation would be kept well aware of its existence. Similar radio shows used studio bands, but Jimmy was a versatile swing band that could play a wide range of material, from pop ballads and novelty songs to dance numbers with occasional hot solos.

At first the musicians in the band had an easy life, because the Los Angeles musicians' union imposed a period of restriction on outside bands that prevented them for the time being from working anywhere but on radio. This gave them essentially a two-day week. Jimmy and his wife Jane rented a house in Burbank, and Jimmy joined the Lakeside Golf Club, where he did a lot of golfing and social drinking.

He also found time to develop the band. He hired Tutti "Toots" Camarata as second trumpet and arranger, and with him worked at developing a distinctive band sound. He also started playing more alto and less clarinet, a suggestion that had originally come from Tommy on the grounds that Goodman had got there first on clarinet, but nobody was featuring alto.

The band also worked on a couple of films. They appeared in a comedy musical called *That Girl From Paris*, starring soprano Lily Pons, and provided the soundtrack music for the Astaire-Rogers musical, *Shall We Dance?* For this, it being Hollywood, the band was augmented to fifty pieces, mostly strings.

Fud Livingtone, who by this time had joined as fourth saxophone, did the arrangements and conducted. At one rehearsal a soft-spoken gentleman politely suggested to him that one of the numbers could be a little slower. Fud, equally politely, explained that that was the way he felt it. "I understand, and I think the arrangements are wonderful, but I wrote the music," said George Gershwin.

A similar thing happened on the same film to Bob Eberly, who was on the set only as a visitor. A man came up and said he admired his singing and asked if he would sing a chorus if he played the piano. The amiable Bob agreed, and they did a chorus of 'They Can't Take That Away From Me'. Bob complimented the man, a little condescendlingly, on his playing and walked away to join Jimmy. "How'd you like George?" said Jimmy. Bob nearly fell through the floor. However unrecognisable Gershwin may have been in person, his name was capable of stunning musicians.

Decca had kept up its contract with the band when Jimmy took it over, and from time to time they went into the studios to produce a batch of records. Two outstanding sessions took place in August 1936, the first when they backed Louis Armstrong on four numbers, the second when they backed Louis and Bing and singer Frances Langford on a medley of numbers from *Pennies From Heaven*, the film that had brought Louis to Hollywood.

The union's mandatory waiting period came to an end, and the easy days were over. From then on life became whirl of one-nighters up and down the west coast, from Washington State down to San Diego, spending nights on the band bus and somehow grabbing enough sleep to get along on roads that were long, bumpy and deserted. Sometimes they could hardly find the small towns they were to play in, and while they were playing in one place the town fire siren went off, and everybody left the dance-hall to go and see the fire. The band stopped playing till they came back.

Meanwhile, on the other side of America, Tommy was setting out to show the world that he could have a better band than the one he had left to his brother. It helped that he didn't have to start from scratch. At about the time of the split-up, a pianist and arranger he knew called Joe Haymes was leading a band at the McAlpin Hotel in New York, playing polite "hotel swing".

Joe, a former trapeze artiste and self-taught pianist, wasn't having a great deal of success with his band, and apparently it didn't take much persuasion from Tommy for Tommy to take most of it over. (Joe Haymes seemed to make a habit of doing this. Only one year before he had turned over another of his bands to the leadership of Buddy Rogers, and for the rest of his life he simply assembled ad hoc groups for recording, then became a studio musician, first in Hollywood, then for CBS in New York).

Of the Haymes band, Tommy hired the entire sax and trumpet sections, the trombonist, pianist and guitarist, and a talented young arranger called Paul Weston. He did this in September 1935, and immediately got MCA to become the band's agent (although he would feud with them for years), and headed for the Victor company, where the recording director was his old acquaintance, Ed Kirkeby, of the California Ramblers.

Kirkeby signed up the new band for Victor, and Tommy asked him for an advance to get things going. "Sure," said Ed. "But better still, let's record right away – how about next week?" So on the September 26, Tommy and his new band did that. Their first-ever recording was called 'Take Me Back To My Boots And Saddle'.

Two weeks later, the band was back in the studios, recording three numbers as the backing band for tap-dancer, singer and Hollywood star Eleanor Powell. At this time the band still sounded a little rough (not surprisingly), but it had a lot of energy and some interesting arrangements, some from Paul Weston, and some from one of the band's alto-players, Noni Bernardi, who among other numbers arranged the one that was to become Tommy's theme, 'I'm Gettin' Sentimental Over You' (later in life he became a member of Los Angeles City Council).

Among his other musicians, Tommy had a good clarinetist (Sid Toneburn) and drummer (Sam Rosen), and an outstanding Bix-influenced trumpeter, Sterling Bose, who had been in the Jean Goldkette and Ben Pollack bands, and would go on to play with Ray Noble, Benny Goodman, Glenn Miller and Bob Crosby.

Tommy himself had by this time become a master of the trombone, and had developed two distinct styles – the smooth poised sound for which he was famous, and a rougher "jazzier" style of great power and effectiveness, that he mainly used when playing with his band-within-a-band, the Clambake Seven. Both his styles can be heard on his famous 1937 record 'Marie', the smooth style in the first chorus, before the vocal, and the rough one after Bunny Berigan's impassioned trumpet solo.

Tommy had formed the Clambake Seven almost immediately he had a band of his own, both recording with it and using it in live performance. The very first track it recorded, in December 1935, was 'The Music Goes 'Round And Around', which became the hit of the season.

It was in that same month that the Goodman Trio first appeared live on-stage with the Goodman band, although they had made their first recordings the previous July. So who first had the idea of a band-within-a-band is not quite clear. Possibly the true originator was Ben Pollack, who occasionally used to feature small groups from his band on-stage.

Tommy's idea in forming it seems partly to have been to add variety to his band's stage appearances, and partly as a gesture towards the hot jazz he enjoyed playing. His uncertainty as to how far the public wanted hot small-group jazz is reflected in the fact that almost every recording the Clambake Seven made features a vocal by Edythe Wright.

Early in 1936 the band made its New York debut, a one-nighter in the Blue Room of the Hotel Lincoln. The performance was attended by many people from the music business. Two leading music publishers who were going there, Jack Bregman and Rocco Vocco, invited Cork O'Keefe to come along and be at their table.

Cork, remembering his last meeting with Tommy, when he tried to patch things up between the brothers, was nervous. Taking the bull by the horns, he went and stood by the bandstand to greet Tommy as he came off at intermission, bracing himself for the confrontation.

When Tommy came off and saw him, he was struck dumb, and the expression on his face was such that Cork laughed out loud. Tommy threw his arms around him, came and joined him with the others at their table, and they settled down to what became a hilarious evening.

Soon afterwards, the band got a longer New York job, at the French Casino. This was strictly a dance-hall job, which kept the band working each night until 3 a.m. This was bad enough, but Tommy, wishing to make a good impression on the dancers and the management, would always make them play on for an extra ten or twelve minutes. Until drummer Sid Weiss (who had replaced Sam Rosen) got fed up with this and put an noisy alarm clock under the stage where nobody could easily get to it, set for three o'clock. It went off like a fire-alarm in the middle of 'The Very Thought Of You' and took five minutes to run down.

Tommy at this stage kept improving his personnel (all his life he changed musicians almost as much as Benny Goodman did). He brought in drummer Dave Tough to replace Sid Weiss (Tough was so good that this was probably nothing to do with the alarm clock). Bud Freeman came in on tenor saxophone, beginning a long association that Freeman would describe as "fired twice, quit three times", and trumpeter Bunny Berigan, who had played with Tommy around the radio studios, joined from the Benny Goodman band.

Hearing Jack Leonard singing on a radio broadcast with a band led by Bert Block, he impulsively hired him without even meeting him. At around the same time, from the same band, he hired trumpeter Joe Bauer and arranger Axel Stordahl. Stordahl would make a huge

contribution to the success of the band and, a few years later, to the rise of Frank Sinatra. Leonard, Bauer and Stordahl also used to sing with the band as The Three Esquires, so the astute Tommy got himself a vocal trio as well.

From Joe Marsala's dixieland band he snatched guitarist Carmen Mastren, who would win three "best guitarist" polls during the next four years. Tommy's main concern was always musicianship. Some years later, when needing a trumpet-player, he asked the band for suggestions. "How about so-and-so?" suggested somebody. "He's a nice guy." "Nice guys are a dime a dozen," Tommy snapped. "Get me a prick who can play." What he wanted were musicians who enjoyed playing, not those who played, as he once put it, "like a fat man on a full stomach".

Tommy's was unique among the top swing bands in never striving for a strongly-identifiable band sound. He wanted (and got) a band filled with highly competent musicians that was adaptable enough play a wide variety of material, and felt that to have a "Tommy Dorsey sound" would limit the jobs the band could get and make it a prey to passing fashion. In a way he was right – his was by far the most versatile of the great swing bands – but not having that identifiable sound meant that it never built up the huge following that Goodman or Miller had.

After the French Casino booking, the band set off on the road, building its reputation (and its bank balance – one-nighters could earn a lot of money). Jack Leonard later recalled, "We paid our dues, playing ... in every city and hamlet, in ballrooms, tobacco warehouses, any place that had a roof." Gene Traxler, the band's bass-player through all its early years, remembered "Tommy always made the long bus-trips bearable by stopping to play ball; or, if we were near his home in Lansford, we would go by his home and his mom and sister would cook Pennsylvania Dutch pot pie for the whole band."

In Texas, during the summer of 1936, the band became for eight weeks the summer replacement on a Ford-sponsored weekly radio show for that polished dance orchestra, Fred Waring's Pennsylvanians (probably the longest-lived of all big bands, it was formed in the early Twenties and was still going strong in the Seventies – Waring, something of a martinet and a prolific hard worker, also published hundred of stock arrangements, ran a monthly magazine, *Music Journal*, ran an annual music workshop, ran a hotel, "The Shawnee Inn", in six hundred acres of ground in Pennsylvania, and invented the Waring Blendor).

It was during that time, while the band was also playing a two-week engagement at the St Anthony Hotel in San Antonio, that Tommy took so much trouble supervising the setting up of microphones for a broadcast that the engineer finally said, "Why are you so worried about it?" "Because," said Tommy, "this is going to the brother."

In New York, sponsors and advertising agencies were making plans for the new radio season. The Depression now seemed to have lifted, radio was big, and its biggest stars, bigger now than even the bands, had become the comedians – Jack Benny, Burns and Allen, Eddie Cantor and Fred Allen were all at the top of the ratings.

The Brown and Williamson Tobacco Company decided to take a chance with comedian Jack Pearl, and needed a band for the show. It would only have one number each week, but nonetheless the feeling in the agency was that it wouldn't hurt to have a really good band. Reports were filtering back to New York of the Tommy Dorsey band's success on the road,

and so they were hired.

Unfortunately, Jack Pearl flopped. He was a late survivor of the old vaudeville tradition of ethnic comics (like Chico Marx's Italian act). Jack Pearl, playing a prevaricating character called Baron Munchausen, was a German comic. One of his stock sayings, "Vas you dere, Sharlie?", had recently caught on as a catch-phrase, but nonetheless the time for his type of comedy had passed. He was dropped from the show and Tommy, whose band's popularity was surging upward, took over. *The Tommy Dorsey Show*, sponsored by Raleigh and Kool cigarettes, was launched, and it was this show that gave him the tag, "The Sentimental Gentleman Of Swing".

The opening number on the band's first show was 'Song Of India', and the featured number in that show was the band's biggest-ever hit, 'Marie'. Both had been recorded in January 1937, both featured trumpet solos by Bunny Berigan, who was shortly to form his own band, and both were released on one 78. (When Berigan left, and Tommy wanted the band to play 'Marie', he found he had to score the chorus that had been Bunny's for three trumpets to generate an equivalent level of power and excitement).

The famous arrangement of 'Marie' (including the famous chanting of other song-titles behind Jack Leonard's vocal) had been the big number of a little-known black band called Doc Wheeler's Sunset Serenaders. During their tour in 1936, Tommy and his band had been headlining a show at Nixon's Grand Theatre in Philadelphia, in which the Sunset Serenaders also appeared. Tommy heard and liked the arrangement, and bought the rights to use it from Doc Wheeler for fifty dollars.

'Song Of India' and 'Marie' both spawned a string of successors for the band. From 'Song Of India' descended a line of swung classics that included 'Liebestraum', 'Humoresque', Mendelsshohn's 'Spring Song' and Rubinstein's 'Melody in F' (partly all these arose from a Whitemanesque desire to prove that swing was respectable), and the 'Marie' treatment of chanted titles was given to 'Who', 'Yearning', 'Sweet Sue', 'Blue Moon', 'How Am I To Know?' and 'East Of The Sun'.

Dancewise, 1937 was the year of the Big Apple, a sort of swing square-dance, and Tommy recorded a number with that title with the Clambake Seven that August. (The term "The Big Apple" seems to have first occurred a little earlier, as slang for New York City, in a song by Cab Calloway.)

The radio show was a hit, the records were selling well, and the band began the first of many bookings it would have at the Pennsylvania Roof in New York, later the Statler-Hilton. Morale in the band was high, and Tommy was enjoying himself. As well as being a martinet, he could also be a cheerful and entertaining companion, cracking jokes and swapping yarns. In fact, his rehearsals were always somewhat unpredictable. Tommy might that day feel like being a raconteur, or he might be giving the band a pep talk that a football coach would envy.

One place he liked to go on Wednesday nights after the broadcast was the famous Onyx Club on 52nd Street, where he would sit in on jam sessions playing trombone or cornet. The Onyx was owned by Joe Helbock, who had been a successful bootlegger during Prohibition, and who loved jazz and jazz musicians. For this reason he had been a regular customer at Plunkett's in the Twenties, and had been a friend of the brothers, especially Jimmy, since around 1925.

In the summer of 1937, after a year and a half working with Bing on the radio in California, Jimmy decided it was time for his band to move on. With Tommy doing so well it was time that the Jimmy Dorsey band appeared to the public as something more than a backing band. It was time for it to develop a style and reputation of its own.

A three-month itinerary of one-nighters across America was planned, bringing the band back to New York in September. The going would be rough, but it would earn some money, get the band into shape and give the Rockwell-O'Keefe publicity boys something to write about. Jimmy's ambition was probably given further impetus by the fact that at many of these one-nighters fans would come up to the bandstand and request 'Marie' or 'Song Of India'.

When the band eventually reached New York, Jimmy found that Cork O'Keefe had been busy. Building on the band's radio exposure with Bing, which had built it a following, he had got it a solid string of bookings, starting in New York at the New Yorker Hotel and the Paramount Theatre. Hotel engagements got the band air-time, which increased its audience further. Demand for it increased, and its price soon rose to $12,500 for a week at a theatre.

When Jimmy first arrived back in New York, he got an invitation to a party from Joe and Mrs Helbock. So did Tommy. It was common knowledge that their feud had run out of steam, and in any case their differences had always been musical, not personal, and Helbock had planned the evening as a celebration, and a public confirmation that there was at least an armistice.

The party was attended by many musicians, including members of both bands, and by several leaders of bands big and small, including Artie Shaw, Joe Haymes, Lenny Hayton and Wingy Manone, and it turned out to be a great success. From then on the brothers would support each

James Reese Europe with his Clef Club orchestra of 1914.

Paul Whiteman

Bix Beiderbecke

Paul Whiteman conducting his band.

Coleman Hawkins

Louis Armstrong

Fletcher Henderson and his 1937 rhythm section: Israel Crosby (bass), Fletcher Henderson (piano), Lawrence Lucie (gtr) and Pete Suggs (drums).

Andy Kirk (left) and his Clouds Of Joy, in 1937, with pianist Mary Lou Williams.

Chick Webb

Lucky Millinder (second left) and his band of around 1941.

Cab Calloway

Jack Teagarden

Jimmy and Tommy Dorsey in 1934.

The Dorsey Brothers band 1934. Singers Bob Crosby and Kay Weber are seated in foreground, and the trombonist behind Kay is Glenn Miller. Brother Jimmy, at the right-hand end of the sax section, eyes brother Tommy.

Earl 'Fatha' Hines

Earl Hines and his 1933 band.

Jimmie Lunceford

Jimmie Lunceford fronting his band in 1936.

Benny Goodman

Benny Goodman among his band during the filming of 'The Big Broadcast Of 1937'.

Bunny Berigan, fronting his band in the late
Thirties.

Lionel Hampton

Gene Krupa

Harry James

Bennie Moten and his band around 1929. Singer Jimmy Rushing stands behind pianists Bill Basie (left) and Bennie Moten (right). Behind Basie stands arranger and trombonist Eddie Durham. At the left is trumpeter Hot Lips Page and at the right, with the baton, is Bennie's nephew, accordionist Buster Moten.

Bob Crosby leads his 1938 band behind singer Marion Mann.

Count Basie

Lester Young

Count Basie and his band at the Famous Door in 1938. Tenor-players Herschel Evans and Lester Young are at the left and right ends of the sax section. Buck Clayton takes a solo.

Glenn Miller

The Glenn Miller band in 1940. Tenorists Tex Beneke and Al Klink trade fours on 'In The Mood'.

Artie Shaw

Roy Eldridge solos in front of the 1945 Artie Shaw band.

Charlie Barnet

Woody Herman

Ivie Anderson and Jimmy Blanton.

Billy Strayhorn

Al Sears and Johnny Hodges.

Sidney Bechet

Duke Ellington and his band in the early Forties.

other's bands, giving what help they could.

It was in the next year, 1938, that Tommy, continuing to hunt down good musicians for his band, raided the Bob Crosby band for two of its star trumpeters, Yank Lawson and Charlie Spivak. Spivak, after having words with and leaving Benny Goodman, had briefly been with the Dorsey Brothers band in 1935. He had moved with Glenn Miller to join the Ray Noble band when it was formed, and in 1937 had moved to Crosby. Yank Lawson had been with the Crosby band since its formation in 1935, and was regarded as one of its fixtures.

In June 1938, Tommy, while in Chicago, had dropped in at the Blackhawk Restaurant where the Crosby band was playing, and the friends who were there found it curious that he came in rather hurriedly, disappeared from sight for a few minutes, reappeared, and swiftly left. It later turned out that he'd had a brief informal chat with Yank Lawson about defecting.

A month later, when the Crosby band was in California, Yank got a telegram. On the outside of the envelope it said firmly, PERSONAL DELIVERY ONLY. IDENTIFICATION OF ADDRESSEE MUST BE ASSURED FOR DELIVERY. MUST SHOW UNION CARD OR DRIVER'S LICENSE. Inside it said, MUST KNOW IMMEDIATELY YOUR PLANS. HOW SOON CAN YOU ACT. PLEASE ADVISE BY WESTERN UNION. TOMMY DORSEY.

Yank joined Tommy that August, without even asking what he was to be paid, and the Tommy Dorsey band had the most powerful and driving trumpeter it had had since Bunny Berigan. And Charlie Spivak, a rather over-sweet player, joined with him.

A few months later, in January 1939, the brothers' fraternal closeness was demonstrated at the Hotel New Yorker. Tommy was due to finish an engagement there on the 10th, Jimmy to begin one on the 11th. Instead of playing till 2 a.m., as was usual, Tommy and his band, after playing 'Auld Lang Syne' at midnight, segued into the old Dorsey Brothers signature tune (which Jimmy had continued to use) 'Sandman'. Jimmy made his entrance and introduced his own band playing what was to be his new signature tune, 'Contrasts'.

The room was filled with fans and friends, and at a front table, Mr and Mrs Thomas Dorsey senior, who were called on to take bows and got a mighty cheer. Tommy and Jimmy embraced on-stage and began swapping reminiscences, and Mr Dorsey was invited up onto the stage and handed a trumpet, and he played a number with his sons, like in the old days. Mom Dorsey was moved to Irish tears by the whole experience.

As a result of this happy reunion, Tommy and his radio producer, Herb Sanford (later author of the book "The Fabulous Dorseys") had an idea. Tommy had a guest on his radio show every week, and they decided to have not a single guest next week, but the entire Jimmy Dorsey band. The programme, which took the form of a short dramatised biography of the brothers, ended with a reprise of the Dorsey Brothers' Band's biggest hit, 'Honeysuckle Rose' (arranged by Glenn Miller) by both bands together, and a good time was had by all.

By this time Jimmy's band was as big a success as Tommy's, but unlike Tommy's, his personnel had remained fairly stable. Eight of the musicians who had been in his band in 1937 were still there in 1939: Shorty Sherock (trumpet), Bobby Byrne and Don Mattison (trombones), Charlie Frazier (tenor sax and clarinet), Freddie Slack (piano), Roc Hillman (guitar), Jack Ryan (bass) and Ray McKinley (drums).

Tutti Camarata was still there as arranger, and

his arrangements did much to give the band its elegance. Shortly it would acquire more strength by adding a third trumpet and a fifth sax. Bob Eberly was still there, and had become one of the most popular singers of the day.

The band hadn't had a regular girl singer since 1936, when Kay Weber, not having much to do while the band was restricted to broadcasting with Bing, had left Hollywood to return to New York. There she attempted for a while to build up an acting career before joining the Bob Crosby band (and eventually marrying one of its trombonists, Ward Sillaway).

In 1938 Jimmy's band acquired June Richmond, a large cheerful woman who was not a great singer but a crowd-pleasing entertainer. With Jimmy she became the first black artist to appear regularly with a major white swing band. For a while after her the band's girl singer was the young Ella Mae Morse, but she turned out to be too inexperienced (once on-stage she broke down in the middle of a song and giggled "I forgot the words"). She in turn was replaced early in 1939 by Helen O'Connell, a pretty, bubbly green-eyed blonde who became popular with band and public alike. Only a year later she won the *Metronome* poll as best girl singer.

Jimmy was always concerned to present his singers well. In most big bands, the band would play an opening ensemble chorus, then lay back while the singer was given a chorus to let the audience hear the lyric. Jimmy used to build his singers properly into the arrangement, often giving them the very first chorus, and occasionally almost the whole number, such as he did for Bob Eberly on 'I Understand', 'I'm Glad There Is You', 'I Get Along Without You Very Well' and 'Marie Elena'.

It was not till a couple of years after Helen arrived that arranger Tutti Camarata had the idea of presenting numbers with tempo-changes. This came about on a radio series the band was doing (for Twenty Grand cigarettes), when the sponsors wanted a three-minute closing number featuring all the band's stars. Tutti arranged for Bob Eberly to sing the first chorus as a ballad, then for the band to pick up the tempo, Jimmy to play a hot chorus, then for the tempo to slow again for Helen to do a bluesy finale.

The routine was a success, and after the not-unexpected arguments with Decca executives about whether the number should be recorded ("People will break a leg trying to dance to all those tempo-changes"), it was.

The first songs arranged in this way and recorded were 'Amapola' and 'Yours', but the big hit, recorded a month later, was 'Green Eyes'. Later they would do the same with 'Tangerine', also a hit, but not to the same extent as 'Green Eyes'.

Tommy's band continued to develop. In the autumn of 1938 he had been introduced to a vocal group called the Pied Pipers (seven men and Jo Stafford) and had hired them to sing with the band, although for financial reasons he soon had to reduce their number to four by firing four of the men. And in 1939 he made a significant addition to his squad of staff arrangers. To add to Paul Weston, Axel Stordahl and Deane Kincaide he acquired Sy Oliver.

Tommy had for years admired the lazy two-beat swing of the great Jimmie Lunceford band, and Sy Oliver was Lunceford's main arranger. Tommy began buying arrangements from him, and late in 1939 he joined the staff. His arrangements gave the band a powerful laid-back swing it had never had before, with such numbers as 'Easy Does It', 'So What!' and 'Swanee River'.

Dave Tough had left early in 1938 to replace

Gene Krupa in the Benny Goodman band, and although the band had had a string of more than capable drummers since then (including Tough himself for a spell), it wasn't till November 1939 that he again acquired one of the all-time greats – Buddy Rich. Buddy's showy and hard-driving drumming propelled the band to new heights of excitement, and he was featured to fine effect on the band's record of 'Quiet, Please!'

Rich, who became Tommy's favourite drummer, had got his start playing with clarinetist Joe Marsala's dixieland band at the Hickory House on 52nd Street, before going on to play with Bunny Berigan, Harry James, Artie Shaw and Benny Carter. Several members of Tommy's band had been with Joe Marsala, including pianist Joe Bushkin and guitarist Carmen Mastren. After Rich joined him, Joe sent Tommy a telegram: "Dear Tommy, How about giving me a job in your band so I can play with mine?"

Rich was a star, but the band's biggest discovery was to come along in 1940. One night in the autumn of 1939, after finishing a performance at the Pennsylvania Roof, Tommy was driving back to his house in Bernardsville with his singer, Jack Leonard. Jack, who by then was high in the popularity polls, asked Tommy if he'd heard the new record by the Harry James band, 'All Or Nothing At All'. "No," said Tommy. "Why do you ask?" "There's a guy who does the vocal and he scares the hell out of me. He's that good."

Jack and Tommy were not entirely on the best of terms at this time. There had been rumours that Jack was thinking of leaving the band to go out on his own, and whereas he was only thinking this very vaguely, the rumours had reached Tommy and annoyed him. In November 1939, while the band was playing the Palmer House in Chicago, they got into an argument (something to do with the way some of the musicians in the band were being treated), and Jack walked out.

Everyone, including Jack, and possibly Tommy, thought he would soon be back, but it happened that in December every big band in the area was summoned to Chicago by James Petrillo, autocratic head of the musicians' union, to perform for the annual Christmas benefit party sponsored by Chicago's mayor, Edward J. Kelly.

It so happened that the Harry James band was appearing in Chicago, at the Sherman Hotel, so it too was at the benefit. After the benefit, Tommy sent a note to the vocalist who had recorded 'All Or Nothing At All' asking him to come round to Tommy's suite at the Palmer House. He did, and when Tommy showed up hours later was asked to sing. He sang 'Marie', and was offered $125 a week to join the band. He accepted, and a few weeks later the Tommy Dorsey band had a new male singer called Frank Sinatra.

From February 1940, through the next three years, almost half of Tommy Dorsey's recorded output featured Frank Sinatra, and musically for a while the band became less interesting, contenting itself for the most part with backing its new-found star. The number that propelled him into stardom, with the Pied Pipers backing him, was 'I'll Never Smile Again', recorded in April 1940.

The bobby-soxers went wild over it and him, screaming and sobbing at his appearances with the band. The record stayed at number one in the Hit Parade for weeks, and Tommy began putting Frank's name above everyone's on the publicity, above Connie Haines, who was also singing with the band at that time, above the Pied Pipers, even above Buddy Rich, who was not best pleased. He and Frank took against each other, and their time together in the band was punctuated by ferocious and often physical fights.

The advent of Sinatra onto the scene was a straw in the wind. From then on, singers began to become a bigger draw with the pop-buying public than bands, and the glorious era that had begun with the ODJB, when fans listened to the music rather than the words, and instrumentals regularly topped the Hit Parade, was coming to an end.

CHAPTER 11

black bands of the thirties

During the Twenties and Thirties in America there was a great respect and friendliness between black and white jazz musicians. Quite naturally, and without having anything much in mind beyond the music they loved, they led the way in inter-racial acceptance, paving the way for integration in other fields.

At the the same time, in the wider entertainment industry, black musicians often felt that they were getting a financial raw deal, as they saw white bands making vast amounts of money out of music that they knew they had done much to develop, played by men who were often their musical inferiors.

They saw Benny Goodman rise to fame using the arrangements of Fletcher Henderson. They saw fine bands like Duke Ellington's or Jimmie Lunceford's working for a fraction of the fees demanded by Tommy Dorsey or Harry James.

Part of the problem was that America is, after all, a predominently white country. The white majority of the day preferred to listen to white bands, so those were the bands that the men running the music business put most of their financial backing and promotional energy into pushing. And the more they pushed white bands to the white audience, the more the white audience preferred them.

Radio, which was enormously influential, catered hardly at all to the black audience. Black bands who got regular air-time were rare and fortunate. White bands, even poor ones, were given all the national exposure, and as a result of their fame were able to command much larger fees. As far as most of the great white audience knew, even the best black bands might not have existed.

The black audience, not able to hear much black music on radio, depended much more than Whites did on buying records, which at least had the fortunate effect for posterity that black bands got to do rather more recording than they might otherwise have done.

In the hurly-burly of the music business, sometimes even quite well-intentioned white musicians inadvertently took advantage of their black contemporaries. Gene Krupa adapted Earl Hines's composition 'Piano Man' into a feature for his own band, altering the lyrics only as much as necessary to turn it into 'Drummer Man'.

Somehow no royalties for it ever reached Earl Hines and Gene, running into him one time, tried rather shamefacedly to apologise. He said, "As a matter of fact, Earl, I never made a cent out of that record I made." "Then we both got screwed," said Earl.

Earl Hines, who had an enormous influence on the development of jazz piano, was also a bandleader for twenty years. A tall, extroverted, cigar-chomping character, he enjoyed being a showman, sitting at his piano set in the dead centre of the stage and the band, and beaming at his audience. He took pride in presenting a good show, and his band of the early Thirties was one of the very first to achieve the sound of a band of the Swing Era.

His name really was Earl Hines, or rather, Earl Kenneth Hines, and he was born in Duquesne, on the outskirts of Pittsburgh, in 1903. His parents were both musical, and as a young boy he studied the cornet briefly with his father, who was a member of a fourteen-piece brass band, before giving it up at the age of nine to begin piano lessons with his mother. He followed these by further lessons from teachers in Pittsburgh, and began playing there professionally when he was fifteen, working in a small band accompanying a cabaret singer called Lois Deppe. With some of his earnings he took further lessons from two local jazz pianists.

Quite soon he had developed into a remarkable player. In only a few years, by the time he was twenty-two, he would have transformed jazz piano, building on everything that had happened before him – on ragtime and stride and the jazz style developed by Jelly Roll Morton. The style he evolved for himself was at once hard-driving and rhythmically loose, and he used more complex harmonies than anyone had before, making use of the full orchestral capabilities of the instrument.

If Earl had been white, his enormous gifts would have given him the chance of a brilliant career as a classical pianist. He seems to have considered this, but being black in the early Twenties made it impossible. Nor was making a living as a solo jazz pianist really feasible, because at that time the dance and jazz fields were dominated by bands, big and small.

The obvious course open to him was band-work and, going to Chicago in 1923 at the suggestion of ragtime pianist and composer Eubie Blake, who suggested he get away from Pittsburgh and into the big time, he embarked at the age of nineteen on a succession of jobs with established bands.

He also quite soon got to know Louis Armstrong. Louis happened on him playing 'The One I Love Belongs To Somebody Else' on a piano newly installed in the black musicians' union hall. Naturally he was impressed by Earl's playing, and the two soon became firm friends (going on to make some of the outstanding small-group recordings of the Twenties and early Thirties, and indeed of all time).

Earl's first band job was with Sammy Stewart at the Sunset Cafe. He went on to play with Erskine Tate (in a band that also had Louis Armstrong in it) at the Vendome Theatre, and with a band led by violinist Carroll Dickerson, which took him on a forty-two week tour.

In 1926 the Dickerson band returned to Chicago to begin a residency (again at the Sunset Cafe), and again Louis Armstrong joined it. Also in the band was Louis' lifelong friend from New Orleans, drummer Zutty Singleton.

Although Dickerson himself wasn't much of a musician, his bands played an important part in the development of early jazz, mainly through their association with Louis. Not only wasn't he much of a musician, he was also over-fond of the drink, and in time the Cafe management fired him, making Louis the leader and Earl Hines the musical director.

This big band was the first that Louis led under his own name, but it didn't last long, because in July 1927 the Sunset Cafe was temporarily closed by the Feds for violating Prohibition.

In December of that year, Earl and Louis and Zutty got together again. They formed a small band and opened a dance-hall of their own, called the

Usonia, hoping that Louis' name would pull in the crowds. Unfortunately, a large and lavish new dance-hall and cabaret called the Savoy opened nearby at the same time (with a band again led by Carroll Dickerson), and within a few weeks the Usonia went bust, leaving the three friends scuffling for work.

In early 1928, Earl went out of town to work for a short while. Returning, he was annoyed to find that Louis and Zutty had accepted the offer of rejoining Carroll Dickerson at the Savoy, which was now the most important venue on Chicago's South Side, without waiting for him. A few weeks later, when there was a vacancy in the band for a pianist and they asked him to join them, he refused, and joined Jimmie Noone's little band at the Apex Club instead. That summer, with Noone, he recorded some exceptional small-group jazz.

Then he heard that the Peerless Theater, a silent movie house at 3955 South Parkway Boulevard, was to be converted into ballroom and cabaret, and renamed the Grand Terrace. He got himself the job of providing the house band and when the Grand Terrace Ballroom opened on 28th December 1928, Earl and his first big band opened with it. It was his twenty-fifth birthday.

His band would spend most of the next eleven years as the Grand Terrace's resident band, playing three shows a night there. Its policy was modelled on that of Harlem's Cotton Club, so while the band got to play only a limited amount of out-and-out jazz, it did get valuable experience in a wide variety of jazz-influenced styles.

With Hines's reputation already established through the fine recordings he had made with Jimmie Noone and Louis, it was hardly surprising that the Victor recording company at once gave the new band a recording contract. It recorded five sessions during February 1929, and one in October, making twelve big-band numbers in all, of

which only nine were released.

It had such a comparatively high failure-rate because, quite frankly, the records weren't very good. Earl's piano-playing was excellent, both swinging and inventive, but the band itself, although playing with a fair amount of energy and bounce, was under-rehearsed. Furthermore, it had no consistent sound of its own. There were echoes in its playing of almost everything that was around at the time – King Oliver, Jelly Roll Morton's Red Hot Peppers, Don Redman, even Guy Lombardo ("The Sweetest Band This Side Of Heaven").

Part of the problem was that Hines was, as he said himself, primarily "a band pianist". By which he meant that he was not a pianist-composer-arranger like Ellington, or a pianist-arranger like Fletcher Henderson. Setting the band's style was not his forte. As a result, he would be, like Benny Goodman later, dependent on finding good arrangers.

After the October session, Victor did not renew the band's contract. Quite apart from the records not selling, Wall Street had crashed, the Depression was starting, and the record industry was entering its serious slump.

When the band next returned to the record studios, it was three years later and for Brunswick, a record company that had been around in a small way since 1916, but had taken on a new lease of life in the early Thirties when it was bought by a large conglomerate called Consolidated Film Industries, which also owned Columbia records.

Their first session was in June 1932, and it is immediately obvious from hearing the records that the band had improved immensely. For a start it had dropped the old-fashioned tuba and banjo in its rhythm section for the lighter and more swinging bass and guitar.

The bass-player, Quinn Wilson, gave the band a fine rhythmic drive, as well as becoming one of the band's most talented arrangers, and among the other arrivals were trumpeter Walter Allen, who played (and sang) in the Armstrong tradition, and clarinetist-altoist-violinist Darnell Howard, who had played with King Oliver and come strongly under the influence of Jimmie Noone in his clarinet-playing, which was rich and warm.

There was also another clarinetist (and altoist), the truly outstanding Omer Simeon, who was born in New Orleans in 1902 but moved to Chicago with his family when he was fourteen. Fluent and warm in the lower register, more biting and intense in the upper, he was Jelly Roll Morton's favourite clarinetist and can he heard on many of the Red Hot Peppers records, for instance 'Black Bottom Stomp' and 'Doctor Jazz'.

In 1927 he also played with King Oliver, and went on to play with Luis Russell and Erskine Tate before joining Earl Hines in 1931. Later he would go on to play in the Horace Henderson and Jimmie Lunceford big bands, and spend the latter part of his career, after the Second world war, working in small New Orleans-style groups such as those of Kid Ory and Wilbur de Paris.

On drums, Earl had the tasteful and swinging Chicagoan, Wallace Bishop, steady as a rock, who had also played with Morton and Erskine Tate, and he had a useful arranger in Henri Woode, who had come to him from a successful Omaha band called Lloyd Hunter's Serenaders. In their first session for Brunswick the band recorded an up-tempo flag-waver called 'Sensational Mood' that Woode had originally arranged for Lloyd Hunter. The number already shows clearly the rhythmic drive that would soon become the hallmark of the band.

By the time the band recorded for Brunswick again, in February 1933, it had acquired a major arranger (and useful tenorist), Jimmy Mundy. Mundy was born in Cincinnati in 1907, and had trained as a classical violinist. While still in his teens

he toured with an evangelist's orchestra, playing violin and, by this time, tenor.

He began to study the craft of arranging after he moved to Washington to work in 1926, and in 1932 Earl Hines heard an number he had written and arranged for a band led by a drummer called Tommy Myles. The number was 'Cavernism'. Earl liked it, hired Jimmy Mundy away from Tommy Myles, and recorded the arrangement at their first session together (and again, with improvements, eighteen months later, when the band started recording for the new Decca label).

At the same session he first recorded 'Cavernism', the band also recorded its first version of a delightful tune written by Hines himself, 'Rosetta'. That too the band would re-record in 1934 after switching to Decca, by which time they were really getting into their stride.

By then they had also acquired a promising trombonist who hailed from Savannah, Georgia – James Osborne "Trummy" Young. Trummy was twenty-one when he joined the band, raising the number of trombones to three, and he was already well on the way to developing the smooth full tone that he would later use to such good advantage with Jimmie Lunceford (not to mention the rougher but just as full tone that he would develop to play with Louis Armstrong in the All-Stars during the Fifties and Sixties).

In spite of the way the band was swinging by now, its records couldn't have sold well, because Decca too dropped them, and it was two more years before they got back into the studios again, this time recording for Vocalion (which oddly enough was now owned by Brunswick).

This break in its recorded output was partly compensated for since, from 1934, regular radio broadcasts began from the Grand Terrace (a radio announcer in those days gave Earl the nickname "Fatha", which he used for the rest of his life).

The band had also by then begun making wide-ranging tours between its residencies at the Grand Terrace, so its national reputation continued to grow. Some evidence of how hard it could swing at this time is that it was about the only band in the mid-Thirties that Chick Webb was nervous about competing against at the Savoy Ballroom. Hines's showmanship and musicianship, and his band's excitement and energy made Chick dig out his number one book, containing all his hottest numbers.

At the beginning of 1937 the Grand Terrace moved, and the band with it, taking over what had been the famous Sunset Cafe, but which had by now fallen on hard times. At the new location the ballroom was known as the New Grand Terrace, but oddly enough this was nothing to do with the move – it had been calling itself that since around 1932.

The Hines band's personnel changed only slowly, and in its two years away from the recording studios (from February 1935 to February 1937) the only major change was that Jimmy Mundy had gone off to become a staff arranger for Benny Goodman, and had been replaced by tenorist and arranger Budd Johnson.

Budd, originally Albert J.Johnson, was a Texan who had worked with a number of local bands there before moving to Chicago in 1932. When he joined Earl he had already been in Louis Armstrong's big band, and would go on to work with both Fletcher and Horace Henderson. In the Forties he would become one of the most important arrangers in introducing the rhythms and harmonies of be-bop into the big bands, doing arrangements for Buddy Rich, Woody Herman, Billy Eckstine and Dizzy Gillespie.

When Budd joined the band he found that its standards had begun to slip a little. Second-rate numbers, mostly from the Grand Terrace shows, were cropping up more and more frequently in its repertoire and, following the trend of the Swing Era, solos were becoming shorter (more emphasis being placed on arranged ensemble-work). There was a slight feeling in the band of fatigue and disillusion, leading to sloppy playing, although it could still produce fine work. Among its best records from the 1937-38 period are 'Pianology' and 'Rhythm Sundae', both of which have sparkling piano work from Earl.

Budd, acting as Earl's musical director, took things in hand, and soon the band's playing began to improve again, becoming ever more relaxed, while continuing to swing powerfully.

In July 1939, by which time the band had changed record companies again and was recording for the Victor company's cut-price label, Bluebird, it recorded two outstanding numbers. One was 'G.T. Stomp', composed by Earl and Budd Johnson as a cheerful finale for the Grand Terrace show. The other was the more ambitious 'Grand Terrace Shuffle', a number closely resembling Count Basie's 'One O'Clock Jump', with composer Budd playing tenor in a style resembling Lester Young.

At the end of 1939 the band ended its long association with the Grand Terrace and began to base itself in New York. Possibly Earl made this move out of a feeling that the Swing Era was to some extent passing him by, and it was time to try and compete with the big names – Goodman, the Dorseys, Miller, Lunceford and Basie.

In this he had some success, because in 1940 it recorded what was to be its greatest hit, latching onto the current craze for adapting boogie-woogie piano rhythms to big-band instrumentation. 'Boogie-Woogie On St Louis Blues' is a charging and powerful piece of swing, arranged by Earl himself, and it brought the band national fame.

A recent addition to the band at this time was a

handsome young singer called Billy Eckstine, and now that the public's attention had been attracted to the band, his singing with it brought it more hits, notably 'Jelly, Jelly' and 'Stormy Monday Blues', recorded in 1940 and 1942.

By this period the band's personnel had started constantly changing and, following the trend of the time, it had grown by 1942 to sixteen pieces, with seven brass and five reeds. It was in 1942 that clarinetist Omer Simeon rejoined. He would stay until 1950, during the same period making a great contribution to the Forties jazz revival by recording in small bands led by trombonist Kid Ory.

Having larger sections allowed arrangers to play more complex chords, and several members of the band, including Billy Eckstine and Budd Johnson, were becoming aware of the new experimental sounds of be-bop, with its strange new harmonies and fast choppy rhythms.

At that time be-bop was still mainly being played by a new generation of ambitious young musicians in informal jam sessions at after-hours spots. The most influential of these was Minton's Playhouse, a club in Harlem at 210 West 118th Street, run since 1940 by ex-bandleader Teddy Hill. Billy and Budd and others started telling Earl, by now an old man of thirty-eight, that he ought to get some of this young blood into his band.

Among those others was George Dorman "Scoops" Carry, an alto-player from Little Rock, Arkansas, who had studied music at the Chicago Conservatory and the University of Illinois. Before joining Earl he had played with (among a number of smaller bands) Lucky Millinder, Fletcher Henderson, Roy Eldridge and Horace Henderson, and it was generally known that he knew what he was talking about when it came to reed-players (after leaving Earl in 1947 he would leave the music business, study law, and become an attorney in Chicago).

Budd had decided to leave the band, so Earl would need a tenor- player. Because of the wartime draft, good young musicians were getting scarce, and Scoops prevailed on Earl to consider giving one of the young boppers a try, a saxophonist called Charlie Parker. "But he plays alto," said Earl, who had heard Parker very briefly a year or so before in Detroit in the Jay McShann band. "That's not going to help us much." "He plays tenor too," said Scoops.

Earl, who all his life took a fatherly interest in encouraging up-and-coming young musicians, took little convincing. After the band finished their gig one night (they were appearing the the Savoy), he set off with Scoops and Billy and Budd Johnson (and Count Basie) to Minton's.

Charlie, although hard up and ragged, was on fine form that night, improvising chorus after chorus. Earl was impressed. He asked Bird if it was true he could play tenor. Bird said yes. Did he have a tenor? No, in fact the alto he was playing wasn't even his. "All right," said Earl, "I'll buy you a tenor." He stripped a ten-dollar bill off the impressive roll that bandleaders liked to carry when they were out scouting talent, and told Charlie to buy himself a clean shirt and be at the rehearsal studio tomorrow.

As well as Charlie, Earl by now had in his band quite a few of the be-bop generation – drummer Shadow Wilson, trombonist Benny Green, and a trumpet section of Benny Harris, Shorty McConnell, Gail Brockman and the other main ringleader of the whole new movement, John Birks "Dizzy" Gillespie. And a little later, on the advice of Billy Eckstine, he would hire the young Sarah Vaughan as his girl singer (and second pianist).

Fellow-bandleaders warned Earl that he had overdone it, that these young hipsters regarded his band as an out-of-date joke and he was sitting on a powder-keg, but Earl remained unalarmed. Charlie

Parker in particular turned out to be just as remarkable on tenor as on alto, and had such a good musical memory that he only had to play his part in an arrangement once to know it off by heart.

This was somewhat offset by his tendency to stay up all night jamming at places like Minton's, then oversleep and miss the band call. Fined by Earl for missing shows, he decided one day that he would sleep under the bandstand so as not to miss the matinee. He did, but failed to tell anyone he was there, or to wake up, and remained missing until the matinee was over, when he crawled out red-eyed.

Musically, the band was a strange exciting jumble, playing in a bewildering mixture of old and new styles. Between sets, Charlie and Dizzy would find a quiet corner to practice together, playing exercises from a trumpet book and an alto book, then swapping books, becoming fluent at playing complex chord-patterns.

Unfortunately, it never got recorded. This was indirectly because of the rise of the juke-box and the disc-jockey. Having caught on with the young swing fans from around 1934, by 1937 there were 150,000 juke-boxes in America (Bunny Berigan disliked them so much he used to jam their coin-slots with chewing-gum). During the same period, radio stations realised that playing records over the air was a much cheaper way of programming than paying a band and venue to broadcast live.

Both of these phenomena were robbing musicians of work, and their common factor was records. James C. Petrillo, a power in the union, the American Federation of Musicians, saw the danger and, in order to redress it, demanded from the record companies that they pay musicians a higher royalty for making recordings.

The record companies refused, and from 1st August 1942, Petrillo ordered all musicians to stay out of the recording studios until the AFM's demands were met. This ban lasted until the autumn of 1943 when Decca capitulated. Founded only in 1934, it had a much smaller back-list than the older giants like Victor and Columbia, but in 1944 they too followed suit.

Unfortunately this was almost exactly the period during which Earl's exciting and innovatory big band existed. By the time the recording ban was over, the two factions within the band (the old and the new) had so exasperated each other that it became a shambles, riven by internal squabbling. "It's still the best big band in show business," Scoops Carry told Charlie Parker. "It's a jail," said Charlie.

Earl's fellow-bandleaders had been right. It had been a powder keg, and in 1943 it collapsed, with musicians quitting in all directions. Earl, disillusioned, fired most of the remnant and replaced his reed section with an all-girl string group. Not only was this band a flop, the girls were almost as much trouble as the boppers. It lasted only a couple of months.

Earl, who could always make a living playing piano, did have another try at leading a big swing band during 1946 and 1947, but it tended (like most bands of that time) be be heavy-footed and overblown, and it was probably with some relief that in 1948 he rejoined Louis Armstrong, who had also just quit leading a big band, in the newly-formed All-Stars.

He would stay with Louis until 1951, and spend the rest of his life leading trios and quartets, or performing solo, playing as well as ever until within a few days of his death in 1983.

Louis, incidentally, remained curiously on the sidelines during the Swing Era. In spite of his reputation among musicians, and his continuing development as a singer and trumpeter, the various big bands he led added nothing much to the development of swing, being almost entirely confined to backing his singing and playing.

Probably the best that worked under his nominal leadership was actually the Luis Russell band, which he fronted from 1935 to 1943, but even that is a much poorer band than Russell had been leading three or four years earlier. It was improved in the summer of 1937 by the addition of three musicians who had been with Russell before – trumpeter Red Allen, clarinetist Albert Nicholas and trombonist J.C. Higginbotham, but still, on record at least, they get little chance to shine.

Part of this comes from Louis' surprising vein of selfishness (or maybe uncertainty) about his audience. He was the star, and he was not about to have anybody in his band who might compete for his applause. (It was friction arising from this attitude that caused Earl Hines to leave the All-Stars in 1951).

Why he worried about this in his big band days is inexplicable, because as always he himself was magnificent and beyond competition. Such Thirties numbers as 'Our Monday Date', 'You're a Lucky Guy', 'Harlem Stomp' and 'Wolverine Blues' are all well worth hearing, but to the young fans of the Swing Era he was an old-timer from years ago, and he made no attempt to compete with the new big name bandleaders, black or white.

A leader who did more than compete was Jimmie Lunceford. On November 18, 1940, probably the greatest collection of great swing bands ever got together to perform were brought to the Manhattan Center in New York for a marathon performance (eight in the evening to four the next morning) MC'd by disc-jockey Martin Block.

The twenty-eight assembled bands included Benny Goodman, Glenn Miller, Count Basie, Glen Gray (the Casa Loma), Les Brown, Will Bradley, Sammy Kaye, and Guy Lombardo. Each was

scheduled to play for fifteen minutes, and every one stuck to its allotted time, except one. The audience of six thousand set up such a shouting and cheering and hollering "More!" that the show had to be held up while the Lunceford band played several encores.

Not only was it among the most exciting big bands of all time, with a joyful swinging beat, it was also far ahead of the others in sheer showmanship. The various sections would stand for ensemble passages, moving their instruments in choreographed unison – the saxes weaving from side to side, the trombones stabbing towards the ceiling, the trumpets spinning in the air. And the band's enthusiasm in playing, expressed in constant ad-libbing between the band-members, all kidding and shouting and cheering each other on.

On top of which it was probably the most disciplined musically of all the great swing bands, and the man responsible for this was the big smiling figure of Lunceford himself, standing placidly in front of the band with his baton (he was one of the few non-playing, non-singing leaders).

James Melvin Lunceford had been born in Fulton, Missouri, in 1902. His family moved to Denver, Colorado, when he was a child, and there he learned to play several instruments, including the alto sax and violin, and learnt the fundamentals of theory from Wilberforce Whiteman, Paul Whiteman's father.

After playing alto in a few local bands (and violin in a society dance-band), he went on to study music at Fisk University in Nashville, Tennessee (where he was also a star athlete), then did a post-graduate course at the City College of New York.

While there he played odd dates with several bands, including Elmer Snowden's Washingtonians, and even formed a small band of his own for a while. But the band wasn't successful, and in 1926 he left New York and went back to Tennessee to take a job as director of athletics (and music teacher) at Manassa High School, in Memphis.

There he formed a dance-band from among his students, calling it the Chickasaw Syncopators. Several of these had been on his track team as well, among them drummer Jimmy Crawford, then aged seventeen. He also acquired a local bass-player of around the same age, Moses Allen.

The Chickasaw Syncopators became proficient remarkably quickly, because in December 1927 they were asked to record for Columbia records, and made two sides in a Memphis studio.

As the band began to make a name for itself, news of it reached his old colleagues from Fisk University, and several of these came to join it, among them mathematics major and altoist Willie Smith, pianist Eddie Wilcox and trombonist Henry Wells.

When selecting musicians for his band, Jimmie always insisted on good musicianship, good character and intelligence. He was a firm disciplinarian, but he was also consistent in his likes and dislikes. This gave his men a feeling of security, and many musicians stayed with the band for years, making its roster of personnel very stable.

The Syncopators recorded another two titles in Memphis in June 1930, this time for the Victor company. Sitting in on this session was a young trumpeter from Zanesville, Ohio, whose name was Melvin James Oliver but who was known to everyone as Sy.

Sy at around this time was playing with the prestigious Alphonso Trent Orchestra. Jimmie had seen the Trent outfit in action, and been impressed by its flashy uniforms and general stage presentation, as well as by its sophisticated arrangements, all of which allowed it to pull down jobs in major white hotels and ballrooms.

Jimmie realised that that was more the sort of band he wanted, but he also realised that some of the musicians in the Syncopators would never be good enough. He decided to leave teaching and Memphis, and move to a more thriving metropolis where he could find enough good musicians to build a better band.

It was agreed between them that the band should be jointly owned by Jimmie, Willie Smith and Edwin Wilcox, and wishing to steer clear of New York City until the band was ready, but not to be too far away from it, they settled on going to the resort town of Buffalo, at the other end of New York State.

The nucleus of the Syncopators that had stayed together were unfortunate enough to reach Buffalo during the autumn of 1930, just as the Depression was really beginning to bite, and just as hot bands were going out of fashion.

As he tried to build up and maintain the new band, Jimmie found work desperately scarce. Musicians he had found would leave to join lesser bands with steady work. It helped a bit that he could play almost every instrument in the band, enabling him to fill in some of the gaps in his line-up himself until a replacement could be found.

He kept a meticulous list of promising young players, and as things slowly improved and his band got offered better jobs, he would send for them to join him. Trombonist Russell Bowles, whom he found working in a Buffalo theatre band, came in to replace Jimmie himself during one of his stints filling in on trombone, and at around the same time he brought in another Fisk graduate, Earl Carruthers, to play baritone sax.

He found two fine trumpeters – Eddie Thompkins, a native of Kansas City who had played in various local bands and graduated from the University of Iowa somewhere in between, and nineteen-year-old Tommy Stevenson from Pittsburgh, the first of his line of high-note trumpet men.

According to Sy Oliver, it was Tommy Stevenson who had the idea of the trumpet section waving derby mutes in unison in front of and around their horns, an idea later borrowed and used incessantly by Glenn Miller. The only trouble, said Sy, was that all the trumpet section would remember to do the routine except Tommy himself.

Sy Oliver joined the band in 1933, at around the same time as a poor reader but exciting soloist, tenor-player Joe Thomas, and now the first famous Lunceford band, no longer called the Chickasaw Syncopators, was more or less complete.

Sy, as well as being a trumpeter, had turned out to be an outstanding self-taught arranger – Jimmie had been much impressed by the scores he had been doing for a band called Zack Whyte's Chocolate Beau Brummels, which in spite of its name was successful around the eastern states from the mid-Twenties to the mid-Thirties, and had several well-known jazz names pass through it, including pianist Herman Chittison, tenorist Eddie Barefield and trombonist Vic Dickenson.

Sy himself had been born in 1910 in Battle Creek, Michigan, and the name was appropriate because he was notorious for being temperamental, hard to handle, and apt to settle arguments with his fists. However, the band felt that Jimmie would be able to handle him, being not only a strong-minded leader who knew his music, but a former athletics coach as well.

Sy it was who really set the band's style, turning it into a fluent outfit that concentrated more on section work than on soloists, and which could turn its hand to playing anything from ballads and waltzes to hot stomps. In this he had the help of Willie Smith and Eddie Wilcox, both talented arrangers as well.

Right from his first days with the band, Sy began turning out scores that became fixtures in its library – 'Swanee River', 'My Blue Heaven', 'Four Or Five Times', 'Organ Grinder's Swing', 'On The Beach At Bali Bali', 'For Dancers Only', 'Margie', 'Cheatin' On Me', 'Dream Of You' (which he also wrote), and 'By The River St Marie'. He also wrote for the band a number that Jimmie rejected because he didn't like it. Sy did, though, and later he sold it to Tommy Dorsey, who had a huge hit with it – 'Yes, Indeed!'

One odd thing about Sy's work was that, against the prevailing trend, he liked to write for the band to play in two-four time rather than four-four. Somehow, because of the expert relaxed phrasing of the band, they still sound like a swing band doing this, although drummer Jimmy Crawford was never really happy with the idea. "What's wrong with two beats?" Sy once asked him. "There's two missing," said Crawfie.

After establishing itself in Buffalo, in the spring of 1933 the band headed for New York. Jimmie and Willie Smith and Edwin Wilcox had met an agent and entrepreneur called Harold Oxley, and a deal had been arrived at whereby he would take over control of the band in exchange for finding it engagements. From then on he was effectively its owner, and Lunceford simply the front man, although still musically the boss. (The rest of the band weren't told about the change. Jimmy Crawford, who had been with Jimmie from the start, was shocked to find out years later that he had been employed by Oxley all that time, and not by Jimmie, who was simply on a salary like everyone else.)

Oxley got the band a series of bookings at the Lafayette Theatre in Harlem, and they were an immediate success. (After arriving in New York Jimmie rarely played any of his instruments again, having decided he was not good enough for his band. As did Sy Oliver about six years later, relinquishing his trumpet to concentrate on arranging.)

In May 1933 they were invited to make a couple of test recordings by Columbia. The numbers they chose, a rip-roaring helter-skelter called 'Flaming Reeds And Screaming Brass', and a slow number called 'While Love Lasts' (the first half sugary sweet and the second half lightly swinging) seem well-chosen to demonstrate the band's range and versatility, but for some reason Columbia decided not to offer them a contract, and the tests were not released until LP's came out years later.

It was, however, their great good fortune that Irving Mills was looking for a band to follow Cab Calloway into the Cotton Club. Duke was not available, and the appearance on the scene of a polished band like Lunceford's, which could play any of the types of number liable to be required for a show, was good fortune all round.

The band set off on an extended tour of New England, returning to open at the Cotton Club in January 1934. Its engagement there lasted for eight months, complete with air-time, and it built up a considerable reputation, to the relief of the club management, who had been extremely dubious about this unknown and relatively untried band.

They were so happy with it, in fact, that they invited it back to do the spring show of 1935, again beginning in January. This was the show that introduced the dance Truckin' (and the song that went with it), and by the middle of that year the band had become so successful that the *Amsterdam News*, Harlem's weekly newspaper, commented, "Lunceford-Lunceford-Lunceford. That's all you hear in Harlem now."

It was at around this time that a struggling young team of would-be songwriters, Saul Chaplin and Sammy Cahn, were asked to write a speciality number for the band. The number they came up with, 'Rhythm Is Our Business', became the team's first-ever success and the band's signature tune. Chaplin and Cahn went on to write more songs for Lunceford, for the Casa Loma, and for Andy Kirk and his Clouds Of Joy.

The song they wrote for Andy Kirk was 'Until The Real Thing Comes Along', and that was an even bigger hit than 'Rhythm Is Our Business', but their biggest came in 1937 when they adapted an old Yiddish folk-song, 'Bei Mir Bist Du Schon'. This became a million-seller for the Andrews Sisters and went on to be recorded by the Casa Loma, Chick Webb and Benny Goodman.

On the back of their success at the Cotton Club, the Lunceford band would spend the rest of the Thirties touring all over America (and once to Sweden, in 1937), although, being black, it obtained very few well-paid or prestigious engagements and few, if any, residencies. This meant a lot of hard work and long gruelling distances travelled for very little financial reward.

Gradually over the years the band got better and better, the rhythm getting ever stronger and more laid back, and the sections playing ever more tightly together (they took great delight in ribbing each other, the brass cheering if the saxes made a mistake, or vice versa).

The personnel changed only slowly. One of the first to go, early in 1935, had been star trumpeter Tommy Stevenson, whose high-note work was getting such applause that he demanded equal billing with the band and, not getting it, he quit, never to be quite such a big star again.

He was replaced by Paul Webster, a Kansas City trumpeter who had worked briefly for Jimmie in 1931, but not playing high notes. He soon mastered the upper register, however, and was a more than adequate replacement for Tommy – not quite so flamboyant and exciting, but rather more musical. He can be heard to good effect on the band's recording of 'For Dancers Only'.

In 1935 the trombone section was increased to three by the arrival of Eddie Durham (trombonist, guitarist and arranger), who shortly would be such an important part of the new band on the scene, Count Basie's. His arrangements used by Jimmie include 'Oh, Boy!', 'Hittin' The Bottle', 'Harlem Shout' and 'Lunceford Special'. When he left in 1937 to join Basie his place was taken by a member of the Earl Hines band, Trummy Young, who by now had developed into a singer as well as a trombonist.

The Lunceford band was always fond of vocals, not only ballads by clarinetist-altoist Dan Grissom (unkindly known in some quarters as 'Dan Gruesome'), but jivier numbers sung by Willie Smith, by trombonist Henry Wells, or by Sy Oliver, who had not much voice, but a pleasant rhythmic way of phrasing. And sometimes by the three of them chanting together, as on numbers like 'My Blue Heaven'.

Trummy had not much voice either, but his quiet laid-back delivery, sung almost in an undertone, was very effective and popular. He even worked on the writing of some of his numbers, notably 'Tain't What You Do (It's The Way That You Do It)', which he co-composed with Sy Oliver.

In 1939 Sy Oliver left to join Tommy Dorsey (who could offer a much higher salary than Jimmie would ever be able to), and although the decline didn't set in all at once, the band began to flounder. At times during the next two years, trying to keep the band's personal sound alive and developing, Jimmie would have as many as eight arrangers on the payroll at once, but their scores were mainly forgettable and the morale of the band began to suffer.

Up till then they had been held together by a strong co-operative pride, in spite of the low salaries which were all Jimmie could afford. But once the music began to lose its edge, the pride began to crumble, and the former stalwarts began to leave.

Sy Oliver may have been right when he said that part of Jimmie's problem was that he had gone out of his way originally to hire intelligent musicians. "But so many of the guys were so intelligent that, as they matured, they realized there were other things in life more worthwhile than traveling all year and living in bad hotels."

Gerald Wilson, who had replaced Sy Oliver in the trumpet section left. So did Trummy Young, off to lead a band of his own. And worst of all, in 1942 Willie Smith left to work in the white band formed by Charlie Spivak. The next year even Jimmy Crawford left, to go and work in a small band led by Ben Webster.

Lunceford carried on through the war years, but his spark had gone. He allowed the repertory of the band to deteriorate badly, recycling the band's old hits in ever-poorer re-creations, using exactly the same charts. It had acquired a serious case of the most deadly ailment that can attack a swing band – formula.

Some people feel that by the beginning of 1947 it was beginning to show faint signs of recovery, with an influx of new musicians and a new recording contract, albeit with a very minor label called Majestic, but in July that year Jimmie suffered a heart-attack and died while doing an autograph-signing session in Seaside, Oregon.

The band struggled on under the joint leadership of tenor-player Joe Thomas and of pianist Edwin Wilcox, who had stuck with the band to the end, but in 1950 it folded, and only the records remain to tell us how good the most polished swing band of them all was in its heyday.

CHAPTER 12

white bands of the thirties

When Bob Crosby left the Dorsey Brothers' band in 1935, at the suggestion of Cork O'Keefe, it was to lead a band made up mostly of musicians who had recently quit working for Ben Pollack. The nine ex-Pollack men were Yank Lawson (trumpet), Joe Harris (trombone), Matty Matlock and Gil Rodin (clarinets and altos), Eddie Miller (clarinet and tenor), Deane Kincaide (tenor), Gil Bowers (piano), Nappy Lamare (guitar) and Ray Bauduc, whom Pollack had hired as a drummer so that he himself could move out front and act like a band-leader.

In 1934, during the few months between leaving Pollack and acquiring Bob Crosby, it was mainly the serious and capable Gil Rodin who had held the band together. He was its musical director, and this was his real value to it, because although he sat in the reed section playing clarinet and alto, he never became any more capable of soloing than he had been back in the Ben Pollack days. In 1940, when *Down Beat* began publishing transcribed solos by famous jazz musicians, the Crosby band, as an in-joke, got the magazine to print a "special" solo by Gil Rodin. The first twelve bars of it consisted of a single held note.

After they left Ben Pollack, the band had come to New York to struggle for work. Gil Rodin managed to get them a radio series, "The Kellogg College Prom", for which they were led by Red Nichols (Rodin knew that he himself was no leader), and they also recorded ten sides backing a wealthy singer from Alabama, whose real name was Frank Tennille, but who worked under the name of Clark Randall.

Then, in 1935, with the sudden success of Benny Goodman, they all realised that they were in a good position to set up as a name band themselves. The question was, whose name? They thought of their old colleague Jack Teagarden, who at that time was playing in the Paul Whiteman band. Jack liked the idea, but suddenly realised that his contract with Whiteman wouldn't allow it.

Gil Rodin went to see Cork O'Keefe at the Rockwell-O'Keefe agency. He told him that the band was proposing to form itself into a co-operative and was looking for representation. Cork said he would be happy to represent them. He liked the co-operative idea, and suggested that the stockholders in the corporation be the band members, his office, and the leader, whoever that turned out to be.

He suggested three names – Johnny Davis, who was a scat-singer with Fred Waring's Pennsylvanians; Harry Goldfield, a rather corny trumpeter with Paul Whiteman; and the singer with the Dorsey Brothers, Bob Crosby. Gil had met Bob when he'd been to see the Dorsey Brothers at the Palais Royale, and had liked him. So Bob it was, and he turned out to be a fine front-man. He had a delightful sense of humour, and was popular with customers and musicians alike.

As well as Gil Rodin, the band had at least two other talented arrangers, Deane Kincaide and Matty Matlock, and because Ben Pollack had gone out of his way to hire jazz musicians, the Crosby band had from its beginning a swinging style of its own, a sort of big-band dixieland, extensively featuring numbers from the previous decade.

This was quite a bold policy because, fashion being what it is, the music of the Twenties was regarded as corn on the cob by the young fans of the Swing Era. Rodin and his colleagues were among the first to realise that the jazz repertory had permanent value, and they did a lot to prepare the way for the jazz revival that was to come along at the end of the Thirties.

The band's ability to play jazz-flavoured numbers was helped by the fact that no fewer than four of its twelve members came from New Orleans – Matty Matlock, Eddie Miller, Nappy Lamare and Ray Bauduc.

Its three non-Pollack members were trumpeter Andy Ferretti, trombonist Artie Foster and, most importantly, bassist Bob Haggart. Haggart was a strong player, one of the first bassists to play solos, and his arrangements and compositions did much to give the band its style and success. Among his numbers were 'My Inspiration' and 'I'm Free' (later retitled 'What's New?').

He and drummer Ray Bauduc would also provide the band with one of its biggest hits (and certainly its most unexpected), a duet by Haggart (playing bass and whistling) and Bauduc (drumming both on his drums and on Haggart's bass-strings). The composition, one of their own, was called 'The Big Noise From Winnetka', and was one of those pieces, like Coleman Hawkins's 'Body And Soul', that had been used in live performance as a bit of light relief or an encore,

then got recorded on the end of a recording session, got released, and caught the public fancy.

Bob Crosby sang with the band fairly often, and although mostly he recorded rather dire pop songs, he was a better singer than he has been credited with being. He had a natural singing voice at least as good as Bing's (slightly richer, if anything, and with the same easy, approachable delivery), but never seems to have made much effort to develop it (for instance, he had an interesting vibrato, but never got it properly under control). Possibly he was only too well aware that he could only ever be regarded as a copy of his staggeringly popular elder brother.

Besides, he was an amiable character, and not greatly ambitious. This was probably why he made such a success of leading the same band that Pollack had had such difficulty with. He just let them get on with it, and enjoyed their music. As they did. There is a feeling of enjoyment in the Bob Crosby band's playing that no other swing band achieved. Others were musically more ambitious (although rarely more talented), but few seemed to have quite such a good time.

The co-operative nature of the band is highlighted by the number of its members (besides Bob Haggart) who composed numbers for it. For instance, 'Loopin' The Loop' (Nappy Lamare), 'Air Mail Stomp' (Gil Rodin), 'The Big Crash From China' (Ray Bauduc), 'Five Point Blues' (Yank Lawson), 'Big Foot Jump' (pianist Bob Zurke, who would join in 1936), and the band's signature tune, 'South Rampart Street Parade' (Haggart, Bauduc, Crosby).

Several of them too were singers, besides their leader – Joe Harris, for instance, on the band's record of 'Beale Street Blues', Eddie Miller on 'It Was Only A Dream', and Nappy Lamare on a dozen sides, notably 'Milk Cow Blues'.

The first New York engagement that Cork

O'Keefe got the band was at the Hotel New Yorker, early in 1936. Its drive and enthusiasm won it immediate approval from both public and critics (always excepting the few who regarded its two-beat style as old-fashioned, and even they tended to criticise the band's musical taste, not the talented musicians in it).

From the New Yorker it went across town to the Silver Grill of the Hotel Lexington, and there Kay Weber joined them as their girl singer. There too they changed their pianist. Being the close-knit band it was, the Crosby band changed its personnel less than any other big band (with the possible exception of Duke Ellington during the Thirties), but Gil Bowers left and was replaced by a top jazz pianist and old associate of the Austin High School Gang, Joe Sullivan.

He joined in May 1936, and whether or not the two events are connected, it was during the previous month that the band had recorded its first two out-and-out dixieland sides, Kid Ory's 'Muskrat Ramble' and a new number, 'Dixieland Shuffle', both arranged by Bob Haggart.

These sold well, and led to the band making many others, although it should be remembered that such numbers accounted for less than forty of its recorded sides out of a total of well over three hundred. Many of the rest were rather dismal pop-sings of the day, sung by Bob Crosby, or whoever was the band's current girl singer (Kay Weber was followed by Marion Mann, Teddy Grace and others).

There were also quite a few numbers that were straightforward swing, such as 'For Dancers Only' and 'Christopher Columbus', and in June 1936 they accompanied the fourteen-year-old Judy Garland on her first-ever record session. The two sides they made that day were 'Stompin' At The Savoy' and 'Swing, Mister Charlie'.

Joe Sullivan, as well as being a swinging pianist,

was a big, powerfully-built man, but unfortunately he had contracted tuberculosis, and in December 1936 had to go into hospital. He was sent to the Dore Sanatorium in North Moravia, California, and was to remain there for ten months, his place in the band being taken by the hard-drinking, hard-driving pianist Bob Zurke.

Zurke, whose real name was Boguslaw Albert Zukowski, was from Detroit, where he had been born in 1912. His wild, blues-influenced stomping playing added even more excitement to the band on such numbers as 'Little Rock Getaway'.

All was not plain sailing for a band sounding just that bit different. Towards the end of 1937 they toured across America to appear the the Palomar in Los Angeles. They were accompanied on the bill by a chorus-line with the unromantic name of the Hudson-Metzger Girls, and got a lukewarm reception.

At around this time they fell out with the Rockwell-O'Keefe agency, having a difference of opinion with them about their charges, and signed with the powerful Music Corporation of America. MCA immediately booked them into their top New York spot, the Hotel Pennsylvania. Unfortunately Benny Goodman had just finished a highly successful run there, and again they were received with little enthusiasm.

Then things began to pick up. They played an engagement at the Blackhawk Restaurant in Chicago, and were lifted by enthusiastic audiences to play at the top of their form. At around the same time their record of their signature tune, 'South Rampart Street Parade', recorded in November 1937, became a hit, and they were on their way.

With the success of its dixieland numbers, and influenced by the examples of Benny Goodman and Tommy Dorsey, the Crosby band too established its band-within-a-band. The Bobcats was much more of a New Orleans-style jazz band than either the Goodman small groups or the Clambake Seven, although it usually departed from the classic New Orleans front line of three instruments – trumpet, trombone and clarinet. The Bobcats tended to have four, the fourth being tenorist Eddie Miller.

Miller was from New Orleans himself, and his style of playing was somewhere between Coleman Hawkins and Bud Freeman. He had the fire and attack of Hawkins, but the smooth tone of Freeman, and it is a tribute to his musicianship that he was the first to find a way of improvising a fourth voice in the traditional line-up without muddying up the overall sound.

The Bobcats were usually led by the fiery trumpet of Yank Lawson, and its clarinetist was the fluent and driving Matty Matlock. The two played well together, weaving around each other's improvisations and spurring each other on, but in 1938 Matlock decided to play less, and devote more of his time to doing arrangements for the band, and his place as lead clarinetist was taken by a newcomer, also from New Orleans (and from the Pollack band), Irving Fazola.

His real name was Irving Henry Prestopnik, and he took the name "Fazola" from three notes of the tonic sol-fa. Born in 1912, he studied C-melody saxophone and clarinet from the age of thirteen, and from his later teens played professionally with local New Orleans bands including those of Louis Prima and Sharkey Bonano, before coming north and joining Ben Pollack in 1935. Among several other bands he had played in before joining Crosby was the band newly-formed by Glenn Miller in 1937.

His tone was warmer and less driving than Matty Matlock's and he tended to sound best on the band's slower numbers, like 'My Inspiration', although on the fast ones he could at times easily

be mistaken for Benny Goodman.

Faz was all music. Once, when he was with the Pollack band, the car he was in, driving the 150 miles from Indianapolis to Evansville, Indiana, skidded into a ditch in rain and poor visibility, and rolled over. Faz, who was no lightweight, was flung clear. Trumpeter Shorty Sherock hurried over to him and saw he had a nasty gash on the head and was bleeding badly. "Everything all right, Faz?" he said. Faz pulled his clarinet out of its shattered case. "I think so," he said, "but I won't be sure until I've tried it out with a new reed." And he sat there in the rain blowing scales.

In August 1938 came near-disaster when Tommy Dorsey hired away Yank Lawson (and Charlie Spivak) from the band's trumpet section. Yank had been with the band since the Pollack days, and provided it with much of its drive, and his defection was a blow.

Fortunately the band still had a considerable trumpeter in the person of Billy Butterfield, who had joined the previous February. Butterfield, a cheerful roly-poly young man from Ohio (he was born in 1917), could not only play a powerful lead but also beautiful slow ballads. In August 1939 George Simon wrote in *Metronome* that Butterfield was "the greatest all-around trumpeter in jazz today", a remark he received some ribbing for from fellow-writers, but which in later years he still felt was pretty well justified.

Great all-around trumpeter or not, the fact remained that not even Butterfield could inspire the band like Yank Lawson had. Over the next two years it became more and more pedestrian and uninspired. In 1939 it took over the band spot on the *Camel Caravan* radio series, featuring its then-vocalist, Dorothy Claire, as well as Benny Goodman's original singer, Helen Ward, and a third singer who also acted as MC, Johnny Mercer.

Johnny Mercer, one of the all-time great

lyricists of popular music, had been born in Savannah, Georgia, in 1909. Although he enjoyed popular songs (and could remember all the words of both verse and chorus), he had no intention of working in that field until, in 1927, the real estate business his father was a partner in went bust. The next year Johnny headed for New York, leading a precarious existence as a bit-part actor while struggling to establish himself as a lyric-writer.

He eventually succeeded so well that he wrote words for a string of eminent composers, including Hoagy Carmichael, Jerome Kern, Harold Arlen and Duke Ellington. His songs, in every vein from romantic to romping, include 'Laura', 'Goody Goody', 'Jeepers Creepers', 'Tangerine', 'Skylark', 'You Were Never Lovelier', 'That Old Black Magic', 'Jubilation T. Cornpone', 'Satin Doll', 'The Days Of Wine And Roses', 'Moon River' and 'Too Marvellous For Words'.

The line-up of the band, so stable for so long, began to change. Bob Zurke left in 1939 to form his own group, and Joe Sullivan came back. But he still wasn't a well man and in October, after a short stay, he left and was replaced by Jess Stacy, who had finally had enough of being badgered by Benny Goodman.

The difference between the fun-loving Crosby band and the Goodman band, with Benny's constant search for perfection, is well illustrated in a story Stacy himself told. "Between each set he [Benny] had me pounding A's on the piano so the saxes and the trumpets could be perfectly in tune. When I went with the Crosby band I had that habit of pounding A's between sets. Bob looked at me and said, 'If you keep pounding that A, I'm going to give you your five years' notice.'"

Although Stacy could swing, his piano style was nowhere near as hard-driving as that of Sullivan or Zurke, but his ability to play thoughtful impressionistic numbers did add an effective strain to the band's repertoire in such numbers as 'Ec-Stacy'.

Throughout 1940 the band relied more and more on its singers, and a constant stream of them passed through the band – Doris Day, Gloria DeHaven and Kay Starr all did short spells, and there was a rather poor vocal group, an imitation of Tommy Dorsey's Pied Pipers, called the Bob-o-Links.

The trumpet section, still missing Yank Lawson, had in it from time to time such Swing Era stalwarts as Zeke Zarchy, Sterling Bose, Shorty Sherock and Bob Peck, and for the last three months of 1940 the great cornetist, Muggsy Spanier, who the year before had recorded sixteen small-band sides that almost single-handedly kicked into life the jazz revival of the Forties and Fifties.

In the middle of 1941, Yank Lawson left the Tommy Dorsey band (after recording with it such fine numbers as 'Milneberg Joys' and 'Hawaiian War Chant') and came back. At around the same time, from the Charlie Barnet band, came another powerful and exuberant trumpeter, Lyman Vunk.

This gave the band a new lease of life. They stopped backing singers or trying to sound like the other swing bands. The Bob-o-Links left and for a few months the band was its old self again. Then, on December 7, the Japanese attacked Pearl Harbor.

America entered the war, and the men in the bands began to be called up. In 1942, Ray Bauduc and Gil Rodin were both drafted, and several of the other men enlisted.

Bob Crosby could see his band disintegrating, and when, in the same year, he was offered a chance to go to Hollywood and become a movie actor, he told the band that he was going to take the chance and suggested that they make Eddie Miller the new leader of the band. They agreed,

Bob left, and then Eddie Miller was drafted. And that, for the time being, was the end of the Bob Crosby band.

A band that was even more fun to be in than Bob Crosby's was the one led by Rowland Bernart "Bunny" Berigan. One of his trumpeters, Johnny Napton, said "It was a laughing band. You couldn't wait to get on the stand and play." And trombonist Ray Conniff said that his time in the band was "one continuous good time, like a non-stop party". Unfortunately Bunny was so amiable and irresponsible that his band (or bands, because he had several serious goes at being a leader) didn't survive long.

By 1936, when he was still a sideman, he had earned a reputation with musicians and fans alike as the best trumpet-player of the Swing Era. He had played with the Dorsey Brothers and with Benny Goodman, who said that his playing "was like a bolt of electricity running through the whole band. He just lifted the whole thing." In fact he was so popular that he won the 1936 *Metronome* trumpet poll with five times as many votes as his nearest competitor.

With such a reputation, it was natural that Bunny would start thinking of leading a band of his own. Tommy Dorsey and he had become friends in the early Thirties, possibly in Plunkett's bar, and Tommy suggested to him that he sit in with his band for a few weeks, as an extra trumpet-man and special soloist, and study what running a band involved. Then, when he felt ready, Tommy's manager, Art Michaud, would help him form his own band.

Which is more or less what happened. Bunny joined Tommy at around the end of 1936, and at the same time started to make records under his own name with bands assembled for the occasion, trying out musicians and arrangements.

By the beginning of 1937 he had assembled an eleven-piece band. He went into the studios with it on January 22 and recorded four titles, including Edgar Sampson's 'Blue Lou', written for Chick Webb.

At this time he was still contracted to make one more record date with Tommy, and a week later he went into the studios to fulfil his commitment. That day he recorded two trumpet solos that were among the best he ever did – 'Song Of India' and 'Marie'. You get the feeling that he was brimming over with confidence and optimism.

In February he went back into the studios with his eleven-piece band and recorded four more titles, but he realised that it wasn't as good as he wanted, so he started replacing musicians, and by April was making his live debut as a bandleader at the Pennsylvania Roof in New York with a fourteen-piece band, only three of whom, besides himself, were from the previous band.

He also got a recording contract with Victor, and for them over the next two-and-a-half years he would produce the best of his recorded work, numbers like 'Frankie And Johnny', 'Mahogany Hall Stomp', 'Little Gate's Special', and his famous theme 'I Can't Get Started', with its trumpet cadenza at the start, reminiscent of Louis Armstrong's opening to 'West End Blues'.

Louis himself was so enamoured of it that three years later, in 1940, he went into the Harlem record shop run by Danish aristocrat and jazz fan Timme Rosenkrantz and bought five more copies to replace his worn out one. Timme asked him, "Why don't you play this lovely tune, Louis?" "No," said Louis. "That's Bunny's. It belongs to him. You just don't touch that one since he made it."

Outstanding among the newcomers to Bunny's new band were Chicago drummer George Wettling, who spent most of his working life in small jazz groups but had just been in Artie Shaw's first band, a good pianist/arranger called

Joe Lippman, who would go on to join Jimmy Dorsey, and an exciting eighteen-year-old tenor-player named George Auld.

Originally from Toronto, Auld had moved to New York with his family in 1929. He had started out on alto, and in 1931 won the Rudy Wiedoeft Scholarship to study with that musician. Then he heard Coleman Hawkins, came under his spell, and switched to the tenor. He came to Bunny from leading his own small band at Nick's, the famous dixieland tavern that was then at 140 Seventh Avenue South. Auld would go on to play with Artie Shaw and to lead his own big band, and in 1977 would provide Al Pacino's tenor-playing for (and appear in) the film *New York, New York*.

Bunny had a talent for spotting talent, which is one of the essentials for a good bandleader, but he was lacking most of the others. He was terrific as a sideman, as a soloist, as a friend, and as a drinking companion. Music to him was fun, and everybody in his band loved him, but he was totally disorganised. One night he turned up with his band to play a Saturday-night date in Bristol, Connecticut, only to find Gene Krupa's band already on the stand. It turned out they were supposed to be in Bridgeport, forty miles away.

He also had no idea of discipline, not that he didn't make an effort from time to time. George Auld recalled one occasion late in 1938. Life on the road could be hard, and the girl with the band, Jayne Dover, who was quite a good singer with a touch of Mildred Bailey in her voice, was finding the going rough. One night, as they got onto the bus, the only seat left was next to her.

Trumpeter Johnny Napton, who had just joined the band, tried to sit in it and she wouldn't let him, so he started swearing at her. She got up and ran off the bus and Bunny hobbled after her. He hobbled not only because he'd just had more than a few but also because he'd recently fallen

over and broken his ankle, so he had one foot in a cast and was walking with a cane.

"I can't take this any more!" Jayne Dover told him. "All this rotten language, this foul-mouthed talk. I'm through." Bunny talked her back onto the bus, then gripped the post beside the driver and started furiously addressing the seated band. As he spoke, he banged the pole with his cane for emphasis. The cane broke, and this made him madder then ever. "I've had it!" he shouted. "All this language, and the girl singer wants to quit the band, and you're hanging me up in the middle of a string of one-nighters without a girl singer! Now I want to get one thing straight! The first motherfucker that curses on this bus is automatically through!"

The band laughed of course, but Bunny continued, "Well, I didn't mean to put it that way, but I'm serious. I don't want to hear another foul word out of any of you as long as Jayne is sitting on this bus."

He obviously meant it, and the band became very subdued. For about the next 250 miles there wasn't a sound out of anyone. People were even lighting their cigarettes quietly so as not to upset Bunny. Then, at about daybreak, pianist Joe Bushkin came rushing to the front of the bus from his seat at the back. He turned to face all the half-asleep band, including Jayne and Bunny, and yelled, "I can't stand it any longer!" followed by a torrent of profanity that included every bad word he knew and quite a few he'd just thought of. Jayne Dover only stayed with the band for a couple of months.

Bunny continued to find good musicians – Joe Bushkin was one. And Buddy Rich, whose parents were vaudevillians and who had been drumming and tap-dancing on-stage from the age of four, got his first big-band job with Bunny. He would go on to drum for Harry James, Artie Shaw, Benny Carter and Tommy Dorsey before forming the first of his own bands (he went back with Harry James from 1953 to 1966 and entered the Guinness Book of Records in the Sixties as the highest-paid sideman to date, earning $75,000 a year).

Ray Conniff, aged 22, got his first break in the music business when he joined Bunny as a trombonist in early 1938 (getting $60 a week). He already had ambitions as an arranger, and would go on to arrange for Bob Crosby, Artie Shaw and Harry James. He offered Bunny a couple of his arrangements. Bunny liked them and the band began playing them every night. After a while Ray asked if he was going to get paid for them and how much? He and Bunny settled on $35 apiece, but time went by and still he didn't get paid. Every time he raised the matter Bunny would up the price, first to $50, then four more times. But Ray never actually received a cent.

In spite of all the talent he assembled, Bunny was too disorganised for the band ever to sound as good as it might have done, and gradually it became clear that with all the partying and inattention to business, it was not an economic proposition. Bunny began drinking even more heavily ("Bring on the dancing team" was his call for Haig & Haig), and his health began to suffer. In November 1939 he spent ten days in New York City Hospital, delirious and with his joints swollen with oedema. At the end of the month he was out and on the wagon, and the band made one more recording date for Victor. It was to be its last, because early in 1940 Bunny gave up and disbanded.

Almost at once Tommy Dorsey invited him back into his band (Joe Bushkin and Buddy Rich were already there). Bunny went, and played brilliantly, bringing new life into the band at a time when it was mostly restricting itself to accompanying Frank Sinatra. An outstanding example of his playing during this period is 'I'm Nobody's Baby', recorded in April 1940.

But after six months Bunny began to get restless. He left Tommy in August, complaining that he was not getting enough opportunity to play, and that he was fed up of being used by Tommy to lead the band while Tommy hobnobbed with the customers at their tables.

He formed another band, composed entirely of unknowns, and while it had lift and drive, and Bunny was playing as well as ever, it didn't last. Bunny was drinking heavily again (partly in depression over the death of his father), and his unhealthy life, with all the drinking and the one-nighters, began to catch up with him again. He began visibly to lose weight and the spark slowly went out of his playing. Late in 1941 he turned the band over to trumpeter Pee Wee Irwin, who had been his replacement in both the Goodman and Tommy Dorsey bands, and was declared bankrupt.

Doggedly he formed yet another band, and carried on trying, unwilling to let down either his musicians, or his wife and two small children. But by now his health was shot. At an appearance in Pennsylvania, for instance, he collapsed with pneumonia and had to be taken into hospital.

On July 1, 1942, his band was booked to appear at Manhattan Center in New York. The band showed, but Bunny didn't. He was seriously ill in Polyclinic Hospital with cirrhosis of the liver. Benny Goodman, appearing at the Paramount Theatre, brought his sextet to the Manhattan Center and filled in as a gesture of friendship for his first star trumpeter. The next day, Bunny died, with his friend Tommy Dorsey at his bedside. He was thirty-three.

Bunny had been the first of the ex-Goodman sidemen to form his own band, but he was by no means the last. More major bandleaders came out of the Goodman band than out of any other.

The next after Bunny, and a couple of years later, was Gene Krupa. Gene had been born in Chicago in 1909, so was a little younger than members of the Austin High School gang like Bud Freeman and Eddie Condon. The only musician around who was younger than him (by about four or five months) seemed to be Benny Goodman.

Gene's family were poor and Polish and Catholic. None was musical, and Gene was the youngest child – a late child – with two elder sisters, the oldest twenty-three years older than him, and six brothers. As the youngest, he was the apple of his mother's eye, and when he became interested in music it was mostly she who encouraged him.

As a teenager, he briefly studied the alto sax, but while still at school he got a part-time job as a soda-jerk in a small dance-hall. He got fascinated by what the drummer in the band was playing, and started sneaking up onto the stand to play the drums between sets. One of his elder brothers, Pete, bought him a set of drums of his own, and that was the end of his interest in school-work.

Many of his brothers and sisters were discouraging, especially the ones who had already married and settled down. Their attitude was, if he doesn't want to stay at school, why doesn't he get a proper job and earn some money? But his mother made a deal with him, over their objections. She would send him to St Joseph's College, over fifty miles away in Rensselaer, Indiana, and if he really worked there at getting some education, then still wanted go in for music, he could do so with her blessing. As being at St Joseph's would involve paying for board and lodging, this was a generous offer in a poor family.

Gene at that time was also keen on baseball, and part of the reason why his mother suggested St Joseph's was that it was strong on baseball, and she hoped that maybe that would keep him there.

It didn't. After a year he left, came back to Chicago, and started gigging around getting any small drumming jobs he could.

Being younger than Eddie Condon and the others, and being away at St Joseph's during part of 1924 and 1925 meant that Gene didn't get to hear the big heroes of the Austin High School Gang – Louis Armstrong with King Oliver, or the New Orleans Rhythm Kings. Instead, his idols became the Gang themselves and their contemporaries – Bix and Jimmy McPartland, drummers Dave Tough and George Wettling.

Somewhat to his surprise, some members of the Gang heard his drumming and liked it and made themselves known to him. They were all highly idealistic about their music, and regarded any "commercial" playing as selling out. Their ideals were so pure that Benny Goodman and Jimmy McPartland were regarded as defectors for joining the Ben Pollack band, because Ben Pollack made money, and that couldn't be right. You might as well play with a "sweet" band like Isham Jones.

Krupa, needing (like Goodman) to contribute to his family's income, was unable to hold to this high ideal, and began playing with a lot of semi-commercial bands (bands that at least had one or two hot musicians in them) like the Seattle Harmony Kings, the Hoosier Bell Hops and the Benson Orchestra of Chicago.

After work, however, he would set off somewhere with the others to jam. Usually to a grubby little speakeasy called the Goat's Nest, in a filthy old store at 222 North State Street that the young musicians renamed the Three Deuces in honour of one of Chicago's biggest whorehouses, the Four Deuces. Later this became its formal title.

At the Three Deuces the motto was "jazz for jazz's sake". The speakeasy itself was on the ground floor, and beneath it was a big dingy cellar with cement walls, unfurnished except for a beat-up old piano (a little earlier, New Orleans trumpeter Wingy Manone had led a small band there). The young jazzmen were welcome to drop in and play all night if they wanted to, with a floating audience of drinkers lured downstairs by the music. According to clarinetist Mezz Mezzrow, it was the home of the first jam sessions ever held.

Gene now began to hear the great originals – he heard Louis Armstrong and Earl Hines playing at the Sunset Cafe with the Carroll Dickerson Orchestra, which had a drummer from New Orleans called Tubby Hall. There were also two greater New Orleans drummers in town – Zutty Singleton, playing in Jimmie Noone's quintet at the Nest (later renamed the Apex Club), and Warren "Baby" Dodds, playing with his brother Johnny at Kelly's Stable.

Baby Dodds taught Gene more than all the others put together. According to Gene, he was the first great drum soloist, not only keeping time but making the drums a melodic part of jazz. He tuned his drums carefully (as Gene was to do all his life), and could play them so that you could follow the melody.

Bee Palmer, a Chicago-born vaudeville singer and dancer who had introduced the Shimmy to the New York public in 1918, used to hang around with the Gang and come to the sessions at the Three Deuces. In early 1928 she was offered a job in New York at a new night-club called the Club Richman. This was at the time when the centre of jazz was moving from Chicago to New York, and Bud Freeman and Eddie Condon were already there, trying to get in on the scene. Meeting them in Brooklyn, Bee said that she was going to tell the club manager that she'd only take the job if her band was made up of the boys from Chicago.

Eddie went back to Chicago and collected pianist Joe Sullivan, clarinetist Frank Teschemacher and Gene. Bee Palmer had given him their train fares to New York, but unfortunately she was unable to come through with the job. The manager didn't like the Chicagoans' music, and when Bee herself eventually refused to take the engagement because her pianist husband, Al Siegel, wouldn't take it with her, he turned them down with a sigh of relief.

Although by then they had made a few isolated records, none of the young Chicagoans was well-known, and with their uncompromising attitude to what they wanted to play, they found life in the big city hard. Several friends who were already there and working, like Bix and Joe Venuti and the Dorseys, saw to it that they didn't starve (just), and they somehow survived by shacking up all together in one room at a succession of cheap hotels. One would register and the rest would then sneak in.

Gradually they began to get work. Gene found a niche playing in various bands led by Red Nichols (like Benny Goodman and Jimmy Dorsey, he was in the pit bands for the two Gershwin shows, *Strike Up The Band* and *Girl Crazy*). He recorded with Nichols and his Five Pennies, and in various pick-up groups that included Coleman Hawkins, Glenn Miller, Fats Waller and Bix.

In 1931, when he was twenty-two, he left the security of the Five Pennies and spent the next four years, through the grimmest days of the Depression, playing in a succession of rather uninspiring big bands – with Irving Aaronson & his Commanders, in the band organised by Benny Goodman to back singer Russ Colombo (after which he swore he would never work with Goodman again), and with Mal Hallett, whose hard-driving New England dance-band also provided eating money for Jack Teagarden for a while. It was from Hallett's band that John

Hammond brought Gene back to Benny Goodman in 1935.

With Benny he became a star. Trim and well-built, he had dark and romantic good looks, with black hair that was slightly longer than usual in those days. Benny, while an exciting clarinetist, was far from being a strong stage personality, and in reviews of the Goodman band's performances, nine times out of ten it was Gene who got the column inches.

Fans came to know the "three Krupa faces". As described by writer Arnold Shaw, "For dreamy pop ballads his eyes got a faraway look and his lower jaw hung open loosely, as if he were in a stupor." For bouncing middle-tempo tunes that skipped along lightly, "Gene's face had the dazed look of a guy dreaming through the window of a railroad train." And for the loud, up-tempo killer-dillers "there was the ecstatic expression ... Gene's head jerked, his mouth clicked open and shut, and he would leap up, furiously thrashing his arms about." His drumming, complete with face-pulling, gum-chewing and hair flying wild, was so violently physical that it was once estimated he lost three pounds weight during every performance.

Part of this was conscious stagecraft. Gene was well aware of the importance of putting on a good show, and in contrast to the public image of him as some sort of inspired maniac, he was a careful and methodical craftsman, well known in the business as one of the few musicians who was absolutely punctual and reliable.

Nonetheless, his popular image as the wild man of swing did not endear him to Benny Goodman, and in March 1938, within two months of the Goodman band's resounding success at Carnegie Hall, they had their final row and Gene left.

He at once set about assembling a band of his own, an idea he'd been considering for some time. He found musicians, bought arrangements, and started rehearsing. He also got agents to represent him (Art Michaud and Johnny Gluskin, who were also the agents of Benny's biggest rival, Tommy Dorsey), and in less than a month he was in the Brunswick studios making his band's first four recordings. Helen Ward sat in to do the vocals, and on tenor he had the outstanding Vido Musso.

The first number they laid down, 'Grandfather's Clock', had an arrangement by Gene himself, and the next 'Prelude To A Stomp' was by the capable black arranger, Chappie Willett, who had originally prepared it for the Mills Blue Rhythm Band, and who had made the fine arrangement of "Struttin' With Some Barbecue" that Louis Armstrong's big band had recorded the previous January.

The next day Gene's band recorded two more sides, and the day after, on Saturday, April 16, it made its first public appearance in the Marine Ballroom on the Steel Pier in Atlantic City. About four thousand fans showed up, and greeted the band with wild enthusiasm. Probably no other band ever had such a successful start.

Over the next few months Gene continued to improve his personnel. Jimmy Mundy came in as chief arranger. He had done arrangements for the Earl Hines band, and later for Benny Goodman (he arranged Benny's 1936 hit, 'Swingtime In The Rockies'). Jerry Kruger, one of the first white singers to try and sound like Billie Holiday (with imperfect success), came in briefly as the first regular girl singer, but soon was replaced by Irene Daye, a rather better singer who based her style on Mildred Bailey. For a male singer Gene acquired for a while the one and only Leo Watson, the greatest scat-singer in jazz.

Leo Watson was born in Kansas City in 1898.

Working originally as a solo singer, he moved to New York in 1929 and teamed up with a small group that became famous as the Spirits of Rhythm but from time to time also recorded as the Five Cousins or the Nephews (some, if not all of them, were genuinely related to each other).

The Spirits of Rhythm played guitars, mostly of a small Spanish variety called tiples, and with Leo Watson (who also did a little drumming) their regular venue became Joe Helbock's Onyx Club on 52nd Street, where a procession of fans came to hear Leo's amazing torrents of improvised mouth-music, making great leaps from bass to falsetto and back again, and always swinging.

When Vido Musso left in October 1938, Gene acquired another useful tenor-player in Sam Donahue, who had just been leading his own band for five years, and in 1944 would take over the U.S. Navy Band from Artie Shaw and have for a couple of years a band to rival Glenn Miller.

At around the same time he acquired another Sam, also on tenor, Sam Musiker, and a little later trumpeters Shorty Sherock and Corky Cornelius. Corky and Sam Donahue became serious rivals for the hand of the attractive Irene Daye. Corky won, and when, early in 1941, he left to join the Casa Loma band (which was still going the rounds under the name of Glen Gray & the Casa Loma Orchestra), she went with him.

Her replacement was Anita O'Day, and suddenly the band began to liven up. Until then, in spite of Gene's attempts to hire the best and most promising young musicians around, he had somehow never managed to build a band with much life. In spite of the undoubted power and excitement of his own drumming, the band as a whole remained somewhat bland (a blandness emphasised in its recorded output, which tended to feature his drumming rather less than the band's live performances did, concentrating instead on far too many numbers that were either ephemeral and rubbishy, or had already been hits for other bands).

Anita was something else. Her real name was Anita Belle Colton, and she had been born in 1919 in Kansas City. She had adopted the name O'Day in her teens when she was competing in dance marathons, and began singing professionally (and playing drums a little) in Chicago clubs when she was nineteen.

Where the typical girl singer with a big band presented herself as feminine, even cute, Anita came across as a hip and knowledgeable chick with attitude. Rather than wearing ball-gowns such as other singers wore, she appeared on-stage in tailored outfits resembling the uniforms worn by the men in the band.

Her voice was crisp and musical and laid-back, and her approach to singing was also different to any band-singer before her. Instead of interpreting the lyric of a song as a sort of dramatic performance, acting out the feeling of the words, she used the words and the melody as musical raw material, improvising on the notes in an abstract way like a horn-player. (In 1942 Gene was pleased to come across a new song almost without words, called 'That's What You Think', which suited Anita's technique perfectly, and she and the band made a fine recording).

Her cool approach took audiences a little while to get used to, but with Gene's co-operation she won them over by concentrating at first on sophisticated and often humorous novelty songs. On quite a few of these songs she sang in duet with Gene's other great acquisition, Roy Eldridge, who joined the band a couple of months after she did.

David Roy "Little Jazz" Eldridge was generally regarded by musicians and fans to be the most influential trumpeter of the Thirties, as Louis

Armstrong had been in the Twenties, and as Dizzy Gillespie would be in the Forties. But whereas Dizzy was directly influenced by Roy, and indeed started out sounding rather like him, Roy was not directly influenced by Louis. At least, not at first.

Born in Pittsburgh in 1911, he began playing the trumpet professionally when he was sixteen. At that time he admired and tried to emulate the playing of Red Nichols. "I liked the nice, clean sound he was getting," he said. "I was doing all right playing in that style until I got to St Louis."

He got to St Louis in around 1927, and the trumpeters he heard there, influenced by Louis Armstrong, were playing in a much more guttural manner, using lip-trills and much vibrato. Roy began developing a rougher tone, but more importantly, he came under the influence, not of another trumpet-player, but of Coleman Hawkins. He loved Hawk's torrents of improvisation, and one exercise he set himself in those days was to learn by heart his tenor solo on Fletcher Henderson's 1926 recording of 'Stampede'.

With this and similar exercises, he set himself to perfecting a trumpet style which would have the speed and range of a saxophone. This was difficult, because the trumpet is technically a less flexible instrument than a saxophone or clarinet (also it uses more breath, so a trumpeter's phrases have to be shorter), but somehow the determined young Roy managed it.

Another difference is that a trumpet naturally plays arpeggios (the bugle-like chains of notes that are produced simply by blowing with more or less pressure, without using the valves). Players like Louis tended to construct their solos around arpeggios, but a saxophone more naturally plays scales, and players like Hawkins based their solos more on those, playing long lines of notes that suggested, rather than stating directly, the underlying harmony.

In 1930 Roy moved to New York and began playing in various bands, including the one led by Teddy Hill, but having got as far as he had, playing faster and higher than any trumpeter before him, and improvising in this new way, he was chagrined to find that with all this formidable technique there was still something missing. Somehow other less accomplished trumpeters were getting a response from audiences that he wasn't.

It was at this stage, in 1932, that he finally went to hear Louis at the Lafayette Theatre in Harlem (he'd listened to some of his records at around the same time he was learning 'Stampede' and not been much impressed). Hearing Louis he finally found the missing piece of the puzzle. What Louis was doing, but he wasn't, was giving his solos dramatic structure. He was telling a story, building his solo all the way through instead of simply playing in a straight line.

Having heard Louis at the Lafayette, Roy set about learning to put what he had found out into practice. He left New York while he did so, working in Pittsburgh and then Baltimore before returning in 1935 to rejoin Teddy Hill. His first recordings with Hill that year attracted immediate attention. He was hailed as the new thing.

In the words of Humphrey Lyttelton, "Were it not for the grotesqueness of associating the word 'philistine' with any creation of Louis Armstrong's, one could say that, in the mid-Thirties, the jazz world was waiting for a David to overthrow the Goliath that Armstrong's decade-long domination represented. The diminutive Roy Eldridge, ambitious, bursting with a sense of his own ability and scared of no-one when it came to a musical fight, had just the temperament to fill the role."

Towards the end of 1935 he joined Fletcher Henderson, staying with him for about a year before beginning to lead a series of small bands of his own, playing various residencies. Mostly these were around New York, but it was when both his band and the Krupa band were in Chicago early in 1941 that he and Gene got talking and Roy suddenly said, "Hey, I'd like to play with your band." "Would you?" said Gene in surprise. "Yeah, I would." And that was that. Roy folded up his little band, and in April 1941 Gene was overjoyed to have the most electrifying trumpeter in the game join him.

Naturally, Roy at once became the star of the band, not only playing the trumpet and singing, but occasionally sitting in on drums (which he also played well) when Gene wanted to lead the band from the front.

With Roy and Anita in it, the band roared to new heights of success. Almost as soon as Roy had joined they recorded their famous vocal duet 'Let Me Off Uptown', and within the next two weeks Roy had recorded a pyrotechnic version of 'After You've Gone', and a magnificent slow Benny Carter arrangement of Hoagy Carmichael's 'Rockin' Chair', on which he both played and sang.

Gene later recalled the recording of 'Rockin' Chair'. "It was a rough date," he said. "We were playing at the Pennsylvania Hotel, and we had to make quite a few takes. You can imagine how hard it was on Roy's chops. He finally made it, though. But to show you how conscientious a guy Roy was, we played the tune again that night at the hotel and this time Roy missed the ending. I looked at him and I could see big tears in his eyes. Then I looked at his lip – it looked like a raw hamburger."

Roy and Gene developed a close and understanding relationship. As Roy once said, "Gene never turns or glares at you if you have a bad lip or hit a bum note. He just lets you play the way you know best. He never drives you."

For some reason, Roy never developed anything like a close relationship with Anita O'Day.

The tensions between them eventually became so bad that it started to affect the whole band, and it was something of a relief all round when Anita left around the end of 1942 to get married and, a year later, to join Stan Kenton.

It was only a few weeks after she left the band that disaster struck. Gene was arrested on a charge of possessing marijuana. Whether or not he ever actually smoked marijuana is not clear, it would hardly be surprising if he did, because it wasn't even illegal in the U.S.A. until around 1937, and many musicians, including Louis Armstrong, smoked it habitually.

In Gene's case, however, what is clear is that the stuff he was arrested for possessing wasn't even his. A valet whom he had just fired, on his way out of the theatre where the band was playing, slipped it into Gene's topcoat pocket in his dressing-room. The cops, who used to hang around the most famous bands looking for such evidence, saw him do it, and waited. As bad luck would have it, a young fan offered to help Gene out as a temporary valet, and carried the coat for Gene to his hotel, where the cops pounced. Using a minor to transport dope.

Gene was immediately arrested and spent ninety-four days in gaol. (When his appeal came up eighteen months later, the valet, who had cooled off, cleared Gene of even knowing that the dope was in his coat, and he was finally exonerated.)

The immense publicity that the arrest generated did Gene's reputation no harm at all. A year later, in January 1944, he was voted top drummer in the annual *Metronome* readers' poll, capturing more votes than all the next ten in the list put together. But by then he had no band. Leaderless while he was in gaol, it had folded.

Set adrift, Gene eventually (and hesitantly) accepted an offer from Benny Goodman to rejoin him. He tried out the idea by playing a few USO shows with Benny, and the reception he got from the servicemen was so enthusiastic that he did rejoin, just as the band was beginning a two-month stay at the Hotel New Yorker.

After the two months, as Benny's band set off on the road, Gene made a sudden decision to take up another offer and became Tommy Dorsey's drummer. Tommy was appearing at the Paramount Theatre. In a review in *Down Beat* of the band's performance there, Frank Stacy wrote, "As for Krupa, his drumming is amazing. No other white drummer can compare with him in technical virtuosity, savage intensity, and feeling."

But more sensational than such reviews was the reaction of the first-night audience. As the bandstand rose into view, they had no idea that Gene would be on drums. On seeing and hearing him, the surprised whispers grew into a torrent of cheering, whistling and clapping, and the whole house stood to applaud him. Tommy motioned Gene to take a bow, and he stood up, still drumming, and crying like a child.

He was still with Dorsey in mid-1944 when his acquittal came through. This gave him a new lease of life and he left Tommy and formed a new band of his own, with a string section in it (following Tommy's example). Strings did not really sit with the Krupa style, and no more successful was his new idea of spending a lot of time out in front of the band, in tails, conducting. "I guess I must have had the idea I was Kostelanetz or something," he said later.

Gradually the band got into better shape. Over the next few years Gene fired the strings, went back behind his drums, and hired two very rhythmic bop-oriented singers, Buddy Stewart and Dave Lambert. With them the band recorded the first bop scat record, 'What's This?', pointing the way forward to such groups as Lambert,

Hendricks and Ross.

He acquired a good bop-influenced tenor-player, Charlie Ventura, who as a band-leader in the late Forties would have some success in making bop accessible to the dancing public. And with Roy Eldridge gone, Anita O'Day came back for a spell, making the band swing even harder. With her, they even made a couple of records that sold well, 'Boogie Blues' and 'Opus One'.

But by now it was 1947, and swing was a stale potato. Gene struggled to keep his band together and to incorporate the new sounds. He hired a hip young baritone player called Gerry Mulligan, and together they wrote some "modern" arrangements for the band. One of them 'Disc Jockey Jump', even had some success. But in 1951 he finally had to give up the struggle, and that was the end of his career as a big band leader.

Another ex-Goodman sideman, however, managed to keep his big band together even into the 1980's – Benny's star trumpeter, Harry James. After Gene left to form his own band, naturally rumours began to spread that Harry was thinking of doing the same. Harry denied this in the spring of 1938, saying "Benny's too great a guy to work for". He was a cheerful and enthusiastic young man.

However, within a few months he did decide to leave. Part of the problem was 'Sing, Sing, Sing'. In the wake of the Carnegie Hall concert, audiences expected the band to play this number as its big finish every night, featuring Harry's string of hot choruses. More and more he was finding the responsibility a strain, to the extent that he would sit there worrying about it during the whole show. He begged Benny to at least put it earlier in the show, so that he could get it over and feel better on the rest of the numbers, but Benny wouldn't meddle with his big finish.

In January 1939 Harry left to go out on his

own. Benny gave him his blessing, and even some financial backing in return for an interest in Harry's band.

The band made its first appearance on March 9, at the Benjamin Franklin Hotel in Pennsylvania. To everyone's surprise, given Harry's reputation as a searing hot player, the band played surprisingly softly (as hotels tended to demand), only swinging out during its last set.

Harry was always very aware of playing for dancers, and he was aware that many swing bands (especially the up-and-coming Glenn Miller) were playing too fast for comfortable dancing in their attempts to be sensational.

Like Gene, he had filled his band with promising newcomers but, like his idol Louis Armstrong, he tended at first to use his band almost entirely as a background to his own trumpet-playing. This worked well enough, because Harry could play in a wide variety of styles – straight and swinging, fast and slow, hot and sentimental – but it did mean that its arrangements were not as interesting as those of other bands. But the public liked it enough to keep it going (just).

As well as being a fine trumpeter, Harry knew how to lead and present a band. With his circus background, his tastes in band uniform were sometimes a little bright (for instance, red mess jackets with wing collars and white bow ties), but his personal manner was relaxed and informal. This was true both on-stage and off. His easy manner and straighforwardness gave him a friendly rapport with his musicians that other bandleaders must have envied.

One of his promising newcomers, who became a close friend, was not a musician, but a singer – Frank Sinatra, who joined the band when it was six months old, in July 1939.

The previous month, Harry and his then wife,

Louise Tobin, were lying in bed when she drew his attention to a young singer broadcasting from a local New York radio station, WNEW. The broadcast was coming from a club called the Rustic Cabin, in Englewood, New Jersey. Harry was immensely impressed by the voice, but failed to note the singer's name, so the next night, after his band's last show at the Paramount, where they were appearing, he drove to the Rustic Cabin to track him down.

The manager at the Rustic Cabin said they didn't have a singer, "But we do have an MC who sings a bit." Harry met Frank, who crooned a few songs for him. Harry invited him to call into the Paramount and discuss things further. Frank did. They made a deal. And Harry gave him a one-year contract to sing with the band.

The only disagreement they had was over his name. Harry though it wasn't memorable enough and wanted him to change it, but Frank insisted that his cousin up in Boston was doing all right leading a band and calling himself Ray Sinatra, and being Frank, he won the argument.

In spite of his cockiness, Frank at first wasn't all that confident as a singer. The first two numbers he recorded with the band, 'From The Bottom Of My Heart' and 'Melancholy Mood', sound quite shy and tentative, albeit musical. Harry's confident encouragement was just what he needed, and their friendship grew.

The band, still establishing itself, ran into some rough times. They had been booked into the famous Palomar Ballroom in Los Angeles in the Autumn of 1939 when it unexpectedly burned down (during a residency by the Charlie Barnet band). Hastily the band was rebooked into the Los Angeles restaurant, Victor Hugo's.

This was a mistake. The manager there complained that the band played too loud and he didn't like Sinatra's singing. Eventually he rushed up to the bandstand while Sinatra was singing 'All Or Nothing At All', fired them without letting them finish the number and refused to pay them. Everybody in the band was broke, and Frank's wife Nancy, then expecting daughter Nancy, used to cook up great heaps of spaghetti to feed them all.

It was not much later, in November 1939, that Tommy Dorsey came headhunting Frank. Frank was the biggest commercial asset the band had, but Harry, a little worried by the shaky patch it was going through, and aware of the imminent arrival of Frank's new baby, nobly released him from the five months remaining on his contract and let him go. Fortunately for Harry it wasn't long before he happened on another fine singer, Dick Haymes.

Gradually the band began to find its own sound. By the middle of 1940 the ensembles were better, and besides Harry himself it had a number of good soloists, including tenorists Sam Donohue and Vido Musso.

Vido was still having trouble with the English language. Once on the band bus, when the musicians were playing word games to pass the long uncomfortable hours, he challenged the others to name a bandleader whose initials were E.C. After they all gave up, he proudly announced he was thinking of Exavier Cugat.

It was on the James band bus towards the end of 1941 that there was another Musso incident. The band was headed for Canada to play a tour there, and as Vido had been born in Sicily, and as Canada was then at war with Italy, it was suggested to him that when they reached the border it would be simpler if he simply said he was born in New York City.

Vido agreed, then fell asleep. He was wakened by a customs officer tapping his shoulder and asking where he was born. "Sicily," he mumbled. Then, waking up enough to realise he had created a situation, he added, "You don't have to worry.

MCA straightened it out so I could come in." "MCA? Where's that?" said the officer. Vido couldn't believe his ears. "Hey, Harry!" he yelled. "This dumb son-of-a-bitch doesn't know what MCA is." Vido didn't make it across the border.

During the war years the band continued to develop, sometimes moving quite far from swing. For the dancers Harry would play waltzes, tangos and rhumbas. In the autumn of 1941 he added a string section, which he would retain until the end of the Forties, performing trumpet-virtuoso numbers like 'The Flight Of The Bumble Bee' and 'Carnival In Venice'.

He also began featuring girl singers, the most successful of whom was Helen Forrest, who'd left Benny Goodman "to avoid having a nervous breakdown". With Harry she did some of her best work, including ballads like 'I Cried For You', 'Skylark' and 'I've Heard That Song Before', which became Columbia Records' biggest seller to date, selling one-and-a-quarter million copies.

His formula of sentimental numbers featuring his horn and Helen's emotional voice, interspersed with occasional swing numbers, was paying off. In the summer of 1942 a poll run by the Martin Block radio programme, *Make Believe Ballroom*, voted Harry's the number one band in America, even above the amazingly popular Glenn Miller.

During the next year, however, there was a falling-off. Harry seemed to lose interest in having the band swing, and it began to sound stiff and plodding. The band had been brought to Hollywood to appear in the film *Mr Co-Ed*, a piece of froth that was released in Britain as *Bathing Beauty* and starred Esther Williams and Red Skelton (as well as giving Harry a brief speaking role), and a big fan of the band (and of Harry) was Betty Grable, who used to book a table almost every night at the Astor Roof, where the band was playing. With Harry's reciprocal interest in Miss Grable, it is perhaps not surprising that his mind wandered from his band for a bit.

On July 5, 1943, they married, an event that caused great excitement among movie fans and swing fans alike. A disc-jockey, as they were beginning to be called, made a crack about a song called 'I Want A Girl Just Like The Girl That Married Harry James', and the station received so many requests for the non-existent song that he was made to go away and write it.

More and more he seemed at this stage to be losing interest in the band. Possibly this was partly due to the troubles he was having (like all the big bands) with having his musicians drafted, but partly he seemed also to want to broaden his own performing career. In 1945, as well as leading the band on the Danny Kaye radio show, he acted as a stooge and as a comedian of sorts. Away from performing he bought racehorses and began to spend more and more time at the track.

At the end of 1946, by which time he had increased his string section to two dozen, the bottom suddenly fell out of the big band business. Many bands folded, and Harry announced that he was disbanding too. But then he had an enormous change of heart. He streamlined the band, reducing the strings to four (and not giving them much to do), and employing a number of young musicians who were hot to play.

This band really swung, and their enthusiasm spread to Harry himself, who admitted at the time that they excited him more than any band since his first. He cut his fees by half to keep going and, helped by long residencies (forty weeks a year) in Las Vegas, embarked on a long career of outlasting the Swing Era. No longer at the height of musical fashion, he played more jazz in those later years than he had when he was at the top, continuing until a few days before his death in 1983.

CHAPTER 13

count basie

The first black swing band to make any appreciable impression on the mass white audience was Count Basie's, and its rapid rise to fame was largely due to the efforts of John Hammond.

William Basie was born in Red Bank, New Jersey, in 1904. His mother was a pianist, and after a while playing drums in a local children's band, he studied piano with her, as well as having some lessons from a local teacher, a Mrs Holloway.

Coming to New York in his teens to hang around the music scene, he one day dropped into the Lincoln Theatre, at 58 West 135th Street, in Harlem. This had been built in 1915 on the site of a previous (and smaller) theatre. It presented silent films with stage acts in between, and it had just become a member of the newly-formed TOBA vaudeville circuit.

TOBA, the Theatre Owners and Bookers Association, was founded in 1920 to present black vaudeville artistes in front of black audiences in a chain of theatres across America. Originally there were thirty- two theatres in the chain, but the number grew to more than eighty, mainly in major cities and mainly in the South, South-West and mid-West. Notorious for its gruelling schedules and low pay (it was known in the business as "Tough On Black Asses"), it nonetheless provided fairly steady employment for many performers, including blues singers like Ma Rainey and Bessie Smith, and variety singers like Ethel Waters.

Once inside the Lincoln Theatre, young Bill Basie discovered an equally young musician accompanying the stage acts and the film by "beating it out on the organ". It was the stride pianist Fats Waller. Fats, born and bred in Harlem, was only three months older than Basie himself, but he was already a far more accomplished player, and from then on Basie was there every day in the front row, hanging onto Fats's every note, fascinated by the easy way his hands pounded the keys and his feet manipulated the pedals.

Fats got used to seeing him there, and one day offered to teach him how to play the organ. He invited Basie into the pit, and Basie began by sitting on the floor at Fats's feet, watching them work the pedals and imitating them with his hands. After a few days, he sat beside Fats, watching and learning.

One day, between shows, Fats excused himself and left Basie alone practising. Listening craftily from the door, he decided Basie was ready, and next day started letting him play during the film at the early show. Basie took to following Fats all over town, wherever he played, listening and learning.

Soon Basie himself began getting work on the TOBA circuit, and he spent most of the Twenties touring all over America, sometimes as a solo pianist, sometimes acting as musical director and accompanist for singers, dancers and comedians.

In 1927 he was with a touring show called the Gonzelle White Show when it got stranded without funds in Kansas City, which by this time had a strong and flourishing musical tradition of its own. Basie liked the music he was hearing there, decided to stay for a while, and got a job playing piano in a silent movie house.

In the summer of 1928, while he was still playing in the movie house, he was asked to deputise for the pianist of Walter Page's Blue Devils, a band regarded in the flourishing south-western music scene as second only to that of Alphonso Trent.

Walter Page was one of two south-western bandleaders who would be important in Basie's musical development, the other being Bennie Moten, and the careers of all three became closely entwined.

Walter Sylvester Page had been born in Gallatin, Missouri, in 1900. His family moved to Kansas City when he was still quite young, and there he learned to play tuba and bass, moving on to also learn saxophone, violin, piano, voice, composition and arranging. By the early Twenties he was playing from time to time in bands led by Bennie Moten.

Bennie Moten was older. Born in Kansas City in 1894, by the time he was twelve he was playing baritone horn in Lacy Blackburn's Juvenile Brass Band. His mother, like Basie's, was a pianist, and he studied piano with her, and later with two men who were disciples of the great ragtime pianist and composer, Scott Joplin.

In his teens he worked as pianist with various local bands, and by 1918, when he was twenty-four, he was leading a ragtime trio (the B.B. and D. Band) at a club called the Panama Club.

By the beginning of the Twenties the Moten group had grown to a quintet, and it continued to grow. By 1923 it was a sextet, by 1925 an octet, and by 1927 a ten-piece band.

Between 1923 and 1925 these bands made records for a small label called Okeh, which produced black music for the black audience, making what were known in those days as "race" records – a euphemism that the black community had been happy to hit on.

The records made by the smaller Moten bands of those days are rather uneven in quality, showing influences that range from ragtime to King Oliver, with some of the cornier effects of the Original Dixieland Jass Band thrown in. But some sides – 'Vine Street Blues' and 'Tulsa Blues', for instance, both made in 1924, show that his bands could on occasion be tightly-knit and relaxed.

In 1923 Walter Page joined a local septet led by a trombonist called Ermir Coleman. They toured all over the south-west, even down as far as Texas, and Page always spoke highly of this band, singling out pianist Willie Lewis as a particularly fine musician. (Lewis, after touring Europe, South America and North Africa in the early Thirties with Sam Wooding's Symphonic Syncopators, would settle in Paris from 1935 to 1941, becoming the most prominent black American bandleader in Europe).

Good or not, the band broke up in 1925 when Ermir Coleman decided to leave music and go into politics. Walter Page, deciding to become a leader himself, took several members of the band to form his own (including, for a while, Ermir Coleman himself).

Wanting to lead a big band, he led this small group around the South-West until he managed to get the backing he needed, from a group of Oklahoma businessmen, and in the spring of 1927 built it up to eleven pieces, calling the new band the Blue Devils.

Among its members at the start were several names that would go on to become well-known in the Swing Era – trumpeter Oran "Hot Lips" Page (no relation), trombonist (and future arranger) Eddie Durham, altoist and clarinetist Buster Smith, and drummer Alvin Burroughs, who had been with Alphonso Trent and would go on to join Earl Hines. All the rest, at one time or another, would become members of the Count Basie band, and the least known of them, Buster Smith, was always cited by Charlie Parker himself as one of his main Kansas City influences.

Once the band was formed it started working small towns within a fifty-mile radius of Oklahoma City. In the town of Shawnee they got a summer job in a dime-dance club called the Riverside that lasted four months. They did so well there that the band bought a great big touring car (a Stoddard-Dayton), and used it to drive round Texas for two weeks before coming back to Oklahoma City.

Walter Page's Blue Devils came to regard the south-west as their territory. They toured all over Texas, and in Kansas City won battles against the prestigious bands of George E. Lee and Jesse Stone.

By this time Bennie Moten, who seems to have been a shrewd businessman, was leading the most famous band in Kansas City, a position he had reached by being the only band-leader there who had managed to land a recording contract with a major company. The company was Victor, and for them his band, which was in fact a co-operative, like the Casa Loma, turned out anywhere from eight to a couple of dozen sides every year from 1926 to 1932.

The Blue Devils would have liked to challenge Moten in a band contest – but Moten was too cautious to get involved in any such thing.

In July 1928, when the Blue Devils were passing through Kansas City, they acquired a new pianist – Bill Basie, and in 1929, back in Oklahoma City, they acquired singer Jimmy Rushing. But neither stayed long. Bennie Moten was usually generous towards other bandleaders, often, for instance helping them towards bookings that his band had been offered but could not take. But, as already noted, he was an astute businessman, and his generosity did not prevent him from making financially tempting offers to members of this new and threatening band.

Early in 1929 both Basie and Eddie Durham left the Blue Devils to join Moten, and towards the end of the same year Jimmy Rushing and Hot Lips Page followed them. It says a lot for Basie's playing in those days (and for Moten's modesty) that a piano-playing leader would hire him as pianist and give up playing himself, which is what Moten did. From then on he mostly restricted himself to leading.

Basie's piano style was already developing the wonderful deceptive spareness that other pianists (including Oscar Peterson) have tried without success to imitate. Basie had his own explanation for how this style developed.

In around 1930, when he was touring with Moten, the band stopped off in Toledo, Ohio, and went into a local bar which sold cigarettes and sandwiches and candy and so on. Basie noticed there was a good piano there, and wishing to show off his prowess as a big-city musician to a couple of good-looking girls who were in there, he sat down and began to play.

The next thing he knew, somebody had gone out and brought in the local pianist whose hangout the bar was. Unfortunately for Basie, his name was Art Tatum.

Basie had heard of this incredible piano-player called Tatum, but had never heard him, and had no idea that this place was his stomping-ground. When Art began playing he was totally stunned. Right then and there decided to give up any ideas he might have had about becoming the fastest-fingered stride pianist that ever breathed. "I could have told you," said one of the girls at the bar.

The Blue Devils, with the defectors replaced, carried on. For a while at this time they had an eighteen-year-old drummer who had been born in Chicago, raised in Alabama, and become a drummer and tap-dancer in carnivals. He would later become one of the Basie band's greatest assets – Jo Jones.

In 1931 (by which time Jo Jones had gone again) Walter Page felt that the Blue Devils were ready for New York and the big time. He started considering the matter, but before he could arrange anything he fell foul of the musicians' union in Kansas City. He had offered a job to a pianist, then found that the man was on seriously bad terms with another member of the band, and withdrew the offer. The union fined him $250 for reneging on an agreement.

This put the band in severe financial difficulties. Unable to continue with it himself on the meagre salary which was now all it could afford, he turned it over to one of his trumpeters, James Simpson, to lead it through its remaining bookings. Page played for a few months in various small groups, and then he too joined Bennie Moten.

The Blue Devils, forming themselves into a co-operative, continued touring the south-west, still a hard-swinging band (and still avoided by Moten in battles), but financially they found the going rough. Eventually, in 1933, they attempted to open up new territory for themselves by touring Kentucky and West Virginia, but they weren't known there, and attendances were poor.

Their morale was already low when they arrived to play at a club in Martindale, West Virginia, and found that a booking-agent had tricked them into accepting a share of door-receipts as a fee. Receipts were around thirty dollars a night. They owed money to a taxi company, and the company had the police impound their instruments (returning them only

for the job each night), and eventually they were thrown out of their hotel.

That was the end of the Blue Devils. They struggled back to Kansas City by train, some lucky ones having borrowed money for fares, the others riding the rods of frieght trains, like hoboes. Four more of them joined Benny Moten, among them Buster Smith and a tenor-player who had joined in 1932 – Basie's future star, Lester Young.

Lester Willis Young, born in Woodville, Missouri, in 1909, was one of six children. His father, Billy, was leader of a carnival band, touring rural America in all sorts of medicine shows and tent shows and circuses. As a result the family tended to move around, although when Lester was still an infant it moved to New Orleans, where it remained based for most of his childhood, and where he loved hearing the bands in the streets.

The Young band was mainly made up of members of the family. As soon as one of Billy's children was old enough to learn an instrument, he or she would be taught one. Lester learned the rudiments of violin, trumpet and drums.

When he was ten his parents separated and Billy, with half of the six children – Lester, his younger brother Lee and his younger sister Irma – moved to Minneapolis. There Lester began his professional career as a musician, playing drums (and doubling as a handbill distributor), touring all over Kansas, Nebraska and South Dakota.

When he was thirteen he got fed up with the drums, because they were too much trouble to take around. Also because by the time he got them packed up after a show, all the girls would have disappeared. He took up the alto sax.

He continued playing in the family band until the autumn of 1927, when his father announced that he was taking the band touring the South that winter. The shy and sensitive Lester, aware of the unpleasantness that could face a black band playing in the deep South, begged his father to reconsider. But Billy wanted to spend the winter somewhere warmer than the mid-West, and insisted. Eventually the family band went and Lester doggedly stayed.

He joined a local band, Art Bronson's Bostonians. At first he played baritone sax, but the band had a rich dilettante tenor-player, who only showed up if he felt like it, and Lester, in another of his rare displays of initiative, offered to become the band's tenor if Bronson would fire the other man. Bronson did, and Lester was at last playing the instrument best suited to him.

On leaving Bronson he played for a while with, of all people, King Oliver, by then an old man of forty-six, unable to play all night but still, according to Lester, having a rich full tone. After that, he drifted around for a while, still basing himself in Minneapolis, which he regarded as home, and it was there that he joined the Blue Devils.

His style on tenor, already formed by that time, was so individual that it is hard to discern any influences on him, but he did later admit to two, both at about the time he took up the instrument. Rather surprisingly, both of these were white, and neither played the tenor. They were Jimmy Dorsey on alto and Frank Trumbauer on the obsolete C-melody sax (pitched half way between alto and tenor).

Although he became a much greater and inventive improviser than either of these, and their influence is hard to detect in his mature playing, he did learn from both of them to construct a solo so that it built logically, to tell a story. And from both he learnt that the saxophone could be played cleanly and clearly, without mooing or clucking.

The understated style he developed, without the heavy vibrato of Hawkins, and with an emphasis on inventing new melodies in his solos, rather than exploring the underlying harmonies of the piece, was entirely his own, and he sounded like no-one else. That is, until the Forties, when every cool young tenor-player in America started to try and imitate him.

Not only the Blue Devils, but even the well-established Bennie Moten band was having a hard time around 1932. Part of its problem was that it had made the switch from playing in 2/4 time to playing in the looser, lighter 4/4 style, and its fans were finding the new rhythm unfamiliar and difficult to dance to. Even without this drop in popularity, there were the other problems a touring band had to face, such as promoters who would suddenly vanish with the proceeds of the box office.

Altoist Eddie Barefield later remembered the hard life the band was having at that time. "We were stranded in Zanesville, we were stranded in Columbus, we were stranded in Cincinnati, and we were stranded in Philadelphia."

What happened in Philadelphia was that, after the band had spent a week playing at the Pearl Theatre and putting rooms, food, whisky and rent all on the tab until pay-day, they found out that a man who had lent them money to buy band uniforms the last time they were in town had attached the box office receipts, and taken not only the money but also the band bus.

Bennie got hold of a local promoter who helped them out. As Barefield recalled, "They got a big old bus and took us over to Camden, New Jersey, to a pool hall, and this guy took a tub and one rabbit and made a big stew. We got a lot of bread, and stood around and sopped up this stew and ate this gravy. I always called it cat stew because I couldn't figure out where this guy got a rabbit. I always kid Basie and say that we ate cat stew that day."

The reason they were taken to Camden, New Jersey, was that Victor had recording studios there and they were booked to do a session. This session, on December 13, 1932, would turn out to be the best the Moten band ever did. While never the swinging outfit that the Blue Devils had been, it was more disciplined. It had come a long way during the previous few years, and an amazing way from its beginnings as a semi-ragtime band.

Partly this was because it now had an army of outstanding soloists (in addition to the men from the Blue Devils it also had the nearest thing in Kansas City to Coleman Hawkins – tenorist Ben Webster), but mainly it was because of trombonist Eddie Durham, who had become an outstanding arranger.

The scores he wrote set off the soloists to their best advantage, using the riff-based style that was to become the hallmark of Kansas City swing, using short repetitive figures developed from the melody for the whole band to harmonise. And the band itself had a looser, more powerful rhythm than any other band had developed at that time, lifted by Walter Page's solid four beats in the bar on his bass.

On such numbers as 'Moten Swing' the band can be recognised quite clearly as the forerunner of the Basie band of a few years later, especially as it has vocals by Jimmy Rushing, and in spite of the fact that at this time Basie's own busy piano-playing still marks him clearly as a disciple of Fats Waller. (The band is also helped on this session by the absence of Benny Moten's nephew Buster, who had joined it in 1928 as front man and accordionist).

It was unfortunate that this was the last recording session it made. Victor, cutting back because of the slump in record sales, dropped their contract. It also never got paid for making the session, and after recording it they just had enough money to make it back to Kansas City.

With all its problems, the personnel of the band kept changing, and many names that would become famous passed through. Early in 1933 Eddie Barefield was replaced by Earl Bostic, whose alto would become one of the most popular sounds of the late Forties and the Fifties. And Ben Webster was replaced by Herschel Evans, whose Hawkins-style tenor would provide such a magnificent contrast to Lester Young in the first great Basie band.

Even with all these great players, things remained rough for the band, and the situation wasn't helped by Eddie Durham leaving to go to New York and work as arranger for the Harlem big band of singer Willie Bryant, although he did compile quite a stack of arrangements to leave behind him when he went.

For a short period in 1934 Moten even got Kansas City singer and bandleader George E. Lee, who was also going through a lean time, to come in as co-leader, hoping that Lee's popularity would help. It didn't help enough. Bookings remained poor, and later the same year most of the band elected to go with Basie and play an engagement he'd obtained in Little Rock, Arkansas.

As the Moten band struggled, Basie had from time to time been getting odd jobs for small bands of his own. One of them included Lester Young, and it was from this band that Lester went in 1934 to take up his ill-fated position with Fletcher Henderson. When that failed, after only a few months, he came back, not to Kansas City, where he might be seen as a failure, but home to Minneapolis, where he got a job in a club calling itself the Cotton Club.

Meanwhile, in Kansas City, Bennie Moten was beginning to sense that the tide was turning (he was getting offered better bookings). He re-formed his band, and soon got a choice engagement for it, at the Rainbow Ballroom in Denver. At last he was on the way back. But he needed a tonsillectomy, so he sent the band on ahead to Denver while he stayed behind to have it. On April 2, 1935 the surgeon severed one of his jugular veins and he died on the operating table.

Walter Page and Bennie's nephew, Buster Moten, tried to keep the band going, but only a few weeks later, in the summer of 1935, they had to call it a day.

After the demise of the Moten band, Basie carried on working around Kansas City, first as a solo pianist, then with a trio. Then, with the help of altoist and arranger Buster Smith, he formed a nine-piece band, which they named the Barons of Rhythm. It was composed mostly of ex-Moten men, including Walter Page and singer Jimmy Rushing, who did a lot to keep up everybody's morale as they struggled to establish themselves.

Eventually the band managed to land a residency at the Reno Club, with Basie as leader.

This club was quite an elaborate one by Kansas City standards. It was situated on 12th Street in Kansas City, between Cherry Street and Locust Street, and it was segregated, with separate dance-floors, bars and dining areas for black and white patrons. Basie's band was of course playing for the black patrons, and the bandstand they had was so small that Basie's piano had to stand on the floor, and a hole had to be cut in the shell over the stage to accomodate the neck of the bass.

Although Basie's residency there would be a fairly long one, and the band's reputation would quickly grow, at first the musicians in it had a tendency to come and go (usually to be replaced by others who had been with Moten and/or the Blue Devils). Two who came were trumpeter Hot Lips Page and tenorist Herschel Evans.

A bonus for Basie in playing at the Reno Club was that the club had a link to a Kansas City local radio station, W9XBY, and as the band's reputation grew, it started making nightly broadcasts.

This was to change Basie's life in several major ways. One was that a radio announcer one night observed that swing already had an Earl and a Duke, and it was high time it had a Count as well. So Basie became Count Basie. In his autobiography, written just before his death in the Eighties, Basie admitted that he'd never felt the name really suited him. He'd always rather hoped for some nickname like "Arkansas Fats".

It was also radio that brought Lester Young back to him. Still at the Cotton Club, in Minneapolis, Lester had started tuning in regularly after work to listen to the Barons of Rhythm on W9XBY. He thought that everything about the band sounded fine – except the tenor-playing of Herschel Evans.

He couldn't stand Herschel's playing, so strongly reminiscent of Coleman Hawkins. After all, it was only a couple of years since he had had the unhappy experience of having Hawk's playing thrust at him by Leora Henderson.

The normally shy and self-effacing Lester again acted out of character. He sent Basie a telegram, asking him if he could use a tenor-player. The exact text has been lost, but Basie remembered it as being "strange and convincing". He took up Lester's offer.

Lester joined the band and loved it. This became the happiest time of his life. He would play all night, jam around Kansas City all day, then fidget to get back to work again next night.

Bassist Walter Page left the band for a while, going off to play with the Jeter-Pillars Orchestra, an outfit led by altoist James Jeter and tenorist Hayes Pillars that had a permanent residency at the Club Plantation in St Louis. When he got there, the band's drummer was Jo Jones, who had been with him in the Blue Devils, and when he returned to Basie, he encouraged Jo to come with him.

Jo did, but the first night he played with the

Barons of Rhythm, at an out-of-town one-nighter in Topeka, Kansas, he was so scared by the playing of Hot Lips Page and Lester Young (especially on the band's version of 'After You've Gone') that he told Basie he was quitting, and refused to take his money. "I'm going back to school," he said. "I can't play with your band, Mr Basie."

When he went back to the stand to pick up his drums, all the musicians in the band told him he was crazy. "You can't leave," they said. So eventually Jo went back to Basie and said, "All right, Mr Basie. I will play with you for two weeks till you find a drummer." Apart from a brief spell in the Army during the Second World War, he was to remain with Basie until 1948.

During this time his example would revolutionise jazz drumming by shifting the basic pulse from the bass drum to the hi-hat cymbal. This made the rhythm section more subtle and responsive, and freed the bass drum for making accents.

Jo was already playing this way by the time he joined Basie, and moreover was playing a steady four beats in a bar. He well earned the description he was later given – the drummer who plays like the wind.

The next, and biggest, change that radio was to make in Basie's life was that it introduced his band to John Hammond.

Hammond was staying with Benny Goodman in Chicago, where the Goodman band was appearing, and while sitting in his car in a parking lot at 1 a.m. one night, he began fiddling with the radio dial. Accidentally he happened on W9XBY, which was right at the very top of the AM band, almost off the dial.

Although it was only a small station and four hundred miles away in Kansas City, W9XBY did have a powerful transmitter, and the Barons of Rhythm came through loud and clear. At that time the band consisted of Hot Lips Page and Joe Keyes (trumpets); Buster Smith, Lester Young and Jack Washington (saxes); Count Basie (piano); Walter Page (bass); and Jo Jones (drums).

Hammond was bowled over, especially by the economical style of Basie's piano-playing, with its perfectly-timed punctuations inspiring both band and soloists. He told Benny to try and catch the band on the radio. Benny had some difficulty getting the station (he eventually had to use his car radio and drive out into an open space away from buildings to get good reception), but finally he managed it, and liked what he heard so much that on his band's next night off he flew down to Kansas City to hear Basie live.

He wired Hammond (who had gone back to New York) that the band was great, and Hammond told him to tell his agent, Willard Alexander, at MCA. Benny did, telling Willard that John had found this terrific new band led by somebody called Count Bassie, and that he should go to Kansas City and hear it.

Willard agreed to go and hear the band, and a few days later he and Hammond flew to Kansas City. Willard too thought the band was great – "a little rough in spots, but terribly exciting" – and he signed it up.

Hammond had already been in action, telling everybody within earshot about the band, and writing it up enthusiastically in periodicals like *Down Beat*. When he got back to New York from his trip with Willard, he went to the Brunswick company and talked them into offering the band a recording contract, arranging for Basie to get a favourable deal, even including royalties, a rare thing in those days. Armed with the contract for Basie to sign, back he went to Kansas City. "A friend of yours was here to see me, John," said Basie. "Who?" said Hammond. "I didn't send anyone to see you." "Dave Kapp."

Hammond's heart sank. Dave Kapp was the brother of Jack Kapp, head of Decca records. "Let me see what you signed," he said. Basie showed him a record contract. It called for him to make twenty-four sides a year for Decca for three years for a flat fee of $750 a year, and Hammond later referred to it as a "slave contract".

The money had seemed like a fortune to Basie, after years spent in struggling Kansas City bands, but in fact it was below the union minimum. Hammond eventually, with the help of the union, did manage to get the basic fee raised, but otherwise the contract was airtight, and on all the band's early classics like 'Jumpin' At The Woodside' and 'One O'Clock Jump', Basie received a derisory payment and no royalties.

In a way, this was Hammond's fault. He had done so much publicising of this obscure little band in Kansas City that people were rushing to sign it. Joe Glaser, Louis Armstrong's agent, had even got to Kansas City before Willard Alexander to try and get the band on his books. Possibly misled by his association with Louis, he had come to the conclusion that trumpeter Hot Lips Page was the leader, and had mistakenly signed him up instead of Basie.

This, however, meant that Lips was now contracted to Joe Glaser, and so could not remain with the band, who were with MCA. Hammond arranged a replacement for him – William Dorsey "Buck" Clayton.

Buck had been born in Parsons, Kansas in 1911, and spent most of his early career in California. There, in 1934, he organised a big band and took it to play a residency in Shanghai.

Returning to Los Angeles the next year, he led various groups there, and played for several band-leaders, including Lionel Hampton. Unfortunately, while with that band, he mistakenly barged into the hotel room of Hamp's wife, Gladys. Gladys was

not amused and, being the real boss of the band, had him fired. Which was fortunate for Basie, because Buck's beautiful clean tone became such a feature of his band that, as Hammond said, "Lips was never missed".

Now that Basie was in the hands of MCA, it was arranged that the band should leave Kansas City as soon as possible, to become a nationally promoted attraction. First, they were booked for a short season at Earl Hines's stomping-ground, the Grand Terrace Hotel in Chicago.

This presented problems. First of all, several of the nine men in the band had no wish to leave Kansas City, and didn't. Next, John Hammond was ruthless in revamping the band, getting Basie to replace some of his men with musicians that Hammond preferred. He later admitted himself that having to fire one of his men to take on a Hammond discovery "nearly broke Basie's heart".

In the event, those who made it to Chicago from the Reno Club were Joe Keyes, Lester Young, Herschel Evans, Jack Washington, Walter Page, Jo Jones, and Jimmy Rushing, plus a trumpeter who had worked with them there on and off, Carl "Tatti" Smith.

With the additions supervised by Hammond, including Buck Clayton, the band that opened in the show at the Grand Terrace in September 1936 had grown to thirteen men. And it was rough. A nine-piece band had been small enough to work with only the simplest arrangements, often simply riffs, but now something more elaborate was needed.

Fletcher Henderson kindly lent the band some arrangements, but these Kansas City boys were far from being the experienced readers of music that New York musicians were. In fact some of them could barely read music at all. They busked along as best they could through Flecther's arrangements, and in the special numbers for the show, and Hammond was amazed they weren't fired. He later reckoned they were saved by the show girls, who found that whatever chaos was going on in the band, Jo Jones's drumming was the best they'd ever danced to.

While they were in Chicago, Hammond arranged to have one small revenge on Decca. He got a quintet from the band, plus singer Jimmy Rushing, into a studio, and had them record four sides anonymously for Vocalion.

The band was to have been Buck Clayton, Lester Young, Count Basie, Walter Page and Jo Jones, but at the last minute Buck Clayton suffered the trumpet-player's occupational hazard, a split lip, and so the more-than-capable Carl Smith came along instead.

Which was convenient, because by using the genuine surnames of two members of the band, Hammond was able to have the records released as played by "Jones-Smith Incorporated".

After struggling through their Grand Terrace booking, the band embarked on a short tour of one-night stands through New England, to Buffalo, and then to New York City, where they were to make their debut in November 1936 at the Roseland Ballroom. The Roseland at that date was still segregated, with a rigid "whites-only" policy. And it was still a taxi-dance hall, although fortunately for the band the length of numbers wasn't restricted to ninety seconds.

It was at around this time that the *Metronome* critic, George T. Simon, who had heard the band only on radio, published a review that passed into swing legend. "True," he wrote, "the band does swing, but that sax section is so invariably out of tune. And if you think that sax section is out of tune, catch the brass! And if you think the brass by itself it out of tune, catch the intonation of the band as a whole!!"

For the rest of their lives both Basie and Buck

Clayton could quote that review word for word, and as Clayton once said to George Simon, "You know what? You were absolutely right. We did play terribly out of tune."

The reason was actually quite simple. Many black musicians, unable to afford good instruments, were forced to blow horns that simply couldn't be blown completely in tune, because the notes on each horn weren't properly in tune with each other.

At Roseland the band again wasn't a great success. Part of the reason, quite apart from the poor intonation, was that it wasn't what the white swing fans were used to. The popular big bands of that time, both black and white, were becoming slicker, their arrangements more elaborate. Even the most complicated figures were played with machine-like precision.

These new boys from Kansas City were out of a different tradition. They concentrated on simple melodies, as often as not the blues, and prided themselves instead on their endless ability to improvise – not only the soloists, but the band as a whole, building up patterns of riffs as the mood took them. It was more spontaneous, and the excitement came from the individual musicians.

The rest of the reason was that the band simply wasn't yet good enough. After Roseland, it played the Paramount, but still the reception from the fans was lukewarm.

Basie at this time quite naturally became a little uncertain. He began worrying that what the band had been playing was old hat. He got them to try playing some slicker arrangements, more like Goodman or Tommy Dorsey, but after a week or so realised that what they had been playing wasn't old hat at all. That they really did have something new.

Throughout 1937 the personnel kept slowly improving. A guitarist, Claude Williams was added to the rhythm section, but not for long. He also played violin, and John Hammond didn't like the violin-playing. Soon he would be replaced by Freddie Green, and at last the great Basie rhythm section would be complete – Basie, Green, Page, Jones. They were the powerhouse of the band, the purring engine that drove the rest along, Freddie Green's regular chords freeing Basie to punctuate from the piano, spurring the band on with well-placed accents.

In March that year the band acquired the best big-band singer of them all, Billie Holiday. She got on well with the band, being accepted by them as a fellow-musician, and she put up with all the rough times on tour, playing in rough places like tobacco warehouses, where the tobacco dust would rise off the floor from the pounding of the dancers' feet and get in your clothes and your throat.

Sometimes, instead of trying to find hotels, they would rent a house and cook for themselves, and Billie turned out to be an excellent cook. As to her singing, Basie said, "She fitted in so easily, it was like having another soloist. All she needed was the routine, and she could come in with her eyes closed – no cues or signals."

Unfortunately she never recorded formally with the band. She was under contract to Brunswick records, so of course she couldn't record for Decca. All that remains of her with Basie are three airchecks (recordings made of radio broadcasts for copyright-checking). Two are from the Savoy Ballroom and one is from the Meadowbrook Inn in New Jersey, and it is quite clear from these that the Basie band was a wonderful setting for her.

She stayed with the band until early 1938 when either she quit because John Hammond kept insisting she should sing the blues ("Too many bosses in this band," she said) or else he fired her because she wouldn't.

While she was in the band, in July 1937, trombonist Eddie Durham joined it, and was considerably annoyed to discover that among the band's small library of arrangements were the ones he had made for the Moten band just before leaving it. One was for a light-hearted number called 'Blue Balls', that had been cobbled together by Buster Smith, Hot Lips Page and himself, and was regarded by the Moten band as a bit of a joke. Basie, when his band played it in a broadcast from the Reno Club, had been asked by an announcer what its title was. Glancing at the time, he said on the spur of the moment, 'One O'Clock Jump'.

Swallowing his annoyance, Eddie Durham got together with Basie, and they began turning out arrangements tailored to the band's own unique style – producing numbers like 'Time Out' and 'Swinging The Blues'.

It was in January 1938 that John Hammond, doing everything he could to build up the band's reputation, managed get Basie, Lester Young, Buck Clayton, Freddie Green and Walter Page involved in Benny Goodman's Carnegie Hall concert, a project in which he was not otherwise involved.

After the concert, that same evening, the whole band went to the Savoy Ballroom to engage in a battle of the bands with Chick Webb. They acquitted themselves well, but when the patrons voted on the way out, Chick Webb, the local band with already a string of hits, won comfortably.

Only a few weeks later, however, the band began a short residency at the Savoy, and at last it became a hit. The Savoy dancers took to its music with delight. But better was to come. Willard Alexander had got it booked into a jazz club called the Famous Door, which had several addresses over the years, but in 1938 was in a cellar at 66 West 52nd Street.

Why the Famous Door was so-called is unclear, but there really was such a door. After the club was opened in 1935, trumpeter Wingy Manone went to a lumberyard, and bought and shellacked a door. It was set up on a small platform near the bar and the club's backers signed their names on it. Over the years so did scores of musicians and celebrities, and whenever the club moved, the door moved too.

The 1938 club was not large, maybe twenty-five by fifty-five feet, and before Basie only small bands had played there. But Willard Alexander had the idea that such an intimate setting would be a good place to feature the band. The fact that the audiences would be small was of minor importance. The important thing to Willard was that the Famous Door had a radio link.

The club owners weren't keen on booking the band, so Willard offered them a deal. He pointed out that the club would do much better business if it had air-conditioning, and offered to lend them the money to instal it if they would book Basie. They agreed, but would only pay the band about $1,300 a week. Willard agreed.

By this time the band settled down – Ed Lewis, Buck Clayton and Harry Edison (trumpets); Dicky Wells, Benny Morton and Dan Minor (trombones); Earle Warren (alto); Lester Young and Herschel Evans (tenors); Jack Washington (baritone); Count Basie (piano); Freddie Green (guitar); Walter Page (bass); Jo Jones (drums). Plus singers Jimmy Rushing and Helen Humes.

Basie had at last got what he wanted – a fourteen-piece band that could work together like his nine pieces had, with everyone in it thinking and playing as one.

From the moment it opened at the Famous Door, musicians flocked to hear it. Basie made the most of the contrasting styles of his two tenor stars, seating his sax section in the front row of the band, with Herschel Evans on the left and Lester Young at the right, as if keeping them separated.

The two played their parts with relish.

For instance, ostentatiously turning their backs on each other's solos during 'One O'Clock Jump'. But in fact a strange exasperated friendship grew up between them, well illustrated in the exchange reported by Billie Holiday. Herschel one day said, "Why don't you go buy an alto, man? You only got an alto tone." Lester, tapping his forehead, replied, "There's things going on up here, man. Some of you guys are all belly."

The engagement at the Famous Door, originally for six weeks, extended to three months, and when it was over, the band was famous. The records it had already started recording for Decca sold in their thousands – records that included such classics as 'Blue And Sentimental', 'John's Idea' (in honour of John Hammond), 'Texas Shuffle', 'Doggin' Around' and 'Jumpin' at the Woodside'.

Basie turned out to be a natural leader. With his laid-back manner, his speech as spare and seemingly casual as his piano-playing, he could appear diffident, and he always remained very much one of the boys, but nonetheless it was always quite obvious that he was in charge. Mostly he controlled the band by joking and kidding. On rare occasions he could get mad and explode, but mostly his attitude to troublemakers was, "I'm not going to fire you – you're going to fire yourself".

With such relaxed leadership, the band was a happy, friendly one. The members gave, each other, or themselves, nicknames – Harry Edison called himself "Sweets", because that was just about the opposite of what he was, a rough brash practical-joker.

Most of the names however came from Lester Young, as gifted at tagging people as he was playing tenor. If Lester gave you a name, it stuck. Basie became "The Holy Main"; green-eyed Buck Clayton, "Cat-eye"; guitarist Freddie Green, "Pep";

Jo Jones, "Samson". The band's manager, whose name was Henry Snodgrass, became "Lady Snar", but then, Lester addressed everyone, male or female, as "Lady This" or "Lady That". "Lady" herself, Billie Holiday, who had had that name since her teens, gave Lester his name, "Pres".

Once established, the band's personnel remained almost unchanged for three years. When it did change, tragically the first to go were its two tenor stars. Early in February 1939, while the band was playing at the Crystal Ballroom in Hartford, Connecticut, Herschel Evans collapsed onstage from an unexpected heart ailment, was taken to hospital, and died. For a while Chu Berry came into the band, on loan from Cab Calloway, then Herschel was replaced in the band by another fine Texan tenorman, George Holmes "Buddy" Tate.

Shortly afterwards, the trumpet section was increased to four by the addition of Shad Collins, replaced a year later by high-note man Al Killian. And the saxes acquired a second altoist, Tab Smith, increasing their number to five. Then, at the end of 1940, Lester Young left.

Why he quit is unclear. He was certainly happier in the band than he had been, or would be, at any time in his life. The story that he quit because Basie wanted him to record on Friday the Thirteenth (of December) can be ignored, because Lester at that time in his life was eager to play any time, anywhere, night and day.

What seems most likely is that at that time the band was having something of an unsettled time. Basie was at odds with MCA, whom he claimed were handling the band sloppily, planning tours so that it had to travel up to five hundred miles between one-nighters, failing to book them into venues that had radio links, and leaving them loafing around for weeks on end without work. He was so unhappy with the state of affairs that he had even threatened to break up the band and go and

work for Benny Goodman, and what was making the band even more nervous was that he kept going off for odd weeks to appear as a featured guest with Goodman.

The vulnerable Lester, who had had an unsettled childhood in a broken home with incessant travelling, possibly had regarded the band as the first real home he ever had, and fearing from all the growing tensions in it that it was ceasing to be a safe refuge, it would have been quite in character for him to take the bull by the horns and quit before it collapsed around him.

As it happens, he needn't have bothered. A month after he quit, Basie bought himself out of his contract with MCA for ten thousand dollars, and peace was restored.

The irreplaceable Lester was replaced briefly by the workmanlike Paul Bascomb, and then by the amazingly fluent and exciting Carlos Wesley "Don" Byas.

Byas had been in one of Buck Clayton's bands, as well as being with Lionel Hampton, Don Redman, Lucky Millinder and Andy Kirk. At that time he was a disciple of Coleman Hawkins (there weren't yet any Lester Young disciples), but in the mid-Forties would come under the influence of Charlie Parker and become an important figure in the transition from swing to bop. For the time being, however, the band had lost the wonderful contrast between Hawkins-style playing and Lester.

Don Byas stayed with the band until December 1943, when he gave Basie his notice in the most tactful way possible. The band was appearing at a theatre, and between shows Basie was sitting peacefully playing solitaire in his dressing-room when Byas quietly opened the door. "Basie," he said, "in four weeks I will have been gone two."

Basie knew that Lester Young was in town (he had been off in California playing in his brother Lee's band, and had come back to New York in a group led by singer-guitarist-pianist Slim Gaillard), so he sent Jo Jones out to find him. Jo found him in a 52nd Street bar, bought him a beer, and simply said, "Now, don't forget. We're at the Lincoln Hotel. Be at work tonight at seven." And at seven, there he was. Lester was back.

The band continued playing well, but America was now at war, and like other band-leaders, Basie began to lose men to the armed forces. In the autumn of 1943 the U.S. Government had issued a "work or fight" edict, which required men to go into industry or risk being drafted.

As Buddy Tate later recalled, "A lot of musicians beat the draft by saying, 'Well, I didn't get it – I was on the road.'" But one night, when the band was appearing at the Plantation Club, in Watts, Los Angeles, an FBI man, who had been posing as a young zoot-suited fan, suddenly produced his badge and said to Jo Jones and Lester Young, "Be at this address at nine o'clock in the morning or we'll come and get you and you'll go to jail for five years."

So on September 30, 1944, Jo and Lester were inducted into the U.S. Army. Jo coped with army life well enough, but for the shy and gentle Lester it was a disaster.

During basic training at Fort McLellan, Alabama, while negotiating an obstacle course on New Year's Day 1945, he fell on his backside, injuring himself just enough to require minor surgery. While in hospital, he was routinely interviewed by the camp psychologist, whose report described him as being in a "constitutional psychopathic state manifested by drug addiction (marijuana, barbiturates), chronic alcoholism and nomadism." The doctor came to the conclusion that he was "a purely disciplinary problem and that

disposition should be effected through administrative channels".

Returned to duty, he was almost immediately arrested by the MP's, probably alerted by the psychiatrist's report, for possession of marijuana and barbiturates. Among his possessions they had found several home-made cigarettes, two bottles of pink liquid, and some pills that he had bought on the base.

At his court martial on February 16, Lester (who had told the Army on induction that he had smoked marijuana for eleven years) was sentenced to dishonourable discharge, forfeiture of pay, and a year's detention in disciplinary barracks.

He served ten months, and was released in December 1945, sadder and even more withdrawn. He never rejoined Basie, and never again played with the total delight and rapture of those glorious years with the band.

Jo Jones rejoined quite straighforwardly on his release from the Army in 1946, but by then the Basie band, like almost all the big bands, was struggling hard to survive. Being as popular as it was, it managed to last until 1950, when Basie disbanded it and formed a sextet.

At least, it was to have been a sextet, but after it had been together for about a month, when they showed up for a gig, there was Freddie Green with his guitar. "Say, Pep," said Basie. "You're not on this gig, are you?" "You're workin', aren't you?" said Freddie. "After I gave you the best years of my life, you think you're going to leave me now?"

He stayed with the sextet (now a septet), anchoring its rhythm section, and when, a year later, Basie reformed his big band, Freddie continued performing the same function, as he was to go on doing for the next thirty-six years.

CHAPTER 14

artie shaw

During the Swing Era, three bands in turn held the title of most popular band, in terms of record sales and positions in polls. From 1936 to mid-1939 it was Benny Goodman. From mid-1940, until he disbanded in 1942, it was Glenn Miller. But for about a year, from the middle of 1939 to the middle of 1940, it was Artie Shaw. After Miller disbanded to enter the American Air Force, Goodman and Shaw ran neck and neck until 1946.

Ten years later, *Billboard* magazine polled America's disc-jockeys as to their all-time favourite records – Shaw's 'Stardust' came top, his 'Begin The Beguine' third, his 'Summit Ridge Drive' eighth, and his 'Frenesi' fifteenth.

Arthur Jacob Arshawsky, the only child of immigrant Jewish parents, had been born in the Lower East Side of New York in 1910. When he was about seven the family moved to New Haven, Connecticut. When he was ten he learned to play the ukulele, and when he was twelve he took up the alto saxophone, teaching himself.

A highly intelligent child, he was attracted by the challenge of learning to play an instrument, but on his own admission didn't have much idea at first that music was anything more than a way out of the world he was raised in, which was poor, and where he suffered from anti-semitic bullying.

When he did realise its power, he became hooked. He began listening to all the records he could lay his hands on, mostly jazz, and practising eight hours a day.

Always an idealist, he would spend the rest of his musical career trying to create music that aspired to a romantic ideal of perfection. This would repeatedly conflict with the day-to-day realities of the music business, and cause him again and again to break up whatever band he was leading, only to start afresh a little while later.

While learning to play, he started hanging round Johnny Cavallero's dance-band, a local band that had in it another future bandleader, Tony Pastor. Tony was a local lad, some three years older than Artie. He played tenor sax, and the two became friendly.

In the Sixties, Tony remembered Artie being impressed by his playing ("I could play a whole-tone scale in those days," he said, "and I guess Artie must have thought I was a genius or something"). His hero-worship even extended to carrying Tony's tenor to the railroad station for him when the band was going off on a date.

Artie formed his own first band in 1924, while still at school, calling it the Bellevue Ramblers (after the California Ramblers) and playing gigs in suburbs of the city like Liberty Pier, Savin Rock and Banham Lake. He was by now so wrapped up in music that at fifteen he was expelled from school for not working.

He shortened his name to Art Shaw to mark

the new life in music he intended to embark on, and set off to take up a job in Kentucky. The job failed to materialise and he worked his way back home by playing in a travelling band.

He then went to Johnny Cavallero to apply for a job in his band, which by now also had in it an alto-player and clarinetist called Rudy Vallee, just back from nine months in England playing in the Savoy Havana Band. Vallee would go on to lead his own band, the Connecticut Yankees, and become the most popular American singer of the late Twenties. He was the first to realise that the new popular songs of the day needed a less openly emotional and more intimate delivery. Developing such a style, he became the first crooner.

Art played for Johnny, who was satisfied, and asked him if he could read. Art, a voracious reader of books all his life, felt mortified. "Of course I can read," he said. Johnny stuck a piece of music in front of him.

Art had never thought of reading music. "I can't do anything with that," he said. Johnny pointed out that a musician who couldn't read music would be useless in a band. "Hold the job for a month," said Art. Johnny was sceptical, but did, and in a month Art was back, able to read music as well as books.

He joined the Cavallero band in the summer of 1925, and played with it in New Haven and then in Florida. It was while he was with Cavallero that he took up what was to be his principal instrument, the clarinet.

Leaving Cavallero in 1927, he worked around Cleveland, Ohio, for a couple of years, first in the bands of Joe Cantor and Merle Jacobs, then in a band led by violinist Austin Wylie, for which he was musical director and arranger, two jobs at which he turned out to be more than competent, establishing a considerable local reputation.

With him in the Austin Wylie band was his old friend from New Haven, Tony Pastor, and in 1929 they both joined Irving Aaronson's Commanders, which was basically a theatre band. Art played clarinet and alto, and Tony played tenor.

When the Commanders visited Chicago, Art sat in on jam sessions with the local musicians. At around the same time, endlessly exploring, he discovered the music of Debussy and Stravinsky. Both would influence his music later.

In 1930 the Commanders came to New York, and Art decided to stay there. While waiting for his New York musicians' union card to come through, he sat in with various groups, mostly with the one led by Willie "The Lion" Smith at a Harlem speakeasy officially named the Patagonia but known to everyone as "Pods' and Jerry's", after its two owners, Pods Hollingsworth and Jerry Preston. The Lion's playing, and his knowledge of music of all kinds, became another considerable influence on Art.

After getting his union card, he worked around New York in a succession of prominent dance-bands, including those of Paul Specht, Vincent Lopez and Roger Wolfe Kahn. In 1931 he played a season with Red Nichols at the Park Central Hotel, and that autumn began a year of radio studio work for Fred Rich, a pianist and leader who frequently gave work to hot musicians, including from time to time Bunny Berigan, the Dorsey Brothers and Benny Goodman.

For the next few years he would work mainly in the radio studios, and, like Benny Goodman, became well known as a talented and reliable player. By 1933 he was New York's "first call" alto-player, making around $300 to $400 a week, very healthy sum for those days.

Then disillusion set in. It suddenly struck him that instead of devoting his life to the art of music, he had become nothing more than a salesman. Working almost entirely in radio, which was controlled by commerical sponsors, he was prostituting his talent by using it to sell soap and cigarettes.

Disgusted with the music business, he left it and resumed his education, enrolling for extension courses in Literature and Philosophy at Columbia University. He married his first wife, a young woman called Jane Kahn, but her father so disapproved that he high- handedly had the marriage annulled without consulting either of them.

Soon after, he married again, and with his second wife, Marge, bought a farm in Bucks County, Pennsylvania. This was an area much favoured by writers, some of them famous. In 1932 the humourist S.J. Perelman had moved there, and in 1936 so would both George S. Kaufman and his collaborator Moss Hart.

Art Shaw spent a year there, attempting to write a novel based on the life of Bix Beiderbecke, but he couldn't manage to get anything on paper that lived. He came to the conclusion that his feelings about music and life had not yet matured enough. In the autumn of 1934 he returned to New York and again began to freelance around the radio and recording studios.

In the autumn of 1935, in the wake of Benny Goodman's success at the Palomar in Los Angeles, Goodman's friend Joe Helbock, owner of the Onyx Club, decided to promote a concert at the Imperial Theatre in New York to celebrate the birth of swing. He asked Art if he would help to fill out the programme by getting together a small group and performing one piece.

Exploring music in his own way, Art wrote a piece called 'Interlude In B Flat', for the unorthodox line-up of a string quartet, a rhythm section, and himself playing clarinet.

To his surprise, the piece was greeted with enthusiastic applause, the audience shouting for more. Helbock asked the group to play another number, and Art pointed out that all they'd prepared was the one piece. All they could do, and did, was to play 'Interlude In B Flat' again.

In the wake of this success, Art found himself being badgered by Tommy Rockwell, the other director of the Rockwell-O'Keefe Agency, to form a band. Rockwell-O'Keefe had been representing the Dorsey Brothers and, following the brothers' split in May, were still representing Jimmy, but the split had made them nervous and they were anxious to have another band on their books to compete with MCA's Benny Goodman.

In the spring of 1936, Art gave in to Rockwell's urging and formed a band, expanding the line-up he had played with at the Imperial Theatre by adding a jazz front line (trumpet, trombone and tenor).

Tommy Dorsey and Benny Goodman were recording for Victor, Jimmy Dorsey was recording for Decca, so Art was snapped up by Brunswick. He made his first records for them in June 1936, beginning with 'The Japanese Sandman' and 'A Pretty Girl Is Like A Melody'. Unable to find dance-band arrangers who were used to scoring for strings, he handled most of the arrangements himself.

The band made its live debut a little later, at New York's Lexington Hotel. By this time the original tenor-player in the band had been replaced by Tony Pastor. His pianist had become Joe Lippman, who also contributed arrangements, and would go on to become a great arranger for Jimmy Dorsey. Joe brought into the band as first violin (and yet another arranger) a fellow-Bostonian, Jerry Gray.

Jerry, who would go on to become Glenn Miller's number one arranger, hadn't been quite sure what sort of band he was being hired to join. Suspecting that it was some sort of polite society dance-band, he showed up bringing his accordion as well. In spite of Art's interest in unorthodox line-ups, he never asked Jerry to play the accordion.

Far from being a polite society outfit, the band definitely swung, and Art himself had become as fine a clarinetist as Goodman. Not quite as fast and fluent, but with more control, and with a somewhat fuller sound. Unfortunately, the overall sound of his band was rather diluted by the somewhat syrupy string-section, and the public, already used to the brasher, brassier bands of Goodman, Berigan and Tommy Dorsey, were not entirely enthusiastic.

Even the band's theme was unconventional. Suddenly reminded by the producer, at the band's first radio appearance, that it would need a theme, Art reacted against the tradition that a swing band should have a song for its theme – Goodman's 'Let's Dance', Tommy Dorsey's 'I'm Getting Sentimental Over You' – by hastily penning a moody instrumental, 'Nightmare'.

After getting a tepid response at the Paramount Theatre in New York, the band embarked on what was intended to be a long residency at the Hotel Adolphus in Dallas. So few people turned up that after four weeks they were cancelled. Returning to New York, disillusioned with the public's response, but determined now to succeed, Art said to himself, "If they want loud bands, I'll give them a loud band."

He fired the string section and built up the band to fourteen pieces, using a conventional swing-band line-up and calling it "Art Shaw And His New Music". For a while Jerry Gray continued to provide Art with arrangements, while earning a living playing his violin in a society dance-band, but eventually the polite music he was expected to play got on his nerves and he went back home to Boston.

Shortly afterwards, Art and his band migrated to Boston too, embarking on a long residence at the Roseland-State Ballroom while he worked to get the band into shape. The owners of the Roseland-State, the brothers Cy and Charlie Shribman, had a well-earned reputation for backing and nurturing new and struggling bands.

The important thing, Art realised, was to find his band an identity of its own. Soon he decided that the key for him was clarity and simplicity, and he began working to create such a sound.

It was hard going. The band was doing so poorly that he couldn't afford to keep regular members. Musicians kept coming and going, some of them inept and some of them drunks. But he soldiered on, making a batch of records every month or so for Brunswick (none of which satisfied him), and broadcasting twice a week from the Roseland-State, all of which at least kept the band's reputation growing.

While still at the Roseland-State, he hired Billie Holiday as the band's singer. He had admired her singing since 1933, when she made her first recordings, backed by a group that included Benny Goodman. He had even told her, when he first formed his band in 1936, that he would like her to record with it some day, but she wasn't impressed. She had heard much the same thing from Benny.

But early in 1938, having heard she had left the Basie band and was looking for a job, he drove to Harlem and found her and told her, "Come on." She said he was crazy to think of taking a black singer with his white band, especially as he was planning a tour that would include the South, but she was game to try it, and came back with him to Boston. Next day they rehearsed, and that night she sang with the band.

Once they went on tour, life with the Shaw band became a lot tougher for Billie than life with

Basie had been. Artie's young white musicians were somewhat in awe of her, and she missed the camaraderie of her friends like Lester and Freddie Green. And Art himself was never easy to get along with, being a rather crustacean character who didn't seem to like people much.

On the bandstand, his announcements were few and brief, but off the stand he would talk your arm off about how clever and well-read he was. Talking about his efforts at writing, Billie once heard him say, "Geez, I went up to the Catskills, I went up to the mountains for two months, and it snowed. I stayed there and I wrote. I didn't shave for about two months. Before I came back to New York I looked just like Jesus Christ." After that, whenever she got the chance, Billie used to say, "Jesus Christ, His Clarinet and His Orchestra." She took to riding in any vehicle but his to get away from his constant self-promotion.

But worse than all that for her were the constant humiliations of being black in a white band. The clubs where she wasn't allowed to sit on the stage with the band, but had to come on to sing and go off when she'd finished. The bookers and club-owners who kept telling Art he ought to have a white singer. The difficulties finding accomodation, with Billie having to stay in a black hotel, segregated from the rest of the band.

She took all this in her stride – it was no more than she expected – and the southern portion of the tour went fairly smoothly for the first couple of nights. Then there was trouble.

It was at a local dance-hall in the South, possibly Kentucky. Billie had just finished singing 'Travelin'', and sat down to loud applause. But just as Art was about to give the downbeat for the next number, a customer near the band yelled, "Let the nigger wench sing again!"

The unfortunate fact was, he meant no harm. He liked her singing and was rooting for more.

"Nigger wench" was his normal vocabulary, and intended without insult. But that was not what it would have meant in Harlem. He yelled it again, and Billie called him a motherfucker.

Over the roar of the band, he (and Art) only saw her lips move, but the word was clear enough. The customer couldn't believe it, and a riot started. Fortunately Art had prepared for such an emergency. The band bus was parked nearby, and they got Billie hustled out and into it and away. But that was the end of that night's performance.

As in Billie's time with Basie, there were contractual problems about her recording with the band. When she joined Art, they were both recording for Brunswick, but at about that time, in February 1938, his contract ran out and he moved to Victor, recording for their low-price Bluebird label.

Jerry Gray had started to arrange for the band again once it had followed him to Boston, and Art and he discussed tunes to do for their first Bluebird session. A tune the band-members enjoyed playing at jam sessions was Cole Porter's 'Begin The Beguine', and they decided on that.

Jerry wrote the arrangement, the short stabbing chords he placed at the beginning being designed to grab the attention of dancers and get them on the floor. The band recorded it in July 1938, against the wishes of their recording director, and the Victor company, deciding that the name "Art Shaw" lacked something, changed it to "Artie Shaw", and released the record under that name.

At this first session for Bluebird, in July 1938, Billie did record one side, a beautiful version of 'Any Old Time'. How they managed to get away with this is not clear, but the record was released. It was they only side she ever recorded with Artie's band.

The pressures being exerted on him to have a

white singer were added to by his need to have a singer he could record with, and in September 1938 he hired nineteen-year-old Helen Forrest, whose demo record he had heard. This was her first big-band job, and she became one of the better canaries. She found Artie a hard taskmaster, but he was more consistent than, say, Benny Goodman, and the band enjoyed working for him.

He still kept Billie on, he and the bandmembers contributing from their pay-checks to pay her wages, and she was generous and encouraging to the young Helen, urging Artie to get arrangements specially made to frame her singing.

At around this time the band was playing a prom at the University of Indiana, and they played 'Begin The Beguine'. To their surprise, it was greeted with wild applause. Unknown to Artie, the Bluebird record had been released and become an enormous hit. At last the band had arrived. "After fourteen years," said Artie, "I was an instant celebrity."

As a result of this success, the band was booked for a long engagement in the Blue Room of the Hotel Lincoln in New York, at a fee of $25,000 a week. It opened there on October 26, 1938. The hotel had a radio link, and the band started broadcasting two nights a week. This led to further problems for Billie. The broadcasts were sponsored by Old Gold cigarettes, and they refused to let a black sing on their show.

She was now in the depressing position of having stuck with the band while it was struggling, and now that it was a hit she felt shut out of its success. Furthermore, the manager of the Hotel Lincoln, asked Shaw to tell Billie to use the freight elevator, so that customers wouldn't get the idea there were black people staying at the hotel.

He did, which was a little out of character, as the anti-semitism he had suffered from as a child made him a lifelong anti-racist. Possibly he was fearful of imperilling his newly-won success, but Billie felt he should have told the manager where to stuff the freight elevator. Charlie Barnet would have. What upset her more than anything was that this took place in the North, where racial prejudice was less expected.

Although Artie could only use Billie's singing part of the time, and although he also had Helen Forrest with the band, he made no effort to fire her. But by December 1938 she had had enough, and quit, swearing she would never work with a dance-band again – a vow she kept.

'Begin The Beguine' was followed by a string of other hits – 'Indian Love Call' (with a vocal by Tony Pastor), 'Back Bay Shuffle', 'Non-Stop Flight', 'Yesterdays', and of course, 'Nightmare'.

By now the band (and Artie) were in demand everywhere. As well as the band's residence at the Hotel Lincoln, and its radio broadcasts, Artie was invited to appear as featured solo clarinetist in a Carnegie Hall concert being given by Paul Whiteman, whose band was still a respected outfit, though long dropped off the pace.

The band was fast becoming a favourite with the college crowd, and becoming viewed as in direct competition with Benny Goodman himself. By the end of 1938 its personnel had remained fairly stable for a year and a half, and in Artie's own words, "They were able to almost breathe together".

It differed from other swing bands, like Goodman and the Dorseys, in playing fewer out-and-out jazz numbers. Its repertoire mostly consisted of the better pop songs of the day and original compositions. Also, its arrangements were less riff-based and more ambitious than those of the other bands. They were also fuller and more complex because, apart from Artie himself, the band did not rely on its soloists.

In January 1939 Buddy Rich left Harry James and joined the band, replacing dixieland drummer George Wettling, who had briefly replaced the band's original drummer, Cliff Leeman, who in turn had gone off to join Tommy Dorsey. (During the Swing Era, *Down Beat* and other magazines used to run a monthly column recording the moves of key sidemen from band to band, so that serious fans could keep up.)

The band was now so popular that it was sent for by M.G.M. to go to Hollywood and make a film – *Dancing Co-ed*, starring Lana Turner. Artie didn't much enjoy Hollywood. It hadn't really occurred to him that on a film set the director is the boss, nor that he would be expected to deliver some over-colourful dialogue.

Faced with a line in the script where he was supposed to address an audience with "Good evening, hepcats and alligators", he instead said, "Good evening, ladies and gentlemen." The director, S. Sylvan Simon, told him to read the line as written, but Artie objected that he detested jive talk, never used it, and after all, was supposed to be playing himself.

After a number of such encounters he went to the producer and offered to return both his and the band's fees in return for being dropped from the film. Naturally, to do so would mean writing off all the footage already shot, and the studio refused. What they did do was save themselves any future argument by reducing his dialogue to a very small minimum.

Between him and the young Lana Turner there was little rapport, with him making not very funny jokes about not playing for her if she wasn't going to dance well, and she not understanding they were jokes at all.

While in Los Angeles, the band was also booked to appear at the Palomar Ballroom, and while it was there, Artie, who had not spared himself for three years in his efforts to build a successful band, collapsed during a performance from illness and overwork.

It turned out that he had agranulocytosis, a rare and usually fatal form of anaemia. He was unconscious for five days, and in hospital for several weeks. In his absence, Tony Pastor led the band, and when he returned the fans turned out in force to welcome him back.

Naturally a loner, Artie's celebrity had made him even more reclusive, feeling that everybody wanted to use him, but in Hollywood he found other celebrities, and two became his friends – comedian Phil Silvers (whom he had met in New York) and the seventeen-year-old Judy Garland.

Feeling that there was at least something about Hollywood he liked, he bought a house in Los Angeles, at the top of Coldwater Canyon, approached by a treacherous winding road that would deter casual callers. Its address was Summit Ridge Drive.

Phil Silvers, who played clarinet enough to get along, was envious of Artie's musical talent, and of his learning. He continued to read omnivorously, and to Silvers would endlessly elaborate on, for instance, the philosophy of Friedrich Nietzsche – that the strong man (Artie Shaw) is morally superior to the common mass of slaves – he is not bound by any laws in fighting for his individuality against the petty restraints of rigid society.

This arrogant disdain, coupled with his sensuous clarinet-playing, brought beautiful women flocking around him. His charisma was one thing he had that Benny Goodman lacked. Judy Garland fell desperately in love with him, although he regarded her as merely a moonstruck little girl.

At that time he was involved with Betty Grable

(his second marriage having been over for some time). She was in New York, appearing on Broadway in the hit show, *Dubarry Was A Lady*, and Artie complained that he was sick of being separated from her. "What does she really want?" he asked Silvers. "The gold pants? The tinsel? Or me? I make enough to take care of her." "Did you ever tell her that?" "No," he admitted. Silvers suggest he write and tell her, and he did.

With Buddy Rich aboard, the band had become even louder and more driving, and during 1939 it knocked the Goodman band off the number one spot in the annual *Down Beat* poll, beating it by forty-seven votes (out of several hundred).

Benny, who had not started out with any particular ambition to lead the number one band, had by now got used to the idea, and was not too pleased. Meeting Artie in a restaurant one night he growled, "Forty- seven votes, huh?"

Artie, for his part, was more bemused than delighted. This sort of enormous popular success was not what he'd really had in mind. It was all starting to feel irrelevant to the music he wanted to create. Even the vast amounts of money he was earning seemed unreal. He took to buying himself a Patek Phillippe watch every month so as to see something real and tangible.

Furthermore, the part of him that wanted to be a reclusive man of letters was feeling neglected and uneasy. He felt that the press viewed band-leaders as gum-chewing idiots, and disliked being regarded as such. He started to feel he might die without ever doing anything he really wanted to do.

Cashing in on his success, Rockwell-O'Keefe were booking him to play eight shows a day, and what made this even worse was that dance-hall managers kept insisting he play his big hits exactly the same way as he'd recorded them, because that was what the fans expected.

He was coming to loathe the fans. He wanted them to listen to his music, but all they did was scream. Teenagers would skip going to school to attend his concerts, which was madness. When he bought an expensive new limousine, they wrote their names all over it, and even scratched them into the paintwork. He began to feel he was no longer a human being, but an object to be celebrated.

At one dance, a fan got so excited that he leapt off a balcony and broke his leg. Others, jitterbugging mear the stage, kicked his clarinet while he was playing. At which point a journalist asked him for his opinion of jitterbugs. "They're a pack of morons," he said, only at somewhat greater length.

This remark of course got plastered all over the press, and didn't do a lot to win him friends among the fans.

Eventually, in November 1939, while the band was appearing at the Pennsylvania Hotel in New York, he decided he had had enough. He had got where he wanted to be, and had worked to be, and then found it wasn't. He quit.

The band was to continue without him as a co-operative, and Tony Pastor was asked to lead it. But a year earlier Cy Shribman had offered Tony backing of fifty thousand dollars if he wanted to set up his own band, and he decided he would rather take up Cy's offer than have a band full of partners, so he left.

The Artie Shaw band struggled on for a couple of months under the leadership of George Auld, who had joined alongside Tony Pastor on tenor about a year previously, but early in 1940 it folded.

Artie retreated to Mexico, stayed there for two months, then returned to his house on Summit Ridge Drive. He had become intrigued by the South American rhythms he had heard in Mexico, and brought back with him a batch of new tunes, one of which was 'Frenesi'.

With Phil Silvers, he visited M.G.M. They went onto the set of *Two Girls On Broadway*, starring George Murphy, Joan Blondell and Lana Turner. Lana made a bee-line for Artie. She looked radiant in a long flowing gown, and he was bowled over, but tried not to show it, remembering their lack of rapport on *Dancing Co-ed*.

Disdainfully he arranged a date for that night, later asking Silvers to come too in case she turned out to be a bringdown. Lana asked if he would take her to hear Guy Lombardo, and he did. The Lombardo band, in awe of him, played dismally, but Artie and Lana didn't care, too busy agreeing that show-business was crap and they'd both be happier on a desert island with each other.

They hired a plane that very night and eloped to Las Vegas to get married, Artie giving Phil Silvers his car-keys to drive back to Summit Ridge Drive. There Phil found a special delivery letter from Betty Grable in New York.

When Artie phoned him at five the next morning to announce that he and Lana were back and married, Phil told him about the letter and Artie asked him to read it over the phone. "Darling," it said, "this is what I've been waiting for. I've just handed in my notice to the show. Let's get married tomorrow."

Betty, being resilient, eventually recovered from the shock of Artie's marriage. Not so Judy Garland. It only served to fuel her growing fear that she was unattractive to men.

Artie and Lana, meanwhile, had looked at each other in the cold light of day and more or less said, "Who are you anyway? I don't know you?" It turned out they had almost nothing in common and the marriage lasted less that six months.

At this point Artie was considering forming a sixty-five piece band, but events were to modify this intention somewhat. The Victor company insisted he honour his contract with them by making more records, so in March 1940 he returned to the studios with a thirty-two piece pick- up band (including strings). One of the six numbers they recorded was 'Frenesi', and this too became a tremendous hit.

Two months later, in May 1940, he went into the studios with a similar pick-up band, and recorded five more numbers, including 'April In Paris' and 'King For A Day'.

These too had considerable success, and this led him to organise a new band with five or six brass, his clarinet, four saxes, four rhythm and nine strings. The strings, he felt, would give him much more range musically.

This was all very well, but the two sets of musicians in the band, the jazz-based brass, reeds and rhythm, and the classically-based strings, found each other strange and alien. The two groups too to isolating themselves on the two band buses. Furthermore, Artie began to find the band too big and cumbersome to give him the freedom he had hoped for.

To give himself more freedom, he began to experiment with various smaller groups within the band, naming them after local telephone exchanges – the Chelsea Three, the Gramercy Five, and the Trafalgar Seven. Of these, only the Gramercy Five made records, so it is the one best remembered. With them, in September 1940, he recorded a number he had written that had no title. Asked for one after the session was over, he called it 'Summit Ridge Drive'.

With this band he appeared in another film for M.G.M. – *Second Chorus*, starring Fred Astaire. This time the dialogue was more congenial to him, and he ended up with a fair-sized speaking role. Cornetist Bobby Hackett, soon to join Glenn Miller, ghosted on the sound-track for Fred

Astaire, and Billy Butterfield, Artie's featured trumpeter, ghosted for Fred's co-star, Burgess Meredith.

It was with the full band, in September 1940, that Artie made one of his most popular records, 'Stardust'. Over the year it was together, the band worked for only six or eight months, but even giving himself that much breathing-space, Artie began to feel the need for more time to learn about music, so at around the end of March 1941, he again disbanded.

Two months later he re-formed, this time with fifteen strings, and with Basie's old Kansas City colleague, Hot Lips Page, on trumpet.

Again he had a black band-member, this time not a singer, who could be regarded as somehow separate, but a musician sitting right there in the body of the band.

This inevitably led to problems when a southern tour was planned. The Rockwell-O'Keefe office phoned to ask Artie if he could find a substitute for Lips on the tour. Artie said that they were booking his band, not telling him who he should have in it. They phoned back a while later to say it was all right, Lips could be in the band, but at some of the venues he would have to sit a little way away from the rest of the band. "How far?" asked Artie. "Oh, say fifteen feet." Artie cancelled the tour, saying later, "I wasn't fighting for Lips, I was fighting for sanity."

The band stayed together for about six months, and Artie found it the best he'd ever had. He also felt that his audiences were improving. Instead of jitterbugging and screaming, they were starting to listen. In fact, he'd have kept that band together for quite a while if the Japs hadn't attacked Pearl Harbor.

The attack took place on the morning of Sunday, December 7, 1941. That night, the band was appearing in a show at Providence, Rhode Island. A dance act was on-stage when Artie was summoned to the wings and asked to make an anouncement that all military personnel were to report to their bases immediately.

After the dance act, he did, and three-quarters of the audience got to their feet and left. Suddenly everything he was doing seemed to Artie to be totally disconnected from the real world. He led the band into 'Stardust', and whispered to the musicians in the front row, "You're all on two weeks' notice. Pass it round." It was a very dismal rendering of 'Stardust'.

The band actually stayed together a little longer than two weeks. They did three more recording sessions, the last on January 21, piling up a backlog of records for Victor. Then they did disband, and in April 1942, Artie enlisted in the U.S. Navy.

Seeing he was Artie Shaw, the Navy gave him a band to rehearse. It was entirely composed of enlisted musicians, and as far as Artie was concerned, they were hopeless.

Struggling with the unfamiliar situation of having to do everything through proper channels, he got permission to form a band of hand-picked musicians, and did.

This was of course not the sort of high-powered leading-edge band he had had in civilian life, but it was a competent band, its repertoire containing a fair number of well-known jazz numbers as well as his hits from the past.

One of its first assignments, in the autumn of 1942, was to play at Pearl Harbor itself, to audiences of soldiers, sailors, paratroopers and marines. It went on to tour all round the Pacific, Artie insisting all the way that it play for the enlisted men, not for officers' dances.

A performance that impressed him deeply was one aboard the Navy's biggest aircraft-carrier, the U.S.S. Saratoga. The band was lined up on the hydraulic platform used to lower aircraft from the flight deck into the interior of the ship, and as they started to play they descended (like the rising stage of the Paramount in reverse) into a cavernous metal-walled area crammed with service personnel. The echoing cheer that went up was like nothing Artie had ever heard, and suddenly he realised what importance his music had for those men in that situation.

From then on he oscillated between pride in what he was doing and inability to handle the service situation of not being in control. For a start, this was one band he wouldn't be able to disband on a sudden impulse. He also hated the unpredictable ways officers and men would approach him, their attitudes ranging from, "Hey, wow, it's Artie Shaw!" to "Who the fuck do you think you are!" In the spring of 1943, from a combination of pressure and total exhaustion, he had a nervous breakdown.

He was sent to Guadalcanal to recuperate, then sent off touring the Pacific with the band again. Towards the end of 1943, after about a year of touring, he became near to collapse again, and was shipped home to San Francisco.

The band was taken over by tenorist Sam Donahue, who had been with Gene Krupa, Harry James and Benny Goodman, as well as leading a band of his own before being drafted into the Navy. Under Donahue it was an splendidly powerful band, eighteen strong and using the heavier beat that swing bands had started to use in the mid-Forties.

When it was posted to England in 1944, British musicians were unaware of the changes that were taking place in swing. American records were almost non-existent in Britain, because of the war and because of Petrillo's recording ban, so they had heard little of the bigger bands and more driving beat. When men of the R.A.F. Dance

Orchestra (unofficially known as the Squadronaires), proud of their ability to do a workmanlike imitation of Glenn Miller or Tommy Dorsey, were booked opposite the Donahue band for a two-band session at the Queensbury Club in London, they felt as if they'd been hit by a truck.

The Navy hospitalised Artie for three months, then discharged him. It was February 1944, and there he was in civilian life, completely at a loss. He could see no future in anything, and felt totally apathetic. After a short period in analysis, he came to realise that it wasn't his fault if he couldn't fit into the music business, that he had an artistic personality, not an entertainment one, and that perhaps he'd been right in his other ambition, to be a writer. So that autumn he assembled a band.

This time there was no string section.

It was to be a straightforward eighteen piece swing band – four trumpets, four trombones, one clarinet, five saxes, piano, guitar, bass and drums.

With this band, it was his intention to take more time over recordings – to reach for perfection. In line with this policy, it had in it some outstanding musicians – Barney Kessel on guitar, Dodo Marmarosa on piano, and Roy Eldridge on trumpet.

Artie's pursuit of perfection is illustrated in a story told by Roy himself. In July 1945 the band was attempting to record a version of 'Someone To Watch Over Me', and there had been so many bad starts and unusable takes that they were up to about take thirty-eight (usually four would be a lot). One of the sax-players said, "Artie, maybe if we went onto something else – leave this alone for a while – it would work out better." Artie looked at the whole band and said, "Anybody who doesn't like the way I'm running this band can pick up his horn and leave." Roy took the mouthpiece out of his trumpet and stood up, and

Artie yelled, "I didn't mean you!" With that band Artie recorded what he thought was one of his best sides ever, 'Summertime', with a beautiful solo by Roy in which, unusually, he plays growl trumpet. He used to play the number that way in rehearsal, but was most reluctant to commit it to record, fearing that people would accuse him of stealing Cootie Williams's routine. But Artie prevailed.

He kept this band together for about fourteen months, but then began to suffer again from the pressures of the big band business, and the feeling that he was a commodity selling commodities. In November 1945 he disbanded what was to be his last full-time big band.

He continued to get married – to Ava Gardner, then to Kathleen Windsor, author of the Forties best-seller, "Forever Amber". Neither lasted.

In 1947 he decided to pursue his long-standing interest in classical music, and to play no improvisation for a year, to see what would happen to his clarinet tone. It changed, becoming mellower.

In 1948 he was asked to be the featured performer at the opening of a new jazz club in New York, Bop City, and agreed provided he was allowed to play his own music. The management agreed, but were less than delighted when he showed up with a forty-piece classical orchestra, who playing left the hipsters bemused.

Towards the end of the Forties, he decided that he'd seen what classical music was about, and that he would now retire to a quiet life and concentrate on his writing. He bought a farm in Duchess County, New York State, and settled down to do just that.

To pay for the farm he briefly put together a big band, but as it didn't play standards, it flopped. Irritated by this, and as a cynical private joke, he assembled the worst possible band he could. To his horror, it was a success everywhere it played. One club-owner even told him, "This is the best band we've had here since Blue Barron." Blue Barron had a band that was a poor imitation of Kay Kyser (and his College of Musical Knowledge), a novelty band that was quite corny enough to begin with.

Disgusted, in 1951 he decided to quit the field of music one and for all. He settled on his farm, happily raising a dairy herd of Holsteins, marrying another actress, Doris Dowling (who also didn't last), and writing his autobiography, "The Trouble With Cinderella: An Outline Of Identity".

In 1953 he formed a band briefly and did a tour through Texas and Oklahoma. Then, those being the witch-hunting days of Senator Joseph McCarthy, when middle America feared there were Reds under every bed, he was summoned before the House Un-American Activities Committee to explain why he'd attended two communist meetings in 1946.

He explained that this was at a time when America and the Soviet Union had only just finished being allies, and that the communists were proposing an international peace conference, which he thought was a good idea, and any time the Republicans thought of arranging an international peace conference, he'd attend that too. He was cleared, but the whole business had disgusted him with America, so after re-forming a version of the Gramercy Five and making the last musical tour he would ever make, he reluctantly sold his farm, where he had been happier than anywhere, and emigrated to live in Bagur, on the east coast of Spain, in a house that he designed himself.

CHAPTER 15

duke ellington - part two

Of all the big bands that had been famous and influential in the Twenties, only Duke Ellington's stayed at the top into the Thirties (and the Forties, Fifties, Sixties and Seventies). Paul Whiteman, Fletcher Henderson, Jean Goldkette, Ben Pollack, the Casa Loma – not all disbanded, but all lost popularity. Ellington, on the other hand, went from strength to strength.

The first years of the Thirties, however, were rather unsettled ones for him, both musically and privately. For a start, his marriage to Edna had foundered in around 1929, and he was now involved with a small, sweet-natured dancer called Mildred Dixon, who with her partner, Henri Wesson, had opened at the Cotton Club on the same night as Duke. He remained on fairly friendly terms with Edna, and never divorced her, although this was possibly because being married protected him from being expected to marry anyone else.

Mildred was living with him in a three-bedroom apartment on fashionable Edgecombe Avenue, Harlem. Late in 1930 Duke suddenly insisted that, instead of visiting New York, his family – father J.E., mother Daisy, his son Mercer (then eleven years old) and kid sister Ruth (eight years old, younger than her nephew Mercer) – should give up their house in Washington and come to live with him and Mildred.

It was an odd and rather high-handed decision. For a start, J.E. took some persuading. The move would involve him giving up his job, and at the age of forty-nine he felt in no way ready to retire. Furthermore, it placed Mildred in the odd situation of being in effect a daughter-in-law in her own home. But neither Mildred nor J.E. could resist Duke's courtly determination, and the move took place.

High-handed though it was, the move undoubtedly sprang from good-hearted family loyalty. Duke felt protective towards his little sister Ruth, he respected his father, and he doted on his mother, showering her with furs and flowers, and generally treating her like a duchess.

Daisy, for her part doted on him. She must have done, because although an extremely correct and proper Victorian lady, she was apparently able to ignore the fact that her son was not only living in sin, but also working in an environment thronged with gangsters, pimps, prostitutes and gamblers. In her eyes, her wonderful son could simply do no wrong.

This family move took place shortly before the band went to Hollywood to film *Check And Double Check*. When the film was finished, it returned to the Cotton Club, as it would continue to do from time to time right through the Thirties. But its great days there were now over. For one thing, Cab Calloway's band had become the club's favourite. For another, Ellington was beginning to get restless there. He wanted to do more than perform for shows, and felt he needed a change if his music was to develop.

On February 4, 1931, his band's contract at the club ended, and on February 13 it began an engagement at the Oriental Theatre in Chicago. The producer there asked for the band to have a girl singer (at the Cotton Club they used the singers from the show). Duke hired Ivie Anderson, who at that time was also in Chicago, singing with the Earl Hines band at the Grand Terrace ballroom.

Ivie had been born in Gilroy, California in 1905. She had singing lessons as a young girl, and began performing in Los Angeles night-clubs when she was sixteen. In 1925 she worked for a while at the Cotton Club, and after touring in the famous black musical *Shuffle Along*, returned to Los Angeles.

There she sang with various bands, including one led by drummer Sonny Clay, which in 1928 took her on a tour of Australia. She also toured as a solo performer, and in 1930 began her short stay with Earl Hines.

Ivie would stay with Ellington for eleven years, leaving only when her asthma became too bad for her to continue touring, and in many ways would be the best regular singer he ever had, her light jazz-inflected voice fitting into the band better than the more trained voices he tended to hire later.

She also fitted well into the band in off-stage life, being very much one of the boys, and from all accounts a considerable poker- player (Ellington once said that he couldn't write really well for a musician until he knew how that man played poker).

It was during Duke's engagement at the Oriental Theatre that his manager, Irving Mills, always the hustler, announced to the press that a new long work – a rhapsody – would be premiered by the band tomorrow night.

Ellington, who worked well with Mills, and was just as much a hustler, let on that this was all a great surprise to him, and said that while had been considering new directions for his work to take, and had certainly been thinking about writing longer compositions in an impressionistic vein, this announcement took him completely by surprise. However (he said), he liked working to a deadline, and would see what he could do. And sure enough, next night there was the band performing the first of his many extended compositions – 'Creole Rhapsody'.

The only thing wrong with their little scenario was that in fact the band had recorded 'Creole Rhapsody' a couple of months earlier, before it had even left the Cotton Club. Irving Mills had arranged for them to record it for Brunswick, but as the band were actually contracted to Victor, they worked under the name of The Jungle Band.

The Brunswick recording lasts a little over six minutes, and it was released on two sides of a 78. By the time the band came to record it for Victor, under its own name, in June 1931, it had grown to over eight minutes, and had to be released on two sides of a twelve-inch 78. It says a great deal for Irving Mills's powers of persuasion that he managed to get Victor to do this, especially in view of the poor state of the record business at that time, because 'Creole Rhapsody' is by no means a conventional big band record.

It has changes of tempo, and shifts of rhythm, and a number of different themes weaving in and out, with unusual, slightly dissonant harmonies. The critics of the time greeted it enthusiastically, as the best attempt so far to create jazz in a more complex form than the popular songs and blues that were its usual raw material. Unlike such efforts as 'Rhapsody In Blue', which was essentially light classical music tricked out with some of the rhythms and voicings of jazz, this piece was rooted in jazz.

As well as 'Creole Rhapsody', the great Ellington classics kept appearing. 'Ring Dem Bells', which was the big number from *Check And Double Check*, appeared in 1930 (nobody seems able to explain how come the tubular bells on the original recording were played by the seventeen-year-old Charlie Barnet).

Also in 1930 came probably Duke's most famous number, 'Mood Indigo', which he recorded (as so often) three times within three months for three different record companies. The first two did not use the whole band, but a septet – Art Whetsol (muted trumpet), Tricky Sam Nanton (muted trombone), Barney Bigard (clarinet), plus the rhythm section, and of all the dozens of version of it that Duke was to record over the years, they remain the best – still and simple and haunting.

Who wrote the number is not clear. Duke once claimed he wrote it in twenty minutes while waiting for his dinner the night before the first recording session. But most of the theme came from Barney Bigard, who, after the tune had been around for twenty-eight years, successfully sued to have his name added to the copyright (he hadn't bothered earlier because nobody had any idea it would grow into not just a hit but a standard).

Bigard in turn admitted that the first strain of it came from his old New Orleans clarinet teacher, Lorenzo Tio Jr., who used to play virtually the same number under the title 'Dreamy Blues' (which, oddly enough, was the title used on some issues of the first recording). One thing alone is sure – the spare, simple classic arrangement was Duke's alone.

Late in 1930 came the complex and rousing 'Rockin' In Rhythm', which seems to have been evolved in rehearsal for a theatre show in Philadelphia by the whole band, with the largest contribution coming from Harry Carney, and other ideas coming from Barney Bigard, Johnny Hodges, and bassist Wellman Braud.

Most of Ellington's work was evolved in rehearsal in this way, with contributions from all concerned, but 'Rockin' In Rhythm' was so much an on-the-spot creation that, although the band played it for the rest of Duke's life, and it kept slowly changing, it never got written down.

In 1931, for some reason, the band recorded far more popular songs by other people than originals by Ellington. Maybe this was because leaving the Cotton Club had unsettled Duke (among other things, depriving him of the deadlines that helped him work), or maybe it was because Irving Mills thought recording already-known numbers would be a good idea in the tottering state of the record industry.

Whatever the reason, among the numbers the band recorded that year (apart from the two versions of 'Creole Rhapsody') were 'Them There Eyes', 'Rockin' Chair', 'Twelfth Street Rag', 'The Peanut Vendor', 'Limehouse Blues', and a four-minute version of 'St Louis Blues', with a rather formal vocal by Bing Crosby, on his best behaviour in the fast company he was keeping.

Early in 1932, however, Ivie Anderson recorded her first number with the band. It became a big hit and gave the whole coming era its name – 'It Don't Mean A Thing (If It Ain't Got That Swing)'.

By 1932 the band's personnel had hardly changed for about three years, and after 1932 it was not to change for another three years, and then not much, but in that year the last member arrived to make the classic Ellington line-up complete – trombonist Lawrence Brown.

Lawrence Brown got his first name from the

town he was born in – Lawrence, Kansas, where his father was a minister. He was born there in 1907, but when he was seven his family moved to California, first to Oakland, then briefly to San Francisco, then to Pasadena.

There they lived next door to the church, where his father preached and his mother played the organ, and from early childhood Lawrence had a feeling for music. Enough to know that his father, who fancied himself as a singer, wasn't very good.

Lawrence was the middle one of three brothers. The eldest, Merrill, became a competent classical-style pianist, and Lawrence and his younger brother studied piano at Pasadena High School, and then the violin. Young Lawrence found the violin too difficult, but fortunately the school had a wide choice of instruments available, so he tried the tuba and, for a short while, the saxophone.

It so happened that the leader of the church choir was a trombonist. He used to leave his trombone in the church all week, and seeing it there when he was cleaning up the church gave Lawrence an idea. Or rather, two ideas. The first was that you didn't see as many trombonists around as other musicians, the second was that he liked the sound of the cello, and he'd been taught that the trombone was the violin of the brass instruments, so maybe if he learned the trombone he could find a way of playing it sweetly, like a cello.

At Pasadena High, which had excellent musical tuition, he learned proper trombone technique, and was exposed to a wide range of music – the school orchestra, for instance, habitually staged operettas.

He became so good that a men's club in the town selected him to play as soloist on their local radio show, and while he was at the radio station he was heard playing by the famous Twenties evangelist, Sister Aimee Semple McPherson.

It was only a year or so since Sister Aimee had opened her temple alongside Echo Lake, in Los Angeles – the Angelus Temple, which as well as having a rotating electrically-illuminated cross on the top, visible for fifty miles, had her living quarters, a broadcasting station, a theological seminary, and an auditorium seating five thousand.

There she mounted her spectacular productions – pageants, lantern-slide lectures on the Holy Land, shows, circuses and, above all, healing sessions, in all of which she "substituted the cheerfulness of the playroom for the gloom of the morgue". She herself was much given to raising her arms in the spotlight, clad in flowing white, and moaning "Come ... come ... come ...", in her rich throaty contralto.

She was so taken by Lawrence's playing at the radio station that she summoned him to appear at the Angelus Temple. He appeared there and played to a packed house next Mother's Day.

It was all very well playing for Aimee Semple Macpherson, but his father was deeply disapproving of any form of secular music. Lawrence's older brother Merrill had gone on from the piano to also play the organ, and became sufficiently good to be offered a job playing in a Sacramento movie theatre. His father said "No!" so firmly that Merrill gave up any idea of a career in music and went off to spend his whole working life in the post office.

Lawrence, having a tendency to bloody-mindedness, reacted differently. He had started slipping out to play at local dances, and when he was nineteen his father gave him an ultimatum, "Either behave yourself and quit disgracing me, or get out!" Lawrence left home and turned professional.

By now his own personal cello-like trombone style was almost formed. He played with various small bands in cheap dance-halls, then with bigger bands such as Paul Howard's Quality Serenaders, the house band at the most important cabaret in California, Sebastian's Cotton Club, just across the street from the M.G.M. lot.

In 1930, still at Sebastian's Cotton Club, he was a member of the Les Hite band, during the time it was being led by Louis Armstrong (and when the band's drummer was Lionel Hampton). And he was still with the Hite band at the club early in 1932, a year after Louis had left, when the Ellington band came to Los Angeles to play an engagement at the Orpheum Theatre.

Irving Mills came into the Cotton Club, heard Lawrence, and decided that he should be in Duke's band. His main reason seems to have been Lawrence's sweet tone, because Irving, like many people in the music business in 1932, had come to believe that what people wanted during the Depression was sweet music, a romantic escape from their troubles.

Lawrence presented himself to Duke, who said, "I never knew you. Never met you, never heard you. But Irving says get you, so that's that." And Duke's instinct to trust Irving was right. He now had three trombones, so the trombone section could voice full chords, and Lawrence's sweet smooth tone gave Duke another voice to work with, contrasting with Juan Tizol's clean classical tone and Tricky Sam Nanton's humorous or impassioned growling.

Lawrence originally only intended to stay with the band for a year: he'd just bought a great big sixteen-cylinder Cadillac convertible, and touring with Duke would mean he'd have to put it up on blocks and not use it. In fact he stayed until 1951, when he quit because he was fed up with touring, only to rejoin in 1960 for another ten years.

Touring was only one of the things Lawrence didn't like. He was by far the touchiest band-member Duke ever had. He didn't like the idea that he was making less money with Duke ($70 a week) than he had with the Les Hite band. He believed that the band ought to be a corporation. He objected when phrases from solos he had played turned up later in new Ellington compositions, and on one occasion seriously angered Duke by saying, "I don't consider you a composer. You are a compiler."

Much of his grouchiness seemed to stem from feeling as he got older that he had chosen a trivial way of life. He had some regrets about not studying medicine, which he had studied briefly in his later years at school, but quit because he didn't think he could face the way he would feel if one of his patients died. He also may have had regrets about not being a solid citizen like his father, whose attitudes he more and more seemed to share as the years went by. A lifelong teetotaller, the band's nickname for him was "Deacon".

Grumpy or not, the last member of the early-Thirties band was now aboard. Or at least, almost the last member. Duke had more fears and superstitions than any other six people put together. He wouldn't wear certain colours, especially green. He thought that giving shoes as presents was unlucky, as they might cause the recipient to walk away. He felt that the number thirteen was unlucky, and with Lawrence Brown in it, his band would have thirteen members (apparently Ivie didn't count in this total). Another musician had to be found.

By good fortune, just at the time Lawrence was to join, who should come looking for his old job back but his old friend, one of the original Washingtonians, Toby Hardwick.

After he had been in his taxi-cab accident in 1928, and been replaced in the band by Johnny

Hodges, Toby had worked around Atlantic City for a bit, then, on impulse, taken a boat to Paris. There he got work with Bricktop, that same Ada Smith who had got the Washingtonians their first job in New York.

She had gone to Paris in 1924, sang at a club called Le Grand Duc for a while, then graduated to running it, and in 1928 had opened her own famous club, "Bricktop's", in the Rue Pigalle. After playing there and at other clubs around Europe for a couple of years, Toby had come back to New York and started leading a band at the Hot Feet Club, on West Houston Street in Greenwich Village.

The Hot Feet Club had a show modelled on the ones in the Harlem nightspots, offering good jazz and spicy entertainment by black performers for white audiences. Toby's band there by all accounts was an excellent one, which is hardly surprising when it had musicians in it such as Chu Berry and Fats Waller.

Unfortunately, the owner of the Hot Feet tried to start a similar club in Chicago, and got eliminated by the incumbent gangsters. So the Hot Feet closed, and Toby came to see if Duke wanted an altoist.

Now the band could be, and became, fourteen, and it would remain almost unchanged right through the Thirties. Art Whetsol, Freddy Jenkins, Cootie Williams (trumpets); Tricky Sam Nanton, Lawrence Brown (trombones); Juan Tizol (valve trombone); Barney Bigard (clarinet and tenor); Johnny Hodges (alto, clarinet and soprano); Otto Hardwick (alto and bass sax); Harry Carney (baritone, clarinet and alto); Duke Ellington (piano); Fred Guy (guitar and banjo); Wellman Braud (bass); Sonny Greer (drums); Ivie Anderson (vocals).

Toby's return to the band brought it more good fortune than anyone expected. He had news that in Europe the band's records had won it an international reputation. The scale of it had astonished him, and the news was undoubtedly a surprise to Duke, who was barely aware that his records were being released in Europe, let alone that dance-band fans and musicians were eagerly awaiting each new release, and that critics were learnedly discussing them.

He was beginning to be aware, however, that some serious musicians in America regarded his band as more than just another Harlem dance-band. In that very year, 1932, the Australian-born composer Percy Grainger had organised a concert for the band at Columbia University in New York, and he also arranged for Duke to lecture on jazz at New York University, where he was head of the music department.

There is a story that at the lecture Grainger expounded to the audience on the influence Delius had had on Duke's music, and that on his way home Duke stopped off at a music store and bought a hundred dollars worth of Delius records, not having wanted to admit that he'd never even heard of Delius.

It took Toby some time to convince Duke and Irving Mills that the Ellington band really did have a reputation in Europe, but when Mills realised that there was a flourishing market to be opened up, he began sending transatlantic letters and cables, and soon it was announced that in 1933, by arrangement with British band-leader and impresario Jack Hylton, the Ellington band would appear for two weeks at the London Palladium.

The band, plus dancer Bessie Dudley, who had appeared with them at the Cotton Club, sailed for England on June 2 on the S.S. Olympia, and the voyage was a pleasant rest for all of them but Duke. Far from being the world traveller he would become in his later years, his superstitous fears took hold of him. He had been deeply influenced in his boyhood by reading a book about the Titanic, and was terrified of being afloat. It had been a standing joke in the band that he wouldn't even take the Hoboken ferry.

His fears became worse when someone told him that during the hours of darkness the ship was often steered by an automatic pilot. He couldn't possibly imagine how an automatic pilot could see an iceberg, so every night he stayed awake, drinking and playing cards and nervously keeping watch.

The ship docked safely at Southampton on Friday, June 9, and the band were greeted by Jack Hylton, Henry Hall (leader of the BBC Dance Orchestra), symphony conductor Basil Cameron, and a platoon of press photographers.

The whole entourage took a train to Waterloo, where they were greeted by thirty-seven more photographers. After which it was discovered that their hotel had no room for a party of eighteen – at least, not Blacks. After some scuffling around, Duke was found a room at the Dorchester, and the rest of the band were got in somehow at various lesser hotels.

That evening, Jack Hylton gave a reception for them all at his grand Mayfair mansion, in the middle of which Duke was whisked away to do a nine o'clock radio interview with the BBC.

The show they were in at the Palladium was not theirs alone. Far from it. They were presented as top of the bill in a conventional variety programme that included comedian Max Miller, and they were restricted to forty minutes, during which they played eight numbers (plus a couple of encores).

The band, in grey tails with grey satin facings, opened with 'Ring Dem Bells' and, as Ellington remembered years later, at the end of it the audience stood up and applauded for what seemed like ten minutes. This so unnerved the

band that when it came to the next number they were shaking so much they could hardly play.

The rest of the programme included Bessie Dudley, in black satin shorts, dancing the snake-hips to 'Rockin' In Rhythm', Ivie Anderson singing 'Stormy Weather' and a rather forgettable song called 'Give Me A Man Like That', and two more up-tempo band numbers, 'Bugle Call Rag' and 'Whispering Tiger'. The two encores were 'Some Of These Days' and 'Mood Indigo'.

The show got good audiences. At the end of the first week they had almost equalled the Palladium record, and the biggest sensation of all was Bessie Dudley. The serious critics, however, were not entirely pleased. This was pandering to commercialism – where were the numbers like 'Creole Rhapsody'? (Much the same thing was said when Duke made his next visit to London, in 1958, and on subsequent visits, but Duke always played for the public, not for musicologists).

The journal *Melody Maker*, had been afraid that his programme might be too commercially-slanted (and too short) at the Palladium, so it had arranged for the band to play two special concerts at the Trocadero cinema, Elephant and Castle, for Musicians' Union members only.

These again did not entirely please some of the critics. For the first half of the first concert, Duke got the band to play some of his moodier and more impressionistic pieces, like 'Blue Ramble', but, sensing that the audience was not responding as warmly as he would have liked, in the second half he reverted to more popular items, such as 'Dinah' (with a vocal by Sonny Greer), Lawrence Brown's trombone feature, 'Trees', and a recent composition, 'Sophisticated Lady'.

Duke, who, like both Louis Armstrong and Sidney Bechet, liked to have an image or a situation in mind when composing, said that 'Sophisticated Lady' was "dedicated to all lady school-teachers who travelled and learned an spent holidays in Europe". The words that got added later by Mitchell Parish were, he said, "Wonderful. But not entirely fitting my original conception."

Despite the misgivings of the critics and the difficulties with hotels, the trip was a success. British dance-band musicians were stunned at the virtuosity and drive of the band, and socially they were lionised.

Lord Beaverbrook invited them to appear at a party he was giving at his palatial London home, Stornaway House, just behind St James's Street. Jack Hylton's band was was to play soft music till midnight, when the Ellington band would take over.

Two of the sons of King George V were there, both Ellington fans. One was Prince George, Duke of Kent (who was killed in an air crash during World War Two), and the other was the Prince of Wales (who went on to become Edward VIII and abdicate). Duke, with his natural grace, treated them as equals. Or almost – when Prince George asked him to play 'Swampy River', Duke, not knowing who he was, brushed him off by saying he didn't do requests.

Later, they got on better, playing piano duets together. Duke was complimentary about Prince George's playing, and even more so about the playing of the Prince of Wales, who did a spell on drums. "And it wasn't just Little Lord Fauntleroy drumming," said Duke. "He had a hell of a Charleston beat." As the Charleston had by then been out of fashion for some eight years, this may or may not, like many of Ellington's remarks, be as straightforward as it seems.

The band's trip continued with a tour of Britain, playing for dancing at the Grafton Ballroom in Liverpool and Green's Playhouse in Glasgow, and giving concerts in Hastings,

Harrogate and Blackpool. The band then made short tours of France and Holland, and set off back to the States.

The trip was a watershed in Duke's career. From then on he knew that with the serious support he could expect from cultured Europeans, he could afford to be more ambitious in his music (without neglecting the commercial side). He acquired a taste for travel, realising it could be an inspiration to him. And he realised that, in Europe at least, it would be possible for him to be accepted socially by sophisticated and titled people, even royalty.

One of the cultured fans he had met in England was the composer Constant Lambert, who had written in the *New Statesman* such praises as, "I know nothing in Ravel so dexterous in treatment as the varied solos in the middle of the ebullient 'Hot And Bothered', and nothing in Stravinsky more dynamic than the final section."

More lasting in effect than Constant Lambert's reviews, however, was the habit his wife had of referring to 'Mood Indigo' as 'Rude Indigo'. Little more than a month after his return to America, Duke produced a rather sombre, reflective piece with brooding trumpet by Cootie Williams and a wordless vocal by trumpeter Louis Bacon (Ivie Anderson's husband), calling it 'Rude Interlude'.

Determined as he had become to write more serious music, back in America there was a living to be earned. Even for a band as well-established as the Ellington band, things could be tough in the early Thirties. His son Mercer, who for a while became the band-boy, remembered on one occasion in Cleveland conplaining he was hungry, and receiving from Duke the reply, "What? Didn't you just eat yesterday?"

Irving Mills was a tower of strength. He pioneered tours through Texas and the Deep South, areas that few New York bands, especially black ones, ever visited, and overcame the problems of segregation by hiring for the band two Pullman cars, plus a van for baggage, which could be shunted into a siding at whatever town the band was appearing in, and serve as their hotel. Duke's was the only band, black or white, to travel in such style.

Trains were the one mode of transport that Duke thoroughly trusted, and his affection for them found an outlet in two of his best compositions, the amazing up-tempo tour-de-force 'Daybreak Express' that the band recorded at the end of 1933 (and never again, and nor did anybody else dare to try it), and in 1947, 'Happy Go Lucky Local', originally part of his 'Deep South Suite'.

Early in 1934, Duke's mother, Daisy, fell ill. At first she refused to go to hospital, possibly out of puritan fear of being examined by a male stranger, but by September it was clear she had cancer. She went back to Washington for treatment and was eventually sent to the Providence Hospital, a research centre in Detroit. There, on May 27, 1935, she died.

Duke, who had spent the last three days of her life beside her, was devastated. For a long while, everything in life seemed pointless to him. He gave her an elaborate funeral, burying her in an iron casket weighing half a ton, designed to last for ever and costing $3,500. The flowers cost another $2,000.

Although he kept busy during the next few months, it was only because he had to. All he was really doing was going through the motions. During the next year his usually-prolific recorded output fell to only sixteen sides, most of them perfunctory and poor. But there was one exception. Alone in his small room in one of the band's Pullman cars, during another tour of the South, he slowly composed his next extended work, based on memories of his childhood, and intended as a tribute to Daisy.

It was called 'Reminiscing In Tempo', a thirteen-minute composition in three parts (though to fit it onto two 78's it had to be split over four sides), and in the same fairly slow tempo throughout. He was hurt and dismayed when those same English critics who had encouraged him to extend himself dismissed it as "a long rambling monstrosity ... pretentious and meaningless". This hostile reception discouraged Duke from writing similar extended compositions for quite some years.

On the other hand, the great musicologist Gunther Schuller, writing in 1989, calls it "one of Ellington's greatest master strokes", praising the way Ellington developed and intertwined his musical themes, and saying that, "It is hard to think of any work in the classical literature that is so uniquely – and so successfully – geared to a specific group of players".

It broke a lot of new ground. Not only was it longer than the conventional big band piece, the phrases within it were of unusual lengths, such as $6\frac{1}{2}$ bars or $3\frac{1}{2}$ bars, instead of the usual 4 or 8. It was in the jazz idiom, but the solos were written, not improvised – although always in the personal style of the performer (it would have been hard for even Duke's musicians to improvise within such an unusual and complex framework).

Opinion has remained divided, but undoubtedly one of the main reasons for the critics' coldness was that it didn't swing. This was no accident. At the time it was written, the Swing Era had suddenly blazed into life, and he was trying to steer as far away from it as possible.

This was because it had put him in an uncomfortable situation. Just at a time when he was beginning to experiment with subtler and more complex music, here was this new breed of big bands bouncing out a simple, direct form of dance-music that had grabbed the public by the ear. Somehow he had to find a way of creating music of his own that had the power and immediacy of swing, without losing the subtlety of Ellington. Either that, or become regarded as a back number.

One thing that helped him was the sheer quality of his soloists. In March 1935, before the Swing Era even started, he had begun recording with small groups from within the band, and although these were never featured as a "band within a band", he would produce dozens of these sides over the next ten years, under the nominal leadership of such band-members as Johnny Hodges, Barney Bigard, Harry Carney, Cootie Williams and Sonny Greer. This helped identify them as stars to the listening public.

The first of these sessions featured a newcomer to the band, cornetist Rex Stewart, who had joined from the Fletcher Henderson band in December 1934. When a new member joined the band, Duke almost always gave him a lot of solo space, fascinated by the new addition to his tonal palette. Rex was no exception. From his arrival he added a quirky and indivdual new sound, his cornet so highly vocalised that at times he seemed to produce sounds rather than notes, and capable of virtuoso torrents of fast fingering. He would go on to produce such Ellington masterpieces as 'Trumpet In Spades' (1936) and 'Boy Meets Horn' (1938).

'Trumpet In Spades' had the alternative title 'Rex's Concerto', and was part of another Ellington technique for publicising his key players. In 1936 he recorded 'Cootie's Concerto' (later known as 'Echoes Of Harlem') and 'Barney's Concerto' (later known as 'Clarinet Lament'), and in 1940 he recorded 'Concerto For Cootie', which became a popular hit after words

were added and it became 'Do Nothing Till You Hear From Me'.

Over the next two years, the band, while still having basically the same personnel, had acquired three more major talents. The first of these, and possibly the greatest of all the talents that ever joined Duke's musical caravan, was Billy Strayhorn.

Billy, born in Dayton, Ohio, in 1915, had been raised in Hillsborough, North Carolina, and in Pittsburgh, and received a thorough musical training. An accomplished pianist, he had ambitions to be a song-writer, and in December 1938 he brought to Duke a song he had written when he was only seventeen – 'Lush Life'.

This witty song, so full of world-weary disillusion, would be an amazing composition at any age, but at seventeen it borders on the unbelievable. Its harmonies are so unexpected that it is notoriously one of the most difficult of all popular songs to play.

Duke was bowled over, not only by the song, but by Billy himself, a small, round-faced bespectacled man, gentle and affable, but totally self-possessed. Immediately Duke co-opted him into the Ellington organisation, moving him into the apartment on Edgecombe Avenue. In the words of Duke's sister, Ruth, "Billy became a brother".

The band, beholding this new arrival, promptly nicknamed him "Swee' Pea" after the baby in the *Popeye* strip. This was something of a band habit. Johnny Hodges had already received the alternative nickname "Jeep" in the same strip, and in the Seventies altoist Harold Minerve would be known as Geezil, from a mad Popeye professor who had a similarly ferocious fringe of whiskers.

Billy turned out to also have a broad range of culture. He was knowledgeable in literature and the fine arts, and Duke came to depend on his knowledge and guidance, both musically and artistically. Nor was he prepared to have Billy aboard as simply a song-writer. Within three months of his joining, the band recorded the Strayhorn song 'Something To Live For', with Billy at the piano. He would go on to develop a piano style very similar to Duke's, but rather less percussive and more romantic.

Duke also decided that Billy should become an arranger. One day he handed him two numbers and demanded they be arranged by ten the next morning. Billy had never thought of arranging, but as he said, "What could I do? I learned fast."

Over the next thirty years, Duke and Billy, as composer/arangers, became so close that, collaborating by phone, they would often find themselves having written identical passages. It became hard to tell where one left off and the other began, although some members of the band, such as Lawrence Brown, claimed that they could always recognise Billy's harmonies, because they were richer, and more interesting to play.

In the summer of 1939 the band acquired its next major innovator. It was appearing in St Louis, and Johnny Hodges wandered into an after-hours club where an informal group of musicians were jamming. When he heard the bass-player, he became so excited that he rushed off and brought back Billy Strayhorn to hear him. Once Billy had heard him, the two went to Duke's hotel, and woke him out of bed. Duke, wearing an overcoat over his pyjamas, accompanied them to the club. He too was bowled over, and the bass-player joined the band. His name was Jimmy Blanton.

Not much is known about Jimmy Blanton, because he died of TB only three years later, when he was twenty-four, but in those three years with Duke he revolutionised bass-playing.

He had been born in Chattanooga, Tennessee, half Black and half American Indian. His mother played piano and led a local band, and young Jimmy studied violin and theory with an uncle, as well as doubling on piano and alto. So he had an excellent musical grounding.

Having played his first professional gig at the age of eight (in a local store, on violin) and gone on to play in local bands, in his teens studied music at Tennessee State College. There he took up the bass, working with the college band and in local groups, and although totally unheard of in the music world at large, soon became the best bass-player in jazz.

He lived for playing bass, would happily jam in clubs for hours for nothing, and practised incessantly. And he had invented a new way of playing.

In the early days of bass-playing, the bass's function was mainly rhythmic, to give a sharp edge to the basic beat. Even the notes didn't matter much, because the piano or guitar could supply those. Most players in those days simply played on the first and third beats of the bar.

As the feeling of swing began to emerge, bassists like Steve Brown with Jean Goldkette, and Walter Page with his Blue Devils, began playing on all four beats. This allowed them to play more notes, and it became the style to walk up and down the notes of the relevant chord – a technique known as "walking bass".

Jimmy Blanton, having played the violin from an early age, thought like a violinist. On his bass he played invented counter-melodies, plucking not only on the four beats, but on eighths and sixteenths and anywhere else that seemed appropriate. In other words, he played the bass as if it was a musical instrument. It helped that he also had a strong rhythmic beat and a full rich tone.

Duke's bass-player in the band at the time was Billy Taylor, who had replaced Wellman Braud back at the end of 1934. He did not fire Taylor, but brought Jimmy into the band alongside him. Oddly enough, when Braud left the band, Duke had replaced him then with two bassists – alongside Billy Taylor for a long while had been Hayes Alvis.

Hayes Alvis had been one thing – Jimmy Blanton was another. In January 1940, after Jimmy had been in the band for about four months, Billy Taylor walked off the stand and quit in the middle of a set at the Southland Cafe in Boston, saying, "I'm not going to stand up there next to that young boy playing all that bass and be embarrassed."

The final arrival in the 1940 Ellington band, still regarded by many as the best Ellington band of all time, was Ben Webster. Although Ben had been with the band for a few months in 1936, now he joined permanently, and at last Duke's wasn't the only major band not to have a featured tenor-player (during the late Thirties, the tenor had come more and more to be the dominant instrument in jazz, at last supplanting the trumpet).

Benjamin Francis Webster, another part-Indian, was born (in 1909) and bred in Kansas City. Having studied music at Wilberforce University and played professionally, it was at first as a pianist. It wasn't until relatively late in life, at the age of twenty-one, that he took up the tenor.

His progress on it was formidable. Basing his style firmly on Coleman Hawkins, within a year he was in the Bennie Moten band, and he went on to play with Andy Kirk before, in 1934, taking the place of Hawkins himself in the Fletcher Henderson band, when Hawk went off to Europe.

By 1940 he had ceased to be a Hawkins clone, and developed a voice of his own, especially on ballads. Never the amazing explorer of harmonies that Hawk was, on ballads he developed a rich,

sensuous, compelling technique, sometimes voicing so softly that his notes drifted away into puffs of breath.

Oddly enough, in spite of his expertise with ballads, his first big hit with Duke was an all-out stomping solo on the number 'Cotton Tail', one of the outstanding tracks of the whole Swing Era.

By 1940 Duke had got it all together. As well as his own subtleties of composing and orchestration, he had a band that could bring any dance-hall alive. In addition, he had in 1939 made another European tour – to Sweden, Belgium, France, Holland and Denmark (but not Britain – the British musicians' union weren't having American musicians coming over playing music that our boys could play just as well).

Even more than in 1933, the enthusiastic and knowledgeable reception he got in Europe filled him with heart and resolve, and during the next two years he created (and recorded) an amazing string of masterpieces – 'Cotton Tail', 'Concerto For Cootie', 'Rumpus In Richmond', 'Sepia Panorama', 'In A Mellotone', 'Warm Valley'.

There was 'Harlem Air-Shaft', his impression of the sounds and voices drifting from a Harlem tenement. There was 'Morning Glory', which was actually composed by Rex Stewart, but Duke won the copyright off him in a game of poker. Perhaps most outstanding of all, there was 'Ko-Ko', an incredible piece of compressed arranging, using increasingly unsettling harmonies, that nonetheless to even the untrained listener quite clearly follows its basic pattern, the twelve-bar blues.

It is an indication of how far the Swing Era had trained an audience to listen and appreciate pure instrumentals, with no words, that Duke could happily play a number as complex as 'Ko-Ko' at a perfectly ordinary dance gig, and have it received with loud applause. You can hear him do just that on the unplanned recording of a concert he gave at the Crystal Ballroom, in Fargo, Illinois, in November 1940.

At the Fargo concert there had been one major and disturbing change in the band. The week before, Cootie Williams had left to go and join Benny Goodman. Although he would eventually return, this was the first of the defections by major Ellingtonians that would bedevil the band during the late Forties and early Fifties. In the meantime, however, he had been replaced by another future Ellington star, Ray Nance.

Ray Nance, a small, lively, cantankerous performer, played trumpet and violin, and sang and danced. He could do a wicked impression of Louis Armstrong without making a single sound, and was such an all-round entertainer that Duke nicknamed him "Floorshow".

Born in Chicago in 1913, he studied piano from the age of six, took lessons on violin, taught himself trumpet, and marched as drum-major with his high-school band. From 1932 to 1937 he led his own sextet in various Chicago clubs, then joined Earl Hines (1937-38) and Horace Henderson (1939-40). At the beginning of 1940 he went solo as a night-club entertainer for eight months, then joined Ellington.

He would stay with the band until 1963, and until Cootie returned in 1962 took over the growl-trumpet role that Cootie in turn had inherited from Bubber Miley. While his playing was never so dramatic and forceful as Cootie's, he could take even more liberties in delaying or advancing the rhythm, and when he had been in the band for only a couple of months was fortunate enough to create one of the band's classic solos – he was the featured trumpeter on 'Take The A Train'.

'Take The A Train' was written by Billy Strayhorn. Its name came from the fact that in addition to the A Train, which for years had taken passengers from central Manhattan to Harlem, the New York subway system had recently introduced a D Train, which set off in the same direction, but after touching the edge of Harlem at 145th Street, suddenly veered off into the Bronx, taking a number of confused passengers with it. Thus the slogan, "If you want to get to Harlem, take the A Train".

How it came to get written is that in 1940 a dispute had arisen with ASCAP, the powerful American Society Of Composers, Authors And Publishers. This for years had controlled copyright, and collected royalties for its members, and almost every songwriter of note had become a member. They had not much option.

In the late Thirties, feeling full of power and confidence, it decided to drastically raise the fees that radio stations had to pay to broadcast ASCAP numbers. Radio decided to fight back.

ASCAP, being somewhat snobbish, had neglected the large area of music that included blues, country-and-western, and rhythm-and-blues. The radio stations formed their own copyright organisation, BMI (Broadcast Music Inc.), and set about mopping up songwriters in those fields, offering the added inducement of a small fee for broadcasting records (ASCAP had ignored this growing field as small beer). Soon they had enough songs in their catalogue to offer ASCAP an ultimatum – from mid-1940, only BMI songs would be played on the air.

Duke was a member of ASCAP, so this put him in considerable trouble. It was bad enough for other big bands, most of whom couldn't even broadcast their themes, but for the rest of their programming they could at least hurriedly get arrangements made of BMI numbers. Duke's repertoire, however, was substantially his own, and he could broadcast none of it.

The answer was twofold – Billy Strayhorn and

Mercer Ellington. Mercer, by now twenty-one, had studied trumpet and saxophone and arranging, and studied at New York's Institute of Musical Art, and, with very little encouragement from Duke, in the late Thirties had started intermittently leading small bands of his own.

Neither he nor Billy were members of ASCAP, and for the next year, until the dispute was settled (ASCAP gave in, having been losing some $300,000 a month in royalties), Duke had them turning out numbers for the band. Mercer said, "It was a great day for both Strayhorn and I ... I mean it was a tremendous – like a gold era."

Many of the numbers they wrote were outstanding, and became part of the band's standing repertoire. Mercer wrote the heavily-rocking 'Things Ain't What They Used To Be'. Billy wrote 'Johnny Come Lately', 'Passion Flower', 'Raincheck', 'Midriff', 'After All' and 'Chelsea Bridge', a beautiful romantic number, played exquisitely by Ben Webster, and which was Billy's musical interpretation of a Whistler nocturne he had admired (and which unfortunately turned out to be of Battersea Bridge).

He also wrote 'Take The A Train', in which he tried as far as he could to recreate the feeling of the old Fletcher Henderson band. Duke (and the audiences) liked it so much it became, and remained, the band's theme. Ray Nance's solo remained an integral part of it, right to the end.

CHAPTER 16

glenn miller

Alton Glenn Miller (who hated his first name) was born in Clarinda, Ohio, in 1904. He was the second of four children, having an elder brother, Deane, a younger brother Herb, and a sister Irene.

His father, Lewis Elmer Miller (who also used his middle name), had a succession of jobs – at various times he was a homesteader, a carpenter, a school janitor and a railway bridge foreman. In pursuit of work he moved his family from state to state around the Middle West, and although they were often poor (at one time, in Nebraska, they lived in a turf-roofed hut), he was an amiable, easygoing man, and the family was a close and fairly happy one.

The dominant member of the family was Glenn's mother, Mattie Lou. She was a god-fearing woman, a staunch member of the Women's Christian Temperance Union, and she drilled into her children the virtues of hard work and high standards. Determined they should have the fullest possible life, she scrimped and saved to give them all a good musical education.

When Glenn was eight, his father, who had just landed a job with the Union Pacific Railroad, bought him a mandolin. He played it for a while, but it wasn't really for him, and within a couple of years he had traded it in for a cornet.

His brothers Deane and Herb both became capable trumpeters, but Glenn turned out out to be the outstanding musician of the family. When he was twelve the family moved to Grant City, Missouri, and there he took up the trombone, playing it in the Grant City Town Band.

Most of his later boyhood was spent in Fort Morgan, Colorado, and there he helped pay his way through school by the usual jobs of delivering papers and working as a soda-jerk. Graduating at seventeen, he didn't attend the ceremony to pick up his diploma (Mattie Lou went for him), because he was off in Laramie, Wyoming, auditioning for a job in a band.

He didn't get it, but he must already have been a competent trombonist, because in the same year, 1921, he got his first professional job, playing in the dance-band led by the popular but corny clarinetist Boyd Senter.

His mother was not too happy about music as a profession, and exerted pressure on Glenn to continue his studies. As a result, in 1923 he got himself accepted as a student by the University of Colorado. He went there, but music was too great an attraction. He cut classes to play in a local band led by Holly Moyer, at first on campus, then all around Wyoming. As a result he got poor grades, and after three terms he left.

He continued touring for a while with the Holly Moyer band, not only playing trombone but also arranging, then tried to join a band based at the University of Texas. Although this band was fronted by the Texan singer, Smith Ballew, it was actually the band of Jimmy Joy, whose claim to fame was that he could play two clarinets simultaneously. This became one of the best hot bands in the South-West, but in the Thirties, as hot music fell from fashion, would switch to becoming a sweet dance band, with great local success.

Glenn failed to get into Jimmy Joy's band, but did get into another south-western band, led by one Tom Watkins. Touring with that band, he arrived in Los Angeles, which in the mid-Twenties, because of the growth of Hollywood, had a booming entertainment industry – the town was swarming with ambitious young actors, composers, writers, artists and musicians. As a result, it was also swarming with night-clubs and dance-halls. Glenn decided to stay there a while, and got a job in the band at the Forum Theatre, led by Max Fischer.

He was still in Los Angeles when Ben Pollack arrived there in 1925 to take over the band of the ailing Harry Bastin. He hired Glenn as trombonist and arranger, the idea being that Glenn would arrange the more commercial material while Fud Livingstone handled the jazz numbers.

The Pollack band in 1925 was heading for success, and it was the best possible band for Glenn to be in at that time. When it went to Chicago in 1926, he went with it. But he was burning with ambition, and certain things began to gnaw at him. He heard Tommy Dorsey, and began to realise that he would never be the greatest trombonist in the business. Worse, by 1927 there were men in the Pollack band like Jimmy McPartland and Benny Goodman, who were better on their instruments than he was on his, and younger. Frustrated, for a while he started drinking, and when drunk turned out to have a fearsome temper.

Still, the Pollack band was by now the best hot

band in the country, and in 1928, when it went from Chicago to its first New York engagement, at the Little Club, he went with it.

When the Little Club engagement ended, the band, not yet properly established in New York, found the going rough. Like the other members of the band, whenever it was going through a lean period Glenn would freelance around.

He played with the Dorsey Brothers from almost the time he arrived in New York. This was long before they formed their full-time band, but Glenn played in the pick-up bands they got together for recording, and again did some of the arrangements.

He was freelancing and unavailable when Ben Pollack suddenly got an important engagement for his band at the Million Dollar Pier in Atlantic City. Glenn not being available, Ben hunted round for a replacement and discovered Jack Teagarden.

Jack's playing did nothing for Glenn's sinking morale, and the next job he took was as an arranger, not a player, working at the Paramount Theatre for the large semi-symphonic band of Paul Ash, part of whose stock-in-trade was his handsome, dramatic, bushy-haired appearance. He had a large female following and his band played mainly in big movie-houses, both for the silent films and between them.

At this time too he got married, to a girl he had been going steady with at the University of Colorado, Helen Burger. Now he had responsibilities as well as problems. He and Helen moved into an apartment on 29th Street, in the Queens district of New York City, and he set about establishing himself firmly in the floating pool of musicians working in the radio and recording studios.

Among the groups he recorded with in 1929 was an odd outfit called the Mound City Blue Blowers, assembled by an ex-jockey and hustler called Red McKenzie, who loved jazz and wanted to play it but had never had time to learn an instrument. So he organised record sessions of good musicians under his leadership and joined in singing and playing the comb-and-paper.

The Blue Blowers session that Glenn was on had the outstanding line-up of Pee Wee Russell (clarinet), Coleman Hawkins (tenor), Eddie Condon (banjo), Jack Bland (guitar), Pops Foster (bass) and Gene Krupa (drums). And of course Red McKenzie. They recorded two fine titles, 'Hello, Lola' and 'One Hour', and in such fast company Glenn plays well in the ensembles and doesn't disgrace himself in his two solos.

In 1930, like Benny Goodman, Jimmy Dorsey and Gene Krupa, he was in the theatre bands led by Red Nichols for the Gershwin shows *Girl Crazy* and *Strike Up The Band*.

In 1931, among his other work, he appeared on two recording sessions organised by Benny Goodman, but his career, like the careers of so many hot dance musicians at this time, seemed to be at a standstill.

It was now that a name from his past reappeared – the Texan singer, Smith Ballew, who had been fronting the Jimmy Joy band when he tried (and failed) to get a job with it. Smith had arrived in New York in 1928, and in the following years had made a number of records with various bands, including Duke Ellington and several put together by the Dorsey Brothers. Now he had the idea of leading a band of his own. He asked the efficient Glenn if he would help him form the band, rehearse it, play in it, write arrangements, and generally act as musical director.

This looked to Glenn like a good career move. The pay was good, Smith was offering him a share in the profits, and becoming in effect a band-leader would move him away from competing for work with other trombonists. He took the job.

It didn't turn out as well as they hoped. The band opened in New York and then set off on a long tour that took in cities like New Orleans, St Paul and Pittsburg. It was a pretty good band, but Smith Ballew's name wasn't strong enough to pull in the customers. They suffered a succession of cancelled dates, and by the time they reached Denver, early in 1934, Smith was ready to call it a day.

At this point Glenn heard that the Dorsey Brothers were preparing to form a permanent band. He called Tommy, offering his services. Tommy was glad to accept, and Glenn joined the Brothers, bringing with him a considerable portion of the ex-Ballew band.

As well as playing trombone, he arranged several numbers for the Dorseys. 'St Louis Blues' and their extended version of 'Honeysuckle Rose', which was issued on two sides of a 78, are his, but as an arranger he wasn't really so at home with such Dixieland numbers as with more straightforward swing. Two of his best of these are 'Stop, Look And Listen' and 'By Heck'.

Once some of his arrangements he was already using the fade-out and fade-in device that he was later to use so effectively with his own band, and obviously he did have good ideas, but his arrangements at this time tended to be fussy and cluttered, often interfering with the soloist.

Musician that he was – and he was – it must have been becoming clear to him at this time that not only was he not in the top rank of trombonists, he wasn't in the top rank of arrangers either. More and more it was becoming clear to him that his true metier was band-leading.

He was temperamentally well-equipped for the job. In the words of his friend, music journalist George T. Simon, "He was an exceptional executive. He made decisions easily, quickly and rationally. He was strong-willed, but that strong will almost always had a clear purpose. He was stubborn, but he was fair. He had intense likes and dislikes, though he'd admit it when he was proved wrong. He also had great confidence in himself. His attitude was that if he couldn't run a band properly, then he had no business having one."

Working for the Dorseys, he became more and more frustrated at not being his own boss. Also the money they were paying wasn't enough to make up for their continual bickering. In the spring of 1935 he left their band, and by way of trying out his ideas got together a pick-up band for a Columbia recording session with Smith Ballew.

The band had fourteen pieces, including a string quartet, and it included some outstanding players – trumpeters Bunny Berigan and Charlie Spivak, clarinetist and altoist Johnny Mince, tenorist Eddie Miller, pianist Claude Thornhill, who would go on to lead a fine band of his own in the Forties, and drummer Ray Bauduc. Certainly Glenn knew how to pick good musicians, which was why the Dorseys had invited him to help form their band in the first place.

They recorded two numbers backing Smith Ballew's singing – 'A Blues Serenade' and 'Moonlight On The Ganges' – and two up-tempo numbers arranged by Glenn – 'In A Little Spanish Town' and 'Solo Hop', the latter dispensing with the strings. These were the first records issued under Glenn's name, and whereas they are competent and cheerful, they bear little sign of the famous Miller sound. That would take him a while to develop.

By good fortune, just at the time of this recording (April 1935), he was approached by the Rockwell-O'Keefe office with a proposition. The well-established English band-leader Ray Noble wanted to work in America, but had been prevented by the American musicians' union from

bringing over musicians he knew. He needed somebody who knew the best American musicians and where they were to be found, and Rockwell-O'Keefe suggested Glenn.

He and Ray Noble met, and it was arranged that Glenn would put together the band in New York while Ray went off to California to write some new songs – among songs he had already written were 'Goodnight, Sweetheart', 'Love Is The Sweetest Thing', and 'The Very Thought Of You'.

From these titles it can be seen that Ray Noble was basically a "sweet" band-leader, but he wanted a band that could play hot numbers as well. His plan was that, as well as hiring the band and playing the trombone, Glenn would arrange the hot numbers while he (Ray) arranged the ballads. These would be sung by his regular vocalist, Al Bowlly, the one band-member he had been allowed to bring into the country. Apart from his manager Bill Harty, who was also his rather unswinging drummer.

Glenn assembled the band with as much care as though it were his own. On trumpets he got the pure-toned Charlie Spivak and the powerful Pee Wee Irwin (good enough to later replace Bunny Berigan in both the Goodman and Tommy Dorsey bands).

Alongside himself on trombone he put the man who would become his favourite trombonist, Wilbur Schwichtenberg (later to change his name to Will Bradley and become not only a member of the Miller band, but the leader of an enjoyable boogie-woogie big band of his own).

In the reed section were Bud Freeman on tenor, and Johnny Mince on clarinet. And on piano again, Claude Thornhill.

It was with Johnny Mince, in the days of the Ray Noble band, that the distinctive Miller sound began to be heard, and it came about partly by chance. Glenn had been writing arrangements in which Pee Wee Irwin played his trumpet in unison with the saxes, but an octave above the lead tenor. Then Irwin left the band to go and replace Bunny Berigan with Benny Goodman.

His own replacement in the Ray Noble band was unable to play so high effectively, and Glenn had the idea of getting Johnny Mince to play the same unison line on his clarinet, at the same time getting one of the violinists, who doubled on sax, to replace Mince on alto, thus keeping the number of saxes to four. This trick, refined a little further, would be the basis of the sound the public came to identify with Glenn Miller.

At this time he was taking a course in arranging from a teacher called Joseph Schillinger, and as an exercise he wrote a gentle haunting melody. He had words put to it by Eddie Heyman, who had written the lyric to 'Body And Soul', and it acquired the title 'Now I Lay Me Down To Weep'. Al Bowlly said he thought it was the most beautiful melody ever written, but the lyric was so depressing that the number lay unused.

George T. Simon had a go at rewriting the lyric, renaming the song 'Gone With The Dawn', but even that came out too gloomy. It wasn't till many months later that Glenn, who had always wanted to use the tune as a band theme, got Mitchell Parish (who wrote the words of 'Stardust') to have a go, and the tune was firmly and finally named 'Moonlight Serenade'.

Thanks to the musical good taste of Miller and Noble, the band turned out to be musical and tasteful. But it was never really a relaxed outfit, the problem being that several of the musicians made it plain that they trusted and respected Glenn more than they did Ray (or his drummer/manager, Bill Harty). This often made the atmosphere rather uneasy.

Nonetheless, Glenn and Ray worked well together. Both were perfectionists, rehearsing endlessly, and taking especial care on recording dates to get every effect exactly right. Although ballads remained the band's forte, it recorded several good swinging numbers, notably 'Way Down Yonder In New Orleans' and 'Dinah'.

Glenn had now definitely decided that he wanted a band of his own, and in the autumn of 1936, once the Ray Noble band was up and running, he left it. Unfortunately for Ray, quite a number of the best musicians in it, whose allegiance had been to Glenn rather than to him, drifted away soon after, and in 1937 Ray broke up the band and went to Hollywood with Bill Harty to begin a successful career as a musical director in radio (also becoming a stooge to Charlie McCarthy on the Edgar Bergen show).

By mid-1936 the Swing Era was a year old, and following Benny Goodman's enormous success the band scene was becoming over-crowded, the bands populated by the tens of thousands of musicians who had become hooked on dance-music during their youth in the Twenties.

Of the leaders in the popularity stakes, after Goodman, the Bob Crosby band was up and running. Charlie Barnet was becoming well established. Bunny Berigan was thinking of forming a band, which would undoubtedly do well. Woody Herman had taken over several key players from the smooth sweet band of Isham Jones, which had just folded, and was planning a blues-influenced new band. Les Brown's Duke Blue Devils (named for Duke University, where he had formed it) was a year old. Artie Shaw's first band had just made its debut at the Lexington Hotel. And there were now two Dorsey bands instead of one.

Any band that Glenn put together was going to have to be distinctive and different. One thing he did know, his plans for his it did not include featuring himself on trombone. "I can't compete against Tommy Dorsey," he told George T. Simon. However, it was Tommy's manager, Art Michaud, who also agreed (with Tommy's blessing), to become Glenn's manager. With George Simon's help, Glenn started driving round to clubs and hotels searching for promising young musicians.

They found altoist and clarinetist Hal McIntyre playing in a small town in Connecticut. They went to a seedy hotel on West 42nd Street to hear a young Texas tenor-player called Johnny Harrell, and were asked to leave by the waiter (who doubled as MC) for ordering coffee instead of drinks. They left, taking Harrell with them.

Glenn already had a reputation in the business of being a strict disciplinarian, and as soon as he had gathered enough musicians he had them hard at work rehearsing, in a second-story room on West 54th Street called Haven Studios. He himself was patient and tireless, playing over difficult passages on his trombone to give the band the phrasing he wanted.

He managed to land a one-session recording contract with Decca, and in March 1937 he took the first real Glenn Miller band into the studios. At least, it was mostly the Glenn Miller band. Feeling that he hadn't yet got all the good men he wanted, he also brought in a few experienced friends, including guitarist Dick McDonough, and an entire trumpet section of Charlie Spivak, Sterling Bose and Manny Klein. Unable so far to find a drummer to his liking, he enrolled the amateur services of his friend George T. Simon.

The band at this stage had rather a two-beat dixieland feel. Among the five numbers they recorded probably the best two are 'Peg O' My Heart' and 'On Moonlight Bay', both of course arranged by Glenn himself. But the records didn't sell well, and Decca did not extend the contract.

About a month later the band played its first live engagement, a one-night stand at the Hotel New Yorker. There they were heard by Seymour Weiss, President of the Roosevelt Hotel in New Orleans. He liked the band enough to give it a two week booking, starting in mid-June, in the hotel's famous Blue Room.

Just before going he managed to get a more permanent recording contract, this time with Brunswick, and using the same augmented band as before, recorded four more sides.

The booking at the Roosevelt stretched from two weeks to ten (the previous record having been five), and from there it got bookings in other hotels, including the Adolphus in Dallas and the Nicollet in Minneapolis. But even so Glenn wasn't getting the enthusiastic response he was after from his audiences, which in any case remained pretty thin.

He kept making changes to his personnel, in particular looking for what he knew he was still lacking, a good drummer. He also knew he needed air-time to get the band exposure, and in the autumn of 1937 was lucky enough to get an engagement at the Raymor Ballroom in Boston, which had a radio link.

It was during his residency there that the Miller sound began to develop. As the clarinet was essential to its effectiveness, he paid more than usual to hire the rich-toned Irving Fazola away from Ben Pollack. Faz added a lot to the band, but Glenn could afford only a few musicians of his experience and talent. The bulk of the band were young and inexperienced, so much so that at a recording session in December (still for Brunswick, but without the additional experts), it took them five hours to record two numbers, both ballads. They weren't very good either.

These were rough times for Glenn. The band was losing money and making little progress. Some of the band at that stage were heavy drinkers (one member of the trumpet section wrote off one of the band's cars), and his wife Helen, to whom he was, and would remain, close, underwent a serious operation.

During the Christmas season the band made a disastrous tour of New England. There was exceptionally heavy snow there that year, and several of the band's cars broke down en route to gigs. Some of his harder-drinking musicians also broke down during the gigs. The one bright spot was the arrival at last of a good drummer, Maurice Purtill, a 21-year-old New Yorker who had been working with Red Norvo, and occasionally with Tommy Dorsey.

Purtill sparked the band into life, but after only one night (at the Valencia Ballroom in Pennsylvania) Glenn got a desperate phone-call from Tommy saying that his drummer Dave Tough had gone on a bender and vanished, and he had an important date, and for God's sake send Moe Purtill back. Glenn regretfully sent him back.

Morale was low in the band, and to add to his troubles, Glenn by now was having disagreements with his manager, Art Michaud. Also his singer, Kathleen Lane, was being sued for breach of contract by her previous employer, Henry Okun. And so far the band had got him eighteen thousand dollars in debt. He decided that for the time being it was time to quit.

The band had just one more date booked, at the Ritz Ballroom in Bridgeport, Connecticut. That would last into January 1938, and Glenn told his musicians that when the booking was over he was breaking the band up for a while, and he'd call them when he needed them.

Back in New York, several of the better men immediately found themselves other jobs. Irving Fazola went back to Ben Pollack. His star trumpeter, Les Biegel, went back home to the mid-West. And his tenor-player, Jerry Jerome, who was one of his favourites, joined Red Norvo.

Determined to try again, Glenn severed his connection with Art Michaud and got a new manager, the helpful and generous Cy Shribman, owner of the Roseland-State Ballroom in Boston. He worked on some new arrangements, then began to assemble a new collection of young hopefuls around a nucleus of four members of the old band – lead trumpeter Bob Price, altoist Hal McIntyre, bassist Rolly Bundock, and pianist Chummy McGregor, who would become the closest friend in his band that the somewhat austere and forbidding Glenn ever had.

In February Glenn played trombone on a few Tommy Dorsey broadcasts, and in March he began rehearsing again at the Haven Studios. Among the new men was a young tenor-player who had been playing in a band in Detroit, and had been recommended to him by some of the members of the recently-formed Gene Krupa band – Gordon "Tex" Beneke. Tall, dark and handsome, Tex would become one of the mainstays of the band, both playing tenor and singing.

The band also had two featured singers. The girl was Gail Reese, who had sung with Bunny Berigan. The male singer Glenn had acquired in a rather strange and Millerish way. One night in a restaurant he ran into Tommy Dorsey's singer, Bob Eberly. Glenn had always admired Bob's singing, and asked him, half-jokingly, if he had any brothers at home. Bob said yes, he had a younger brother Ray, who had played alto with the Casa Loma band. "If he's your brother, he must be able to sing," said Glenn. "I'll give him a job."

So Ray Eberle, who had never sung a note professionally in his life (and never changed the spelling of his last name), joined the band, and with a bit of coaching from Glenn, performed remarkably well. Glenn even came to believe he was better than his brother.

At this stage he also began chnging the rhythm

of the band. Previously he had liked the two-four beat of dixieland, or the smoother two-four beat of Jimmie Lunceford. But now the Basie band had emerged on the scene. Glenn was one of its most devoted fans and became a firm convert to the smoother four beats in a bar.

Smoothness became more and more what he was after. A band that swung enough to attract the hot band fans, but was smooth enough to also attract the sweet band fans. Competent musician that he was, Glenn's poverty-stricken childhood had given him a healthy respect for money, and all his hard-won expertise was harnessed to the pursuit of it. Once, in the days of his success, he confronted jazz journalist Leonard Feather about a hostile criticism. "Why do you review my band from a musical point of view?" he protested. "I'm a businessman." From which we can deduce that he knew what music was, but he wasn't going to let that get in the way of success.

On April 16, 1938, the new band made its live debut, back at the Raymor Ballroom in Boston again, on a six week booking. Again it was received with only mild enthusiasm, but the band did get to broadcast nationally on the NBC Blue network several times a week.

They also broadcast from their next long-term venue, the Paradise Restaurant in New York. Their first engagement was for two weeks, but over the following months the band would return there fairly often. Unfortunately the Paradise was a typical Broadway nightclub, catering to out-of-town businessmen.

The band was still playing quite a lot of jazz in those days (towards the end of their stay at the Raymor the new band had made its first record date, and one of the four sides they recorded was a spirited version of 'Dippermouth Blues', with Glenn playing King Oliver's famous cornet solo on his trombone). But the Paradise Restaurant's clientele weren't keen on such stuff, so Glenn's was only the number two band there, playing mainly to back the entertainers in the floor-show. The number one band was Freddy Fisher and his Schnickelfritzers, a joky band playing cheerful corn.

Having to play the dull arrangements for the show dispirited the band, with the result that when they broadcast they tended to sound dull and uninspired. Some of them began to drift away to other jobs, among them singer Gail Reese. She was a good singer, but her going turned out to be a blessing in disguise.

While in Boston, Glenn had heard two blonde sisters singing with the Vincent Lopez Orchestra, Betty and Marion Hutton. They had been a great hit, especially Betty, but when Gail left, in September 1938, it was Marion that Glenn hired. He felt that she would be easier to handle than the strident and hyperactive Betty (who went on to noisy and short-lived fame and fortune in Hollywood).

Marion was popular with musicians and public alike, bringing a lightness and joy into the band's performances that it had previously lacked. She had a likable girl-next-door quality that Glenn at first tried to capitalise on by renaming her Sissy Jones (the attempt only lasted about a week). One step further, wrote George T. Simon, and he might have been featuring the only girl singer wearing a Girl Scout uniform.

All the same, Marion's presence wasn't enough to make the band a success. Its personnel continued to change (Glenn still needed a good brass section and a good drummer), and by February 1939 Glenn was ready to quit and settle for making a living as a session trombonist.

Back from a discouraging tour of North Carolina, he took the band back into rehearsal at the Haven Studios, and there, on March 1, 1939 (his thirty-fifth birthday), things began to look up. Glenn was stunned to get a call from his booking office to say that his band had been chosen to play the summer at the Glen Island Casino in New Rochelle, at the inner end of Long Island Sound.

By 1938 the Glen Island Casino had become so prestigious that a band playing the summer there was almost bound to become famous. How the booking had come about was that Glenn and the band had recently played a one-night stand at the Iona Prep School, in New Rochelle. The evening had been a fair success, and the student who had booked it, an enterprising young man called Tom Shiels, had dashed straight off to see the management of the Casino, telling them that they simply had to book the band for the summer. It was on the way to being a huge success (he said), and was bound to pack in the customers during the whole season.

As it happened, the Glen Island management had already heard the band and quite liked it, even though they heard it at the Paradise Restaurant, where Glenn (and the band) knew they were well below par. Young Tom Shiels's enthusiasm was just the shove they needed, and they made the booking.

A summer booking at Glen Island was so prestigious that, as soon as it was announced, the band was also booked for a lengthy engagement at the Meadowbrook Inn, in Cedar Grove, New Jersey. To appear there first.

The Meadowbrook was one of the major venues of the Swing Era. Whatever band was there made ten radio broadcasts a week, and Glenn's band could be heard audibly improving as he used the booking to whip it into shape. He added an extra trumpet and an extra trombone to build his brass section up to eight – bigger than most other bands had at that time. The biggest improvement, however, came from his at last getting hold of a

good drummer. Dave Tough had made his way back to Tommy Dorsey, and Maurice Purtill returned to Glenn.

Things now really began to move. The implied success of the Glen Island booking also enabled Glenn to move from Brunswick to the bigger and more prestigious Victor record company (although they did only hire him to appear on their low-price Bluebird label).

In April 1939, while the band was still appearing at the Meadowbrook, it made no fewer than three recording sessions for Victor. Among the numbers it recorded at the first session was the definitive version of its theme, 'Moonlight Serenade', composed and arranged by Glenn Miller.

The tune's new title had been chosen to complement another number that Glenn had written the arrangement for 'Sunrise Serenade'. This was recorded at the second session, and the two numbers were released on the two sides of one 78.

At that same session it also recorded another of its famous numbers 'Little Brown Jug'. The Miller sound was now firmly in place, the hits were beginning to pour out, and this was the first.

'Little Brown Jug' was not arranged by Glenn, but by Bill Finegan. Glenn was now beginning to collect better arrangers than he was himself, and Bill was the first. He had been recommended to Glenn by his friend Tommy Dorsey, who had just bought and recorded Bill's arrangement of 'The Lonesome Road'.

For the whole summer, while appearing at Glen Island, the band would go into the Victor studios once a fortnight, recording four new sides each time. Among the hits released were 'Pavane', 'Stairway To The Stars', 'Back To Back' and 'Slip Horn Jive'. To celebrate their appearance at the Casino, Glenn commissioned Count Basie's arranger, Eddie Durham, to write a special number, 'Glen Island Special', and the band recorded it that July.

In August it recorded what was to be the biggest of all its hits. It was based on a riff that seemed to have been around in jazz for ever. It bore a strong resemblance to the second strain of the New Orleans Rhythm Kings' 'Tin Roof Blues', that they recorded in 1923. In 1930 trumpeter Wingy Manone recorded it as a number he had composed himself, calling it 'Tar Paper Stomp' (and again in 1939, calling it 'Jumpy Nerves').

Saxophonist Joe Garland, who'd worked with Jelly Roll Morton in the Twenties, and been a member of the Mills Blue Rhythm Band from 1932 to 1936, took 'Tar Paper Stomp' and built it up into an elaborate big band arrangement lasting some eight minutes, calling it 'There's Rhythm In Harlem'.

In 1937 he took this arrangement to Artie Shaw. Artie liked it, but felt that it was too long to be of much commerical use (it would have needed two sides of a twelve-inch 78 to get it out on record, and only classical music was considered worthy of twelve-inch discs). He gave it back to Joe, and Joe brought it to Glenn.

Glenn liked it too, enough to cut it to three minutes, simplify the arrangement, and record it, retitled 'In The Mood'. It success was instant. Fans would gather round the bandstand, clamouring to hear it. They loved the tenor exchange between Tex Beneke and Al Klink, one of the young newcomers to the band. And they loved Glenn's gimmick, which he had started experimenting with back in his days with the Dorsey Brothers, of letting the band's sound die away to a whisper, only to come roaring back in again.

Well aware of staging and presentation, Glenn by this time had also adopted the trick of having the various sections flourish their instruments in unison (always giving due credit for the idea to Jimmie Lunceford). He always demanded good stage deportment, musically and otherwise. Al Klink, asked later in life by a radio interviewer why the Miller band wasn't considered by many fans to be a swing band, replied, "We were all too scared to swing."

There was no doubt that its appearance at Glen Island was the making of the band. So hard did they work to consolidate their success that in the middle of the season Marion Hutton collapsed from exhaustion. She soon bounced back, and in the meantime was replaced by the young Kay Starr.

By the end of its summer there, what with the records it was making and with its having the facility to plug them on the radio, the band was well on the way to being the most popular in America. (No wonder the Glen Island Casino only paid its bands a pittance.) In a poll conducted by New York's radio station WNEW in the autumn, Glenn Miller, almost unheard-of six months before, came fourth, behind Benny Goodman, Artie Shaw and Tommy Dorsey, and ahead of all the others.

By December 1939 the band was being offered far more work than it could cope with. In that month, after making regular radio appearances on the *Lucky Strike Hit Parade*, they replaced Paul Whiteman as the resident band on the popular Chesterfield Cigarettes Show.

On January 5, 1940 it opened at the Café Rouge of the Hotel Pennsylvania in New York, replacing the Artie Shaw band there after Artie decided to quit the band business and go to Mexico.

While Glenn was still appearing there, the band also got a booking to play the Paramount Theatre. So it was doing three radio shows a week, which meant rehearsing new numbers each time.

It was doing two sets a night at the hotel, totalling five hours on weekdays and six on Saturdays and Sundays. And it was doing four and sometimes five shows a day at the Paramount.

On top of this, during the first two months of 1940 the band went into the studios and recorded almost thirty sides, including another massive hit 'Tuxedo Junction', which Glenn had bought from the black bandleader who wrote it and first recorded it, Erskine Hawkins.

When Artie Shaw folded up his band, Glenn, who was finding himself with less and less time to do arrangements, snapped up his Bostonian arranger, Jerry Gray. Jerry would do more than anyone to develop and smooth out the band sound that Glenn had conceived. For a start, he took the hotel's telephone number and made it into a hit – 'Pennsylvania 6-5000'. It sold forty thousand copies in its first week of release.

Among the many numbers Jerry would prepare for the band, he arranged 'American Patrol' and 'Anvil Chorus', and both composed and arranged 'Caribbean Clipper', 'Here We Go Again' and 'A String Of Pearls'.

In the autumn of 1940, at the great battle of bands that took place at the Manhattan Centre, and which Jimmie Lunceford won hands down, Glenn at least had the satisfaction of coming second, ahead of both Goodman and Basie.

But still he was not quite satisfied with the band. He brought in bass-player Trigger Alpert, whom he'd heard in the Alvino Rey band, and admired. Jerry Gray, for one, felt that the difference Trigger's arrival made to the band was the difference between night and day.

Still not happy with his trumpet section, Glenn hired two youngsters – the nineteen-year-old Ray Anthony (another future bandleader), and a cheerful stocky twenty-four-year-old, Billy May, who came from the Charlie Barnet band, played strong lead trumpet, and was an even better arranger than trumpeter, having arranged, among other things, Charlie's theme, 'Cherokee' (a number composed the previous year by Ray Noble).

Early in 1941, Marion Hutton, who was married to the well-known music publisher, Jack Philbin, was taken pregnant. A gossip columnist printed the news, which so embarrassed her that she took her maternity leave some months before it was strictly necessary.

Suddenly faced with having to find a temporary replacement, Glenn first tried Dorothy Claire, whom he took from the Bobby Byrne band. Bobby Byrne was furious, the two leaders fell out, and then Glenn decided that Dorothy wasn't right for the band. She went back to Bobby and the dispute blew over.

Then he hired Paula Kelly, who had been singing with Al Donahue's band. She worked out better, and Al Donahue was gracious about losing her. Glenn also decided at around this time that he needed a vocal group (following the example of the Pied Pipers with Tommy Dorsey), and he decided on the Modernaires.

The Modernaires were already quite successful, having appeared with the Charlie Barnet band (with whom they recorded the theme for Martin Block's radio show, *Make Believe Ballroom*). At present they were working with Paul Whiteman, but Glenn offered then a ten year contract (extremely unusual in those days, and an indication of the confidence he now had in his band's future), and they accepted.

Also early in 1941, Hollywood beckoned. This time it was Twentieth Century Fox, headed by Darryl Zanuck. When they approached Glenn, he acted like the astute businessman he was. He knew how much a film appearance could mean in terms of publicity, not only in America but all around the world, but there was no way he was going to have a hot property like his band slipped into a second-rate movie in order to give it more clout at the box office. Nor was he going to get lumbered with the sort of dialogue that Artie Shaw had suffered from in *Dancing Co-ed*. He insisted on a starring role for himself and his band in a major feature, and on his right to vet the script. And he got what he asked for.

Zanuck offered him a two-picture deal, with an option on two more, his fee for the first film, according to *Down Beat*, being $100,000. This may have been true, because when the band went to Hollywood to make the film, he was able to buy himself a ranch in Beverly Hills. The name he gave it was 'Tuxedo Junction'.

Once the deal was signed, the studio moved fast. The film was to be called *Sun Valley Serenade*, it would also star the Swedish Olympic skating champion Sonja Henie, and as well as containing Miller hits like 'In The Mood' and 'Moonlight Serenade', would have new material written by the studio's own hit-writing team, Mack Gordon and Harry Warren.

Shooting started at the end of March and finished in early May, and the film was released in August. It was a smash hit. Gordon and Warren had provided a song that made for a rousing climax. It was 'Chattanooga Choo-Choo', and in the film was danced spectacularly by Dorothy Dandridge and the Nicholas Brothers. With help like that it was no surprise that the band's recording of it became a million-seller and was awarded the world's first-ever gold disc.

A special celebrity screening of the film was given at the Palladium Ballroom (as the Palomar had been renamed when it was rebuilt after the fire), and it was typical of Glenn's tight grasp on a hard-earned dollar that he refused to issue free tickets, even to his own family. The celebrities were not amused.

Two other things happened in August. Marion Hutton returned to the band, and Glenn hired cornetist Bobby Hackett. This rather surprised everyone, because Bobby, a highly talented small-group musician, was not known as a section player. But he played solos in a gentle, thoughtful romantic style that went well with the band. Known for never having a bad word to say about anyone, he was once pressed by a friend to give his opinion of Hitler. "Well," said Bobby, "he was the best in his field."

What surprised people further was that on his first appearance with the band he appeared not in the trumpet section, but sitting strumming a guitar (his first instruments had been the ukulele, and then the guitar). The explanation was that he'd just undergone some painful dental work, and it was a week or two before he felt ready to play his cornet. When he did, he contributed some beautiful solos on such numbers as 'Rhapsody In Blue' and 'A String Of Pearls'.

In 1942 the band made its second movie for Fox, *Orchestra Wives*. This had a similar schedule to *Sun Valley Serenade*, being shot from the end of March to early May and released in September. This time Glenn was the sole star, with supporting roles played by Jackie Gleason and Cesar Romero, and the story was rather more realistic, being set in the big band business.

The big new number in the film, again by Mack Gordon and Harry Warren, was 'Kalamazoo'. It was sung by Tex Beneke, Marion Hutton and the Modernaires, and was nominated for an Oscar. But nobody knew while the film was being made was that back in February, a few weeks before shooting started, Glenn had registered with his local Draft Board in New Jersey.

America's entry into World War Two had had a profound effect on him. Even before the bombing of Pearl Harbor the previous December, way back at the beginning of 1940, President Roosevelt had introduced a peacetime draft.

It didn't affect Glenn himself, because even then he was over the draft age of thirty-five. But his Protestant conscience, instilled into him by his god-fearing mother, made him more and more anxious to do his bit for the war effort. In October 1941 he had begun to dedicate his radio shows to helping it, running competitions for service men and women (the winner to get a phonograph and fifty swing records), and insisting his audience members buy US Savings Stamps if they wanted admittance.

He also had the band recording numbers specifically aimed at a wartime audience, like 'Soldier, Let Me Read Your Letter', 'Keep 'Em Flying', 'Don't Sit Under The Apple Tree' and 'When Johnny Comes Marching Home'.

By February 1942 he had decided that all this wasn't enough, and registered, and in May, after shooting on the film was completed, he had applied for a commission in the Navy Reserve. He waited, and in August heard that he had been turned down. Doggedly, he offered his services to the Army Air Force, and again settled down to wait.

All this time he kept his ambition to enlist hidden from the band. Its morale was already suffering enough from the fact that its young members were all under the threat of being drafted. Bassist Trigger Alpert had been the first to go, although Glenn did manage to get him a six-month deferment, and everybody was feeling unsettled.

Tensions mounted. Ray Eberle, having been held up in traffic, arrived late for a broadcast from Chicago, and Glenn fired him on the spot. There was also pressure from the recording ban being threatened by James Petrillo. Victor, to cover themselves in case it should come to pass, wanted the band to record a backlog of material. In mid-July they recorded thirteen numbers in three days. They would be the last recordings Glenn Miller's civilian band ever made.

On August 1 the recording ban came into force, and on September 10 Glenn heard that he had been accepted by the Army. He would be given the rank of Captain and the task of organising a band to entertain the troops.

He told the band first, then his management team, the Victor company and his Chesterfield Radio Show team. The final Chesterfield broadcast, from the Central Theatre in Passiac, New Jersey, took place on September 27, and was a very emotional event. The band had trouble playing, Marion Hutton broke down in the middle of 'Kalamazoo', and the audience wailed and sobbed. Only Glenn kept calm, handing the show over to his successor, Harry James.

Two weeks later, on October 7, he reported for duty with the Army Specialist Corps at the Seventh Service Command Headquarters, in Omaha, Nebraska.

After basic training at Fort Mead, in Maryland, he received his commission and was assigned to the Army Air Force. At first his job was simply to assemble bands. By the spring of 1943 he had assembled forty-nine of them, sending them to outfits all over the country. Then he was posted to Atlantic City and given the job of forming his own band, with power to recruit men from anywhere in the service.

Hunting out as many of his old colleagues as he could, he unearthed Trigger Alpert, trumpeter Zeke Zarchy, trombonist Jimmy Priddy, and his key arranger, Jerry Gray. Of men from other bands he found pianist Mel Powell (from the Goodman band), guitarist Carmen Mastren (from the Tommy Dorsey band), trumpeter Bernie Privin (from one of the Artie Shaw bands), his old friend, drummer Ray McKinley, who had been with the Dorsey Brothers and had gone on to co-lead a band with trombonist Will Bradley (formerly Wilbur Schwichtenberg), and the clarinetist and tenorist from their band, Michael "Peanuts" Hucko.

He also acquired a twenty-strong string section, all classical musicians and many of them from the Cleveland Symphony Orchestra. With such a large and varied personnel he was able to put together various sub-bands. There was the Marching Band, the American Dance Band, the Swing Shift Band (led by Ray McKinley), the "Uptown Hall Gang" (led by Mel Powell), and "Strings with Wings". (In the Marching Band, the string section doubled on a variety of drums, not always to great effect).

With his personnel almost complete, his operation was moved to the Army Air Forces Technical School at Yale University in Connecticut. It was at about this time that he dropped in on Benny Goodman at the Starlight Roof in New York. Benny started complaining that some of his boys were being difficult over money, and were driving him crazy. Glenn leant back in his chair and said, "Benny, I got fifty-four guys up at Yale, working for twelve dollars and fifty cents a week, and I ain't gettin' no squawks."

It was clear that Glenn enjoyed army life. He had the officer temperament, and it was congenial to him to have his orders obeyed without question. At Yale he started whipping the band into shape, while at the same time embarking on a series of coast-to-coast Air Force recruitment broadcasts.

The Marching Band in particular became extremely exciting, playing superb arrangements of old favourites like 'St Louis Blues' and 'Blues In The Night'. The Air Force Cadets at Yale especially enjoyed marching to it, and it gave a real zest to their parades. The Commandant of Cadets, however, wasn't so pleased. He sent for Glenn and tore him off a strip, eventually saying, "We played those Sousa marches pretty straight in the last war, and we did all right." By this time Glenn had had enough. "Tell me, Major," he said, "are you still flying the same planes as you flew in the last war too?" The band continued to play as it had.

It stayed at Yale for a year, and during that time Glenn began to become increasingly irritable, fretting to take it overseas. At last, in the spring of 1944, it was ordered to England. Leaving behind some of the less good musicians, Glenn arranged to ship twenty string players, five trumpets, four trombones (not including himself), six reeds, two drummers, two pianists, two bassists, a guitarist, three arrangers, a copyist, five singers, two producers, and announcer, two musical instrument repairmen, plus Warrant Officer Paul Dudley, and First Lieutenant Don Haynes, who had been Glenn's personal manager in civvy street.

They sailed for Britain on the NY 8425, formerly known as the liner "Queen Elizabeth", and docked at Gourock, on the Clyde, on June 28. Glenn had flown on ahead to London to hold planning meetings with his boss, Lieutenant Colonel David Niven. He flew to Scotland to escort the band down to London by train, and as they emerged from Euston Station the sirens went off and a V1 landed nearby. The huge explosion brought the war home to the band in a hurry.

Somewhat shaken, they were taken in army trucks to their quarters in 25 Sloane Street. These quarters had been arranged before the V1's appeared in the sky, and now so many had been falling round Sloane Street that it had been nicknamed "Buzz Bomb Alley". Glenn made arrangements to have his band moved somewhere else as quickly as possible. Bedford was chosen, the musicians were transferred there, and the next day a V1 landed in front of 25 Sloane Street, killing twenty-five US military policemen in a truck, and seventy other people in the flattened buildings.

At Bedford, the band was quartered in the Co-Partners Hall, a dingy little place that had belonged to the Gas Board, but which the band found strangely congenial. A land-line was installed connecting it to Broadcasting House, and from there they rehearsed and broadcast over the BBC Home Service. Or at least, they did until the BBC, regarding themselves as the voice of the most powerful nation on earth, asked Glenn if he would stop playing those quiet passages that suddenly got loud again, because listeners might think the station had gone off the air. Glenn told them that he had no intention of doing any such thing, and perhaps it would be better if in future he broadcast only to the American Expeditionary Force. The BBC adopted his suggestion, and stopped his Home Service broadcasts early in August.

Nonetheless, the band had plenty to do. On top of its AEF broadcasts they began to record propaganda programmes at Abbey Road, in halting German, for broadcasting to Germany. And it played concerts for troops all over the country, in all sorts of places and in all sorts of conditions – sometimes from the backs of trucks. It did seventy-one of these in fourteen weeks, with an assortment of singers, both British and American.

But still Glenn wanted to get closer to the action. The allied armies, under Eisenhower, had landed in Normandy on June 6 and were advancing fast across France and Belgium towards Germany. Glenn wanted to be over there, and at last received orders "by command of General Eisenhower" to report to Paris in the middle of December.

Feverishly the band began pre-recording a stack of radio programmes to cover what was planned as a six week trip to Europe. On top of their usual commitments they recorded sixty-six programmes (plus a few extra just in case) in two-and-a-half weeks – a total of thirty hours of material.

On December 12 the band played its last concert in Britain, a live broadcast by the BBC (who must have relented) from the Queensberry Club in London. The last number they played was 'Stompin' At The Savoy'. On Friday, December 15, just before 2 p.m., Glenn took off for Paris, exhausted. The band, equally exhausted, was to follow him three days later.

The aircraft he took off in was a small wood-and-canvas monoplane, a "Norseman". It was an eight-seater, but only three people were aboard – the pilot, Flight Officer John "Nipper" Norman; Major Glenn Miller; and Lt-Col. Norman F. Baessell, executive officer with the US 8th Air Force Service Command, who was bound for Bordeaux with money and several empty crates of wine-bottles, including champagne, to be refilled.

The plane vanished. The band, arriving in Paris three days later, assumed hopefully for days that there had been some wartime foul-up, and that soon Glenn would appear. But he never did.

Many theories were advanced over the years as to what happened to him, but in the early Nineties Roy Nesbitt, the official Royal Air Force historian, finally pieced together the most likely explanation. The Norseman was accidentally hit in the bomb disposal area in the Channel off Beachy Head by a returning plane dumping its unused bombs before landing back in England.

This theory had been discounted for years because the timing of Glenn's flight didn't match the records of timings for returning bombers. Then Nesbitt realised that the American Air Force worked on local time, the Royal Air Force on Greenwich Mean time. That meant that bombs were being dropped right above Glenn's plane just as it was hopping over to France. And three witnesses in one of the returning bombers saw the Norseman underneath them plunge into the sea.

What would he have gone on to do if he had survived the war? Certainly he had already been making plans. He had already opened negotiations with the Paramount Theatre in New York for his first show after he got back, and it seems likely that he would have wanted to lead a larger band than before in civilian life. Something more like his army band, with strings, that could play extended set pieces in concert halls. Some of his band's later arrangements on pieces like 'Oh, What A Beautiful Morning' and 'Poinciana' were already lengthening well beyond the three-minute length of a 78 side. But he didn't just want to lead a band all the time. He had plans to lead one for six months and spend six months doing other things, like going into personal management, or song publishing, or radio production. He even had a project to distribute Coca Cola. When the Swing Era came to an end, Glenn Miller would certainly have found something to do.

CHAPTER 17

charlie barnet

How Charlie Barnet, in his seventeenth year, came to be playing the tubular bells on Duke Ellington's 1930 recording of 'Ring Dem Bells' is a mystery. What is clear is that by that time in his life he had already rejected the lifestyle of his wealthy white family.

Charles Daly Barnet was born in New York in 1913. His mother's father, Charles Daly, had been First Vice-President of the New York Central Railroad, and in the beginning his parents had all sorts of conventional plans for their son. He was sent to Blair Academy, a respectable boarding-school in New York, then on to high school in Winnetka, Illinois. With the idea that he might become a corporation lawyer, his parents had also enrolled him at Yale. But he never went, having already become passionately interested in music.

When he was ten or eleven, his parents had wanted him to take piano lessons, but Charlie at that age was already more interested in drums. They never bought him a drumkit, so he had to make do with banging on pots and pans and his mother's hatboxes. When he was twelve, however, they did buy him a C-melody sax.

There was a Victrola record-player in the house and, listening to it, Charlie became hooked on the sound of the Fletcher Henderson band, in particular on the playing of Coleman Hawkins. Naturally he traded his C-melody sax in for a tenor.

A little later, he discovered the sound of Ellington, and in particular of Johnny Hodges, so he also acquired an alto and a clarinet.

When he was sixteen he left school, got together a quintet and, possibly through his family's connections in the transport business, got it the job of ship's band aboard the S.S. Republic. For a couple of years he led ships' bands, working on the liners of Cunard, Red Star and Panama Pacific. He made Atlantic crossings, and cruises around both the Mediterranean and South America.

When he was eighteen he briefly went back to school, to another respectable New York boarding-school called Rumsey Academy. He played in the school band while he was there, but the lure of the music business remained too great, and he left to join a band called Frank Winegar's Pennsylvanians.

He stayed with them for a year, playing tenor, then left New York to gig his way around the country, turning up at various times in bands in Illinois, Texas and California. He also spent a fair amount of time in New Orleans, soaking up the sounds of the city.

While he was in Texas he played in a small band led by Jack Purvis. Jack Purvis, described by Charlie as one of the wildest men he ever met, as well as one of the greatest trumpet players, had undoubtedly the most extraordinary career of any musician in jazz, and it went like this: born in Kokomo, Indiana, in 1906, his mother died when he was young, and he spent several years in a boys' institution, where he learned to play trumpet and trombone. Returning to Kokomo when he was about fifteen, he played in the high school orchestra and in local dance bands. Then for several years he joined the Original Kentucky Nighthawks, a band based in Lexington, Kentucky, taking time out from the band to study music in Chicago and to qualify as a pilot.

In 1926, aged twenty, he left the Nighthawks to work as a freelance trumpeter and arranger. He is alleged to have played with Whitey Kaufman's Original Pennsylvanians, working with them in New York and Pennsylvania, but whether he did or not, he certainly sailed to Europe in 1928 as a member of George Carhart's band, who were the ship's band aboard the "Ile de France".

He played with them for one night, then vanished into the first class lounge to socialise with famous fellow-aviators Levine and Acosta (Charles A. Levine, with Charles Chamberlin, had attempted to fly the Atlantic just before Lindbergh in 1927). Purvis did not rejoin the band until they docked in France, when he played with them in Aix-les-Bains and Nice, before leaving them (somewhat hurriedly) via the roof of their hotel in Paris.

Arriving back in the U.S., he played with the Hal Kemp band (a hot band that turned to sweetness and success in the early Thirties), at first on trumpet, then on trombone, then on trumpet again. In 1929 and 1930 he made three record sessions under his own name. The first session produced a very fair tribute to Louis Armstrong, disarmingly called 'Copyin' Louis', and the second and third included such eminent musicians as Coleman Hawkins, J.C. Higginbotham and Adrian Rollini.

When the Hal Kemp band sailed to Europe in 1930, Purvis did not go with them, but nonetheless mysteriously appeared to rejoin them in Paris.

By September 1930 he was back in New York, playing with the California Ramblers in a New York restaurant on 47th Street. He worked with other outfits organised by Ed Kirkeby all though 1931, also broadcasting with other bands, including those got together by the Dorsey Brothers, and occasionally sitting in as fourth trumpet with Fletcher Henderson.

In 1932 he was with Fred Waring's Pennsylvanians, and during this period for a while became a harpist. It was shortly after this that (again as a trumpeter) he was in Texas leading the band that Charlie Barnet joined. He set off for California with Charlie, but somehow lost contact with him in El Paso.

At this time he seems to have started using his skill as a pilot to ferry unspecified goods between Mexico and the U.S., but he reappeared in New York in 1933 to rejoin Fred Waring's respectable Pennsylvanians, who were opening at the Roxy Theatre, a truly magnificent new theatre rivalling Radio City Music Hall in size and sumptuousness.

Jack's pride and joy (according to Charlie) was a little moustache that he spent hours waxing and trimming to a fine point. This upset the dictatorial Fred Waring, who wanted his band to resemble clean-cut collegians (on-stage they had to wear sweaters and slacks). He ordered Jack to remove the moustache.

The Roxy, like the Paramount, had a rising orchestra pit, and the band was to rise up in the dark, a spotlight was to pick out Fred Waring as he walked on from the wings and, when he gave the downbeat, the band was to begin playing the *1812 Overture*, opening with a dramatic trumpet solo that only Jack could handle.

When Jack began playing, the spotlight moved to him. He had shaved off not only his moustache but every hair on his head. As Charlie said, "Suddenly he became available to join my band."

This was Charlie's first-ever big band, and Jack Purvis did not stay in it long. He left, and next surfaced in California, writing arrangements for George Stoll's orchestra and for various film-studio bands organised by Warner Brothers. One of his compositions, 'Legends Of Haiti', he scored for a 110-piece band. While in California he also worked as a chef.

In 1935 he drove back from California to New York in a baby Austin, hauling a trailer full of orchestral scores and cookery books, and set about leading a quartet at the Club 18 and the Looking Glass, both on 52nd Street. (During the same year he also recorded with a band led by Frank Froeba, who had been Benny Goodman's pianist for a while).

After touring for two weeks in a band led by Joe Haymes (the band that Tommy Dorsey essentially took over as his own after the split with Jimmy) he disappeared for two years (possibly this was when he organised an ill-fated school of Grecian dancing in Miami).

In 1937 he reappeared briefly in Los Angeles, then in a night-club quintet in Marysville, California. He vanished for a while but rejoined the same quintet in Medford, Oregon, staying with them this time for two weeks.

Next he appeared in San Pedro, California, playing in Johnnie Wynn's band under the name Jack Jackson, but left the band after a week, reappearing a little later, working in a Fresno burlesque hall.

Still in 1937 he began serving a prison sentence for robbery at El Paso, Texas. In prison he formed (and played piano with) the Rhythmic Swingsters, who in 1938 used to broadcast locally on Station WBAP. Temporarily released from prison, he violated his parole and was reincarcerated in Huntsville Prison, Texas, where they kept him until 1947.

There was a rumour that after his release he resumed flying in Florida, but whether or not that is true, in the spring of 1948 a man resembling him was seen in a garden in Royal Place, Honolulu, playing 'The Flight Of The Bumblebee' alternately on trombone and trumpet.

In 1949 he lived briefly in Pittsbugh, where his daughter, Betty Lou, was working for a local radio station. After that he was reported as working as a carpenter, then as chef on a boat sailing from Baltimore, but little more was heard of him before his death, in 1962, in San Francisco. It seems likely that he may yet reappear.

Charlie Barnet, after losing contact with Purvis in El Paso, returned to New York in the spring of 1933. There he bought a library of arrangements from Jan Garber. Jan Garber had led a hot band until the late Twenties, when the sweet band, Guy Lombardo and his Royal Canadians, became an enormous success. At which point Garber went to Canada, took over somebody else's sweet band there, and brought it back to America, where he had great success with it and didn't lead another hot band again until the Forties.

It is said that the Garber arrangements cost Charlie only twenty dollars, but using them he formed his first big band and got it a three-month residency at the Paramount Hotel Grill. This being a hotel job, the band was fairly peaceful, but it did contain some promising young musicians, especially in the trumpet section – as well as Jack Purvis for a while, there were Chris Griffin, who would go on to become part of Benny Goodman's greatest band, and Tutti Camarata, who would go on to arrange for the Casa Loma band, for Jimmy Dorsey, and for the 1938 band of Paul Whiteman.

Charlie also got hold of some additional arrangements by Horace Henderson, which was an indication of things to come, because from the beginning many of the musicians who inspired him most were black. Because his band frequently included Blacks, it never got picked as resident band on a radio series. You couldn't have listeners writing in for pictures of the band and discovering that half of them were the wrong colour. He also, for the same reason, had difficulties in getting the band booked into certain hotels, but in all cases he stuck to his principles.

Having a wealthy background certainly helped him do this, not so much because it meant he wasn't dependent on music for a living, but because it gave him an inbuilt confidence. All his life he was able to remain cheerful and happy-go-lucky. What he mostly wanted to do was have a ball, and it helped enormously in achieving this that he was debonair, handsome, and sufficiently wealthy.

After his first band finished its engagement at the Paramount Hotel Grill, he led it at the Park Central Hotel in New York, at the Glen Island Casino in New Rochelle, at the Hotel Roosevelt in New Orleans, and at numerous other places. But at the beginning of 1935, becoming restless, he broke it up and formed an octet.

This again included some interesting names. On trumpet it had Eddie Sauter, who in the Fifties would co-lead the Sauter-Finegan band, and who already was a promising young arranger. On piano it had Kenneth Norville, who had already adopted the name "Red Norvo", and who would go on to become about the only xylophonist in jazz, leading tasteful and imaginative small groups right through into the Nineties.

This group too used the arrangements of an outstanding black arranger – Benny Carter. But again Charlie became restless, and in 1935 broke

up the octet and left music to take up an offer he had had to go to Hollywood and act in movies.

He had a small part in a light comedy, *Love And Hisses*, and a slightly larger part in a musical, *Sally, Irene And Mary*, based on a Broadway hit, and was sufficiently good on-screen for a studio to offer him a contract to be groomed as a cowboy star. Turning down this tempting offer, he returned to New York and formed another band.

There are certain similarities between the lives of Charlie Barnet and Artie Shaw. Both were serial bridegrooms, but whereas Artie Shaw became notorious for having eight wives, nobody really seemed to notice that Charlie had eleven. Both, too, were given to suddenly disbanding, but whereas Artie did it out of disenchantment with the music business and in pursuit of musical perfection, Charlie, who had the habit mostly in his early years, seems more to have done it out of a lighthearted desire to try something else for a while.

The band he formed on his return from Hollywood in 1936 was again a fairly polite hotel band. Again it was good enough to get a booking at the Glen Island Casino (it was while there that he introduced a new singing group, the Modernaires), and again, after a year or so of touring, Charlie disbanded it.

Although by the mid-Thirties he had become an entremely proficent performer on tenor, alto, soprano and clarinet, he remained a modest man, and seems to have felt that while he admired the great swing musicians, especially the black bands, there was no point in his trying to lead a band that in any way competed with them. He was content to lead straightforward commercial bands, using the best musicians he could find, and have a good time.

In the late Thirties, this changed. The Swing Era was by now well under way, and another leader had appeared on the scene whose music he liked almost as much as Duke Ellington's – Count Basie. In 1938 Charlie got together another band, but this time a swing band, and set about using it to bring the music of Ellington and Basie to the mass white audience. No other swing band-leader so thoroughly devoted himself to playing the music of others.

He himself could play alto in a style reminiscent of Johnny Hodges (which he did when the band played Ellington numbers), and powerful Hawkins-influenced tenor (which he used for Basie numbers). His band were all young and relatively unknown, and as his main trumpet soloist he was lucky to find Bob Burnet, a twenty-six-year-old Chicagoan who had the useful ability to growl like Cootie Williams or Rex Stewart, and to play open horn that was close enough to Buck Clayton to serve.

Charlie had already made the acquaintance of Duke Ellington. In fact it had become his practice, if he heard that the Ellington band was between jobs, to hire it (and his local country club) for a party, at which the band were only obliged to play when they felt like it, and the rest of the time join in as guests. At one of these parties he had signs put up in the entrace-hall saying "No requests. No 'Melancholy Baby'. No anything but Duke Ellington."

Duke, hearing about Charlie's new band, recommended to him the black arranger, Andy Gibson, who had worked with McKinney's Cotton Pickers, with Blanche Calloway (Cab's sister), and with Lucky Millinder. One of the first numbers that Andy re-scored for the Barnet band was Duke's composition, 'Harlem Speaks'.

The new band took a little time to settle down and establish itself. At first it didn't even have a recording contract, except to make what were called "transcriptions" – recordings produced solely for sale or hire to local radio stations. But towards the end of 1938 it obtained a booking at the Famous Door, on 52nd Street, from which the Basie band had recently made its name by broadcasting. Charlie's band made its name there in a similar way, and in January 1939 he obtained a recording contract with Victor, to record, like Glenn Miller, for its low-price Bluebird label.

Shortly after its engagement at the Famous Door, the band had an engagement to appear at the New Penn Club, a roadhouse out in the country outside Pittsburgh. They were rehearsing there one afternoon when a bedraggled young man came in, his shoes all spread out at the sides. He had a sheaf of music manuscripts under his arm and wondered if the band would be prepared to try an arrangement he had written.

This sort of thing was always happening to bands, and usually the arrangements were pretty terrible, but that afternoon the rehearsal had gone well, and they had some spare time, so Charlie said, "Okay, let's have it, we'll pass it out."

The band moaned and groaned, but shared out the sheets of music. Charlie counted them in, and after four bars everybody suddenly sat up straight. After eight bars, they uncrossed their legs, and by the end of the first chorus they were all blowing (as Charlie said) "like they meant it".

The bedraggled young man was Billy May, "who at that time was playing trumpet and trombone in a horrible Lombardo-type band called Baron Elliott" in Bridgeport, Connecticut. Charlie hired him on the spot, as arranger, trumpeter and occasional vocalist, and Billy started turning out a stream of fine arrangements that did much to consolidate the band's reputation, among them 'Pompton Turnpike' and the Ray Noble tune that became the band's romping theme, 'Cherokee'.

By now the band was really swinging. It had

become the band that many people considered the most musical white band of the Swing Era, and it started producing a string of great numbers. At a recording session in September 1939 it made two sides in tribute to Charlie's two idols – 'The Duke's Idea' and 'The Count's Idea' – following these a month later with two numbers called 'The Right Idea' and 'The Wrong Idea', the latter satirising the worst musical habits of sweet bands. It was written (and sung) by Billy May, with the band swooping and whinnying away over an upright ricky-tick rhythm, and Charlie commented ruefully in the late Sixties that "nowadays I've actually run into people who take this record seriously."

Being in the Barnet band was always a lot of fun, and not always predictable. On one occasion they were playing at the Paramount Hotel on West 46th Street in New York, and making a coast-to-coast broadcast for CBS. The next tune they had arranged to play was 'I've Got The World On A String', but the announcer Paul Douglas (who went on to become a successful supporting actor in Hollywood during the Fifties) mistakenly announced 'Avalon'.

Charlie started the band off. Half of it began playing one tune and half of it the other. The brass section, playing 'Avalon', finally won, to Charlie's great relief, and later he smiled proudly in the 52nd Street clubs when musicians praised his new wild introduction.

Charlie's own joie-de-vivre infected the band. Once, on a very hot day, when they were staying in a hotel in San Francisco, several of them decided they would like to go swimming. The hotel had no pool, so they stuffed the cracks around the door of one of the rooms with rags and towels, ran the en suite bath until it flooded the room about two feet deep, and started jumping in from bureaus and couches.

Finally, water began to seep through the ceiling below. The management investigated, and sent for Charlie. Brought to the room, he took one look and said, "Why, you miserable bastards! The least you could have done was invite me."

In October 1939 the band was booked for an engagement at the famous Palomar Ballroom, in Los Angeles. During that engagement (but fortunately not during show-time), the Palomar burnt to the ground. The band lost everything – instruments, arrangements, even most of the uniforms. "Hell," said Charlie, "it's better than being in Poland with bombs dropping on your head."

Both Ellington and Benny Carter, hearing of the band's plight, shipped Charlie batches of new scores, and when the band began its next engagement, it began with two swing originals that Charlie had had written, 'We're All Burnt Up' and 'Are We Hurt?'.

In 1940, while in Hollywood, the band were at a hotel called Peyton Hall, which did have a pool. They nicknamed it "the fish pond", and from this came the title they recorded that year 'Wild Mab Of The Fish Pond'. Who Wild Mab was is not clear, but for years after the release of the record, Charlie became known in the band world as "Mad Mab".

He himself rather went in for obscure titles. The same year he wrote and recorded two numbers 'Afternoon Of A Moax' and 'The Reverie Of A Moax', arranging the first himself and giving the second to Billy May. Both numbers came out kind of Dukish, but who or what a "Moax" is, nobody seems to know, although for a brief while after those numbers were recorded, the band featured a vocal trio called The Three Moaxes.

It was at around this time, back in New York, that Charlie heard from a song-plugger he knew that Benny Goodman was in town and looking for the guy writing the band's arrangements. Charlie knew he could never afford the sort of salary Goodman might offer, so he gave Billy May a great stack of numbers to arrange, and kept him hard at work in a hotel room until Benny left town.

In 1940, when the band was working in New York at the Edison Hotel, the manager there, Mrs Maria Kramer, had the idea of trying to get the Barnet and Ellington bands together to perform a concert piece at the New York World's Fair (then in progress). Billy May wrote a long and ambitious piece, with dramatic changes of mood and tempo, called 'Wings Over Manhattan', but unfortunately the suggested performance never took place, so the Barnet band alone recorded the piece (on two sides of a 78) that autumn, with Charlie playing excellent soprano sax.

Towards the end of 1940, Charlie managed to get the band booked at top of the bill into Harlem's great variety theatre, the Apollo. He had wanted to play there for some time, but the theatre's director and part-owner, Frank Schiffman, had been dubious, not because he didn't like the band, but because it was mostly white. The Apollo had presented white performers before, but never as the headliner.

Charlie finally won by offering to take the pre-Christmas week (traditionally a bad week in the theatre), and to play for a percentage of the receipts, with no guaranteed fee. It was an offer too good for Frank Schiffman to refuse, and he accepted. Not only was the band an enormous hit, it went on to become the most popular white band ever to play the Apollo. And because it had initially played for a percentage, it had won the right to do so at every appearance, a deal otherwise only granted to Ellington, Basie, Cab Calloway and Lionel Hampton.

It undoubtedly helped the band that at that time it had a black singer. From 1939 the band's

girl vocalist had been Mary Ann McCall, a good jazz-tinged singer who had been with Woody Herman. In 1940 she left and was replaced by a young black girl who had started in show-business as a dancer at the Cotton Club in 1933, when Cab Calloway's band was there, and when she was only sixteen – Lena Horne. On her first appearance with the band, after only a minimum of rehearsal, she stopped the show cold.

Inevitably Lena ran into some of the same racial difficulties that Billie Holiday had had with Artie Shaw, but in her autobiography she looked back affectionately on her year with the band, saying that it was with Charlie that she first began to evolve her own personal singing style. Her best recording with the band was the song 'Good For Nothin' Joe', made in January 1941.

From 1939 to 1941 the band's personnel had remained fairly stable, but from 1942 on, mostly because of the wartime draft, it began to change more frequently. Black trumpeter-vocalist Herbert "Peanuts" Holland came into the band, another musician who, like Cat Anderson, had learned to play in the Jenkins Orphanage in Charleston, South Carolina. So did another trumpeter, Neal Hefti, who would go on in 1944 to become part of Woody Herman's most famous Herd, where he would develop into an outstanding arranger (in the Sixties he wrote the theme for TV's *Batman*).

On piano, in 1943, it acquired Michael "Dodo" Marmarosa, who came to him from the Gene Krupa band after Gene was arrested. Dodo, who in 1943 was only eighteen, came from Pittsburgh (the same town that also produced Earl Hines, Mary Lou Williams, Erroll Garner and Billy Strayhorn).

His immigrant Italian family, although working class, set a high value on their native music, and their home was furnished with a piano, a phonograph, and stacks of opera records. Young

Michael was given piano lessons from an early age, and drilled through the exercises of Hanon and Czerny.

A small slight boy (with a large head that got him the nickname "Dodo"), he was something of an outsider at school, denied participation in sports by his constant piano lessons (and his physical ineptitude). His idea of fun was to practise pieces like Bach's 'Two-Part Inventions' till he could play them at double the indicated metronome marking.

By fifteen he had acquired formidable technique and, unknown to his classically-inspired teachers, a burning interest in jazz. Naturally, his inspiration became Art Tatum, and he was one of the very few pianists around to have enough technique to consider emulating him. His touch was clean and precise, his left hand as fluent as his right, and he was both swinging and inventive.

At around the same time, also from the collapsed Krupa band, Charlie acquired the services of Roy Eldridge. With such new talent in it, the band entered a new phase, moving from its discipleship of other bands to lead the way into the big-band sounds of the late Forties.

This new style involved more dissonant harmonies, sudden excursions into double time, and a smoother, more flowing beat. The band's drummer, Cliff Leeman, previously with Artie Shaw and Tommy Dorsey, had obviously learned a lot from the smooth Basie rhythm section, especially Jo Jones.

The band had already begun to move in this direction before the Petrillo recording ban of 1942-43 (we can hear it beginning in two Andy Gibson arrangements from April 1942 – 'Smiles' and 'Shady Lady'), but its absence from the studios during the ban makes the change all the more marked on its return.

In October 1943 it recorded a stunning number, 'The Moose', featuring Dodo Marmarosa's piano, and written and arranged by another young newcomer, Ralph Burns, who came from Newton, Massachussetts, and had studied at the New England Conservatory.

A feature of the new sound was that a new generation of band-members had far more technical proficiency than ever before. In 1944, for instance, the Barnet band recorded an arrangement of Louis Armstrong's classic, 'West End Blues'. When Louis recorded it, in 1928, only he and maybe a couple of other trumpeters could have even attempted to play the opening cadenza. By 1944 the entire Barnet brass section could play it in perfect unison, and with ease. This was the band that in that year gave Charlie an enormous hit with their rendition of his own composition, 'Skyliner'. Fluency and control, such as they now had, allowed bands to play numbers faster, and they did. It was all part of the move away from playing dance music to playing music for listening.

In the years after the war, as the dance-band business declined, Charlie managed to hold his band together a bit longer than most – until 1948. But by 1945 his brief period as the band leading the way had already ended. He had ceded pole position to the band that Ralph Burns had left him to join in late 1944 – Woody Herman.

CHAPTER 18

woody herman

Woodrow Charles Herman was born in Milwaukee in 1913. His family were in vaudeville, and he began singing and dancing on-stage at the age of nine. When he was eleven he took up the alto saxophone, incorporating it in his act. When he was fourteen he took up the clarinet, intending to do the same, but before he got round to that he decided instead to become a dance-band musician.

In 1928, when he was fifteen, he joined a rather obscure band led by Myron Stewart, and shortly afterwards another obscure band led by Joe Lichter, in which he toured Texas. He briefly studied music at Marquette University, and when he was still only sixteen joined a rather better-known band led by Tom Gerun (whose real name was Gerunovitch).

This was an excellent and highly professional band that had with it at the time two good singers – Virginia Simms, who would later shorten her name to Ginny Sims and sing with the Kay Kyser band, and Al Norris, who would change his name completely to Tony Martin. Woody at this time was still spelling his name "Woodie", and by now was also playing tenor sax. Someone once asked him how he sounded then, and he said, "Like Bud Freeman with his hands chopped off."

He was with Tom Gerun from 1929 to 1933, when he tried unsuccessfully to lead a band of his own. After it failed, he spent eight months in the radio band of Harry Sosnick, then two months with Gus Arnheim, who had the top West Coast dance-band of the late Twenties and early Thirties (a band that only a few years later would have an interesting young pianist called Stanley Kenton).

After a brief spell in a band led by Joe Moss, in 1934 he joined the band that would be most important to his career, the Isham Jones band.

The Isham Jones band, which had been around since the Twenties, was by the mid-Thirties one of the best and most popular dance-bands in America. It was outstanding for its full, rich sound, largely the creation of arranger Gordon Jenkins (who later became a successful commercial band-leader himself), and although it played some hot numbers (Don Redman also provided some of its arrangements), it mostly played ballads, many of them written by Isham Jones himself. He was a prolific songwriter, and among his most famous songs were 'I'll See You In My Dreams', 'The One I Love Belongs To Somebody Else', 'On The Alamo', 'You've Got Me Crying Again' and 'It Had To Be You'.

A sombre, long-faced man from Ohio, he was a strict leader who tended to fill his band with untried youngsters. In spite of his cold and remote personality, he managed to build up a musical rapport with his musicians, and was somehow able to get them to phrase in long flowing lines, apparently without breathing. In the words of Gordon Jenkins, "There was a musical affinity between Jones, the boys and myself ... The picture of that big farmer standing up there, moulding seventeen boys (half of whom probably weren't speaking to him at the time) into one gorgeous unit, was something I'll never forget."

Both Gene Krupa and Lionel Hampton (and there were undoubtedly others) said, on forming their bands, "What we really should do is try to sound like the old Isham Jones band." Part of its rich effect was due to the powerful playing of tenorist Saxie Mansfield. Gordon Jenkins used to score his tenor to play in unison with the lead trumpet, only an octave below, which gave the band a sound not unlike a gutsier version of Glenn Miller.

Woody often sang with the band, and also as a member of Isham's hot band-within-a-band, an octet called Isham Jones's Juniors, in which he played clarinet and (by now) baritone sax.

This octet may have been formed by Isham as a reaction to the birth of the Swing Era. Certainly he was aware that a big change was taking place in the world of popular band-leading. He was a fair bit older than leaders like Goodman and the Dorseys, and in 1936 (when he was forty-two), he decided that it was time for him to quit, and broke up the band. (He would form another one in the early Forties, but somehow things were never quite the same).

Woody took several members of the band and, using them as a nucleus, organised his own first band. It was run as a co-operative, and among those who came with him from Isham Jones were tenorist Saxie Mansfield, trumpeter Clarence Willard, bassist Walter Yoder and flugelhorn-player Joe Bishop (the flugelhorn resembles a fat trumpet, being in the same key (B flat) and range, but with a smoother, mellower tone – this band of

Woody's was the first to introduce it into hot music, and it really came into its own with the cool jazz of the Fifties).

Joe Bishop also became the band's arranger, and further arrangements were at first supplied by Gordon Jenkins.

Woody's successive bands became known as his "Herds", which can be a little confusing because this first band was not his First Herd – that came later. This band was identified as "The Band That Plays The Blues", a title it retained into the early Forties.

After six weeks of rehearsals, the band made its debut towards the end of 1936, at the Roseland Ballroom in Brooklyn, following that booking immediately with one at the more famous Roseland Ballroom at West 51st Street on Broadway.

Woody was one of the best of all the leaders to work for. With his background in showbusiness, plus his years of experience with Tom Gerun and Isham Jones, he was a total professional, aware of the high standards needed and in complete control. In addition, however, he encouraged and appreciated his musicians, so that they felt they were working with him rather than for him.

His genial self-confidence also helped. This was well exhibited during the band's second booking, at the famous Roseland Ballroom. The then manager, Joe Belford, a big man built like a brick outhouse, took to bellowing at the band to play waltzes, rhumbas, tangoes and sambas – none of which Woody had, or wanted to have, in the band's repertoire. Grinning amiably, he would yell back at Joe Belford to get lost and quit bothering him. Joe was so disarmed that he not only stopped bothering Woody, he became one of the band's biggest fans.

The band got a recording contract with Decca, making its first recordings for them in November

1936, and over the next few years it would certainly live up to its billing. Among the numbers Woody recorded were 'Dupree Blues', 'Calliope Blues', 'Twin City Blues', 'Laughing Boy Blues', 'Dallas Blues', 'Blues Downstairs', 'Blues Upstairs', 'Casbah Blues', 'Farewell Blues', 'Jumpin' Blues', 'Blue Dawn', 'Blues On Parade', 'It's A Blue World', and the band's first theme 'Blue Prelude', most of them with vocals by Woody himself.

Towards the end of 1938 he also recorded one side with a sextet from within the band, which called itself "Woody Herman's Woodchoppers". The number they recorded was 'River Bed Blues', again with a vocal by Woody. He had a pleasant voice, surprisingly rich on ballads, that never let you down, but never really lifted you up either, and oddly enough, he certainly was no blues-singer. Not even as much as that other "blues-singer" who came out of vaudeville, Mamie Smith.

Even Woody was inclined to admit later in life that the band perhaps played too much blues. In a booking at the Meadowbrook Inn during the band's early days (when they were getting the pitiful fee of six hundred dollars a week for the fifteen of them), they filled their radio shows from there with almost nothing but blues, which, as Woody said "was a little too strong".

It wasn't all blues though, by any means. The band also played and recorded jazz standards like Jelly Roll Morton's 'Doctor Jazz', new pop songs like 'You're A Sweetheart' and old ones like 'Carolina In The Morning', and band originals like 'Herman At The Sherman'. But, naturally enough, by far the greatest hit the band had during its early days was indeed a blues, although not so called – the number jointly composed and arranged by Woody and Joe Bishop, 'Woodchoppers' Ball'.

That was an enormous hit, so much so that Woody's band had to keep playing it for the rest of his life. He became considerably sick of it, and felt eventually that it was old-fashioned and outdated, but nonetheless he regarded it with a kind of grateful affection. As well he might, because it was the brightest gleam in five or six difficult years, during which the band slowly laboured to build up a reputation.

After 'Woodchoppers' Ball' was recorded, in April 1939, things started to get better. They were booked back into the Meadowbrook, this time at a decent salary. Then, in the autumn of that year, the band was booked into the Glen Island Casino to follow Glenn Miller's first fantastic summer there.

It got bookings at other prestigious venues – the Panther Room at Chicago's Hotel Sherman, the New Yorker Hotel in New York, and twice at the Famous Door, on 52nd Street. But still the upward struggle was slow. Another hit, recorded towards the end of 1941, helped. That was Johnny Mercer and Harold Arlen's 'Blues In The Night' (with a vocal by Woody).

This led to occasional movie appearances, usually in simple guest spots, such as in *What's Cookin'?*, made in 1942, in which the Andrews Sisters also had a spot, and in which the band played (of course) 'Woodchoppers' Ball'.

By now Woody, like all the band-leaders, was beginning to suffer from the draft. But he suffered less than most, because when men were taken from him and he had to find replacements, it was well-known in the business that he was a good man to work for. In addition, he was more receptive than most of the top band-leaders to the new ideas of the talented young generation that was knocking at the door.

The feeling had been beginning to grow on him for some time that his band was musically in something of a rut, and that there was more in music than he had been getting out. In 1942, as a step towards changing the band's sound, he hired arranger (and alto and tenor player) Dave Matthews, who had been with Ben Pollack, Jimmy Dorsey, Benny Goodman, and Hal McIntyre (who himself had left Glenn Miller in 1941 to form a dance-band of his own, with backing from Miller).

Dave Matthews could write in an Ellingtonian style, and naturally Woody admired Duke (and his musicians). Temporarily short of good men for a series of recording sessions in 1943, he hired Ben Webster, whose ravishing tenor can be heard on 'The Music Stopped', 'Do Nothing Till You Hear From Me', 'Basie's Basement' and 'Who Dat Up Dere?'.

Also recorded at those sessions, singing 'The Music Stopped' and 'I Couldn't Sleep A Wink Last Night' was an excellent female vocalist who had just joined the band, Frances Wayne, who also happened to be Mrs Neal Hefti.

The Webster sessions worked so well that a year later, for another session, Woody hired three Ellingtonians – Ray Nance, Juan Tizol and Johnny Hodges. Among the three sides they recorded was a delightful version of 'Perdido'.

Being aware of the new musical ideas of his young players, in 1942 Woody had also commissioned a couple of arrangements from Dizzy Gillespie. Dizzy at around that time also played in the band during a booking at the Apollo Theatre, and Woody afterwards advised him to stick to arranging and give up the trumpet. As he said later, "That was one of my strongest decisions."

Like Charlie Barnet, the Herman band changed quite dramatically during the recording ban of 1942-43, with the result that its return on record in 1943 was quite a surprise to those who had not heard it in the meantime.

By 1944 the band was known as the Herman Herd (later, when others came along, as the First Herd). It had grown to eighteen pieces (five

trumpets, three trombones, six reeds, piano, guitar, bass and drums), and not only was it musically adventurous, it was high-spirited and exuberant. Fans began flocking to hear it.

Its two main arrangers had both come from Charlie Barnet's band – Ralph Burns, who with Woody also played piano, and trumpeter Neal Hefti. With Hefti in the trumpet section were two brilliant young brothers, Pete and Conte Candoli, both able to soar brilliantly up into the high register. Blowing for canines, the fans called it.

The Candolis were from Mishawaka, in Indiana. Pete, who was twenty, had already been in a number of bands, including Will Bradley's, Ray McKinley's and Tommy Dorsey's. Conte, who was sixteen, was still at school and had to keep leaving the band to go back there.

Pete, like many of the Herd, had a touch of the comedian. Tall and muscular, he worked out a Superman routine. His wife made him the costume, and when the band played theatres he would leap onstage wearing it, just in time to blast out the bridge of 'Apple Honey' on his trumpet.

He did this for quite a while, and when the first costume wore out his wife made him a second. Comedian Buddy Lester, who was travelling with the band, took over the old one. He was much smaller than Pete, and after 'Apple Honey' was over would come shambling on, wearing the baggy old costume and playing sourly on a beat-up old cornet.

Over more or less the period of the recording ban, Woody had had Vido Musso on tenor, but by 1944 his chair was occupied by Flip Phillips, a white New Yorker with a beautiful touch on ballads, who in the late Forties and Fifties rather overshadowed this talent by playing long honking mob-exciting solos on such numbers as 'Perdido', mainly during impresario Norman Granz's *Jazz At The Philharmonic* tours.

The star trombonist was Bill Harris, who had also been briefly with Charlie Barnet. Bill was from Philadelphia, and had learned piano, tenor and trumpet before deciding on trombone. Early influenced by J.C. Higginbotham, he had developed a style of his own, full of dramatic and unexpected contrasts – he could move fluently from soft purring to loud declamatory shouts and back again. He could play tender ballads, or make great leaps up and down the scale, sometimes jumping as much as four octaves.

Bill too was a natural comedian. He was a tall man, and always harboured an unfulfilled desire to get a pair of those comics' shoes that lock into slots in the stage, so that soloing soulfully out front he could startle the audience by suddenly leaning at impossible angles.

It was Bill who got hold of a life-size rubber dummy that had been used in their act by some dancers. He dressed it in a band uniform, gave it a trombone, and had it sitting in the section next to him. From time to time he would get into a furious argument with it for not coming in when he told it.

Eventually, he and Flip Phillips took it up to their hotel room on the sixth floor. They opened the window, screamed and yelled until a crowd had gathered below, then pushed it out. Hitting the sidewalk, it bounced about fifty feet in the air. They had Nat Wexler, the band-boy, standing by. He caught the dummy on the first bounce and carried it quickly back into the hotel, leaving the crowd startled and amazed.

In the rhythm section, as well as Ralph Burns on piano and guitarist Billy Bauer, there was an extrovert bassist from New York, Greig Stewart "Chubby" Jackson, who brought even more humour into the band (musically, he became a sort of associate leader to Woody, finding new talent for the band, keeping in touch with new musical developments, and occasionally composing).

And on drums there was Dave Tough. Chubby Jackson had at first objected to him being hired, saying he was old-fashioned, but after only a day or so he admitted he had been wrong. Little Davey, with his discreet and rock-solid drumming, adapted easily to the new bop-influenced rhythms.

On top of all this talent there was Woody, who had by now mostly settled on playing clarinet, doubling on alto. His clarinet-playing was pleasant and highly competent, and on alto he could play effective ballads with a hint of Johnny Hodges. On both he always managed somehow to adapt sufficiently to the changing styles of his bands, and not to appear old-fashioned and out-of-place. Always he played something worth hearing.

He welcomed the new sounds deriving from be-bop with enthusiasm, unlike, say, Tommy Dorsey, who wanted no be-bop in his arrangements and forcefully said so on several occasions. Woody went to a men's clothing store in San Francisco and bought the squarest jacket he could find, a loud check with a belt across the back. He sent it to Tommy with a note – "If you want to play that way, why not dress that way?"

By the beginning of 1945, with Conte Candoli mostly off at school, the band acquired another outstanding trumpeter, Saul "Sonny" Berman. Sonny was twenty years old, from New Haven, Connecticut, and was a disciple of Roy Eldridge and Dizzy Gillespie. He shared the solos with Pete Candoli, and would have gone on to great things if he had not died of a heart-attack at the beginning of 1947, while participating in an all-night jam session.

In February 1945, the Herd, which had a new recording contract with Columbia, recorded its first big hit, the up-tempo 'Apple Honey' (this was basically a head arrangement with a few boppish brass figures provided by Ralph Burns and Neal Hefti). A week later, it recorded its second, 'Caldonia', with a vocal (or at least, a chant) by Woody.

'Caldonia' came to the band in a rather unusual way. Written by a New Orleans drummer and singer, Freddie Moore, it had been brought to Louis Jordan, the alto-player and singer who came out of the Chick Webb band in 1938 to lead his Tympany Five to enormous heights of success. Besides instigating the small group line-up that would lead directly to rock 'n' roll, Louis and the Tympany Five were also the inspiration for the long-running Nineties stage show *Five Guys Named Moe*.

Louis and the Tympany Five recorded 'Caldonia' for Decca in January 1945. But for some reason Decca refused to release it until a version had been released by Woody Herman. Maybe they said "by some popular white band", but it was Woody it came to, and he and the band recorded it in February 1945 for Columbia under the supervision of Louis Jordan's shrewd manager, Berle Adams.

Woody's version was a hit. So was Louis Jordan's. But ironically a bigger hit than either was the version recorded in March for Victor by the big band of Erskine Hawkins.

The Herd's own hits began to pour out – 'Northwest Passage', 'Bijou', 'Blowing Up A Storm', 'Your Father's Moustache', 'Wild Root', 'Fan It', 'Back Talk', 'Non-Alcoholic'. Most of those were fast and flamboyant, with virtuoso ensemble passages leading to a crescendo of excitement, from the peak of which the soloist would wing his way upward.

There were also slower and more reflective pieces – 'Laura' (from the Preminger film), 'I Surrender, Dear', 'Panacea', 'Everywhere' (with a masterful solo by Bill Harris), and 'Happiness Is Jes' A Thing Called Joe', on which Frances Wayne delivers one of the best vocals of the whole Swing Era.

Early in 1945, Red Norvo joined the band, playing vibes. He had just finished a stint in Benny Goodman's small groups, and in 1946 Woody gave him musical control over the Woodchoppers. Under Norvo, with the assistance of trumpeter Shorty Rogers (who had joined the band later in 1945), and with the sublime and unpredictable playing of Bill Harris, they recorded ten amazing sides that would point the way forward to the small-group jazz of the Fifties. Outstanding are 'Steps', 'Igor', 'Nero's Conception', 'I Surrender Dear' (substantially a Norvo solo), and 'Fan It' (a hilarious and provocative masterpiece by Bill Harris).

At the end of 1945 the band won the musicians' polls (as opposed to the readers' polls) in both *Metronome* and *Down Beat*, and Flip Phillips, Bill Harris and Dave Tough all won their respective instrumental categories. Unfortunately, by then, Dave Tough had left the band, suffering from his usual combination of ill-health and alcoholism. He was briefly replaced by Buddy Rich, before Woody (or Chubby) found an excellent young Oklahoman drummer, Don Lamond.

Then along came Igor Stravinsky. Living in France, had heard some of the Herd's records during 1945, and he sent Woody a wire saying that he had been very moved and was writing something for the band. Not long afterwards, he arrived in New York and presented Woody with 'Ebony Concerto', saying what a challenge it had been to write for such an unusual line-up of instruments. He had managed, but only by adding a french horn and a harp.

The band was appearing at the Paramount

Theatre at the time, so they arranged with Stravinsky to rehearse the piece in a room on the top floor between shows. For the first rehearsal, the band put on respectable dark blue suits, shirts and ties. Stravinsky arrived in a sweatshirt and a pair of slacks, with a towel round his neck.

A routine began where they would rehearse for an hour and a half while the movie was showing in the theatre. When they were due back onstage a buzzer would go, and down they would troop to play another show. Stravinsky would go out to Sardi's restaurant and drink a little champagne.

After the show, the band would climb the stairs, meet Stravinsky, and start rehearsing again. And so on. After three days, when the band were slowly going under from exhaustion, somebody thought to explain to Stravinsky that they were also doing shows. "Oh, you're doing shows?" was all he said. "How lovely." And during the next show he came and listened.

The rehearsals continued, somehow the band managed to learn the piece, albeit with some simplification, and in March 1946 they performed it during their first appearance at Carnegie Hall. In August they recorded it.

Neither performance was entirely a success. Rhythmically it owed more to ragtime than to swing, and Stravinsky had used only those elements of jazz that interested him. The band found it difficult to cope with its immense technical demands and at the same time play with the feeling and vitality the piece cries out for. As Woody said, with his usual honesty, "We were no more ready to play it than the man in the moon."

At around the time of 'Ebony Concerto', the band played another engagement at the Hotel Sherman in Chicago. While they were there, a woman by the name of Lady McGowan took over a suite and several other rooms. She became a great fan of the band, coming every night to the Panther Room to listen to them, and one night throwing a big party for them in her suite, with champagne and caviar laid on.

A day or so later, the management decided to check up on her and discovered that there was no such person as Lady McGowan. All her trunks and suitcases were empty, and she had vanished leaving behind a tab of four thousand dollars. She was never traced.

Ralph Burns wrote his six-minute composition 'Lady McGowan's Dream' in her memory, and the band recorded it in September 1946, the day before recording the first three parts of his even longer and more ambitious piece, the four-part twelve-minute 'Summer Sequence'. The fourth part wouldn't get recorded for another fourteen months, when the First Herd had been replaced by the Second.

The First Herd's success proved its undoing. Recording executives, agents, managers and sponsors crowded round Woody, pressing him to broaden his appeal to reach a wider audience. To some extent he gave in to this towards the end of 1946, playing more pop tunes, and even adding a vocal group. He was also plagued by the hits the Herd had recorded. At concerts and dances, fans clamoured to hear the same tunes over and over, making it hard for the band to explore new territory.

At the end of 1946, exhausted, Woody broke up his great band. After nearly twenty years of hard work without a break, he felt it was time he had a holiday.

He didn't take much of one. During February and March 1947 he made about ten quartet recordings, playing his clarinet with a rhythm section that included Don Lamond on drums. In April, May, and August he got together pick-up bands to record another eighteen titles. And in September he formed the Second Herd.

This was a bold thing to do at a time when the big band era had just died, and almost every band in the country had folded. For a while, almost alone, the Second Herd kept the flag of big band jazz flying.

Shorty Rogers was back in the trumpet section, and Sam Marowitz was back on alto. Walter Yoder was still on bass, and Don Lamond was back on drums, but apart from that the Second Herd was all new faces.

This was the band that contained the amazing saxophone section of Al Cohn, Zoot Sims and Stan Getz (tenors), and Serge Chaloff (baritone) – the section that would become immortalised by their recording (as a featured quartet) of the Jimmy Giuffre number 'Four Brothers'.

Once, when the Second Herd was playing at a party, a lady asked Woody if the band could play something Jewish. "Well," he said thoughtfully, "we have some arrangements by Al Cohn."

In its way, the Second Herd was even wilder than the First. Many of the band, including the "four brothers", were under the influence of firstly, Lester Young, and secondly, Charlie Parker (as every serious young musician was in 1947).

And now, in this post-war era, there was a new attitude among the serious young musicians and fans. The hepcat had given way to the hipster, and after thirty years of hot music, suddenly the thing to be was cool.

The cool attitude was this. The new music was difficult, and if you could appreciate it, you were in. If not, forget it. But because the new music was so amazing, its amazingness went without saying. It was as surplus to requirements to express excitement as to go round saying that water is wet.

In a way this attitude wasn't new in the jazz world. Back in the Twenties in Chicago, Eddie Condon's highest praise for a piece of music he liked was, "It doesn't bother me." But in the Forties it became a whole philosophy of life. The hipster was indifferent to anything but the music and his fellow-hipsters (male or female). The trick was to stay free and keep the big, fat, safe, cold world of the squares at arm's length.

Part of this attitude of being an insider, aware of good things that the square world didn't and couldn't share, came from the drug world. Charlie Parker was a user, and he played like a god, so if you wanted to play like a god maybe the thing to do was become a user yourself. Many young musicians in the Forties became addicts, and the Second Herd had its share. The most notorious, in fact the band's pusher, and unfortunately also its most gifted musician, was baritone-player Serge Chaloff.

Born in Boston in 1923, Chaloff had been taught piano and clarinet formally (his mother was a teacher at the Bopston University School of Music), but he had taught himself to play the baritone. Influenced by Harry Carney and by Count Basie's baritone-player, Jack Washington, he acquired a full rich tone, coupled with fast and dexterous fingering.

In 1939, at the age of sixteen, he turned professional, working in various minor bands before, in 1945, joining the Boyd Raeburn big band. Boyd Raeburn, a cheerful and straightforward musician who played all the saxes from tenor down to bass, had led a rather boring commercial dance-band from 1933, but in around 1942, after getting an injection of bright young talent, it suddenly and briefly blossomed into a forward-looking experimental group. In 1944, before it had had time to make much impact, it lost all its music and most of its instruments in a fire at Palisades Amusement Park, New Jersey. It never really recovered its momentum, and Serge Chaloff, joining in 1945, soon left to join the big band being led by tenorist George Auld.

It was while with Auld that he came under the influence of Charlie Parker, and although his style remained swing-based, he still absorbed enough of the new ideas in harmony, melodic contruction, and rhythm to make him a serious force among the young white boppers. Unfortunately, it was at this time that he also acquired his habit.

In the Herman band he was a liability. He was inclined to nod off while smoking in bed and set the mattress alight. Once in a hotel room he had an air-pistol and to get some target practice put a phone-book against the door and potted at it. He damaged the door, and the manager, furious, made him pay twenty-four dollars to have it replaced. Serge reluctantly paid, but insisted that in that case the door was his, and got vibraphone-player Terry Gibbs to help him unscrew it and carry it down to the band bus.

He also introduced other musicians in the Second Herd to hard drugs, mostly heroin. The band started to both look sloppy and sound sloppy, and in spite of Serge's brilliance (he had won the *Down Beat* and *Metronome* polls on baritone) Woody decided he would have to go. Since he came from Boston, Woody decided to fire him the next time the band got near Boston, which would be at a famous dance-hall at Nutting-on-the-Charles.

He told Serge in advance that this was to happen, and Serge was distraught, needing his band income to feed his habit. The dance-hall backed onto the River Charles, and at intermission on the band's last night there, Serge called Woody's attention to a mass of torn-up paper floating in the water. It was the band's baritone book, which only Serge knew by heart. Woody was stuck with him for a while longer.

One night, on a gig in Washington, D.C., the band was sounding even worse than usual. Half the men, including Serge, were stoned and Woody, fed up, started to yell at him there on the bandstand. Serge, spaced out, simply got more and more laid back – "Hey, Woody baby. I'm straight, man. I'm clean," he kept repeating over and over. Woody got so mad that he snapped, "Just play your part and shut up!"

He was so depressed that night that after the gig he went for a drink at an after-hours club called the Turf and Grid. It was jammed full, and he had to fight his way to the bar. Finally, hot and sweating, he got his drink, but as he raised it to his lips, he felt somebody pluck at his arm and heard this voice whining, "Hey, Woody baby, whadya wanna talk to me like that for? I'm straight, baby. I'm straight." It was Serge.

Woody was livid. Then he remembered something that violinist Joe Venuti had once done, and did it. He unzipped himself in the dark club, with everybody packed tight together, and peed down Serge's leg. It took a while to sink in, but when it did Serge let out a howl like a banshee, and rushed away and shut himself in a phone-booth. Not long afterwards, Woody ran into Joe Venuti and confessed what he had done. Joe was horrified. "Woody!" he said. "You can't do things like that. I can do things like that, but you can't. You're a gentleman."

Woody finally got rid of Serge in 1949, and disbanded the Second Herd later the same year. It had produced such fine numbers as 'Keen And Peachy' (a remake of an earlier Herman recording called 'Fine And Dandy'), 'Lemon Drop', 'Keeper Of The Flame' and 'Autumn Leaves' (one of the themes from 'Summer Sequence', re-recorded with a magnificent tenor solo by Stan Getz).

Soon after it disbanded there was a Third Herd, and a Fourth, and a Fifth, and a Sixth. The number of fine musicians that passed through the various Herds reads like a "Who's Who" of modern jazz, but the music got further and further away from the dance-hall.

Woody continued leading Herds until his death in October 1987, forming his last in 1986. Some years before his death he was walking up Seventh Avenue in New York with guitarist Jimmy Raney and they ran into Artie Shaw, then out of the band business for years. "Hi, Woody," said Artie. "What are you up to these days?" "Well, the band is in town for a couple of dates," said Woody. Artie looked surprised. "Oh, do you still have a band?" he said. "Well," said Woody, "some guys dig ditches; I have a band. It's what I do."

CHAPTER 19

ride-out

There were many reasons why the big band era ended so abruptly after the Second World War. The war itself was responsible for many of the problems facing the bands. Not only did they have difficulties in keeping regular personnel, with musicians continually being drafted, the US Government had also, as a wartime fund-raising measure, imposed a tax on places of entertainment.

This was particularly hard on ballrooms.

Other places of entertainment, such as theatres, cinemas and hotels, could if necessary do without bands altogether. Ballrooms could not, and the tax hit them hard, coming on top of the huge fees that top bands were demanding by the time the war ended in 1945.

Such leaders as Tommy Dorsey, Benny Goodman, Harry James and Artie Shaw were asking for a guaranteed $4,000 dollars a night, or else sixty per cent of the takings (less entertainment tax), whichever was the greater. In big high-profile ballrooms the basic fee could rise as high as $7,500 a night.

The war had caused an enormous boom in dancing, but those high fees meant that as soon as there was the slightest dip in demand, the ballrooms, already suffering from the tax, would find themselves in financial straits.

After the war, demand did fall away. After ten years of swing, its very popularity had meant an enormous increase in the number of bands. There may have been as many as twenty thousand in America at the height of the boom. Naturally, many of these were not very good. Quite a few were sweet bands, or peaceful hotel bands, that had suddenly declared themselves to be swing bands in order to jump on the band-wagon.

This meant that much of what was being played, on bandstands and over the radio, was pretty boring and repetitive. Certainly such band-leaders as Barnet and Herman were exploring new avenues, but the feeling among the general public by 1946 was that swing was getting played out, and it was time for something new.

There was a similar feeling among many musicians, who were getting tired of playing the same old riffs and changes night after night. But the problem with developing something new was that swing was rooted in jazz, which was where its new musical ideas mainly came from, and jazz itself had made a dramatic development.

The be-bop movement had started growing up among young black jazz musicians at the beginning of the Forties, being developed mainly at jam sessions in after-hours New York clubs, notably Minton's Playhouse in Harlem and Monroe's Uptown House on 52nd Street.

The two men most influential in the growth of bop were altoist Charlie Parker and trumpeter

Dizzy Gillespie. As Diz once explained it, "Some of us began to jam at Minton's in Harlem in the early Forties. But there were always some cats showing up there who couldn't blow at all but would take six or seven choruses to prove it.

"So on afternoons before a session, Thelonious Monk and I began to work out some complex variations in chords and the like, and we used them at night to scare away the no-talent guys.

"After a while, we got more and more interested in what we were doing as music, and, as we began to explore more and more, our music evolved."

Much of what they were doing, apart from playing very fast, involved using the higher intervals of chords, such as ninths and thirteenths. This gave the music a strange quality of seeming to be in two keys at once, and allowed it much greater emotional expressiveness. It also permitted the use of new and unfamilar key-changes, modulating from one chord to the next. These new changes, to the ears of older musicians, sounded wrong. Cab Calloway, for instance, accused Diz, when he was in his band, of playing "Chinese music".

Charlie Parker, a much more instinctive player than Diz, expressed his own discovery of the power of the new music this way: "I was jamming in a chili house on Seventh Avenue between 139th and 140th. It was December 1939. Now I'd been getting bored with all the stereotyped changes that were being used all the time at the time, and I kept thinking there's bound to be something else. I could hear it sometimes but I couldn't play it. Well, that night I was working over 'Cherokee', and, as I did, I found that by using the higher intervals of a chord as a melody line and backing them with appropriately related changes, I could play the thing I'd been hearing. I came alive."

Bop's leading practitioners in the early days included drummers Kenny Clarke and Max Roach. The drummers were important, because much of what was new in bop was its rhythmic approach. Bop groups took their rhythm from the bass, rather than the drums, freeing the drummer to elaborate on the rhythm in counterpoint with the rest of the band.

This led to drummers playing mostly on their hi-hat and ride cymbals, using their side and bass drums for accents and punctuations. The music became filled with asymmetrical accents and patterns, and this, even more than the harmonic innovations, made bop hard for swing-era musicians to play. This suited many of the young black boppers, among whom the idea had grown up that the whole swing era had been built on white musicians stealing black musicians' ideas, and making a lot of money from them.

Because part of the music's genesis had been a desire to keep away outsiders, it always retained something of this quality, for listeners as well as musicians. To appreciate bop became a sign of hipness, a sign that you were a member of life's inner circle.

In the jazz world at the same time there was a big revival of the sounds of the Twenties, and jazz fans split into two camps, each sneering at the other. The boppers labelled the others "mouldy figs", and accused them of hiding in the musical nursery, unable to appreciate what was really happening. The mouldy figs complained that bop didn't swing, and that it was a jarring unmusical noise.

The ultimate effect of bop on jazz, which in the form of swing had been the dominant form of popular music, would be to split it in two. As musicians and the more knowlegeable fans went deeper and deeper into musical complexity, the simple rhythmic appeal of jazz faded further and further away, leaving the way open in the Fifties for a music to appear that was direct and approachable, and almost nothing but rhythmic appeal – rock 'n' roll.

With the massive success of rock, jazz was freed from any obligation to be widely popular, and became more and more a minority interest, with those who played it moving ever further into experimental self-absorption. The rhythmic joy stayed largely with rock, the musical inventiveness with the successive developments of jazz.

In the mid-Forties, some established bandleaders tried to make use of the new musical ideas of bop (with varying success). Some did not. Tommy Dorsey, for instance, wanted no part of it.

Benny Goodman had a brief flirtation with it, employing tenor-player Wardell Gray in his band. Wardell was only about a year older than Parker and Gillespie so, although he had started out as a swing musician, he was able to adapt to bop enough to become an important transitional figure. But Benny, whose musical approach was firmly rooted in Twenties Chicago, had no hope of adapting. His flirtation with bop was brief.

Charlie Barnet and Woody Herman were perhaps the most successful of the white bands in their attempts to move with the times, although there were others. The bands of Boyd Raeburn and Claud Thornhill, both basically dance-bands, dabbled briefly. Thornhill, who had been Ray Noble's pianist when Glenn Miller was working with the Noble band, co-opted two young white boppers, baritone-player Gerry Mulligan and altoist Lee Konitz.

Using arrangements by Gil Evans, the Thornhill band recorded several bop standards, including 'Anthropology', 'Donna Lee' and 'Yardbird Suite', but although they were well-received by the cognoscenti, they left the dancing public, if not cold, then certainly lukewarm.

A bandleader who for a brief while had more success was Charlie Ventura. He was a tenor and baritone-player from Philadelphia, who had been in the ill-fated Gene Krupa band. In 1946 he had formed a big band of his own, but shortly was forced to reduce it to an octet. In 1948 the octet adopted the slogan "Bop For The People", and began using clever arrangements in which voices and instruments played well-known bop themes in unison.

These numbers largely featured Charlie Ventura's own playing, and although that was more in the swing than the bop idiom, the octet had only a brief success with the public, and in 1949 it gave up the unequal struggle.

The only band to have a considerable amount of popular success with the new sounds was that of Stan Kenton, who developed a brand of music all his own, which he labelled "Progressive Jazz".

Stanley Newcomb Kenton had been born in Wichita, Kansas, in 1911. All his life he had a vein of obstinacy that showed itself early when his mother wished him to take piano lessons. Young Stanley refused, preferring to play ball instead. It wasn't until two cousins paid a lengthy visit to his house, and played jazz incessantly, that he realised that maybe there was something to be said for this music idea after all.

He learnt to play the piano, and grew into a tall rangy adult, well over six feet, fizzing with nervous energy and confidence in his own rightness. During the Thirties he worked as pianist and arranger in various dance-bands on the West Coast. In 1934 he was with a band led by a jazz clarinetist called Everett Hoagland, and stayed until Hoagland got the job of head of the arranging department at the RKO film studio. In 1937 he joined the prestigious Gus Arnheim band, then played in bands led by Gil Evans and Vido Musso and Johnny "Scat" Davis (a comedian-singer-trumpeter who'd made a reputation as one of Fred Waring's Pennsylvanians, then gone out on his own).

In 1941 Stan formed a band of his own, which made its first live appearance on May 30 at the Rendezvous Ballroom in Balboa Beach, California. Right from the start he was determined to do something different, his taste running to something big and blasting, with large sections of brass and saxophones playing innovatory and dissonant progressions of chords. The main fault his bands had was that, being so big, they were difficult to make swing, and tended to sound heavy and ponderous.

He chose excellent musicians, and his bands were usually at their best when he gave the men in them free rein to improvise. At the other end of the scale, they were usually at their worst in his "concert works", which could be mind-numbingly turgid and pretentious.

In 1941 his band had a conventional fourteen pieces, but by 1944 the number had grown to eighteen, with five trumpets, five trombones and five saxes (one of whom was Stan Getz). As well as the fourteen there were two singers, one of whom was Anita O'Day.

By 1949 it had grown to twenty pieces, and with it Stan appeared in a prestigious concert at Carnegie Hall. Later that year he fell ill, and temporarily disbanded, but was back in 1950 with the biggest band he ever had, a forty-three-piece aggregation including strings, an oboe, a bassoon and a french horn. It was called the Innovations in Modern Music Orchestra, and during 1950 and 1951 he undertook two nationwide tours with it, before having to face the fact that it was too big ever to pay its way. After that he led more conventionally-sized bands of around twenty pieces.

During the mid-Fifties his was the most popular and fashionable big band around (thus inadvertently opening the door wide for the coming of rock 'n' roll), but the audiences he could command were not on the same scale as those Goodman and Miller had commanded in their heyday.

The new sounds coming into swing in the years immediately after the war were not the only reasons why its audience drifted away. For a start. the recording ban of 1942-43 had had an unexpected side-effect. Barred from using musicians in those years, the big record companies had done a lot of recording using singers backed by vocal groups.

Coming on top of the great success of Frank Sinatra with Tommy Dorsey, this drew the public's attention firmly to singers. Most fans found it easier to identify with a singer as a popular idol than with an instrumental soloist, let alone with a whole band. Someone using words created a much more personal image. So from the mid-Forties on, solo singers became the stars.

They didn't even need big bands to back them. A quintet would do, or even a trio. Clubs and radio shows also began to find, in the wake of the success of Louis Jordan, that even without a singer, a small group could pull the public in just as well as a big band. Why pay fifteen musicians when you could pay five?

With all these circumstances massing against them, the demise of the big bands was stunningly swift. In January 1947, within a period of four weeks, many leaders broke up their bands, among them Les Brown, Benny Carter, Benny Goodman, Tommy Dorsey and Harry James. Some of them would form big bands again later, but rarely on a permanent basis.

Benny Goodman formed his short-lived bop band later the same year, but after it disbanded in 1949 he spent the rest of his life organising ad hoc bands and small groups for tours or special occasions, playing basically old favourites from his days at the top.

Hollywood, always behind the times, had decided to make a film of the lives of Tommy and Jimmy Dorsey at around the time that Tommy disbanded. Highly fictionalised, and with the two brothers rather unconvincingly playing themselves, *The Fabulous Dorseys* nonetheless contained a fair amount of their music, including performances of 'Marie', 'Green Eyes', 'Never Say Never', 'The Object Of My Affections' and 'Dorsey Concerto', and on the back of the publicity the film brought him, Tommy was able to re-form his band and, with some difficulty, keep it together.

Jimmy's band, from around 1943, had become more popular than Tommy's, so he managed to avoid disbanding in 1947. But as the years went by he was the one who found the going hardest. In 1953 he eventually disbanded, and what he did next was to join Tommy. After eighteen years, there was again a Dorsey Brothers band. People who knew Jimmy (who had become a leader only reluctantly) said that he hadn't looked as relaxed and happy in years.

They were together till Tommy choked to death in his sleep in 1956, too exhausted by the effort of keeping the band alive to wake up. Jimmy, so emotionally tied to his brother, was devastated. He even found it impossible to tell their mother himself that Tommy was dead. To Cork O'Keefe he said, "I don't think I'll last out the year." He didn't (although turning out to have cancer didn't help). He survived Tommy by only six months.

Bob Crosby, whose band had broken up back in 1942, spent the years after the war working as a compäre and singer on radio and television, occasionally getting together a band to recreate his hits of the past.

Charlie Barnet, after breaking up his band in

the late Forties, took a similar course, dabbling in music-publishing and the restaurant business, and re-forming his band for occasional concerts or recording sessions.

Artie Shaw, who in 1954 had quit music for good and emigrated to Spain, continued to marry. His wife for several years was Evelyn Keyes, another movie star (and like his friend Judy Garland, a former MGM actor). They parted, and in the early Seventies both returned to America, where Artie lived a hermit-like existence for some eleven years before emerging in 1983 to form a new band. He only directed the band having long given up playing, and for much of the time it was led by clarinetist Dick Johnson. It played recreations of his best-known pieces, Artie having reconciled himself to the idea that, whatever his original intentions, he had created a piece of Americana that was an important part of many people's memories.

Gene Krupa managed to keep a band together until 1951. After it folded, he toured for a few years as a member of Norman Granz's "Jazz At The Philharmonic", then spent the rest of his life (he died in 1973) running a school of percussion and occasionally getting together small groups for one-off engagements.

Another surviving ex-Goodman band-leader, Harry James, succeeded in soldiering on, helped by his forty-weeks-a-year resdidences in Nevada, until his death in 1983.

There was a third ex-Goodman leader, who didn't form his first band until the Swing Era was almost over, but who would go on from there to lead bands right into the Nineties – Lionel Hampton. From 1937, while he was still playing in Benny Goodman's small groups, Hamp had had a contract with Victor records to assemble and direct small groups in their studios. In 1940 he left Benny and formed a big band of his own. When planning it, he seemed uncertain what sort of band he wanted to have, changing his mind almost daily, and the band he eventually assembled in a way reflected this, featuring his delicate and thoughtful vibes-playing on ballads, and roaring away with simple but effective riffs on the up-tempo numbers, in what at times was effectively big-band rock 'n' roll.

With Hamp's fame established before he started, and with his enthusiastic showmanship on-stage, the band quickly became a sustained success. It boasted a parade of outstanding musicians over the years. Some were famous already, and some became famous, among them trumpeters Cat Anderson, Al Killian, Kenny Dorham, Fats Navarro, Idrees Sulieman, Quincy Jones, Nat Adderley and Joe Newman; trombonists Booty Wood, Britt Woodman and Al Grey; altoists Marshall Royal and Earl Bostic; tenorists Dexter Gordon, Illinois Jacquet, Lucky Thompson, Arnett Cobb, Al Sears, Frank Foster and Johnny Griffin; guitarist Wes Montgomery; bassists Charlie Mingus and George Duvivier; singers Dinah Washington and Betty Carter. And of course Hamp himself, playing vibes, drums and piano (hammering the keys with two fingers as if they were mallets), and singing.

His band held the attendance record at Harlem's Apollo Theatre for years, and it was always exciting. Even if it did tend to repeat its most famous numbers at every performance, they were always worth hearing, and always different, because of the quality of his soloists – 'Hey, Ba-ba-re-bop', 'How High The Moon', 'Stardust', 'Air Mail Special' and of course 'Flying Home'. If any one man could have kept the Swing Era alive single-handedly, it was Hamp.

Of the black bands that were actually around at the height of the Swing Era, both Louis Armstrong and Earl Hines disbanded theirs in 1948, coming together as members of the Louis Armstrong All-Stars.

The All-Stars, with its devoted audience of mouldy figs, kept performing until Louis' death in 1971, but Earl Hines left it in 1951 (Louis had never been happy about having another flamboyant personality in what was, after all, his band), and spent the rest of his life leading small groups of his own, with considerable success, in terms both of popularity and of critical acclaim.

Jimmie Lunceford died in 1947, and his band folded. Lucky Millinder and Erskine Hawkins managed to keep their bands alive into the early Fifties, giving them more and more a heavy rhythm-and-blues beat, but then they too gave up.

Count Basie managed to keep his band together until 1950, when he disbanded it and formed a smaller group that ranged in size from a sextet to a nonet. In 1952, missing having a big band, he re-formed and embarked with his new band on a gruelling series of tours and recordings to re-establish himself.

Only Basie and guitarist Freddie Green remained from the old band, and the new one was rather different. Its emphasis was more on written arrangements and less on inspired soloists and arrangements developed in performance. Rather than having the wild easy swing of the first band, it became a shining well-oiled machine, capable of generating considerable excitement, but tending to become slick and predictable.

It established success with the production, in 1957, of the album *The Atomic Mr Basie*, which contained beautiful numbers like 'Li'l Darlin'' and 'Whirly-Bird', all composed by his then arranger, Neal Hefti.

From then until Basie's death in 1984 (latterly he played piano from a wheelchair), the band continued to tour the world with enormous success, although Basie once claimed that if, by magic, he could have just one night again with his first band, he would retire happy.

Duke Ellington never disbanded. Partly he was helped to survive by revenue from the many numbers he had composed and from the many recordings the band had made, but nonetheless it went through a very lean period from the mid-Forties to the mid-Fifties.

After Cootie Williams had left the band in 1940, more of the big names followed. Clarinetist Barney Bigard left in 1942 to lead groups of his own, and in the same year bassist Jimmy Blanton died of TB. In 1943 tenor-player Ben Webster left, also to lead groups of his own, and in 1945 cornetist Rex Stewart left to tour with "Jazz At The Philharmonic". The same year trombonist Tricky Sam Nanton had a stroke, and though he returned to the band, he died in 1946 while on tour in California. Toby Hardwick left that May, and in 1949 guitarist Fred Guy left to become the manager of a ballroom. With the new Blanton-inspired style of bass-playing, the guitar had become somewhat redundant in the band, and Duke never again used one.

In 1951 came the biggest blow of all. Johnny Hodges, Lawrence Brown, Sonny Greer and tenorist Al Sears (who had replaced Ben Webster) left en masse to form a band of their own. This came about at the instigation of "Jazz At The Philharmonic" impresario, Norman Granz, who during the late Forties had become both rich and influential in jazz. He felt that Hodges in particular was not getting the exposure with Duke that he deserved, and apparently Hodges felt the same. He was also beginning to feel aggrieved at the number of new Ellington compositions based on his improvisations (without payment).

All these losses would have been a blow to any band, but they were even more so to Duke, who composed his pieces so specifically for individual musicians. Additionally, of course, he was suffering from the rapid decline of swing, and for a while there was a real sense that the band was in terminal decline. But Duke was not ready to give up so easily. With Billy Strayhorn's collaboration, he worked more and more on extended pieces, and the band began to appear more often in concert halls than it had.

Gradually he gathered a new choir of voices. High-note trumpeter Cat Anderson joined in 1950, and the Rex-like Clark Terry in 1951. In the trombone section appeared Quentin Jackson, who took over Tricky Sam's role in 1948, and Britt Woodman, who replaced Lawrence Brown in 1951. But it was the reed section that in many ways became the glory of the reviving band. In 1943 clarinetist and tenorist Jimmy Hamilton had replaced Barney Bigard. His pure and almost classical tone was at first disconcerting to jazz-trained ears, but as usual with new and distinctive voices, Duke made excellent use of him. Toby Hardwick had been replaced in 1946 by altoist Russell Procope, who had played with Jelly Roll Morton, Benny Carter, Fletcher Henderson and Teddy Hill. When Al Sears left in 1951 he was replaced on tenor by Bostonian Paul Gonsalves, who had been with Count Basie, and in the big band led by Dizzy Gillespie, but whose life's ambition had always been to play with Duke. In 1955, Johnny Hodges returned, and at last what would be the longest-serving sax section in big band history was assembled – Gonsalves, Hamilton, Hodges, Procope, and Harry Carney, who had never left (and never would). After having a succession of drummers (including Louie Bellson), in 1955 the band also acquired Sam Woodyard, whose beat, stronger than Sonny Greer's, gave the band a new lift and drive.

All was ready for the band to hit the top again, and on July 7, 1956 it happened. At the Newport

Jazz Festival, the Ellington band had been booked to end that day's performance, beginning their set at 11.15 p.m. The previous groups overran their time, and in fact the band did not begin until quarter to midnight. Duke was furious, feeling that the band had been kept waiting around and would be playing to a departing audience, and his anger may have communicated itself to the band, raising their adrenalin. Whatever the cause, after playing a suite specially composed for the occasion, they played a couple of the band's standards, then Ellington called for two numbers from 1938, 'Diminuendo In Blue' and 'Crescendo In Blue', separated, as his announcement said, "By – er – an interlude by Paul Gonsalves."

The audience recieved 'Diminuendo In Blue' with enthusiasm, but nothing like the enthusiasm aroused by Paul's interlude, which was basically straightforward blues tenor-playing. By the sixth chorus the crowd had begun to clap and cheer. By the eighth the applause had grown to a continuous roar. Some of the audience climbed up to stand on their seats. Some began to dance. Photographers rushed to record the exceitement, and promoter George Wein, fearful of a riot, crept up to Duke and asked him to bring the number to an end. But nothing could stop Duke (or the band) now. Paul's solo kept on building for twenty-seven choruses, lasting some six-and-a-half minutes. After it, there was a brief piano solo by Duke, that had rather the same effect of suppressed tension as Jess Stacy's had had in 1938 during 'Sing, Sing, Sing', and then the band came roaring in with 'Crescendo In Blue', layer upon layer of sound, as if there were endless sections to be brought in one on top of the other, and the whole thing climaxed by Cat Anderson's high-note trumpet.

As Duke used to say in later years, when asked his age, "I was born in Newport in 1956." He was featured on the cover of *Time* magazine, and the band was established again, and for ever. From then on, all through the Sixties and into the Seventies, it would tour the world, playing for concerts and dances and film sound-tracks, pouring out an apparently endless stream of suites and songs, old and new. In 1960, even Lawrence Brown rejoined the band, and in 1962, so did Cootie Williams. It wasn't quite the same as the great 1940 band. The arrangements were not quite so closely-integrated and dense, the voicings of the chords not quite so mystifyingly unusual, but the new band swung harder than ever and, being still a band of great soloists, every performance was a new delight.

The whole Swing Era had been a beautiful and exciting time, brought about by the happy coincidence of a fortunate set of social circumstances – the new music of ragtime at the turn of the century, leading to the craze for dancing that caused dance-halls and ballrooms to be built all over America – the excitement of jazz, coming along just as America, full of confidence, was ready to celebrate the end of the Great War and move into a new era of happy irresponsibility – the record industry, spreading the music from coast to coast – Prohibition, giving rise to the thousands of speakeasies that proved a natural home for hot music and dancing – the Harlem Renaissance, bringing blacks and whites together to develop the music further – radio, giving even more work to musicians and helping to make big bands an economic proposition.

And above all, the hundreds of great musicians who took advantage of all this to create a music that will never die. Thanks, of course, to Thomas Alva Edison, inventor of the phonograph, who never thought it would be anything more than just a toy.

bibliography

the music

Walter C. Allen
Hendersonia: The Music of Fletcher Henderson and his Musicians
[Walter C. Allen 1973]

Rudi Blesh
Combo: U.S.A.
[Chilton Book Company (US) 1971]

Walter Bruyninckx
50 Years of Recorded Jazz
[Privately published (Belgium) 1970-72]

John Chilton
Jazz
[Hodder & Stoughton 1979]

John Chilton
The Who's Who of Jazz: Storyville to Swing Street
[The Bloomsbury Book Shop 1970]

Donald Clarke
Wishing on the Moon: the Life and Times of Billie Holiday
[Viking 1994]

Sid Colin
And the Bands Played On
[Elm Tree Books 1980]

James Lincoln Collier
Benny Goodman & the Swing Era
[OUP 1989]

James Lincoln Collier
Duke Ellington
[Pan 1989]

James Lincoln Collier
Louis Armstrong
[Pan 1985]

James Lincoln Collier
The Making of Jazz: A Comprehensive History
[Papermac 1981]

Eddie Condon, with Thomas Sugrue
We Called It Music
[Corgi 1962]

Stanley Dance
The World of Duke Ellington
[Macmillan 1970]

Duke Ellington
Music is My Mistress
[W.H.Allen 1974]

Mercer Ellington with Stanley Dance
Duke Ellington in Person
[Hutchinson 1978]

Peter Gammond
Duke Ellington
[Apollo 1987]

Dave Gelly
Lester Young
[Spellmount 1984]

Dizzy Gillespie with Al Fraser
Dizzy: To Be Or Not To Bop
[Quartet Books 1982]

Rex Harris
Jazz
[Penguin 1956]

Jim Haskins
The Cotton Club
[Robson Books 1985]

Burnett James
Coleman Hawkins
[Spellmount 1984]

Derek Jewell
Duke: A Portrait Of Duke Ellington
[Elm Tree Books 1977]

Max Jones & John Chilton
Louis
[Mayflower 1975]

Orrin Keepnews & Bill Grauer, Jr
A Pictorial History Of Jazz
[Spring Books ca.1958]

Kitty Kelley
His Way: The Unauthorised Biography Of Frank Sinatra
[Bantam Press 1986]

Rick Kennedy
"Jelly Roll, Bix And Hoagy: Gennett Studios And The Birth Of Recorded Jazz"
[Indiana University Press 1994]

Ed: Barry Kernfeld
The New Grove Dictionary Of Jazz
[Macmillan 1995]

W.T.Ed.Kirkeby
Ain't Misbehavin': The Story Of Fats Waller
[Peter Davies 1966]

Alan Lomax
Mr Jelly Roll
[Cassell 1952]

Humphrey Lyttelton
Enter the Giants
[Unwin Paperbacks 1984]

Albert McCarthy
Big Band Jazz
[Peerage Books 1983]

Mezz Mezzrow & Bernard Wolfe
Really The Blues
[Secker & Warburg 1957]

Stuart Nicholson
Ella Fitzgerald
[Victor Gollacnz 1993]

Robert Reisner
Bird: The Story Of Charlie Parker
[Quartet Books 1962]

Ross Russell
Bird Lives!
[Quartet Books 1973]

Brian Rust
Jazz Records 1897-1942 (2 vols.)
[Storyville Publications – 5th Edn. 1982]

Brian Rust
My Kind of Jazz
[Elm Tree Books 1990]

Brian Rust & Allen G. Debus
The Complete Entertainment Discography
[Da Capo Press (US) 1989]

Herb Sanford
Tommy And Jimmy: The Dorsey Years
[Ian Allan 1972]

Gunther Schuller
Early Jazz
[OUP(US) 1968]

Gunther Schuller
The Swing Era
[OUP(US) 1989]

Ed: Nat Shapiro & Nat Hentoff
Hear Me Talkin' To Ya
[Peter Davies 1955]

Arnold Shaw
52nd Street: The Street Of Jazz
[Da Capo Press (US) 1977]

George T. Simon
The Big Bands
[Macmillan (US) 1967]

Marshall & Jean Stearns
Jazz Dance
[Collier-Macmillan 1970]

Rex Stewart
Jazz Masters Of The 30's
[Macmillan 1972]

Richard M. Sudhalter & Philip R. Evans with
William Dean-Myatt
Bix: Man & Legend
[Quartet Books 1974]

Dicky Wells
The Night People
[Robert Hale 1971]

Mark White
**You Must Remember This: Popular
Songwriters 1900-1980**
[Frederick Warne 1983]

the rest

Lester V. Berrey & Melvin Van den Bark -
The American Thesaurus Of Slang
[Harrap (US) 1942]

Ed: Ezra Bowen
This Fabulous Century (Vol.III) 1920-1930
[Time-Life Books 1971]

Ed: Ezra Bowen
This Fabulous Century (Vol.IV) 1930-1940
[Time-Life Books 1971]

Sylvia G.L.Dannett & Frank R.Rachel
Down Memory Lane
[Greenberg Publishers (US) 1954]

Roland Gelatt
The Fabulous Phonograph
[Cassell 1956]

Douglas Gilbert
**Lost Chords: The Diverting Story Of
American Popular Songs**
[Cooper Square Publishers (USA) 1970]

Abel Green & Joe Laurie,Jr
Show Biz From Vaude To Video
[Permabooks (USA) 1953]

Ed: Albert Halper
The Chicago Crime Book 1
[Tandem 1967]

Jim Hol
Some Saxophone History
[Privately Printed London 1982]

Ed: Isabel Leighton
The Aspirin Age 1919-1941
[The Bodley Head 1950]

Emmett Murphy
Great Bordellos of the World
[Quartet Books 1983]

Billy Rose
Wine, Women and Words
[Simon & Schuster (US) 1946]

Jack Schiffman
Harlem Heyday
[Prometheus Books (US) 1984]

Phil Silvers
The Man Who Was Bilko
[W.H.Allen 1974]

Julian Symons
Crime And Detection
[Studio Vista 1966]

Harold Wentworth & Stuart Berg Flexner
Dictionary Of American Slang
[Harrap (US) 1963]

Maurice Zolotow
It Takes All Kinds
[W.H.Allen 1953]

index

INDEX OF VENUES